Will America Surrender?

Books by Slobodan M. Draskovich

THE SERBIAN PEOPLE AND SERBIAN POLITICS
TITO, MOSCOW'S TROJAN HORSE
WILL AMERICA SURRENDER?

WILL AMERICA SURRENDER?

SLOBODAN M. DRASKOVICH

Foreword by General Thomas A. Lane

Introduction by Frederic Nelson

THE DEVIN-ADAIR COMPANY | *Old Greenwich*

Foreword

America is greatly enriched by the presence of exiles from communist countries within our society. Their knowledge of the ruthless communist tyranny is not clouded by ignorance, or hallowed by wishful thinking. They see the world as it is.

Talk with an escapee from an iron or bamboo curtain country about the foreign policy of the United States. It is to him an inexplicable madness. How can this country, once the symbol of liberty to all the oppressed peoples of the world, now consort with tyrants, reinforcing with trade and diplomacy their grip on the subject peoples? Why does the United States side with the dictators against the people?

The refugee finds that in the United States he is expected to speak kindly about communism. He must not disturb the public illusion that the communists are mellowing. If he tells the truth about his experiences, his voice will be excluded from the news media. He will be hidden from the American people.

Dr. Slobodan M. Draskovich is a scholar and political warrior who refuses to be hidden. His understanding of world conflict has not been blunted by twenty-five years of residence in the United States. He knows the enemy and he realizes that the United States has been following a policy of gradual surrender.

In this volume, Dr. Draskovich gives us a wide-ranging and thorough analysis of communist political warfare and western ineptitude. The book is a course in international relations far superior to texts used in our colleges. Readers will find in it a lucid and rigorously reasonable analysis of the political forces on both sides of the world conflict.

If the United States is to survive, it must adopt a policy of waging aggressive and prudent political warfare against communism. Dr. Draskovich tells us why. You had better believe it.

—THOMAS A. LANE

McLean, Va.

Introduction

There have been many books dealing with the Communist threat to the Free World, but most of their writers would hesitate to startle, or maybe turn away, readers with a title like "Will America Surrender?" Not Slobodan Draskovich though! When I first met him in 1957 in my office at the *Saturday Evening Post* he was working on a book which he wanted to call "Tito: Moscow's Trojan Horse." The title shook me, not because I questioned its accuracy but because in those days I still harboured the crypto-liberal illusion that calling a spade a spade could upset the people you were trying to convert. The then current opinion about Tito was that he was a courageous foe of communism who could be relied on to help along with the fragmentation of the Stalinist slave empire. In that book, and in a piece which the *Post* published, Draskovich disposed of that illusion. Liberals, of course, are still befuddled by it.

Nevertheless, when Dr. Draskovich sent me the manuscript of this book, some of those old weak-kneed doubts returned to trouble me. The average American refuses to believe that his country would ever surrender, although a few years back the intellectuals at the Rand Corporation shut themselves into their think tanks to discuss the possibility that America *might* surrender if a Soviet first strike did more than "acceptable" damage. However, Dr. Draskovich is not concerned primarily with military surrender. He is referring to "a policy of concessions to the enemy in most matters of vital national interest; a readiness to compromise on all questions, no matter how brazen the challenge and unmistakable the hostility to the U.S." This process he thinks has been taking place for a long time.

His indictment of the official contribution to surrender centers around this statement: "Our foreign policy since 1933 (the recognition of the USSR by the U.S. under President F. D. Roosevelt) up to the present day has not been one of fighting communism, trying to stop its advance, break its aggressiveness, defeat its drive for world-conquest—but one of seeking compromise, accommodation, as well as active help to communism in various countries under diverse pretenses, explanations and excuses."

Is this too tough? Well, look at the picture. Facing a group of tyrannical bureaucrats who by the most cruel and despotic methods rule a billion people, most of whom detest their communist masters, this country has—from the engineering and technical aid to the then barely viable Soviet dictatorship in the 1920s down to President Nixon's fraternization with the Red satraps in Russia and China—confined itself to vocal deununciation of communism, while managing somehow to come to the rescue of the communists every time their bizarre economics gets them into a self-engendered crisis. President Truman's timely support of anti-communists in Greece, when Britain was forced to bow out, was a notable exception which ought to have firmed up American policy-makers ever since.

Even when popular rage exploded in East Germany, Poland and Hungary, thereby creating an opportunity to shake Soviet domination to its foundations, we, fearful of the Soviet-manufactured specter of universal nuclear destruction, sat on our hands. This is the more remarkable because there is no hard evidence that the ordinary people in this country favor quasi-surrender or appeasement of Red aggression. Indeed, I think Senator Fulbright was right when he warned that the time might come when people will "want to hit the Communists with everything we've got."

However, among the intellectuals, the manipulators of the media, the occupants of the groves of academe and the "radical chic," things are different. What passes for enlightenment in this diverse group includes bland acceptance of negotiation as the means of dealing with communists despite the disastrous results of past negotiation with them; distortions of news so that Anthony Lewis in *The New York Times* could report with a straight face that "Hanoi rejects elections managed by the Saigon administration. It fears its own people would be victims of a bloodbath if left to the control of President Nguyen Van Thieu and his police"; widespread acceptance of the belief that firmness would risk nuclear war and the massacre of untold millions, a terror sold to us by the Communists when we had the atomic bomb and they didn't; reluctance even to appear to "win" against the communists, so that we are supposed to be more concerned with General Lavelle's alleged bombing behind the balk-line in Vietnam than with the possible loss of the whole war; description of potential allies and foes of communism (Greece, Rhodesia, Spain, Portugal, Taiwan, etc.) as fascists and reactionaries, in contrast to *our* new leftish friends.

In this part of his book Dr. Draskovich needs only your morning newspaper to confirm his diagnosis. He could call his book "America *Has* Surrendered" when he is telling off our cognac-scented cognoscenti, as Don Marquis used to call them.

To be sure, it is by no means only the Liberals and their ilk, the Galbraiths, the Mary McCarthys, the old hand-over-China hands, who have sold the pass. Since Mr. Nixon's journey to Canossa, the financial pages have been filled with glowing accounts of the oil we are going to get from China, the caviar from Russia, and the enormous markets about to open for American gadgets, now that "the Cold War is over." American manufacturers already supply the communists with trucks with which to deliver communist war materials to communist troops in Vietnam, and our capitalists look almost goggle-eyed as their expectations rise. I like a recent cartoon in the *New Yorker* magazine showing an irate American business man shouting in desperation, "Don't we make *anything* we can sell to the goddam communists?" Lenin took care of this sort of thing in his prediction that the capitalists would cheerfully destroy themselves.

Dr. Draskovich, after attributing this depressing record of flights to communist propaganda, and Liberal echoing of same, not to mention the dream of profits to be realized from selling every Chinese woman a mini-skirt, does hold out some hope that we shall reverse our field and, in concert with the increasingly rebellious captives of communism, create a tide of opposition sufficient to "sweep communism from power." Otherwise— "Should America betray itself, thus also betraying mankind, it will go down."

I still nourish the belief—and it takes a lot of feeding—that despite the sinister facts so eloquently presented in this book, we shall manage to make it. Paul Greenberg, who does a column for the Boston *Herald Traveler and Record American,* recently reminded his readers that in the past friendly dealings with the communists, like our swap of American wheat for Soviet kind words, have been followed by a "wave of euphoric expectations" —which, when the phoniness of the expectations has been demonstrated, gives way to a "wave of reaction and suspicion." "How long will it be," Mr. Greenberg asks, "before Americans begin asking just what has the President's summitry accomplished?"

However, aside from the traditional belief that God looks with favor upon drunks, idiots and the United States, the odds on any drastic setback to Communism are not impressive. A wide reading of "Will America Surrender?" could help change these odds in our favor. It has been a great experience and an education to read this book.

—FREDERIC NELSON

Truro, Mass.

Contents

Preface: Before You Read

In writing this book, the author has been aware of the fact that the very talk of U.S. surrender to communism is abhorrent to the liberal makers of U.S. policies and of U.S. public opinion. Not because they would consider surrender imaginary as an assertion of fact and unthinkable as a policy, but because U.S. surrender is then a matter of record, and their responsibility in steering the U.S. toward surrender, undeniable.

For that is the gist of the situation. The most powerful country in the world, the United States, has met the challenge of the most aggressive, most ambitious and most ruthless organized force in history, communism, spearheaded by the Soviet Union, with a policy of surrender. And the main success of the total and global war which the communists are waging against the free world, is that they have succeeded in convincing us that the evident is not true.

For while all evidence points to world communism as the main source of trouble in the world and the main problem of our time, the communists have convinced the West, i.e. its rulers and opinion-makers, of the contrary: that communism poses no serious threat to the world, and thus is a non-problem. The cold war, we are told, is just an appendage of the "McCarthy era," the problems of our time are essentially unrelated to communism, and would exist without communism. Therefore our task is not to fight communism, but to collaborate with the communists, since co-existence is the only way to save mankind and solve its problems.

Moreover, the United States, the leading country of our modern age, the only one which can defeat communism and make freedom triumphant in the whole world, has been slandered and discredited as imperialistic, warmongering, inhuman, militaristic, racist, weak, oppressive, opposed to the prevailing trends of the modern world. The trouble with its policies, so we are told, is—contrary to what the title of this book indicates—that the U.S. has tried to boss the world, to impose its will, influence and solutions everywhere, to preserve the imperialistic power of its capitalist class. So, it is not communism we should fear, but U.S. might.

In other words, the view of communism as the main danger and problem of the contemporary world would seem unrelated to political reality—would seem to be extreme, reactionary or paranoid, or all three. And yet, the title of this book is fully justified by reality.

There has never been a time when hard, incontrovertible facts, the plain truth, were so ignored, twisted, misinterpreted, when the gap between what is and what people consider to be true, was so wide and deep. Modern Western man—in spite of all the unique abundance of knowledge and information of the era of electronic mass communications—seems to be the most misinformed man in history, and politically the most illiterate.

It is certain that the very use of the word surrender as applied to U.S. current policy, and victory as the advocated course of policy, is considered disqualifying by the present opinion-makers. But that is a vital part of the problem. The current liberal monopoly of the intellectual, cultural and political market place is such that in the name of freedom and diversity only conformists need apply; in the name of the preservation of the U.S. only advocates of coexistence with communism are considered qualified, and in the name of intellectual probity and honest factual approach, preference is given to those who shy away from facts and are sufficiently trained in the art of personal invective and smear, as a substitute for logical analysis and the proper understanding of issues under discussion.

But there are limits to the power of those who would suppress, deny and defeat the evident. As Goethe told us, that which has happened, cannot be considered as having never happened. (*"Gewesenes kann nicht ungewesen sein"*). Facts do not always necessarily speak a clear and unequivocal language, leading to evident conclusions. However, plain facts can also show great resilience against systematic efforts to twist and misinterpret them. It is Lincoln who gave the well-known immortal form to man's belief that the time for fooling all people was finite.

On that we base this book, which deals with the surrender of the West, especially the U.S.; with the nature of communism and the communist strategy for world conquest; and with the possibilities of U.S. surrender and defeat, as well as with those of the defeat of communism and the victory of the U.S. and freedom in the world.

Until recently, any mention of U.S. policies being policies of surrender was promptly banned from the public place as extremist and alarmist talk, unfit to print and hear.

But, under the pressure of events and some incontrovertible evidence, as well as owing to a number of people of insight, intellectual acumen, knowledge and moral courage, who have written about the U.S. policies of surrender with facts, documents, genuine patriotic concern and regard for the truth, the issue of surrender can no longer be suppressed as imaginary, or extremist or paranoiac. It is very real. And no smear will make it go away.

Our official attitude in the Soviet invasion of Czechoslovakia, the developments in Vietnam and the part which Vietnam is playing in the life of the U.S. and in international politics, the *Pueblo,* EC 121 and Simas Kudirka incidents, and the disgraceful, brazenly proclaimed and boldly carried out civil war activities of the New Left to destroy the United States, are lifting many veils, opening many eyes and clearing many minds to the reality of U.S. non-resistance to multiple communist aggression.

It is therefore becoming increasingly difficult for those responsible for the present state of affairs, to ignore the questions, or answer them with slogans or commonplaces, to evade the issues, as it is to continue as usual. The insistence of the American people on answers seems to be mounting and getting less negotiable, as problems keep piling up and the impression turning into certainty that our most serious problems, with the problem of surrender at the top of the list, are not made of accidental mistakes, but have resulted from concepts, views and practices which are in conflict with the best interests of the United States and the American people.

An era of unavoidable accounting and clarification lies ahead. It is very unlikely that Americans will be satisfied forever with the explanations and excuses given so far, much less that they will allow the policies of surrender to continue.

S.M.D.

Chicago, 1972

PART ONE

The Faith and the Will

"The American people are far ahead of the Administration in their willingness and determination to do what is necessary to defend our freedom against aggression."

RICHARD M. NIXON
(*Chicago Sun-Times,* June 20, 1961)

"There is a remarkable awakening in America as to the issues and dangers involved. This has never happened before in peacetime. People seem to me to be ready for any eventuality: they only ask to be told what is expected of them . . . they sense the danger; they want to join in some common effort; they crave to know what that common effort is; but so far nobody has told them, nobody has summoned them to a supreme effort for the common good . . ."

CHARLES MALIK
("The Challenge to Western Civilization," article
in *The Conservative Papers,* Doubleday Anchor, 1964, p. 17)

"These times demand that our next President be an extraordinary man, dedicated to freedom as Nikita Khrushchev is dedicated to communism."

"Who Shall Lead Us?"
(Political Advertisement for Senator Lyndon B. Johnson,
in *The New York Times,* June 1, 1960)

1 The Faith and the Will

We have reached the most critical juncture in the history of the United States, and on the ability of the nation to find a solution to its chief contemporary problems, its own future and that of the world will depend for centuries to come.

What makes this situation the more dramatic is that both the U.S. and the USSR were never closer to disaster, and at the same time never closer to victory.

The main difference today between the communist world and the West, especially the U.S., is in the realm of the will.

Communism is the most political, most power-seeking, most aggressive enterprise in history. The role of will, of struggle and victory at any price is paramount in it. "Bolshevism . . . can be considered as one of the few successful movements of pure will in history." [1]

Communist successes and Western defeats have been caused not by superior communist ideas or techniques, but by the will which permeates their struggle for power. Their aim is conquest, their ideas are ideas of conquest, their methods are tailored to lead to conquest and so are their techniques. Different as communist leaders are individually, they have one thing in common, the lust for power; they are all aggressors and conquerors. Their stand is never one of doubt; it is always one of being right. They proclaim their concepts, their ways, their yardsticks to be the correct ones, and they work to make their interests prevail. The members of the party, the public, the world, must, by all conceivable means, be impressed, brainwashed, mesmerized into believing that, as Frank Meyer put it, "The cause is advancing, the chariot of History is rolling inexorably on, and the Communist is firmly seated on that chariot." [2]

It is this communist will to power, their extremism and the unconditional, unwavering promotion of communism in the world, which work for communism, in spite of all their crimes, injustice, inhumanity and ineptitude.

It is clear that such a political force in the world can be defeated only by superior force and superior will. And this is the last thing the West so far has been inclined to strive for and display. The West has tried nicer ideas, superior performance (economic, technological, scientific), a kinder spirit of cooperation, efforts to know each other better and remove misunderstandings, cultural exchanges, bridges of trade—but never, never to display a superior confidence in its values, a superior will to win over communism.

Regardless of the causes and factors which have brought this about, it is a situation which cannot endure, because no nation can tolerate it and live.

Nobody can go forward by dropping to his knees and all the time strewing his head with ashes. Humility before God is proper, but humility before Stalin, Khrushchev, Brezhnev, Mao, Chou En-lai, Castro, Kadar, Tito, Ceausescu and their ilk, is disgraceful, inane and inhuman.

In history there have always been those who are rising and those who are declining. The question is who is today playing which role. The old men who have no heart for battle, are very "humanistic" simply because they lack the strength to fight and conquer. They do not want to risk anything and they do not want to conquer anything. But the young ones in history are willing to risk everything because they want to conquer everything there is to conquer.

Is the West willing to play the role of the "old man" in history and leave the role of the young conqueror to the communists?

If Western man is not convinced that the civilization he has created is the greatest thing ever created by mankind, if he lacks the strength to stand by its values and achievements, and, instead, abjectly bows before the charges and slanders of the communists who have done no good and infinitely more evil, he will be destroyed.

Those who are tired of life, competition, struggle, war (of all kinds) cannot survive. The world will be conquered by those who are *not* tired, who possess the vigor to grapple with whatever obstacles and enemies standing in their way.

In human affairs there are no situations which are inalterably favorable or inalterably hopeless.[3] The worst situation can turn into victory if the difficulties, adversities and enemies are met with determination, wisdom and courage. And the rosiest of situations is lost if our will falters, if we cannot muster the will to fight and make the effort required for victory.

When a criminal comes to your home and starts molesting your wife and beating your children, you don't engage him in academic discussion on crime and manners, nor do you try to reason with him, nor do you make a special effort not to raise your voice, nor do you point out to him the moral condemnation by public opinion which his behavior will inevitably bring upon him. No. You do everything to stop him!

That is what we have forgotten in our relations with the communists. We have reduced all the problems which communism creates (especially subversion, imperialism and aggression), to problems of discussion, to an intellectual contest, to an academic debate, where supposedly all we have to do is produce more logical and cogent arguments, and make more convincing recommendations.

But that path of no-will, has led us down and is leading us to disaster. Therefore, the problem is how to arouse and mobilize the *will* of the nation.

Confrontation

To this end, the prime, absolute, vital necessity for the United States is precisely that which U.S. foreign policy rejects, *confrontation*. The first requirement for life, in an individual or a nation, is to confront the world, its dangers, evils and tragedies, as well as its opportunities, challenges and beauty, to see the world as it is. Our undoing is that our foreign policy experts reject confrontation with the world as it is, with reality, with difficulties, with the forces of change and the forces of self-assertion, with the dangers which threaten us and the bright chances which invite us. We are afraid of reality, and thus magnify its threats and by-pass its chances.

Without confrontation there is no freedom and there is no survival. Whoever is afraid of life, will not live, even if all the nuclear forces of the globe are tied by treaties or destroyed by common understanding. The predicament of the West today is precisely that: its leaders lack the courage to confront its enemies, to defend its values and positions and to attack and destroy communist values and positions. We would like to talk where only strength avails, and to compromise where only victory or defeat make sense.

And our problems are multiplying, our troubles growing and our positions deteriorating precisely because and in the measure that we avoid confrontation and try to settle all problems in a "fair and business-like" manner by negotiation.

History is not made that way and the communists who are today challenging the existing order and striving to be the makers of the future, are less inclined to fairness and matter-of-factness than any history-makers of the past.

You don't communicate and negotiate with Mao Tse-tung and any of those who have been raised on Mao's thoughts. You beat them or you surrender to them in the struggle for world power. If we persist on the course of adaptation, negotiation and communication, if we are guided by the defeatist philosophy that "you cannot ignore 700 million Chinese," they will destroy the United States, more thoroughly than any old regime or empire known or no longer known, has been destroyed in history.

We cannot join them. So, we have no choice but to beat them.

Therefore, what the U.S. needs, is not more commissions, more study groups, more money, more police and more troops, but more will to oppose the enemy, more determination on the part of the leaders of the nation to defend America and its values unconditionally. It needs not learned historians and sociologists to describe and explain its downfall, but fighters and leaders to face the enemy, to put liberty and honor above life, and lead the nation to victory.

There can be no struggle for freedom without unconditional commitment. Call it moral courage, or drive, or militant faith, or will; speak of ideas-forces with Fouillée, or "élan vital" with Bergson, or true beliefs with Ortega y Gasset and Eric Hoffer, or "passionate intensity" with Yeats, or virtú with Vilfredo Pareto and James Burnham, or simply leadership,—there is the key to success.

Unless the top of the nation is a repository of the qualities and forces which shape human events and make history, no historic document or program, neither plan nor project, nor our very system itself, will save us. It contains no built-in guarantee for our national existence, regardless of what we do or fail to do. A system is no better than those who make it and especially those who operate it. "Liberty," says Judge Learned Hand, "lies in the hearts of men and women; when it dies there, no constitution, no law, no court can save it."

Therefore, the fate of the U.S. depends on its ability to produce the kind of leaders who can master its problems as the Founding Fathers did in 1776 and who can thus provide the leadership which the U.S. must give to the world or perish.

Conservatism versus Liberalism

In the course of recent years the idea has developed that the chief contest in the U.S. is between liberalism and conservatism, and that the fate of the U.S. depends on its outcome.

Such is not the case. The issue of liberalism versus conservatism does not pertain (or only marginally) to the fundamental problem of the U.S.: to survive and to make history. This is the point which the conservatives have failed to grasp. They have studied every problem and every facet of every problem, they have documented every assertion, produced all the proofs, exposed all the villainy, corruption, treason, fallacy and folly of liberal policies. They have rightly pointed to the alienation of the liberal leaders from the fundamental principles of the U.S. And they have invoked all the noble documents, above all the Bible and the Declaration of Independence, and quoted all the wise men and their choice thoughts, from Confucius, Plato and Aristotle, to St. Augustine, Berkeley, Adam Smith, Edmund Burke, Frédéric Bastiat, Herbert Hoover and Ludwig von Mises. They have confronted corruption with pure morality, internationalism with Americanism, lawlessness with law and order, treason with loyalty, atheism with Christian ethics. Briefly, they have proved all their points.

All except one: that they are resolved to stand for their principles and fight to make them prevail, with the same determination with which the communists are promoting their own schemes. An idea is strong only if it embodies personal commitment. Values and standards which are not defended, lose their validity. If exposure and evidence endlessly accumulate without ever maturing into certitude and impelling to action, they become a source of moral erosion. If a good cause accumulates a record of weakness and failure and a foul cause accumulates a record of efficiency and success, virtue becomes inoperative and evil gathers prestige. It is particularly in times of confusion and crisis that personal commitment (of "fortune, life and sacred honor") outweighs all other factors. For every failure to take a stand worsens the situation and further weakens the will. Sooner or later, we turn not against the enemy, but against those who want to stop the enemy. They, not the enemy, increasingly appear as the "extremists" and troublemakers because they refuse to surrender.

Most liberal attacks on conservatives are as vicious as those of the communists. They unfailingly include defamation. The stigma, clearly implied or barely qualified, is without fail: "fascist!" To this, conservatives react with timidity and deference. For they have apparently not remained unaffected by the confusion which has been created in the realm of our values and standards, and have lost the inner certainty of being right. And this inevitably affects their fighting spirit. Their opposition to liberal policies is mainly academic and respectful. Rebuttals or criticism of those whose attitudes and actions are opposed to U.S. national interests, are too often preceded by a recognition of their patriotism, loyalty, sincerity, noble motives.

Too much conservative writing and action today oozes an acceptance of defeat. There is too much readiness to die, "driven against the wall" by the communists, but not to live, to fight, to win, to defeat the enemy.

The proclamation of lofty principles behind which there is no faith and no will cannot bring about important change. For all the facts in the world, all the documentation, are of no avail if there is no spark to make it into a huge fire of indignation to burn to death the criminal communist conspiracy.

Unfortunately, too many conservatives today behave like the Stoic philosopher Epictetus who had warned his master not to twist his arm, because he would break it. And since his master went on twisting his arm, he finally did break it. Epictetus unquestionably proved his point and won an intellectual victory. But his arm was broken. Too many conservatives today are proving, explaining, demonstrating, that the enemy is destroying America —instead of breaking the enemy.

The liberals have reduced the conservatives practically to "His

Majesty's Loyal Opposition." The function of every loyal opposition is not to radically change policies, but to keep its disagreement within the bounds of respectfully indignant protests and objections, deploring the Establishment's folly, but never threatening its power positions.

Whittaker Chambers and his words charged with gloom, hopelessness and doom:

> ". . . the total situation is hopeless, past repair, organically ir-
> remediable. Almost the only position of spiritual dignity left to
> us, therefore, is a kind of stoic silence, made bearable by the
> amusement of seeing, hearing and knowing the full historical
> irony that its victims are blind and deaf to, and disciplined by
> the act of withholding comment on what we know."

seem to be representative of the mood prevailing among most
conservatives.* Which raises the question, what can you do with a
conservative with whom you may share many views and opinions,
but who tells you that everything is lost?

The vital spark of will which America needs can fly only from
faith, not from despair, be it liberal or conservative.

It is precisely because of the failure of the conservatives in the
realm of will, that their policies (1952–1960 under President
Eisenhower, and recently under President Nixon) have become
indistinguishable from the liberal policies of President Kennedy
and President Johnson, 1960–1968.

The issue which is today at stake transcends the conflict between liberalism and conservatism. It is a belief in the nation itself
which alone can produce the spark of will to save it. The answer
must be sought beyond the liberal-conservative controversy.

It is here that we meet with the problem of the leaders versus
the people, which is the nub of the question of America's future.

---

* It is all right for a liberal nihilist like Gore Vidal to call his latest book *Reflections on a Sinking Ship*, written after *Myra Breckenridge*. That is in
style.

But there is unacceptable incongruity for an outstanding representative of
the revolt against the infamy of communism, like Whittaker Chambers, to
ooze pessimism out of every pore. Characteristically, his last book *Cold
Friday* (published posthumously), was originally entitled *The Losing Side.*
(*National Review*, Jan. 27, 197, p. 79, 91.)

The Leaders and the People

In the long run, no nation is better than the leadership it is able to produce. So, no nation can be exempt from the blame which its leadership may deserve.

In any case, no nation can, for very long, live without adequate leadership, i.e., without having at its top, at its helm, people completely dedicated to the values of the nation and capable of upholding and defending them.

The finest principles and documents on earth are of no avail if those who have risen to the pinnacle and are called to implement them lack the stature to uphold those principles or the courage and strength to face the enemies and brave the difficulties.

The deep and fundamental conflict between the leaders and the people of the United States is unmistakable. And if there is one short statement which contains in essence the truth about it, it is the view presented by Senator William J. Fulbright, chairman of the Foreign Relations Committee of the U.S. Senate in his notorious Memorandum about the muzzling of the military: "In the long run, it is quite possible that the principal problem of leadership will be, if it is not already, to restrain the desire of the people to hit the Communists with everything we've got, particularly if there are more Cubas and Laos'."

In this Senator Fulbright is right indeed. The present situation of the U.S. is heavy with perils because the normal relationship between the leaders and the people, and the normal process by which the nation produces its own leadership, have been severely disturbed: the leadership has been alienated from the people, and standards have been adopted which tend to produce leadership inclined to consider the interests of the world as more important than those of the United States.

Our liberal leaders have failed miserably in their responsibility to safeguard the interests of the United States. They may complain that the people are not "mature" enough, that they are unable to understand and follow into implementation the grandiose schemes of the creators of various New Frontiers, Great Societies, etc., but the plain truth of their incompetence and ineptitude is visible and irrefutable. To admit their responsibility would be suicide. So, they have no choice but to continue "investing in error."

This viewpoint has been unmistakably expressed by Theodore White in his articles on "action-intellectuals" in *Life* magazine (of June 9, 16 and 23, 1967) that while the "action-intellectuals" have greatly contributed to the mess we are in today and that they do not know the way out, there is nothing we can do about it. After all, the liberal "action-intellectuals" are the most brilliant men we have. And since, in spite of their brilliancy, we have drifted to the impasse we are in, where their ideas, theories, premises and systems clash with common sense, with the mood and thinking of the people whom they are supposed to serve and with one another—it means that nothing better can be excogitated.

However, no matter what their concerns and motives may be, the liberal leaders of the nation have no right to bring about the suicide of the U.S.*

There is a gaping chasm between our leaders and the people. The people have faith. They revere the Founding Fathers and they fully understand and carry in their hearts the meaning of 1776. They believe in the country, its fundamental principles, its accomplishments, its right to live and its future. They know that only the spirit of 1776 can save America: faith in God, fearlessness before enemies and difficulties, self-confidence, and the firm resolve that America must be ruled not by other peoples, kingdoms, states or "soviet unions," but must take its fate in its own hands and walk undauntedly to the realization of its aims.

---

* Those people in U.S. public life who have developed a guilt complex, as some Russian nobles had in the 19th century, and feel that the accusations against their parents or grandparents as plunderers, exploiters, robber barons, are true, have no right to implicate the rest of us (the overwhelming majority), to impose on us the obligation of atoning for their sins and complexes. Whether their conscience is rightly or wrongly burdened with the feeling of guilt for the (real or imaginary) crimes committed by their ancestors, they have a way out of the guilt which is oppressing them: 1. distribute their injustly acquired wealth to the people, the poor, the plundered, and 2. stay out of political life.

In such manner they would atone for the sins of their ancestors and they would render a signal service to their contemporaries. As things stand now, the burden is too heavy and unfair to the American people. The people have been robbed by the dads and granddads. Now they have to suffer the liberal policies of the sons and grandsons, which may serve to ease the consciences of a few, but are disastrous for the nation.

The spirit of 1776 gave birth to this great nation. The spirit of Teheran and Yalta, Potsdam and Geneva, Camp David and the Bay of Pigs, Korea and Vietnam, the *Pueblo* surrender, and the case of Simas Kudirka spells the end of this nation.

Obviously there can be no compromise between the two. Which one shall it be?

The issue is not ideology, not liberalism vs. conservatism, nor free enterprise vs. socialism, but whether the thinking, basic sentiments, strivings, concepts and ideals of the people will prevail, or those of its present leaders. The former are life, the latter are death for the nation.

Normally, in the struggle for survival of a nation, its leaders are its strongest part. However, in the U.S. today the leaders are the weakest part of the nation.

The American people, to speak with President Nixon, i.e., to quote his very apt remarks from 1961, when he was Vice-President, are "far ahead of the Administration in their willingness and determination to do what is necessary to defend our freedom against aggression." The trouble is that the verdict is as valid today as it was then.

And this is a thoroughly unhealthy and perilous situation, which cannot be permitted to last too long.

A nation is strong and sound if its citizens are aware of the need for leadership and actively contribute to the selection of the ablest to be entrusted with the affairs of all—and when the leaders are fully aware that their exceptional position is above all a position of moral trust and highest responsibility.

And a nation is deeply confused and morally debilitated if its citizens think that it does not matter who runs the affairs of state, who is at the helm, whether or not the elected officials are doing their duty and their assigned jobs well, and even worse, when the leaders are unable to provide leadership.

In the great debate of 1960 about the National Purpose, John W. Gardner passed a shattering verdict: "We lack leadership on the part of our leaders, and commitment on the part of every American." [4]

To find a way out of this vicious circle, the American people need leaders who above all care about the values which make America, who are not awed by the enemy's might but interested in and also delighted by its weaknesses, and who can muster both the wisdom to find ways to defeat the enemy, and the fortitude to persevere and not be deflected from the task by any force, threat or blandishment.

We need statesmen who will not be dominated by the experts—people "who know more and more about less and less," to use the famous definition of Nicholas Murray Butler, and whose courage decreases as the threats to America increase. We need statesmen who will themselves give the basic direction and determine the meaning of our national policies.

What the People Can Do.

How are those leaders to emerge?

In important historical moments there is a correlation between the emotional condition and spiritual tension of the masses and the intellectual readiness and political availability of the leaders. The one promotes the other. The growing awareness of the vital aspects of the situation and the indignation against the liberal betrayal are conducive to intellectual clarification, to the maturing of political thought and the creation of political strength. Mind and will being intertwined, it is out of the clear U.S. mind, liberated from liberal poisons, and from the stout heart of the American people, that the new leadership must be expected.[5]

But for the "average American" out of whose ranks the new leadership is to emerge, the road is full of formidable obstacles. On the one side, his common sense, his conscience, his patriotism tell him that the country is in mortal danger. On the other hand, he is being constantly taught by most public-opinion makers to find every fault under the sun with America and its accomplishments, to doubt the sanctity of the family, to take a "sophisticated" view of the sacred bonds between husband and wife, and between parents and children, to distrust the "military-industrial complex," to reject "organized religion," to be very "impartial" between right and wrong, to "understand" the destroyers of his country, to find "redeeming social values" in the moral filth which is swamping the literary market and the entertainment field.

Should the liberals be permitted to continue their "business as usual," there would, sooner or later, come a point of no return, at which they would finally and "sincerely," turn to us and ask: "Well, what would you do if you were in my place? You see there is nothing that can possibly be done!" Which, at the end of the line, would be true, of course.

So, the question remains: will the liberals be permitted to bring us to the end of the line?

Nearly ten years ago, I was invited to speak before a small group of about thirty people. In the discussion that ensued, a lawyer, veteran of World War II, said: "I agree wholeheartedly with practically everthing you have said. However, I want to stress that none of us should forget that once the American people start going, there is no force on earth to stop them."

It was my turn to express qualified agreement with that statement. "Once they start," I repeated, "but they haven't yet."

Nevertheless, man's thirst for truth is unquenchable and his striving for freedom is indomitable. They are part of the universal order. They are as indestructible as man himself. If man's tendency to self-deceit encourages the deceivers, his search for the truth dispels the fogs of distortion. Consequently, more and more people refuse to deceive themselves by lullabies of peace in the midst of the most merciless war ever waged, or by warnings against "extremism" and "alarmism." As Confucius said 2500 years ago, when things are going well, it is unbecoming to protest and be against those who run them. But when things are going badly, it is the inescapable duty of true patriots to raise their voices and take action to improve them.

That is why, in spite of the fact that the process of the "commitment on the part of every citizen" has been developing slowly, an important change is taking place in America today. There is a stir in the nation, a healthy uneasiness, a yearning for explanations, for clarity, for sense.

No matter how hard our opinion-makers try to convince us not to look at the world, or not to believe what we see, the pressure of reality in Vietnam, in Red China, in the Soviet Union, in Europe, in the Middle East, in the streets and at the colleges of America, in our armed forces, etc., is growing irresistibly. It cannot be wished or propagandized away. Americans are getting tired of being pushed around in the world and at home and they want to know what is really going on.

The unshackling of the American mind has been set in motion. There are all the time more people who are absolutely sure that two and two make four, even if most radio and television stations, most university professors, most newspaper editors and columnists, most Hollywood stars and directors, most politicians and all the priests and ministers who proclaim that God is dead, to make room for man—tell him that two and two make five.

The American people sense that it is unnatural that the U.S. should be going down all the time and that they should be told that nothing can be done about it, that nobody is responsible, that only right-wing extremists and alarmists view things pessimistically, but that actually things are going fine. And anyway, whatever is happening, is the will of history!

The people can no longer stomach those explanations. So an increasing number of "ordinary Americans" are increasingly asking some elementary questions:

—is it true that there is no alternative to our foreign policy of coexistence and surrender, save nuclear war and global annihilation?

—is it true that our leaders have a sacred obligation to save mankind, but have no obligation to save America?

—is it true that our unilateral disarmament would induce the communists to disarm as gentlemen should?

—is it true that helping communists (Tito, Gomulka, Gierek, Castro, Ceausescu, etc.) is good for freedom?

And finally, what it all amounts to:

—is it true that the best possible and most American thing to happen to the U.S. is to surrender abjectly to communism? Is that the natural logical conclusion and end of what the Founding Fathers dreamed, conceived, created and launched as one of the greatest, most nobly ambitious ventures in the history of mankind?

As people raise such questions, it becomes increasingly difficult to sidestep the issues, and to silence the questioners by means of slander, character-assassination, moral blackmail, distortion or ridicule.

It is not that the communist-liberal tandem is not trying hard. (As the destroyers of all kinds are tearing down America, they are warning Americans about the danger of "repression," which might stop the destroyers!). But in the minds of the people the confrontation between evidence and liberal propaganda is turning in favor of reality, of truth.

After a long time, we are about to overcome the Great Fear, the fear of being morally blackmailed, attacked, vilified, smeared by the communists and their liberal accomplices.

The liberal machine of mind-conditioning and moral intimidation has already been exposed as less than all-powerful. An important step in this sense was made in 1968, so important that the liberal opinion-makers and shapers of our minds have done their utmost to comment on it as little as possible, to treat it as non-news, to ignore it.

That step is the difference between the presidential elections of 1968 and those of 1964. In 1964 the American people gave Lyndon B. Johnson the greatest majority in the history of U.S. presidential elections (43 million, versus 27 million for Barry Goldwater). In 1968, Hubert Humphrey, Johnson's successor, was able to get only 31 million (i.e., twelve million less than Johnson), as opposed to 41 million votes for Nixon (31) and Wallace (10).

There is no need here to go into any elaborate analysis of the difference between the votes for Nixon and those for Wallace. The point is that all those votes were votes of "No!" to the liberal policies of domestic and international surrender.

Another important development is the response of enthusiastic endorsement which Vice-President Spiro Agnew's speeches of slashing criticism of the bias, intolerance and monopoly of the liberal opinion-makers has elicited in the broad masses of the American people. Obviously those feelings and opinions are so strong and widespread that they represent a serious political factor and a political mood to be reckoned with.

The unexpected, but energetic and articulate manifestations of the "hard hats" in New York have confirmed how right Eric Sevareid was when he said in his comments on TV on May 8, 1970 about President Nixon's press conference on Cambodia and the Kent State University, that "a great number of Americans have just about had it."

Besides, the very fact that the American people were able to hear out of the mouth of the Vice-President of the United States, words, opinions, judgments and condemnations which until then were considered as the characteristic of the "right-wing extremists," has done much more harm to the policies, institutions and persons under attack than to Vice-President Agnew and the philosophy expounded by him.

And finally, both the campaign of Vice-President Agnew and the outrages of the New Left have provoked a process of re-evaluation and re-examination of problems, as well as an upsurge of conscience and patriotism among quite a few outstanding liberals. Which is to their credit and to the benefit of America.

I am not saying that we are over the hump. Far from it. We have, to speak with Robert Frost, "many miles to go" before we can safely sleep. But much headway has been made. The turning point will be reached when enough Americans realize that the liberal policies do not serve progress, nor peace, nor the future, nor the "common man"—but are deceit and suicide for the nation, and they therefore must be rejected if America is to live.

The capacity for indignation of the American people and their desire to make history have been dulled by the good life which the U.S. offers to all its people, loyal and disloyal alike. They have been blunted because we have been too successful in material achievement for too long and because we have been taught to believe that a high standard of living is the sense and essence of life, making security more important than liberty.

The victory we must achieve is not over matter, it is not a victory of steel and nuclear weapons over steel and nuclear weapons, it is not a victory over hunger, disease, illiteracy and ignorance, but a victory over the enemy's will. To achieve that victory will be to open the roads leading to all victories. To fail in that test, is to forfeit all chances.

There has never been in history a nation so bent upon self-destruction as the U.S. is today. And part of the problem is that solutions are sought in shortcuts, easy formulas, clever techniques.

The solution, however, of the problem of the fate of America in the last third of the twentieth century, depends on the faith and the will of Americans. Either Americans believe in America and can muster the will to make it victorious, or—if they do not—they will lose.

If the *Communist Manifesto,* and all other communist writings, plus the criminal record of communist rule since 1917, can inspire the communists to more dedication and fervor in their struggle for world domination, than the Declaration of Independence and the achievements of the U.S. can inspire Americans to stand for America and liberty—then communism will win.

That is the question which Americans must answer. Actually, there is no other question, since they are all contained in that one.

Communism was created to change the world by conquering and enslaving it. It has achieved complete mastery over one-third of the globe and has influenced life throughout all continents.

If we persist in letting the communists conquer and change the world, we shall even forfeit the right to interpret events and tell posterity what happened. Communism will have changed the world so thoroughly, that those who lacked the courage to oppose their changes and to make history themselves, will have no place in writing it.

Our assets and the tools in our hands are unique and uniquely powerful. With them the enemy can be smitten into oblivion. But only if there are creative craftsmen to use them properly.

One thing is sure: our fate is in our hands. We have been a spectacularly successful nation. But success has apparently gone to our heads at the same time as it has weakened our will, our moral fiber and our vitality. That is why the United States is the only great power in history that was mortally endangered as soon as it reached its climax.

The task before us is perhaps superhuman. But the mark of a man is to surpass himself. If defeatism is contagious, so is faith; if fear is contagious, so is courage; and if the mood of surrender is contagious, so is the spirit of uncompromising struggle and the resolve for victory. And since there are no alibis in history, the promise which the Founding Fathers made when they founded the nation, must be kept. The Founding Fathers themselves kept it splendidly, to make Americans proud to be Americans and men proud to belong to the human race.

But the question is now, what will the present generation do?

Should we fail in spite of all the gifts received by history, nature and our ancestors, that would be the worst disgrace ever recorded. It would disgrace America and it would disgrace the human race. A country blessed with fearless freedom-loving pioneers, endowed with huge natural wealth and resources, exceptionally fortunate to receive at its birth all the gifts and achievements of Western civilization, a country which through the wisdom of its founders and the courage, industriousness and undaunted spirit of its people rose in one hundred and fifty years from a small colony to the leading power of the world, a country which gave the broadest masses of its population the highest standards of living ever attained and offered the greatest opportunities for everybody— should such a country be unable to find enough sons and daughters to rise in its defense, and thus be destroyed for lack of moral stamina and manly essence, that would indeed be the sorriest spectacle the world has ever seen.

And it will come to pass unless Americans rise in anger to defend their country.

We have been hearing for years about angry dissenters, protesters, rebels, rioters, destroyers. And this anger was considered as a proof in itself that things were not in proper order and indicative of the need for "social change."

But we have never really heard the full voice and mind of angry Americans. To be sure, there have been instances of substantial popular indignation, such as in 1961, at the time of the McNamara-Fulbright witch-hunt against the U.S. military leaders, after Major Knickerbocker disclosed that the U.S. Air Force was training pilots from communist Yugoslavia. And there were the "hard hats" with their spontaneous anger in June 1970 in New York City. And again the gigantic wave of public indignation at the condemnation of Lt. Calley.

But they were all outbursts, flashes, which subsided fast. What we need are angry Americans, who have had enough of surrender, of constantly appeasing our mortal enemy, of trying not to displease our most vicious detractors; we need Americans who can no longer stand the deceit, the treason, the propaganda against America and in favor of the enemy. We need angry Americans who are not willing to tolerate the constant, insistent mind-conditioning about how bad, corrupt, unjust, unfair, unfree, oppressive, racist, America is, and how it must spend all its time apologizing to the world and use all its resources to combat "poverty, hunger, desperation and chaos," but never its enemies, who are entitled to destroy the U.S. to get even for all the evils and wrongs it has done to its own people and to the people of the world ever since 1776, or 1620, or even 1492!

But the voice of angry Americans has not yet been heard. So far we have heard from disappointed Americans, disgusted Americans, disconcerted Americans, amazed Americans, shocked Americans, informed Americans, tired Americans, hopeless, beaten Americans—but not from angry Americans. Either they are not yet angry enough, or they have been cowed under the organized and orchestrated leftist outcry against "extremism" and "fascism," which goes up as soon as the ire of the people starts mounting. Or perhaps they are holding back, still unbelieving at the obvious and hoping for some miracle, or waiting for some catastrophe to shake them out of lethargy and inaction.

In any case, our fate depends on the capacity for righteous anger by the American people.

We have seen in the past few years all sorts of actions by the enemies of America here at home. We have seen riots, looting, bombings, subversion, destruction, sedition, murder. We have seen weird assortments of hippies and yippies, moral degenerates, hopeless innocents, drug addicts, political opportunists, led by enemy agents, drag America in the mud, and glorify the enemy, carrying defiantly the enemy's flag in our nation's capital, under the protection of the authorities! We have seen marches on Washington, the sorry spectacle of "resurrection city" in our capital, the hideous and unspeakably disgraceful demonstrations of May 1971 to "stop the Government," which were a rehearsal for much more serious things to come.

It is time to stop the enemy. We now need massive demonstrations of at least a quarter or half-a-million Americans from all 50 states, of all national origins, all races, all religions, around the Washington Monument, not to threaten or blackmail the Government to surrender to the enemy, but to remind and warn it that it must serve the nation as George Washington did.

We need angry Americans, at least as angry as the destroyers and at least as determined to defend and save America as the destroyers are determined to destroy it!

Otherwise, the nation will not survive. If we are incapable of feeling insulted and aroused by all the outrages of America's enemies, if all we can do is to deplore the situation and its trends, engage in gloomy predictions, proclaiming that "this flat and flabby country was not fitted by history or temperament for the great-power role thrust upon it by the second world war . . ." (Stewart Alsop) or that "America's history as a nation has reached its end." (Prof. Andrew Hacker)—we shall go down and we shall have deserved it.

All the predictions about the bright prospects of peace in the immediate future, in the world and in the U.S., are either communist propaganda aimed at us at the height of the arming of the USSR both in weapons and in aggressive spirit, or they are suicidal lullabies, or wishful phantasies, directly at odds with plain evidence and reality.

The truth is that the forces of destruction and evil are on the march and in ascent all over the world, and the forces of anti-Americanism are so emboldened right here in the U.S., that we are moving toward conflicts of unseen proportions and violence, internally and internationally. Anybody who has the slightest interest about the world he lives in and does not accept unconditional surrender for himself and for America as inexorable fate, can easily see this.

We are engaged in the struggle for the world, faced with forces which hate all that America is and stands for, and want to build a "new world" and "new society" on America's grave and ruins. So, let there be no mistake: when forces are active in the world to destroy the strongest country of the globe, there cannot be peace —unless it be outright surrender. No little gestures, or nice platitudes about peace and the noble disposition of our enemies, or visits to the other end of the globe or "reasonable negotiations" will do. We have let the enemy gain such momentum, go so far, occupy such positions, exert such influence, that they are smelling blood and will not stop. They deem they have it made; they will not shrink from bloodshed. And the more our Government appeases them, the more blood will be shed. They think they have America on the run. They have no intention of letting her fight back.

It is only the righteous anger of the American people that can instill some sense and some fear in the frenzied, demented minds of the enemies of America, and turn the tides.

Everybody has some kind of grudge against America. It is more than high time for Americans to develop a mighty grudge against all those who dislike America and are busy running her down and destroying her.

And since blind anger is powerless, it must be enlightened and guided by knowledge and reason, to become a creative force. We must know why and how we came to this point and we must clearly envisage an alternative to the policy of surrender. To that purpose the following pages were written.

PART TWO

Surrender

2 The Concept of Surrender

"It is a legitimate American national objective to see removed from all nations—including the United States—the right to use substantial military force to pursue their own interests.

". . . It is therefore, an American interest to see an end to nationhood as it has been historically defined."

WALT W. ROSTOW
(*The United States in the World Arena,*
Harper & Row, New York, 1960, p. 549)

"The goal of the Soviets remains victory, while ours remains peace."
RICHARD M. NIXON (February 21, 1968)

To avoid any misunderstanding and possibility of distortion in this age of "scientific" forgery and Orwellian dialectic, let me make it clear that the use of the word surrender does not refer to a formal act of surrender, solemnly signed by the representatives of a power which has lost a shooting war.

Formal acts of surrender do not necessarily express a readiness to renounce fundamental political ambitions nor the failure or abdication of the will to live and actively participate in international life. Brest-Litovsk in 1918, Compiègne in 1918, the battleship *Missouri* in 1945, are some recent examples. The bolsheviks signed with imperial Germany the humiliating terms of the treaty of Brest-Litovsk because they considered it as an unavoidable retreat, without which their regime in Russia could not survive. But they did not renounce their revolutionary aims.

In the forest of Compiègne, German representatives signed on November 11, 1918 the surrender of the German army, but, as the history of Germany in the ensuing years clearly shows, this also was an act of temporary powerlessness, which produced a strong reaction and was used by various groups to rouse German nationalism, and by one group to organize a revolutionary movement (the Nationalsocialist German Workers' Party—N.S.D.A.P.) which threatened to upset the map of the world, and did upset it, although in a way contrary to the intentions of Adolf Hitler.

As for the surrender of the Japanese armed forces on the U.S.S.

Missouri (Sept. 2, 1945), the present state of Japan clearly shows that no surrender of national existence and aspiration to a great role in world affairs was signed away.

On the other hand, history is full of real surrenders of nations too weak to assert themselves, too naive to understand political reality and international life, too spoiled by a good life and loose morals to muster the strength to discipline themselves, to face and defeat their enemies and set their house in order. In most cases, there was no formal surrender. There simply was no longer the will to live, the determination to fight, the pride to assert one's identity against foreign enemies, the noble ambition to be worthy of the ancestors and the responsibility to prepare a better future for the coming generations.

This is the kind of surrender I am talking about. It does not need to express itself in any spectacular moves which would reveal their meaning for everybody to understand. It is a rather complex process where the average citizen is unable to survey the whole field, to connect events and grasp their true meaning, and assess their consequences, but which, in its entirety, amounts to national surrender and suicide.

So, when I am using the word surrender, I am referring to a policy of concessions to the enemy in most matters of vital national interest, a readiness to compromise in all questions, no matter how brazen the challenge and unmistakable the hostility to the U.S. may be, an acceptance of yardsticks opposed to those upon which the nation was founded, compliance with the enemy's policy, willingness to open to public debate the most sacred values and principles of the nation's heritage and to step down or be swept away from the stage of world history.

And this process has been taking place in the United States, no matter how paradoxical it may seem. For a long time, the impressive might of the U.S., its leading position in the world, as well as the uniqueness of the U.S. position in history, were obstructing the view of reality. They still do, especially owing to the preponderance of liberal influence and slant in the ranks of our policy makers and public opinion makers.

But in spite of the reality of U.S. military might and industrial superiority, in spite of all the declarations of everybody's democratic respect for everybody else's rights and universal love of mankind emanating from the U.N., in spite of all the talk about joint U.S.-Soviet efforts for peace, in spite of all the official assurances that we are making progress toward a world of peace, freedom and security—there is one stark and incontrovertible fact: in the war for the conquest of the world, which the communists are waging with increased intensity, subtlety and efficacy, the leader of the free world, the United States of America, is losing because it is surrendering.

There is no other name for a policy which rejects U.S. national interests as its permanent basis, and shuns the idea of asserting U.S. rights and will in the world as a danger to peace* or as contrary to the standards of absolute morality, but adopts as guidelines the enemy's concepts, plans and strategy, because they allegedly offer the only alternative to the "thermonuclear holocaust" which would, they say, destroy mankind! Only surrender and suicide can designate a policy which rejects and penalizes U.S. friends and allies, and helps and supports U.S. enemies in the world.

No matter how our twentieth century will go down in history, what is happening before our eyes is the most fantastic unconditional surrender of a civilization before its enemy, the world has ever seen. And what makes the phenomenon the more puzzling and paradoxical, is that the surrendering civilization is headed by the youngest and most "successful" nation ever to attain the position of leader of the world.

Our planet has seen everything. But this is new. Many nations, states and empires have existed and disappeared from the world because they had spent their energies and capacity for survival, because great conquests and achievements or too soft a life had burned up their energies and exhausted their supplies of vitality, because they did not defend themselves against new, more primitive and far more militant enemies, because they disintegrated in

---

* "Eisenhower deliberately refrained from using America's vastly superior wealth, economic development and technology to create a permanent preponderance of military power over the Soviets that would have made any attack by them unthinkable. He even said (see Merlo Pusey: *Eisenhower the President*) that too strong an America "would itself become a potential menace to the peace." (Edgar Ansel Mowrer, article "U.S. Presidents For Last 18 years in Race for Peace," Long Island *Star*, September 30, 1961.)

corruption, frivolity and lack of civic spirit and public responsibility, because they were unable to change their ways and make the necessary adaptations in periods of historical transition—but no nation has ever engaged on a policy of active suicide as soon as it had reached its peak. The phenomenon is unique.

The more so since, among so many unknowns, imponderables and changing factors of the world scene, the main and decisive one has been there all the time, concrete, glaring, unchanged and growing in strength and hostility to the United States: world communism. In the face of this towering fact of the world and U.S. situation, the natural course for U.S. leaders, who are duty-bound to defend U.S. interests at any price, has been to face the facts of the international situation squarely, to determine U.S. policies accordingly and to stop the enemies of the United States with all the vigor and resources at our disposal.

This is definitely not what has happened.

Let us start with objective, well-known and indisputable facts.

The U.S. emerged from World War II as by far the strongest country in the world. And yet the result of World War II was: a. that the area under communism grew from 200 million people to 900 million, and b. that communist power, which until 1960 was some five thousand miles away from the United States, came (in Cuba) to a mere 90 miles from its shores.

Thus the career of the U.S. as the leader of the world had started with a most unusual paradox: as the country of "liberty and justice for all" rose to world leadership, liberty and justice were brutally crushed by communism in one-third of the world. The causes of this paradoxical development have been cleared in the meantime: while the U.S. military and industrial might was the decisive factor in inflicting military defeat on Hitler and Japan, the absence of U.S. political will in the face of fierce Soviet will to power and conquest, resulted in the spread of communism and the corresponding shrinkage of freedom in the world. The military victory of the United States over Hitler and Japan was accompanied by a U.S. political surrender before the Soviet Union.

It would have been logical to expect that once the euphoria of U.S.-Soviet wartime fraternization had worn off and yielded to the reality of Soviet unchanged revolutionary ambitions and policies, the U.S. course of surrender would also have been radically altered in favor of a policy of elementary common sense.

To shape such a policy, two considerations would appear as beyond controversy and perfectly clear: 1. that the unchangeable objective of U.S. foreign policy is to safeguard the national interests of the United States, and 2. that the Soviet Union is the main historical challenger and aggressor, with the main imperialist and subversive thrust of its policy directed against the United States.

In all vicissitudes and changes of the international situation, those two considerations would be the decisive factors shaping U.S. foreign policy.

One part of President Kennedy's Inaugural Address (January 20, 1961) seemed to have been inspired by this concept:

"Let every nation know, whether it wishes us well or ill, that we shall pay any price, bear any burden, meet any hardship, support any friend, oppose any foe to assure the survival and the success of liberty."

Unfortunately, our policy under President Kennedy (as well as later) remained unaffected by such thinking and sentiments. It is the policy of surrender, of withdrawal of U.S. power before communist power which, instead of being discontinued, remained the rule.

The Record of Surrender

The U.S. won World War II, but President Roosevelt let Stalin be the political arbiter of the war and actively worked to safeguard Soviet interests by telling Stalin that he was determined not to let any regime hostile to the Soviet Union be established along its borders. Stalin had no objections to that resolve. Thus, half of Europe was given to communism.

Moreover, the political defeat of the West in World War II and the corresponding triumph of the communists were institutionalized by the creation of the United Nations. The U.N., as conceived and brought into being, was an admission by the West that communism was here to stay and that it belonged to civilized society and humanity. No restrictions were imposed on the USSR and other communist regimes in the pursuit of their unchanged objectives.

Our anti-colonialist policy, by weakening the position of the West in the world, fitted into Moscow's world strategy, as Lenin stipulated and the Congresses of the Communist International untiringly stressed.

The policy of historical surrender was evident in Korea (1950–1953), where U.S. troops for the first time in history were unable to win a war, because they were prevented from achieving victory. This "refusal of the United States to win the Korean war was a major disaster of the free world," in the estimate of General Douglas MacArthur.

In 1954 we let the French be defeated in Indochina by the communists, and endorsed the decisions of the Geneva Conference on Indochina, which spelled gradual surrender to communism.

In 1955 our enthusiastic participation at the Geneva Conference (Eisenhower-Khrushchev) greatly enhanced the prestige of the Soviet Union.

The next year was marked by the shocking indifference of the Western world to the occupation of Tibet by Red China and the crimes perpetrated against Tibetan freedom fighters, and by the equally intolerable inaction in the face of the anti-communist uprising in Hungary (October 1956) which had excellent chances of succeeding and spreading throughout Eastern Europe.

In the same year we gave Nikita Khrushchev a big propaganda and prestige victory by inviting him to the United States.

In 1960 the intervention of Secretary of State Christian Herter in South Korea against President Syngman Rhee was the decisive factor in bringing about his downfall.

In April 1961 the failure of the anti-communist invasion of Cuba by Cuban patriots, with U.S. official help organizing the invasion and preventing its success, was another communist victory and U.S. surrender, i.e., proof of communist invincibility and U.S. impotence.

This was also the year of the erection of the Berlin wall, which was proof of Western weakness of will and triumph of communist aggressiveness, boldness and disregard for treaty obligations.[6] This boldness may very easily have been instigated by the experience of the Berlin airlift of 1949. For the issue then was not whether land access to West Berlin would be free. It was not. So, the success of U.S. ingenuity, logistics and technology was offset by the defeat of U.S. political will.

In 1961 our State Department also "arbitrated" the issue of West New Guinea (West Irian) by pressuring the Netherlands to yield to the U.N., which in turn gave it to Sukarno, the pro-communist dictator of Indonesia.

U.S. official influence and pressure were clearly used in Laos against the anti-communist and pro-American governments of Premier Samsonith and then Prince Boun Oum, as well as against the most popular nationalist leader, General Nosavan, and in favor of the neutralist Souvanna Phouma, acceptable to the Soviet Union. In 1962 the Geneva Conference on Laos imposed the same kind of "coalition" government which in World War II was imposed on Chiang Kai-shek, decisively influencing the struggle between the nationalists and communists in China.

The Cuban crisis of October/November 1962 is almost generally considered as a major turning point in international relations after World War II, from "total war" to "total peace," to speak with Walt Rostow.[7] The facts of the matter are that the confrontation resulted in a guaranty to the communist regime in Cuba that it would be unmolested and that no Cuban patriots would be helped or even allowed to undertake any action to liberate their country from communism. It also resulted in the dismantling of U.S. bases in Italy and (partly) in Turkey.

The last few years have been occupied mainly with our intervention in South Vietnam, to which a separate chapter is dedicated.

Now, our military actions against communist aggression should not confuse anybody. For important as military actions are, their real and final effect always depends on political decisions and the political framework within which they are implemented.

In Korea our soldiers fought as valiantly as ever, but they were not allowed to win. And Vietnam is the most drastic example of the futility of military action against communist military aggression, as long as it is hampered by our overall foreign policy of collaboration with communism.

In other words, World War II, Korea and Vietnam prove beyond any doubt that military resistance to communism alone, without politically determined opposition, is powerless. Military actions and victories are in vain as long as they are used to promote communist *political* power.

In any case, our foreign policy, for all the exceptions that could be indicated (Greece, Turkey, Iran, Guatemala, Lebanon, Dominican Republic), has been a policy of yielding to the communist enemy, of working actively in his favor (economically, financially, technically, politically, propaganda-wise), and this in the face of unhidden and incontrovertible communist hostility. Our inconceivable and unforgivable trust in the communists has made it possible for their espionage to operate freely and perform services to communism which have, without the slightest exaggeration, changed the course of history. It suffices to mention the delivery of our atomic secrets to the Soviet Union and the key role which the British spies Burgess, Maclean and Philby played in influencing the war in Korea.

At the same time we have used our influence and worked against staunch anti-communists and U.S. allies, from Draza Mihailovich to Presidents Syngman Rhee (Korea) and Diem and Thieu (South Vietnam).

In a historical era where we are faced with the evident and implacable hostility of the USSR and all the communists, we have worked and applied a double standard of politics and morality, not in our favor and against the enemy, but against ourselves and in favor of the communist enemy.

They Know

To make the problem even more perplexing, the excuse of ignorance can hardly be invoked by any of the responsible figures who have been our national leaders in all the years of the decline of the U.S. will to self-assertion.

Who has not, in explaining and analyzing the disastrous course of our appeasement and coexistence policy to uninformed individuals, heard the desperate retort: "All right, even if that is so, don't you think that the men in Washington know that better than you, or at least as well as you do?" Of course they do. And that precisely is what makes the problem so perplexing and so difficult. For there can be no doubt that all or most of those who have had the responsibility to shape and conduct our foreign policy over a considerable period of years, have known the truth about communism. There is practically no leading American political figure who has not, at one time or another, spoken about the aggressive and imperialistic character of communism, its ruthless methods of oppression at home and aggression and deceit in international relations, its unchanged goal of world conquest, its threat to the security of the United States.

In 1935 Hamilton Fish Armstrong, an outstanding expert on international affairs and, as secretary general of the Council on Foreign Relations and editor of the magazine *Foreign Affairs*—for many years influential shaper of U.S. foreign policy—wrote a remarkable booklet entitled *We or They* in which he pointed out the incompatibility between U.S. concepts, principles and interests and those of (both) the fascists and the communists.

As early as February 1940, President Roosevelt had stated that "The Soviet Union, as everybody knows who has the courage to face the facts, is a dictatorship as absolute as any other dictatorship in the world." At this time, Hitler was in full political ascent.

In 1947, two years before the communist conquest of China, Senator Arthur Vandenberg warned against the peril of the U.S. Government being misled by the propaganda that Chinese communists were just "agrarian reformers." Instead, he recommended that "we might as well begin to face the Communist challenge on every front."

Speaking on January 30, 1949 in Salem, Mass., the then Congressman John Fitzgerald Kennedy said:

"At the Yalta Conference of 1945 a sick Roosevelt with the advice of Gen. Marshall and other chiefs of staff gave the Kurile Islands as well as the control of various strategic Chinese ports, such as Port Arthur and Dairen, to the Soviet Union . . . This is the tragic story of China, whose freedom we once fought to preserve. What our young men had saved, our diplomats and our President have frittered away."

During the presidential campaign of 1952, General Eisenhower warned against the Soviet unchanged intent to destroy "democracy in general and . . . the U.S. in particular." He expressed the same thought nine years later (May 1961), that "basic Soviet policies had not changed." [8]

President Truman was quoted as stating, with his customary bluntness:

> "There wouldn't be any cold war if the Russians had kept their word with us. They lied to me 32 times and to President Franklin Roosevelt 16 times." [9]

Even Mr. Dean Rusk, the champion of the "winds-of-change" theory of history, designated the communist global "announced determination to impose a world of coercion upon those not already subject to it," as "the central issue" of the world crisis.[10]

General Earle G. Wheeler, Army Chief of Staff told the American Legion that there had been "no slackening in the Communist aim of world domination." [11]

President Nixon has in the past stood out among U.S. statesmen and policy-makers in his clear awareness of the communist danger and the impossibility of coexisting with it. His position stated in 1964, that

> ". . . The communist goal is to impose slavery on the free world. The United States goal must be nothing else than to bring freedom to the communist world."

is no exception, but a typical example of his thinking on the problem of communism and freedom.

Even more significant is his sharp characterization of the comparative goals of the U.S. vs. Soviet policies (in a speech in Rhinelander, Wisconsin, in 1968) to the effect that:

> "the goal of the Soviets still remains victory, while ours remains peace." [12]

And it is a matter of common knowledge that while pursuing his policy of building bridges with the main subverter of the world and the pillar of the North Vietnamese war effort, the Soviet Union, President Johnson repeatedly called the attention of the public to communist unrelenting aggression and subversion, as he did in his San Antonio speech (September 30, 1967): ". . . I do know that there are North Vietnamese troops in Laos; there are North Vietnamese guerillas in northeast Thailand; there are communist-supported guerilla forces in Burma; and a communist coup was barely averted in Indonesia."

Finally, in his article "In Quest For Peace" (February 1969),[13] which presents the sum of his five years in office, his experience and conclusions about the world situation and its key features, Lyndon B. Johnson pointed to "the existence of totalitarian communist power in much of the Eurasian land mass—power which continuously threatens to disrupt such order as the world had managed to achieve."

Examples could be multiplied indefinitely. These are just a few samples of the clear awareness of U.S. leaders that the world is faced by a force whose basic policy, in spite of all its tactics and pretenses of cooperation and coexistence, is simply to conquer the whole world.

However, in spite of this clear awareness, our policy has been based on ideas which deny the supreme importance of U.S. national interests as the foundation for U.S. foreign policy, and ignore the true nature of the Soviet Union and its communist policies.

Comparing Prime Minister Harold Macmillan's statements and his policies, Malcolm Muggeridge concluded that "there is no correlation between word and deed, between the aspirations ostensibly entertained and what actually happens." [14] This observation fully applies to the views of U.S. leaders which stress the aggressive character of communism, and their policies, which are based on the idea of coexistence with communism.

The first and most important fact to keep in mind in attempting to understand and explain this crucial contrast is that the general attitude, world outlook and public philosophy underwent a rapid and thorough change immediately after World War II.

In World War II, there was not the slightest ambiguity about the military enemy, Nazi Germany and Japan, about the aim, unconditional victory, and about the need not to rely on events and trends, but to strain every bit of our resources and efforts to beat the enemy. All forces had to be mobilized to capacity for the attainment of that goal. And the only answer we were willing to accept from the enemy, was unconditional surrender.

World War II brought about a reversal in American political thinking and political philosophy. When the enemy was Hitler and Tojo, the philosophy was struggle and victory. When after the war the only (remaining) enemy was the Soviet Union and world communism, we started becoming "optimists." Now, our top experts, such as George Kennan, Averell Harriman, Senator Fulbright, Charles Bohlen, Harlan Cleveland, Walt Rostow, Dean Rusk, George Ball, McGeorge Bundy, etc., launched a new philosophy. Reversing the statement of General Douglas MacArthur, the greatest American general of modern times and one of the greatest in history, that "in war there is no substitute for victory," they proclaimed that the concept of victory belonged to the realm of harmless pastimes, to sport (baseball, football, basketball, etc.), but not to the serious business of national and international politics. (They have proven their point in Vietnam, where they have seen to it that the United States would not achieve victory.)

In World War II the magnitude of our task, of the issues and values at stake called for total ruthlessness in the struggle. "I want every devilish, subtle device and every underhanded operation possible to use against the Germans and Japs by the Underground in all occupied countries," was the request addressed by Gen. William J. Donovan, chief of the Office of Strategic Services, to his director of research, Stanley P. Lovell.[15]

Now, all of a sudden, the supreme rule was humanity and morality in our behavior toward the avowed mortal enemy, an enemy who is guided by an absolute disregard for any humanity or morality. The rule of morality is discarded only in our dealing with the strivings of the enslaved peoples for liberty, since they disturb our policy of coexistence with the Soviet Union and world communism. They have to be sacrificed to placate the enemy and attain accommodation with the communists. But in dealing with the communists, we must be strictly moral and must absolutely not use their methods, because "if we do the same, we are the same."

In World War II we were constantly reminded that the tree of liberty needed to be fed with both the blood of the tyrants and of the freedom fighters, and the more (human) lawns were mowed, the better would the grass grow. Now, peace was rapidly becoming more important than freedom, and blood-letting had to stop, allegedly in the interests of humanity. The only blood that could flow freely was the blood of freedom fighters, mowed down by communist secret police or foreign communist occupation troops.

In World War II great emphasis was put on the need for sacrifice of personal comfort, material goods, family happiness, personal interests, for the cause. The new line was that mankind had seen enough, too much, of sacrifice and suffering, and that it was high time to make an end to it all and become "human" again.

In World War II the war effort drew heavily on traditions in the fight for national independence and the freedom of every participating nation. Now, tradition belonged to the scrap heap of history, since the source of war was the nation-state, and all traditions were connected and imbued with the nation-state and its warmaking. The new, atomic age, required that a clean slate be made with the "dead wood" of the past and that all forces and energies be devoted to the building of entirely new, global traditions of coexistence, collaboration and world brotherhood.

The Attitudes and Climate of Surrender

This change of basic outlook assumed many forms. Our leaders took a position on world communium as if it were just a matter of mutual suspicion and misunderstanding and insufficient knowledge about each other, so that the remedy would clearly be to learn more about the other side and be nicer to it. Typical is the recommendation of Kenneth T. Young, former U.S. Ambassador to Thailand, President of the Asia Society, for the solution of U.S.-Asia problems: "Let us all seek some common reality to overcome this legacy of suspicion and divergence." [16]

Not only did we not adopt a hostile attitude toward communism, a position of "either-or," but on the contrary, we exerted the most strenuous efforts to consider and solve all problems in the perspective of one, indivisible mankind, where that which unites us above all ideological barriers, outweighs that which divides us.

We have proclaimed from the most authoritative place that war was "unthinkable" (President Eisenhower), and we have stressed a million times that in a future war there would be no victors, but only losers. We would just have to learn to live together or we would die together. ("One world or no world," in the formula of Arnold Toynbee.) [17]

In that spirit, Franklin D. Roosevelt did not shy away from subordinating U.S. national interests to those of U.S.-Soviet "understanding" and collaboration: "I am determined that there shall be no breach between ourselves and the Soviet Union." That word he kept. And over 800 million people were enslaved by communism.

That Rooseveltian tradition of considering the Soviet Union and world communism not as the enemy, but as partners and allies in the struggle for peace, has never been abandoned. It still pervades the outlook and thinking of our policy-makers.

We have minimized the communist danger, its hostility and subversive virulence.

We have stubbornly refused to see communism's repulsive face. In the presence of communist aggression in Laos and Tibet (1959), all that Mrs. Eleanor Roosevelt was able to say was that such cases (of blatant communist aggression) "create great uncertainty in our minds." [18]

This refusal to face the truth about communism has taken the strangest forms, from espousing Thomas Mann's position that "Communism has some relation to the ideals of humanity and a better future" (receiving in Frankfurt the city's annual Goethe prize), to the "realization" that "communism need not necessarily be totalitarian." [19]

We have, against our best judgment, treated the communists as people amenable to reason and apt to reject ideology in favor of common sense. In his telecast on "Red China: The Roots of Madness," one of the top U.S. liberal experts on that country, Theodore White, viewed it as our "Key problem: to reach the minds of Mao's successors with reason, before the bomb destroys the world." As if the Chinese communists were naughty children enjoying their power unrestricted by law, which the policy of Franklin Roosevelt and after made accessible to them, and not the most cold-blooded despisers of human lives, foreign or Chinese.

We have gone out of our way to defend communists from communism: "Castro . . . is not only not communist but decidedly anti-communist" was the verdict of a famous *New York Times* reporter and expert on Latin American problems, Herbert L. Matthews.[20]

One of the most shockingly defeatist statements on U.S.-communist relations stems from a leading U.S. foreign policy thinker and shaper, Ambassador George F. Kennan. In a television interview in 1967, he paid tribute to the durability and achievements (!) of communism in Russia (50 years) and then said that the U.S. should "not press too hard" for victory in Vietnam, since the Soviets and Red Chinese "cannot afford to let us end this war with some sort of military victory on our terms." Therefore, to strive for U.S. victory "would be harmful to this nation." [21]

Tito's expulsion from the Cominform by Stalin (June 28, 1948) was viewed as a gift from heaven by a West craving for accommodation at any price with communism. This was it! Tito was admittedly a communist, but a different, national, democratic communist, which made all the difference in the world. On a number of occasions, Tito bluntly denounced such nonsense: "There is no such thing as national communism. It was invented by some Western newspapermen." Nevertheless Western propaganda about the blessings of "national communism" has never subsided.

We have praised the human qualities of communist leaders under whose rule dozens of millions of people have been tortured and put to death (Lenin, Mao, Khrushchev, etc.) and given them all the benefits of all doubts. In presenting a family portrait of Nikita Khrushchev two months before his visit to the U.S., the *Chicago Daily News* (June 23, 1959) commented: "One wonders whether any man who loves his grandchildren . . . as much as Khrushchev seems to would dare start a nuclear war that could wipe them out along with virtually everyone else." Very similar views were expressed by President Eisenhower. *The Daily News,* however—apparently to strengthen its argument—added: "Such would-be conquerors as Hitler and Napoleon didn't have grandchildren."

We have outdone the communists in pro-communist fervor. According to *Newsweek* magazine,[22] when Khrushchev arrived in Kabul in March 1960, radio Moscow simply said that "Khrushchev was warmly greeted by thousands of people." But the Voice of

America was in much higher spirits about the visit: "Khrushchev was enthusiastically greeted by half a million people."

We have pronounced ourselves unable to fathom the enemy. Winston Churchill's statement about the USSR being "a riddle wrapped in a mystery inside an enigma," has been used as an excuse for all our wrong moves and all inexcusable ignorance and misconceptions about the Soviet Union. The same attitude has prevailed about Red China, a "maze of imponderables" within a whole complex of "desperately complicated" related problems. (Senator Vandenberg).[23]

Our representatives have made statements pertaining to some of the most important questions of our time, which may abstractly be true, but which, spoken from the political platform, and proclaimed to the whole world under conditions of communist total political war against the free world, amount to statements of surrender. Such is the case, for instance, with the recommendation of Henry Cabot Lodge to the whole world to practice tolerance and realize that "nobody has the infallible truth." [24] Such a statement is the last thing able to move the communists to desist from their attitude of omniscience and infallibility. It is rather bound to confirm them in it, by showing the lack of self-reliance and self-confidence of the free world. In the same category belongs the statement of President Kennedy that today "the U.S. does not have an answer to every world problem."

Faced with implacable communist imperialism and subversion, we have not fought back, nor have we refuted or challenged communist accusation and vilification against the United States. We have instead considered it an important obligation of the U.S. to convince the world that *we* meant no harm, that *we* were not threatening the world and especially the communists. We have substituted emotional pleas for "an understanding of America's heart," that she wants "peace, nothing else" (President Eisenhower's statement on October 4, 1958), for policies based on hard facts and U.S. vital interests.

When Nikita Khrushchev visited the United States, *The New York Times* thought that more important than "any impression we could score with our material might, or even evidence of our unity," was the task of proving to Khrushchev "that freedom here was real" (!)[25]

Worst of all, we have rejected the struggle against communism as historically hopeless or as immoral, and thus advocated accommodation with it at any price.

Harold Ickes, Secretary of Interior in F. D. Roosevelt's administration, reported on a most interesting talk that he had with the then Secretary of War, George Dern, about world affairs and communism: "He feels about Red hunting just as I do and thinks it absurd to deny Communists an opportunity to express themselves . . . He thinks, as I do, that *we are working towards a society of modified communism,* although I believe he would be as unhappy in a Communist state as I. He feels as I do that *it is better to bend to the wind* than to be torn from the trunk of the tree and dashed to the ground." [26]

The same attitude was adopted several years later, in World War II, by Harry Hopkins, Roosevelt's alter ego and possibly the most influential man in the U.S. at that time, who thought "the world is definitely swinging to the Left, that we are in the middle of the revolution and that it would be unwise to try to oppose it." [27]

The important and disturbing thing is that this attitude did not remain confined to people of Hopkins' political hue, but spread over a wider spectrum of political orientation, becoming the prevailing mood among the nation's leaders.

During the presidential campaign of 1952, General Eisenhower spoke of "rolling back the Iron Curtain." But John Foster Dulles, as Secretary of State designate, made it plain, in November 1952, that no such thing was intended at all: "Violent revolt would be futile. Indeed, it would be worse than futile, for it would precipitate massacre." [28]

This attitude ran clearly against the mood and strivings of the oppressed people under communism, who in East Berlin (1953), Poznan (1955) and Budapest (1956) gave unambiguous evidence of their appreciation of freedom and the sacrifices worth bearing for it. Their great chances of achieving freedom were reduced to massacre not because of their shortcomings, or the strength of the communist regimes, but because of the concepts of U.S. impotence and the futility of the struggle for freedom, prevailing in the State Department.

In 1958, during the second Eisenhower administration, the Rand

Corporation, under a research contract with the Air Force, undertook a study on Strategic Surrender which "scientifically" considered the advisability of the U.S. rejecting the traditional concept of victory in a future (nuclear) conflict, and adopting one of "compromise," for humanitarian reasons. In our nuclear age and in the new world strategic situation, victory—so opined the author of the study, Paul Kecskemeti—would require "going to extremes of inhumanity and malevolence never imagined before." And since the U.S. "traditions of humanity and benevolence" exclude "this inhuman alternative to survival," we must realize that "the maxim that 'in war there is no substitute for victory' is totally erroneous." "We shall have to revise some of our deeply rooted traditional attitudes" and adopt "less rigid, more elastic ways of thinking about the international conflict and international harmony."

As David Lawrence aptly pointed out in his column of August 15, 1958,[29] the talk of surrender was nothing new. For

". . . the talk of stopping nuclear tests . . . could result in a 'surrender psychology'; the talk of the horrors of a nuclear war and that America . . . must choose between some kind of 'negotiated' agreement or destruction, is also a kind of 'surrender' talk; . . . the talk of 'disengagement' of American forces stationed in Europe is 'surrender' talk in the guise of peacemaking; . . . the talk of admitting Red China to the UN Security Council and thus forfeiting Chiang's Army of 300,000 men in Formosa involves virtually a military surrender in the Far East; . . . the talk deriding 'massive retaliation' is related to the surrender concept . . . and the talk of appeasing Nasser and giving him what he wants in the Near East is 'surrender talk.' "

In March 1962 President John F. Kennedy made his stupefying statement, in an interview with Stewart Alsop, that in view of the USSR's growing nuclear power, "the day could come when . . . the West would choose a concealed surrender rather than the risk of the ultimate terror of thermonuclear war." Recently, a leading liberal diplomat, economist and thinker, Professor John Galbraith, offered the opinion that the war in Vietnam not only was a war "which our people do not support . . . and . . . we cannot win," but a war we "should not wish to win." [30]

In accordance with this basic stance of avoiding struggle against communism at any price—and, once engaged in a struggle, avoid at any price winning it—we have directed our arrows against anti-communists, trying to oppose and defeat the communists, as in the case of China, where according to President Roosevelt, "the fault lay more with the Kuomintang and the Chungking Government than with the so-called Communists." The same attitude was adopted in the case of many other countries (all of Eastern Europe, Cuba, Vietnam, etc.).

Possibly the most unbelievable and most disgraceful statement on the Soviet Union ever to come from a U.S. official place is the one to which Congressman John Ashbrook called our attention when he discussed the annual report of the Arms Control and Disarmament Agency, which contains the following passage:

> "We benefit enormously from the capability of the Soviet Police System to keep law and order over 200 million odd Russians and the many millions in the satellite states. The breakup of the Russian Communist empire today would doubtless be conducive to freedom, but would be a good deal more catastrophic for world order than was the breakup of the Austro-Hungarian Empire in 1918." [31]

It is, of course, difficult to identify all the various component parts and factors contributing to this general attitude and atmosphere of surrender before the enemy, thus betraying one's world responsibilities and especially the responsibility before one's own people and its future.

The range of motives, processes of reasoning, psychological transformation, intellectual confusion, transvaluation of values, hopelessness, or simply opportunistic reorientation—is very wide. But the decisive point is that in practice, in real life, the results, the consequences are the same.

When Robert F. Kennedy, former U.S. Attorney General, on his fact-finding and good-will political tour (1964) declared in Toronto that

> "We must recognize that the young in many areas of the world are in the midst of a revolution against the status quo. They are

not going to accept platitudes and generalities . . . And we must recognize one simple fact: they will prevail. They will achieve their idealistic goals one way or the other. If they have to pull governments tumbling down over their heads, they will do it." [32]

he was not helping "the young in the world," but promoting unconditional surrender to communism on a world scale as the only reasonable attitude of the West, which had found its champion in Aneurin Bevan some years earlier. Speaking in the House of Commons, Bevan asserted that it was vain to try to stop the Chinese revolution, as it was vain to try to stop the Russian revolution, and concluded:

> "We shall bring upon us a third world war by not realizing that you cannot do anything with these revolutionaries except work with them, help them through their difficulties and not make it necessary for them to oppress their own people." [33]

And while Joseph Alsop is far apart from Aneurin Bevan (and, in all probability, from Robert Kennedy, too) in political philosophy, his consideration of the Soviet invasion of Czechoslovakia, on August 21, 1968, leads to conclusions which have identical political results: "It is horrible to stand by helplessly . . . ," but "the Western powers cannot, in truth should not, come to the rescue." [34] "There is nothing much this country can do about it, except pray for the victims." [35]

It stands to reason that with the shapers of U.S. policy and public opinion holding such views, the practice of U.S. foreign policy was bound to be one of surrender.

It is out of this new state of mind of our policy-makers that the four basic points of U.S. foreign policy naturally emerged: peace, the U.N., anti-colonialism and coexistence.

Peace

War, runs the argument, has always been the worst evil and the chief enemy of mankind, its welfare, happiness and progress. Today, with the threat of global nuclear annihilation hanging over our heads, war looms as a greater and more horrible danger than ever before. If the leading atomic powers in the world used their nuclear weapons in a future war, the result would not be great material damage and casualties in the millions, as in the two world wars, but the annihilation of mankind. Thus, it is vain to speak of victory as a rational aim, since in a nuclear war there would be no victors, but only losers. Clearly, war in our nuclear age has become "unthinkable." And consequently, the main aim of U.S. foreign policy must be to do everything possible to avoid the horrors of thermonuclear war and ensure peace.

U.N.

Since today no world power, and that includes the U.S., is strong enough to ensure peace by its own strength and means, there must be a universal organization which will assume the task and which for that purpose must be above the individual—big and small—nations of the world.

This is the more imperative since sovereign states, with their independent means and policies, have been the main source of all wars in history. Therefore, to ensure world peace, it is imperative that all member-states delegate one part of their traditional sovereignty to that international body. And that is only the first step, which must be followed by many more in the same sense, so that the sovereignty of individual states be restricted all the time, while the power of the international body be increased correspondingly. Typical is the stand of Walt Whitman Rostow, chief U.S. foreign policy planner for several years under President Kennedy:

"... it is a legitimate American national objective to see removed from all nations—including the United States—the right to use substantial military force to pursue their own interests. Since this residual right is the root of the national sovereignty and the basis for the existence of an international arena of power, it is, therefore, an American interest to see an end to nationhood as it has been historically defined." [36]

President Kennedy was evidently expounding the Rostow philosophy when he said in his speech to the U.N. General Assembly on September 25, 1961: ". . . And as we build the international capacity to keep peace, let us join in dismantling the national capacity to wage war." [37]

The international organization to fulfill the noble task of saving mankind from war and guaranteeing lasting peace in the world is the United Nations Organization, based on the fundamental idea of the democratic-communist alliance of World War II, that "antifascism" guarantees an effective and equitable cooperation of all its members, regardless of their political philosophies.

If mankind is to be saved, it must be unified, sovereign states must be liquidated by general and universal disarmament, all national armies must be abolished in favor of a one-world police force which would control all nations and all individuals. While the goal may appear too ambitious and remote today, it must guide the efforts and policies of all sovereign countries, including the United States.

Indeed, too many of our officials are inclined to consider the U.N. superior to the U.S., because the U.N. is supposedly above all and any nations. Walter Lippmann, a leading leftist Westerner, to use A. Sakharov's term, considers the Secretary General of the U.N. as a "father confessor," to whom the representatives of all nations should confess their sins, discuss their problems and take mandatory advice from.

The U.N., we are told, is the "hope of mankind." Its very existence is a boon to all nations, since it keeps their representatives talking, instead of their armed forces fighting. As for communism, it is through the U.N. that its virulence is being toned down and its revolutionary energies are being turned from hostility and destruction toward cooperation.

Anti-colonialism

Mankind, we are told, is going through one of the most revolutionary periods in its entire history. Both in the social order and the international order, forces are at work which irresistibly strive to change the existing conditions inherited from before World War II. These forces are revolutionary in character, they express the realization on the part of the countless millions of underprivileged and underdeveloped in the world of what they have been

missing in life and of their right to all that life can offer. Therefore, their strivings are both natural and irresistible. The "revolution of rising expectations" is a fact. The winds of inexorable
change are blowing all over the world and it would be immoral,
foolish and in the last resort suicidal for the "haves" (headed by
the U.S.) to try to stem the tide of the have nots, resist the winds
of change favoring them, suppress the rising masses, influence the
course of history against those imminent forces and trends.

All the U.S. can and should do, is to go along, to help liquidate
the unjust international order of colonialism, which is no longer
defendable and liveable, and lend all its assistance to the newly
awakened peoples and masses of the world to find their way toward a life of material progress, education and freedom (G. C.
Marshall, R. Kennedy).

This anti-colonial ingredient in our foreign policy is of great
consequence. First, because it is a vital and natural part of our
national tradition of anti-colonialism and self-determination
(Rusk), and second because it is the most efficient way to prevent
those emerging nations from turning to the communists, accepting
their aid, guidance and influence and becoming allies in fighting
and destroying the U.S.

Coexistence (Accommodation and collaboration with "modified"
communism).

The fourth basic principle of our foreign policy, which contains
its essence and from which all others are derived, is coexistence.

While our policy of coexistence has evolved over a period of
years and cannot be ascribed to one author, there can be little
doubt that Walt W. Rostow, as chairman of the State Department's Policy Planning Council, made in 1962 a unique contribution to it with his Strategy plan (of 168 pages), which contained
guidelines for a "new" U.S. foreign policy.

Actually the plan contained nothing new. All the ideas presented in it had been implemented in the previous years. And it
was preceded by moves and events which provided the ideal setting for a bold new thrust in the same direction.

In 1961 the campaign of Secretary of Defense Robert S. Mc-

Namara and Senator William J. Fulbright, chairman of the U.S. Senate Foreign Relations Committee, against U.S. military leaders doing their duty of informing their troops about the communist enemy, bore the unmistakable imprint of surrender. Expressions like "the communist challenge," "communist blackmail," "soviet bluster," "communist threat" were censored from the speeches of high U.S. military officials.[38]

Admiral H. D. Felt, commander in chief of the U.S. forces in the Pacific, was forbidden to describe communist strategy as "subversion and armed revolution." [39] Secretary of the Army, Elvis J. Stahr, was not permitted to state publicly "that the Communists have not abandoned their plans for world conquest." The same treatment of suppression was administered to Secretary of the Air Force, Eugene Zuckert.[40]

Then, in September 1961, the U.S. submitted to the Sixteenth General Assembly of the United Nations, a "program for General and Complete Disarmament in a Peaceful World," (*Department of State publication 7727*), which proclaimed as supreme goal "a world in which adjustment to change takes place in accordance with the principles of the United Nations." The chief objective "toward which nations should direct their efforts" is "the disbanding of all national armed forces and the prohibition of their reestablishment in any form whatsoever other than those required to preserve internal order and for contribution to a United Nations Peace Force."

This "grand design of surrender," in the words of Robert Morris amounted to "no more United States of America." [41] And yet, to the knowledge of this writer, nobody was ever asked to account for this outrageous act in favor of peace on the grave of the United States.

The Rostow Plan was also preceded (in April 1962) by a 286-page State Department document entitled *Basic National Security Policy* filed with a special Senate subcommittee, under the signature of Undersecretary of State George V. Ball. It might have been composed (and probably was) by the same "whiz-kids" censors who in 1961 muzzled U.S. military leaders, for it oozed unmistakable surrender:

—it banned all talk of victory in the cold war with the USSR because such talk was militaristic and aggressive and implied "an all-or-nothing approach which leaves no room for accommodation with the Soviet Union"

—it stressed the vital importance of "communication" between the U.S. and the USSR, which must never be jeopardized by "provocative" statements from American leaders (!), and above all

—any statement which offered the slightest possibility of being interpreted as "a suggestion that the people should overthrow the Soviet government" was absolutely intolerable.[42]

The sum of Mr. Ball's five-hour testimony was that

"We must bring about situations which will be attractive to the Communists and induce them to reject their society for ours. This is a positive policy. It is very difficult and complex. It is not an easy business."

(The communists find attractive only those situations which offer chances for advancing the interests of communist power. How the creation of such situations by the West would induce the communists to reject their society for ours, Mr. Ball never explained).

This suffices to make clear that the task of the Rostow plan was not to innovate anything, but rather to raise the existing practice to the level of principles and guidelines. The plan, whose text was never made public and which was never officially endorsed by President Kennedy, nevertheless became a code of U.S. foreign policy guidelines and has been thoroughly implemented ever since.

The essence of Rostow's "precise, balanced and complete master plan of global objectives and strategies" [43] can be summed up in the following propositions:

1. We must recognize the strength and influence of the Soviet Union (and communism in general) as a world force. It is here to stay and it is also in a position to start a nuclear war, in which—"as we all know"—there would be no winner, only losers. In the words of Secretary of Defense McNamara: "If someone thinks we should have a nuclear war in order to win, I can inform them that there will be no winners of the next nuclear war, if there is one . . ." [44]

2. Besides, communism in the Soviet Union and other commu-

nist countries, is undergoing substantial changes, which make accommodation and collaboration with communism not only desirable, but possible and beneficial. The consolidation of communist regimes and the realization that nuclear war would make an end not only to capitalism but to communism as well, is inducing them to relent strict police controls, to renounce their aims of world conquest by force, and to concentrate on the solution of their internal problems. They are increasingly inclined to lessen tensions, coexist peacefully and collaborate with the U.S. to solve the common problems of mankind (poverty, disease, ignorance, etc.)

3. If these two propositions about communism are accepted as dogmas, then the inescapable first and most important conclusion is that our attitude and policy regarding the USSR must not be struggle, antagonism, cold war and victory, but accommodation. Instead of fighting communism, we must do everything possible to come to terms with it. And to that effect, we must set the greatest store by

4. keeping "communication" with the communists open at all times and at any price.

And this can be achieved if we strictly and absolutely reject any idea of victory over communism. "It will not be a victory of the United States over Russia." "It will not be a victory of capitalism over socialism." The free world will not triumph over "the communist bloc." "It will be a victory of men and nations over the forces that wish to entrap and to exploit their revolutionary aspirations." W. Rostow took care of not identifying the forces which "entrap and exploit" men and nations, nor clarifying the concept of the "revolutionary aspirations" of those same men and nations.

In any case W. Rostow expected "this planet to organize itself in time on the principles of voluntary cooperation among independent nations dedicated to human freedom," which will triumph "on both sides of the iron curtain." And if he does not explicitly state how the betrayal of freedom will make it triumphant or how the West's appeasement of communism will make it wither away, he apparently expects that:

5. This result will be brought about by a fundamental shift of emphasis in U.S. foreign policy, "from the problems of opposing communist aggression to exploiting opportunities in building and extending "a community of free nations."

To this end, the Soviet Union "must be granted its status as a great power," Western free countries must be encouraged to establish closer ties with the Soviet satellites and furnish them aid. But "above all, no encouragement or support must be given to armed uprisings in eastern Europe." For this belongs to the concepts and philosophy of the now surpassed era of the "cold war" and thus must be discarded, since the removal of all factors of mutual suspicion and justified Soviet fear from U.S. imperialism and aggression is vital for U.S.-Soviet collaboration. We must now insist not on that which divides us, but discover and cultivate "areas of overlapping interests with Communist regimes." [45]

In view of the strained relations between the Soviet Union and Red China, and the Soviet fear of nuclear weapons in Red Chinese hands, the USSR might find "that the only logical course is to make a common cause with the United States to establish a minimum framework of order."

6. W. Rostow assigned a place of priority in his master plan to a new U.S. nuclear strategy which would be that the U.S. "would never strike the first nuclear blow unless it were faced with a massive conventional assault, such as a full-scale invasion of western Europe." [46]

In November 1960, after the elections which made Senator John F. Kennedy President, W. Rostow travelled to Moscow (Nov. 27-Dec. 7) "with about 25 other scientists for an international roundtable discussion." There he did his utmost to convince the Soviet representatives that the U.S. and the USSR had "a substantial area of agreement in principle" about the dangers threatening the human race. He pleaded for "maintaining tension at a low level," "pointed to their mutual interest in preventing enlargement of the nuclear club's membership" and "urged joint measures to forestall nuclear war." [47]

The Soviets apparently reacted with much less "idealism." According to *The Chicago Tribune*, W. Rostow heard in Moscow:

> "complaints from Vasily Kuznetsov, soviet foreign office official, that American defensive weapons with 'first strike' capabilities were a source of provocation, because their existence suggested that the United States might initiate a preventive war. Rostow thereupon is reported to have appealed to Mr.

Kennedy to abandon such weapons as the Russians said were making them jittery, among them the Atlas missile and the planned RS-70 superjet manned bomber."

The Chicago Tribune editorial concluded:

"Emphasis on conventional nonnuclear armies and limited war deterrents has since suggested that *the administration accepted this American defense policy which had been made in Moscow.*" [48] (Emphasis added)

It should not be too difficult to understand why Senator Goldwater called the Rostow paper "the most dangerous paper in America," and the Republican National Committee assessed it as "a design for defeat," which would "fulfill many immediate Soviet objectives and thereby clear the road for further American retreat." [49]

The climate of surrender at that time can more thoroughly be understood when we bear in mind the sensational initiative of Secretary of Defense Robert McNamara to codify rules for the conduct of nuclear war, and Secretary of State Dean Rusk's clarification of the basic U.S. foreign policy goal.

In June 1962, Mr. McNamara, speaking at the University of Michigan, made his proposal for a "code of war for the atomic age" and invited the USSR to adopt it. The gist of it was that

"principal military objectives, in the event of a nuclear war stemming from a major attack on the Alliance, should be the destruction of the enemy's forces, not of his civilian population.

"The very strength and nature of the Alliance makes it possible for us to retain, even in the face of a massive surprise attack, sufficient reserve striking power to destroy an enemy society if driven to it. In other words, we are giving a possible opponent the strongest imaginable incentive to refrain from striking our cities."

While this may sound ambiguous, we are obliged to James Reston, a kindred soul, for telling us what, translated "into plain American talk," McNamara, "under the authority of the President," was saying to Moscow:

"Even if you decide to make war, don't forget those United States Polaris submarines wandering under the oceans. You may *wipe out all our military bases and cities*, but we will still be able to destroy, not only your armies and factories, but your whole society." (Emphasis added)

"So, even if we cannot agree on the political organization of the world, or on banning nuclear tests or on a disarmament treaty, let's at least agree, if all fails, on some ground rules for atomic war." [50]

And we owe to another "soul brother" of Secretary McNamara, the leftist columnist Marquis Childs, some invaluable clarifications about McNamara's nuclear doctrine of "controlled response." First, he stresses that McNamara absolutely did not dream of implying that the U.S. would "strike to knock out an enemy's bases," i.e. resort to the "pre-emptive strike" allegedly favored by U.S. "warmongers." On the contrary, McNamara was letting the enemy strike first.

But, more important, the U.S. not only would let the USSR strike first, but even after being hit, it would not retaliate with all its might. It would "respond by hitting only enemy bases." Why? Because "this would theoretically give the enemy an incentive either to stop the war or to limit it to U.S. bases." (!)[51]

It is not known that Mr. McNamara was ever asked to account for his inexcusable ignorance about communism and his unforgiveable stance, much less that he was asked to resign for surrendering, instead of defending, his sacred trust, the United States.

There is no more fitting conclusion to this brief review of the basic concepts and plans of coexistence than to quote from Secretary of State Dean Rusk's programmatic speech about the Kennedy Administration's no-win policy (to the Veterans of Foreign Wars, in Minneapolis). He declared that "the global struggle for freedom and against Communist imperialism is our main business in the State Department" and that the U.S. "intends to win and is going to win" that struggle.[52]

However, victory will not be achieved over the Soviet Union, but "by exploring with the communist world the possibility of reducing the danger of conflagration and finding means of mutually advantageous agreement." [53]

To remove any ambiguity as to the possibility that the U.S. might be the winner, he stated:

> "Let us be clear about what we mean when we say, 'we are going to win' . . . Who makes up the 'we'? Not only 185,000,000 Americans, but most of the rest of the people of the world. And what is the world-wide victory we work for? Not victory of one nation over another or of one people over another, but a world-wide victory for freedom." [54]

In other words, what Mr. Rusk was telling us is that in order to defeat communist imperialism, which is the main enemy of the U.S. and freedom, we must not strive for a U.S. victory over the Soviet Union and communism, but for a compromise between the two. Only such a joint victory of freedom and communist imperialism will ensure the triumph of freedom in the whole world!

Apparently, the Orwellian "newspeak," according to which slavery is freedom, wrong is right and surrender is victory, reigns supreme among the makers of our foreign policy of coexistence with communism.

Surrender on the Domestic Front

The surrender has taken place not only in foreign policy, but on the domestic front as well. The importance of the preservation of the rule of law for any civilized country is too evident to elaborate on. Its function is dual: to protect the rights and freedoms of the individual and to safeguard the vital interests of the country. In the U.S. the importance of the law is even greater than elsewhere, because it is composed of people from many nations and because it was created by a statement of principles, upon which a Constitution was established. Theodore Roosevelt's saying that "nobody is above the law and nobody is beneath the law" is American to its very core.

However, the rule of law is precisely where the other decisive surrender is taking place. It seems that the courage to govern is rather deficient in important segments and posts of our Government. There is certainly no historical example of any country, where professional agitators could have so openly, so brazenly and so freely accused and vilified their own country, spoken with contempt of its laws and order, proclaimed loudly their intention to disrupt the life of whole cities, as well as the center of national defense (the Pentagon), used sit-ins, teach-ins, lie-ins, to paralyze the normal functioning of universities; stopped trains carrying troops to their destination for combat duty; invaded and demolished offices of cabinet members, university presidents, mayors and other public officials; prevented Cabinet members from making their prepared public speeches; obstructed the work of recruiting offices; created such riots, looting, arson and destruction that air traffic had to omit big U.S. cities from their regular schedules (Detroit) and left them looking like Hiroshima after the A-bomb; flaunted their weapons and invaded State capitols unhindered and unpunished, bombed buildings, offices and university research centers, invaded courtrooms and killed judges.*

There has been much talk about the redress of grievances, the idealism and sensitivity to social injustices of youth, about the generation gap, about the need to try to understand what "they are trying to tell us." However, all that is beside the point.

There have always been grievances, unjustified and justified. But the rioters, bombers and destroyers are not interested in any grievances as such, nor the redress thereof. They are interested exclusively in using grievances against the U.S.†

As for idealism, there is a certain amount of it among some of the participants in New Left activities. There are innocents who have no inkling of what is going on, of the real aims pursued and interests served, but who are simply being carried away by the momentum of the movement.

However, idealism which always lends itself passively to be

* In September 1967 Milwaukee Mayor Henry Maier stated that "Milwaukee had verged on civil war" (*Chicago Tribune,* September 13, 1967).
† Jerry Rubin made this perfectly clear when he stated (in his book *Do It*):
    "Give us an inch—and we'll take a mile. Satisfy our demands and we got 12 more. The more demands you satisfy, the more we got . . . Demonstrations are never 'reasonable.' We always put our demands forward in such obnoxious manner that the power structure can never satisfy us and remain the power structure. Then we scream, righteously angry, when our demands are not met." . . . "We've combined youth, music, sex, drugs and rebellion with treason. That's a combination hard to beat."

used for aims alien to the purposes proclaimed, is not idealism, but stupidity, chronic immaturity and irresponsibility.

Certainly, there is not one shred of idealism among the leaders, who know the score and who are cold-blooded plotters and enemies of the U.S. It is they who give their stamp to the activities of the New Left.

All the words and all the actions of the masterminds of civil disobedience, violence and riots have made it clear that their aim is *not* to work for the achievement of full equality for all citizens before the law, or for the solution of real U.S. problems, or any kind of improvement, but to institute complete lawlessness* leading to revolution and the breakdown of the United States.†

The agitation, rioting, disruption and rebellion are being organized and carried out not because the rebels would want to improve the U.S., but because they want it destroyed.

The Yippie leader Abbie Hoffman has summed it up in six words: "We are at war with America."

They have made it clear that they do not have the slightest sense of obligation to the U.S., nor respect for its institutions and laws.

J. Edgar Hoover has quoted as typical the advice of a communist given to his son, always to distinguish between laws which may be obeyed and those which must be violated.[55] That is the position which Martin Luther King adopted and openly proclaimed: when he took over a building in Chicago from its legal owner, he declared it to be a "supra-legal" act.[56]

Stokely Carmichael was less concerned with legal terms: "To hell with the laws of the United States." [57]

Rap Brown set some specific conditions for recognizing in the whites equality before the law: "Honkies can't be equal to me until they serve 400 years under me." [58]

---

* One of the main conclusions to come out of the Black Power "summit conference" held after the riots in Newark, was that "If this country does not come around, then the black people are going to burn it down." Rap Brown thought it necessary to explain that "No one has to tell me how to kill." (*Life* magazine, August 4, 1967, "Newark: Post-Riot Summit for Black Power."

† "Sooner or later the day of the Mau Mau will come" is another basic attitude emanating from the Black Power "summit conference" (*Life,* August 4, 1967).

Their hateful bias against the United States is no secret. Huey Newton branded the U.S. as a nation "dedicated to death, oppression and the pursuit of profits." [59]

Martin Luther King called it "the greatest purveyor of violence in the world today" and made his thought clear when he added: "All over the globe men are revolting against old systems of exploitation and oppression and out of the womb of a frail world new systems of justice and equality are being born . . . We in the west must support these revolutions." [60]

Travelling to communist countries, publicly condemning the U.S., and taking the side of the enemy has been common practice of the New Left representatives, such as Professor Staughton Lynd and Tom Hayden, who joined Herbert Aptheker, the chief theoretician of the communist party of America, in a voyage to Hanoi.

This message was understood and accepted by Stokely Carmichael, who participated at the international communist conference for Latin-American solidarity in Havana (August 1967), where he condemned the U.S. and "exhorted American Negroes to take arms and fight, from New York to California, from Canada to Mexico." [61]

He accused U.S. leaders (President Johnson and others) and British Premier Harold Wilson of being killers who must be stopped: "We are not waiting for them to kill us. We will move to kill them first—or rather, we are working towards that goal." [62]

In 1967 Professor Naom Chomsky, of the Massachusetts Institute of Technology, considered the "possibility of an international brigade to fight the United States Army." [63]

Not to be outdone by the learned professor and educator, Eldridge Cleaver advocated that the USSR "give nuclear arms to North Vietnam to use against the United States in South Vietnam." [64]

The disrupters of America have openly spoken of murder as the only way of solving problems: "A white man's head is made to be busted." [65]

The Black Panthers, who in J. Edgar Hoover's estimate are the most aggressive anti-American force of the New Left, have printed and distributed to children cartoons suggestively depicting the killing of "white pigs" by "black brothers."

Rap Brown called President Johnson "a wild, mad dog" and "an outlaw from Texas." He was not much kinder to the First Lady: "If you give me a gun and tell me to shoot my enemy, I might shoot Lady Bird." [66]

All these attitudes appear in true light when we consider that none of these fire-breathers against inhumanity and injustice has ever uttered one word against the communists, the most inhuman and unjust group in history. According to Martin Luther King, it is the injustices and violence of the West which drive the masses toward communism.

The disrupters, in the words of George Schuyler, never "condemned Viet Cong atrocities against South Vietnam civilians or the slaughters in Nigeria and Zanzibar." [67]

Roy Wilkins, director of the National Association for the Advancement of Colored People (N.A.A.C.P.) was equally indignant against the destroyers, who injected the issue of Vietnam in the civil rights issue: "Is it wrong for people to be patriotic? Is it wrong for us to back up our boys in the field? . . . They're dying while we're knifing them in the back at home." [68]

However, the destroyers of America never felt the slightest remorse for their vile actions and crimes. On the contrary, the lack of firm action on the part of the Government had only served to inflame their destructive lust.

After the armed attack on the courtroom in San Rafael (Marin County, Cal.) where Judge Harold Haley was murdered (August 7, 1970), the *Black Panther* (weekly publication) of August 15 claimed "credit" for the murder.

Unfortunately, the openly seditious and treasonous activities of the New Left have met with little moral and legal resistance and with no political counter-action on the part of the U.S. Government. Instead of exposing their motives and their work for the enemy, masquerading as "moral indignation" against the inhumanity of war, and unmasking them before the American people as enemy agents, the U.S. Government has taken toward them the same attitude as toward the foreign enemy: non-resistance to evil, a tendency to yield, accommodate and reconcile.

The Supreme Court of Earl Warren has supplanted the traditional concept that every citizen, and society as a whole, has a right to be protected from lawbreakers, by a new concept which in practice means that the lawbreakers rate above the law abiding citizens and have a right to be protected from the law.*

By its decision of December 11, 1967, the Supreme Court protected communists in defense plants, thus giving aid and support to the deadly enemy of the United States.

Attitudes and statements of leading U.S. public figures have, regardless of personal motive, heavily contributed to discrediting the very concept of law and order and greatly strengthened the disrupter of America.

The Chicago Tribune (of August 2, 1967), in its editorial "The Harvest" quoted the following examples:

President Johnson said in his speech of August 3, 1965 to college students:

> "I am proud to salute you as fellow revolutionaries . . . We want change . . . I hope you will go out into the hinterland and rouse the masses and blow the bugles and tell them the hour has arrived and their day is here."

Vice President Hubert Humphrey said in his remarks in New Orleans (July 18, 1966) that if he had to live in the slums,

> "I think you'd have more trouble than you have already, because I've got enough spark left in me to lead a mighty good revolt."

And Senator Robert F. Kennedy, who under President Kennedy occupied the post of Attorney General, i.e. chief defender of the law in the United States, stated on August 17, 1965:

> "There is no point in telling the Negroes to obey the law. To many Negroes the law is the enemy."

---

* At the conference of law enforcement in Washington of March, 1967, President Johnson made the significant statement: "It is monstrous that, while more than 8,000 Americans were dying for their country 10,000 miles away in Vietnam, more than 50,000 Americans met violent deaths here in America at the hands of other Americans." [69]

A few more examples are worth citing:

President Kennedy, speaking of protesters, had warned that, "Unless Congress acts, their only remedy is in the streets."

Adlai Stevenson, Governor, twice Presidential candidate and U.S. ambassador to the U.N., declared: "A jail sentence is no longer a dishonor but a proud achievement . . . We are destined to see in this law-loving land people running for office . . . on their prison records."

Secretary of State Dean Rusk said that he would behave like the practitioners of civil disobedience if he were in their position; Senator William J. Fulbright, chairman of the U.S. Senate Foreign Relations Committee, spoke of Saigon, the center of organized U.S. military effort in South Vietnam, as an "American brothel"; Secretary of Defense Robert S. McNamara and U.S. Ambassador Arthur Goldberg stated that the right to dissent was so essential that it must remain unaffected by the anti-Vietnam agitation and subversion in the U.S. (thus ignoring the vital difference between dissent and treason); Senator Robert Kennedy declared himself ready to give his blood to the North Vietnamese; Senator Mark Hatfield stated that our war in Vietnam was an "attack on God"; the Mayor of New York, John Lindsay, stated that the "real heroes" of the war in Vietnam were those Americans who refused to fight in it.

To conclude the list: William Douglas, one of the nine supreme lawyers, judges and defenders of the law in the United States, endorsed violence in his recent book, *Points of Rebellion:* "Violence may be the only effective response in dealing with the so-called establishment."

Powerful encouragement was also given to the rioters by the Report of the National Advisory Commission on Civil Disorders (of March 1, 1968), which is a shocking document of irresponsibility of some high U.S. officials entrusted with making a conscientious study of a grave problem. President (then former Vice-President) Richard Nixon rightly criticized it for laying the blame for the disorders on everybody and everything except the rioters. And while the Report contradicts itself on the question of communist participation and influence in the rioting, it makes a point of formally denying them. When Martin Luther King formulated his subversive plan to "dislocate" a number of big U.S. cities, he invoked the Report to justify his stand.

It is impossible and unnecessary to present here a detailed review of all the instances of surrender on the domestic front. However, there are some which must be mentioned to illustrate the pervasive atmosphere of surrender of the forces of law and order before the forces waging war against the United States.

The case of the official endorsement of the mission of two enemies of the United States to act as U.S. official diplomatic representatives deserves special attention. In its editorial "Enemy Agents as American Envoys," *The Chicago Tribune* of July 17, 1969, gave a succinct account of what happened.

"David Dellinger and Rennie Davis, both under indictment for conspiracy to incite rioting during the Democratic National Convention in Chicago last August, and both leaders of the pro-Hanoi National Mobilization to End the War in Vietnam (MOBE), have been released from the jurisdiction of the Federal District Court here to "negotiate" with the North Vietnamese Communists for the release of three American war prisoners.

"Federal Judge Julius J. Hoffman, in whose court Dellinger, Davis, and six others are scheduled for trial, released Dellinger last week to go to Paris for a meeting with Hanoi's delegation. Dellinger returned from Paris with word that agreement had been reached for Davis and three other anti-war agitators to go to Hanoi and complete arrangements for the release of the prisoners. Judge Hoffman, however, refused to release Davis, saying it would put the court in "the position of entering into foreign relations." Judge Otto Kerner of the United States Court of Appeals promptly overruled Judge Hoffman, and Davis left Tuesday night for Hanoi."

The editorial then stressed that Dellinger and Davis were leaders of the Chicago convention riots and also organizers of a MOBE demonstration against President Nixon's inauguration in Washington. At that rally they "made anti-American speeches," and leaflets were distributed which might have been "printed in Hanoi."

"Dellinger and Davis are enemy agents. Adhering to the enemies of the United States, giving them aid and comfort, is treason, as defined by the Constitution, and in this sense Dellinger and Davis are traitors. Yet they have been released by federal judges, without objection from the justice department, and, according to their attorneys, with the approval of the state department, to act in effect as special envoys of the United States.

"This is disgraceful . . . The United States and its South Vietnamese ally have enough North Vietnamese prisoners in custody to interest Hanoi in exchange negotiations at a proper governmental level, and the services of enemy agents are not needed."

The case does not require comment at this point, for the surrender of the U.S. before its domestic and foreign enemy is too evident.

But the most shocking and disturbing single case of the surrender of the law before the violators of the law is undoubtedly the ruling of Superior Court Judge Harold M. Mulvey (New Haven, Conn.) in the murder-kidnaping trial of Bobby G. Seale and Ericka Huggins, dismissing the charges with the scandalous explanation that

"I find it impossible to believe that an unbiased jury could be selected without superhuman efforts—efforts which this court, the state, and these defendants, should not be called upon either to make or to endure." [70]

A horrendous crime had been committed, in May 1969, the torture and murder of Alex Rackley, member of the Black Panther Party. And nobody was guilty! Not because the accused had been found innocent or the criminals had not been apprehended, but because the court found it impossible to establish guilt and innocence and make any other ruling than that of finding it impossible to make any ruling!* Regardless of the real reason for the incredible decision of Judge Mulvey, Seale's attorney David Rosen was expressing the obvious when he stated that "the system . . . is not equipped to deal . . . with such a situation as the Seale-Huggins case."

There is no evidence that anybody in the Government had thought of the short-range and long-range consequences of the Mulvey ruling. First, it conveys to the Black Panthers the message that they are above the law. And it signals the beginning of the end of the rule of law in a country founded on the rule of law. It should be evident that a country where courts declare that they are unable to dispense justice is in most serious trouble.

When the Supreme Court, on January 23, 1967, declared unconstitutional New York State laws designed to keep subversives off the faculties and staffs of public schools and state colleges, Justice Tom C. Clark dissented. And in declaring in his minority report that, by its decision ". . . the majority . . . swept away one of our most precious rights, namely the right of self-preservation," [71] he pointed to the gist of the problem.

Nothing prospers and grows more wildly than defiance of the law, when unrestricted, unopposed and encouraged by those who should uphold the law. The lawbreakers get the green light and they go from protest to insurrection, from revolt to revolution, from civil disobedience to civil war.

That is where the surrender on the domestic front is leading. As long as this is not realized, all the efforts to correct conditions, redress grievances and meet demands are a sheer waste of time, goodwill and the taxpayers' money. Worse, they are gasoline poured on the communist-fed fires of revolutionary agitation and action against the United States.

It stands to reason that the war against America on the domestic front would not bypass the Army. In 1961/1962 Senator Fulbright joined forces with Secretary of Defense Robert S. McNamara to prevent U.S. military leaders from educating our armed forces regarding the communist threat to their country.

---

* In its editorial of May 27, 1971, *The Chicago Tribune* asked the question: "Is Justice Too Much Trouble?" This feeling was expressed by a number of other newspapers across the country, such as the St. Louis *Globe-Democrat*: "Seale Case-Mockery of Justice," May 27, 1971.

The deletions which Mr. McNamara's civilian experts ("whiz kids") made in the prepared speeches of our highest military leaders unambiguously indicate that they were shielding the communists.

The disruption of our Armed Forces through the war of no-victory in Vietnam is hardly debatable. Unfortunately in the course of that process the military were unable to produce visible and effective opposition to the policy of no-victory.

In September 1969, General Leonard F. Chapman, commandant of the U.S. Marine Corps, facing increasing agitation to provoke racial unrest and conflicts among enlisted men, white and black, issued an order permitting the clenched fist salute of the Black Panthers among Negro marines. It is evident that he was badly advised. To ensure equal treatment for enlisted men, regardless of color and origin, must be an overriding concern of every responsible officer in the U.S. Armed Forces. However, to allow individuals belonging to the ultra-leftist militant organization of the Black Panthers to use their clenched fist salute and the caps of their party uniforms, is neither understanding nor wisdom, but weakness, which disrupts and invites more trouble.

That is what a Pentagon team investigating racial conflicts among U.S. soldiers in West Germany found in November 1970. *The New York Times* published a full page report describing a very unhealthy situation which included the creation of a number of "dissenters'" groups and a protest meeting for "justice," attended by over 1000 black soldiers at Heidelberg University, with the clenched fist salute and closely collaborating with German student "radicals." No wonder "widespread hostility and bitterness among black G.I.'s . . . have seriously affected morale and discipline and threaten . . . to undermine the combat efficiency of the 165,000 man Seventh Army." [72]

After the outrage of Madison, August 7, 1970, Secretary of Defense Melvin Laird did not take the position that the U.S. Army's research facilities must unconditionally be protected from America's enemies, but stated that the incident had forced the Defense Department to reexamine its policy of putting research facilities on campuses and considered building them elsewhere "if federal research facilities on campuses are causing grave problems for university administrations."

Such an attitude, which amounts to withdrawal before the enemy, illustrates how deeply the poison of surrender before the destroyers of America has penetrated.

Even worse, to the point of appearing unbelievable, is the Army's order of July 27, 1970 ("Display of the U.S. Flag During Incidents"), directed at all installations and activities "which by their location can be considered isolated":

> "If violence is indicated which could result in the desecration or improper display of the flag, commanders should not have the flag raised, or if it is already raised and time and circumstances permit, have it properly lowered."

The order is also applicable to flags displayed at Army installations "located on campuses, and are also applicable if college presidents order flags on campus to be flown in any manner not authorized."

It obviously never occurred to those who issued the order that the lowering of the U.S. flag before its enemies—and anybody who desecrates the U.S. flag is an enemy of the U.S.—is the worst desecration possible. Nor did it ever occur to anyone to ponder what effects such an order is likely to have on the student-rioters, as well as decent young Americans.

A country where the flag of the enemy (North Vietnam or Vietcong) is freely displayed in the nation's capital, but where the nation's flag must under certain circumstances be lowered before threat or insult by the nation's enemies, is in grave trouble, especially if the officials responsible for such policies do not realize it.

General Surrender

Domestic surrender includes, besides official policies, the attitudes and behavior of groups as well as individual citizens. The close connection between public duty and private morality has been badly neglected, vital as it is.

A nation can live only as long as those who comprise it believe in it and respect it. Individual self-respect and national self-respect are intertwined and inseparable. As long as a nation respects itself, its policies cannot stray very far from the right path. But if the policy makers and public opinion-makers destroy the foundations of the nation, national self-respect is destroyed and the decline of personal self-respect inevitably ensues. The vicious circle of personal and national decline and self-destruction is set in motion.

Herein lies the essence of our present trouble.

The nation seems to be caught in an orgy of self-destruction in every area of its life. It is not only that its political institutions, law and order are under heavy attack, but the process is being powerfully promoted by our mass communications media, by the movie industry, in literature, education, arts and religion.

Every value, everything sacred to the Founding Fathers and to any man worthy of the name, is proclaimed outdated or unworthy and is sullied, perverted and ridiculed in the most shameless fashion in film after film and radio and television program after program. Every shred of morality, concept of duty, of effort, of human dignity, of discipline and responsibility, the very bases of civilized society, everything that built the nation and holds it together, is constantly exposed to smear and ridicule.

There is a diseased tendency to see, expose, show and put all the glaring lights of publicity and advertisement on the seamy side of life, on the wounds, the sores, the ulcers, the boils. We are mercilessly and savagely exposing all our foibles, magnifying all our weaknesses, suicidally baring every shortcoming of the U.S., while ignoring, justifying and finding excuses for the worst inadequacies, failures, and crimes of the communist enemy.

To read a good part of what today goes under the name of literature, there seems to be no problem and aspect of life worth considering, analyzing, and describing unless it be about failure, degradation, disease—or unless it is confined to man's life only three feet from the ground. Literature has moved from the drawing room, the living room, the workroom, to the men's room.*

---

* Actually, there is a "play" by LeRoi Jones, which would have been inconceivable only a few years ago and in any country at any time except the times of the last spasms of decaying empires of the past, entitled "The Toilet." All its action unfolds in a men's room and there is no doubt that it is exactly where it belongs. The trouble, however, is that the toilet had been put on stage, thus becoming "legitimate theater"!

We present the spectacle of a society sure of nothing, having no absolutes, believing in nothing, respecting nothing, doubting everything, uncovering everything, as if to flaunt its emptiness.

And the most disturbing aspect of it is that everybody is participating in the act; nobody is opposing the destroyers. There is no front and there are no two opposing sides. Everybody is against, the beatniks, the peaceniks, the hippies, the communists, the liberals, the Black Panther movement, the SDS, the LSD addicts, the anti-Vietnam mobs—and the Establishment (the rulers)!

To borrow Hegel's dialectical frame—usurped and disfigured by Marx—there is no thesis (the established order defending itself) and antithesis (the forces of change), locked in combat out of which the synthesis (new order) is to emerge. No, everybody is on the same side, criticizing and protesting, everybody is engaged in tearing down, creating a new society (great!) and engineering social change. Experts, politicians, action-intellectuals, public opinion makers, university professors, columnists, sociologists and psychoanalysts, historians and anthropologists, clergymen and educators, film producers and actors, sports figures and TV performers—vie with each other to see who will do more to destroy America.

Freedom, human dignity and civilization can subsist only if the beast in man, the evil, the weeds, are fought, resisted, uprooted all the time. But when evil and depravity are unopposed and catered to, when the beast in man is unleashed and encouraged, human dignity disintegrates, liberty becomes impossible and the doom of civilization inevitable.

Before making his visits to communist China and Moscow, President Nixon should have seriously pondered the meaning and purport of Leonard Bernstein's "Mass" (performed at the opening of the John Kennedy Center in Washington), of the prison revolt in Attica, and of the riots-looting orgies in Pittsburgh (on October 17, 1971), all happening in rapid succession. While they may seem unconnected as far as the performers are concerned, they express the same suicidal sickness of surrender in the nation, which calls for rapid and drastic cure.

The Balance

Our policy of surrender made possible in World War II and its aftermath the communist conquest of Eastern Europe (1945) and then China (1949). That in itself was a most serious blow to the position and prestige of the U.S. in the world. But since no conclusions were drawn from developments which should have jolted the nation and its leaders into realizing the magnitude of the blunders of appeasement and into changing the course of disaster, the policy of surrender has continued and so has the weakening of the United States.

At the end of the Eisenhower era, a leading U.S. columnist, Joseph Alsop, stated that "according to suppressed soundings taken by the President's own subordinates, the standing of the United States abroad has reached a low unprecedented in recent history." [73]

However, nobody investigated the causes of this grave development to find a remedy. On the contrary. When the U.S. suffered the unforgivable defeat at the Bay of Pigs in April 1961, former President Eisenhower categorically warned against investigating the causes: ". . . I would say the last thing you want to have is a full investigation and lay all this out on record."

Why? Because, he explained, the new Administration was "preoccupied with the most important question there is in the world—preventing establishment of a Communist stronghold in this hemisphere." [74] President Eisenhower did not explain how that most important task could be fulfilled without investigating the reasons for the failure of a major move destined to prevent the consolidation of communism in Cuba!

Most likely it was the clear realization of this state of affairs and its causes that prompted Secretary of the Army Elvis Stahr, Jr., to issue a solemn warning about the inevitable final consequences of our policy of surrender:

"We must firmly draw the line here and now against any further capitulation to the Communists—any further surrender of bits and pieces of the free world . . . If we should allow this nibbling process to continue, it could have but one result—a cumulative defeat which would lead to our ultimate destruction . . . It is time for every American to wake up to that elemental fact." [75]

However, seven years later, a most competent authority, Republican presidential candidate Richard M. Nixon, stated in his acceptance address at the Republican National Convention, on August 8, 1968:

"We are worse off in every area of the world today than we were when President Eisenhower left office eight years ago." [76]

The question naturally comes to mind: how many more eight-year periods of surrender policy can the United States stand?

Today in Vietnam the incredible spectacle of the mightiest military power in the world and in history, being unable to win the war against a small communist country is producing grave domestic problems in the U.S. and alienation from the U.S. in many parts of the world, as well as a general softening of attitude toward communism.

And as President Nixon's "new policy" on Red China, announced on July 15, 1971, is on its way, containing as its basic features the sacrifice of two most valuable and loyal allies, Nationalist China (Taiwan) and South Vietnam, it is safe to predict that the chief and most harmful consequences of our Vietnam policy of no-victory are yet to come.

In Europe a general spirit of neutralism is spreading, as a result of our overall policies of surrender.

France has practically left NATO, thus dealing a heavy blow to an organization which was shaky from the inception, both in the number of its divisions, supposed to stop Soviet and satellite divisions in case of communist aggression, and—especially—in its fighting spirit, or rather the conspicuous absence thereof.

Germany, which already under the "great coalition" government of Chancellor Kiesinger had engaged on a course of "opening" to the communist regimes of Eastern Europe, elected, in 1969, a socialist government. When Chancellor Willy Brandt took over, it was logical to expect that Germany would "depart from

the uncompromisingly anti-communist course of previous conservative governments in Bonn," that the policy of rapprochement
with Eastern Europe would be pursued with renewed vigor, that
the Hallstein doctrine would be abandoned, thus ushering in an
era of conciliation with communist East Germany, above all that a
policy of friendship with the USSR would become a key concern.
In less than two years, the Brandt policy—especially the pact with
Moscow—fully met, if it did not surpass, all the expectations of
the Soviet leaders, as well as communists in all countries behind
the Iron Curtain.

In Italy there is a marked course of "adaptation" to the "trends
of the times" in the leading circles of the chief democratic, conservative and anti-communist force, to the Christian Democratic
Party (especially former prime minister Aldo Moro).

In Sweden there have been noticeable changes in its traditional
neutrality, away from the U.S. The Swedish government has recognized the regimes of North Vietnam (on January 10, 1969) and
Cuba, the two most aggressively anti-American governments in
the world.

The Mediterranean, until recently unquestionably a Western
(NATO) sea, has become a domain of Soviet naval preponderance. The decision (in August 1971) of the Dom Mintoff government of Malta to force NATO out of this strategic island, is a
disturbing and unambiguous sign of the change of the political
mood in the Mediterranean.[77]

But how can we blame Mr. Mintoff for not trusting U.S. might
in the Mediterranean, when the U.S. is ready to surrender its sovereignty on the Panama Canal, which Congressman Daniel J.
Flood has aptly called "the key strategic point in the western hemisphere and the greatest single symbol of United States prestige."?

Even our staunchest anti-communist allies, Spain and Turkey,
are shifting their policies toward accommodation with Moscow,
since they cannot rely on Washington.

As opposed to the hesitant and timorous presence of the United
States, the Soviet might is aggressively spreading. Egypt is becoming increasingly a country under Soviet military occupation.
Libya, a country with a population of less than 2 million, but with
a strategically located huge territory rich in oil, and with the im-

portant U.S. Wheelus Air Force Base (in Tripoli), turned against the United States. The contract for the Wheelus base was not renewed and the U.S. Air Force abandoned it.

Algeria, which could never have achieved "independence" without U.S. influence, is becoming, under the leadership of the "moderate" Colonel Boumedienne, a base of Soviet power in the Mediterranean.

In Asia the prevailing attitude has become one of distrust and cautious but unambiguous dissociation from the U.S. and of "opening" toward Moscow or Peking, or both.

As far as India and Pakistan (with a combined population approximating that of China) are concerned, this was made crystal clear during President Nixon's visit to Asia in July-August 1969. Significantly, the Indian Prime Minister, Madame Indira Gandhi, stressed that "the Chinese did come across the Yalu in spite of heavy U.S. presence," and concluded that the U.S. would not restrict their freedom of action in the future.

The Indo-Soviet Pact of Friendship of August 1971 clearly marked an end to India's non-alignment and put it in the Soviet orbit. Pakistan, regardless of unabated antagonism, tensions, and even war with India, is following the same path of alienation from the U.S. and adaptation to the power realities of Asia.

In Thailand, the very day when President Nixon arrived in Bangkok and after his talks with the highest representatives of the Government (June 1969), it was announced that the troops of Thailand fighting alongside Americans and South Vietnamese would be withdrawn. Worse and most unusual were the comments of Foreign Minister Thanat Khoman on July 18, 1970, to the effect that U.S. policy "is being warped" by the "confusions and convulsions of hippie and yippie culture." According to *Time* magazine, he added the blunt but perhaps not unreasonable observation that the U.S. "is exhibiting signs of derangement and systematic disorder." [78]

In the Philippines, considered as possibly the staunchest U.S. ally in Asia, foreign minister General Carlos P. Romulo on several occasions has spoken with bitterness of U.S. foreign policy, expressing the conviction that "the United States is no longer dependable as an ally." [79] He hinted at a serious re-orientation of Philippine foreign policy in the direction of recognizing the "reality" of world communism. After the general elections of November 11–12, 1969, confirming President Marcos in office, an announcement was made about the withdrawal of Philippine forces from Vietnam.

In the Western Hemisphere, two recent events indicate the unmistakable and ominous trend of developments.

The first is that an avowed Marxist, Senator Salvador Allende was elected President of Chile in free elections. The immediate impact of this event is obviously great. Its historical consequences may be incalculable. The Nixon administration reacted by giving arms to Marxist Allende's government!

The second is that our northern neighbor, Canada, which under Premier Pierre Trudeau, a well-known admirer of Mao Tse-tung, has been moving away from the U.S., in October 1970 recognizing Red China. This recognition represents not a tactical move, but a basic change of policy. For to disapprove of U.S. involvement in Vietnam is one thing, but to establish diplomatic relations with Red China, which is actively involved in our conflict with North Vietnam, is quite another. It was a grave blow to traditional U.S.-Canadian friendship; it established the first foothold for the Chinese Communist regime in the Western Hemisphere; it was a signal success for world communism.

Deplorably, the far-reaching implications of Allende's election and of Canada's recognition of Red China seem to have escaped the attention of our State Department. Or rather the conclusion its experts drew from such development was to advise President Nixon also to move toward recognizing Red China.

In Latin America the vaunted Alliance for Progress is dead. President Nixon's special delegate, Governor Nelson Rockefeller, in 1969 received anything but a friendly reception. Peru's military government of General Juan Velasco (since October 1968) had not only nationalized U.S. property (mines), but adopted an overall hostile attitude toward the U.S.

In Brazil, the largest country of Latin America, comprising half of its population, General Emilio Garrastazu Medici, upon assuming the Presidency (1969) announced a new policy, based on belief in a "world without ideological barriers," which diplomatic observers have interpreted as a readiness to "open trade with China and expand trade with the East European countries." [80]

The contrast between our awareness of communist evil intents and our policies of surrendering to communism, remains to be explained. But one thing appears crystal clear: communist advances have been made possible by our retreats. We have reaped what we have sown.

Our predicament is due not only to communist policies and anti-American propaganda and subversion, but to our own policy of weakness and surrender, which is delighting all U.S. enemies and inflaming their hatred, while it is causing the despair of all our friends and allies, forcing them to realize that they cannot trust us, but had themselves better find some *modus vivendi* with the communists.

There is increasingly less law and order in the United States, and there is increasingly less law, order and respect for the United States in the world. The forces of civil war in the U.S. and of civil war in the whole world against the United States, are marching forward. And the peril is commensurate with the degree of our surrender before the attacks of the U.S. enemies and before the challenges of the modern world.

In all the history of the United States there was no moment and no situation comparable with what we are witnessing today. For there never was anything even vaguely similar to the present incredible lack of the nation's elementary will to assert itself, its fear of hostility, its aversion to success, its intolerance of victory, its reluctance to defend its identity, its morbid tendency to self-accusation and self-condemnation. There seems to exist an inexplicable guilt complex, which impels to self-negation and suicide.

Not only "right-wing alarmists" but the highest civilian and military officials have warned that our military might has seriously declined in comparison with the Soviet Union. Admiral Hyman Rickover has certainly been the most conscientious "Cassandra" of all. Admiral Waldemar F. A. Wendt, commander in chief of the U.S. naval forces in Europe, has stressed that Soviet naval forces are present in all world seas,* and "if we are not alert, we may

---

* This apparently was a cause for rejoicing to Senator Fulbright, chairman of the Senate Foreign Relations Committee, who stated that if the Soviets were building a submarine base in Cuba, "the United States is in no position to bluff them out of it."

As for the Soviet naval expansion, Fulbright rebuked the U.S.: "Americans have long thought that they alone had the right to patrol the world's oceans,

find tomorrow that our strength has been checkmated at sea." [81]

Admiral Elmo Zumwalt, chief of U.S. naval operations has noted that "Russia will become the number one naval force in the . . . Indian Ocean unless checkmated by America." [82]

Secretary of Defense Melvin R. Laird has repeatedly spoken of the Soviet danger. In November 1969 he confirmed the information supplied by Senator Henry Jackson and stated that

> "the Soviet Union is trying for a first-strike capability that would enable it to knock out United States offensive missile bases and prevent retaliation to an attack." [83]

In May 1971 he said that the Soviet Union had "a tremendous weapons momentum." There was "more or less parity in the strategic nuclear weapons area," and at the same time the USSR had greatly modernized its naval, as well as ground forces. Therefore, "the danger from Russia . . . is our principal concern at this point." [84]

At the same time, however, the new (July 2, 1970) chairman of the Joint Chiefs of Staff, Admiral Thomas H. Moorer, while stressing the importance of providing for the security of the U.S., without which "all of (domestic) problems become moot," sounded the bugle of U.S. global withdrawal:

> "We . . . must be prepared for a continual decline in the number and accessibility of our overseas bases.

> "We . . . must be prepared for a possible decision on the part of the United States to reduce or eliminate its presence in some overseas areas." [85]

President Nixon, addressing (July 6, 1971) newspaper editors in Kansas City, spoke of "a sense of defeatism growing in the U.S. . . . from the country's divisions and alienations" and its decline in morality. He warned against the mortal peril of moral decadence which sets in and destroys nations which become

---

and now must realize they can no longer exclude the Russians and others from the Mediterranean, the Indian Ocean and the Caribbean." (*Chicago Tribune*, September 28, 1970, "Soft Stand on Cuba Urged by Fulbright").

wealthy and lose their will to live. The U.S., in President Nixon's estimate, was approaching that stage. He therefore called for "moral reforms in America."

Nine days later President Nixon announced his new policy toward Red China, which strongly expressed a fear of facing the mortal hostility of communism, and the lack of the will to live.

In any case, in spite of all the realizations, recognitions and solemn warnings, the heart of the matter is that, as opposed to communist leaders, there has been no display of American will to stop the rot and decline, to control events and to pursue a policy of U.S. strength and victory.

In the face of this situation, the optimistic lullabies of some liberals are so infantile and irresponsible that they cease to be relevant. For the enemy is systematically implementing its unchanged aim, moving forward with unfaltering will and deadly persistency, while our resolve is getting softer as our situation worsens.

The communists are waging war.

In response to their aggressive challenge, we:

—ignore the real nature of communism and its implacable warfare;

—view problems not from the positions of U.S. interests, but from "one-world" positions;

—proclaim our weakness and powerlessness;

—reject struggle against communism as hopeless.

We are surrendering. America has never been in graver peril.

3   An Open Invitation to Surrender

The Sakharov Plan for U.S.— Soviet Cooperation

"Only . . . socialism . . . will preserve civilization"
ANDREI SAKHAROV

Our review of the problem of surrender would be incomplete without considering the Sakharov Plan, "a bold plan for cooperation and eventual rapprochement between the United States and the Soviet Union," offered by a leading Soviet physicist, Andrei D. Sakharov, under the title "Thoughts on Progress, Peaceful Coexistence and Intellectual Freedom," and published on three full pages of *The New York Times* of July 22, 1968.

The Soviet invasion of Czechoslovakia on August 21, 1968, deprived the Sakharov Plan of immediate actuality. But its ideas, its approach, its arguments, indicate the general line of Soviet strategy and of their appraisal of Western inability to understand communism and oppose its drive for world power, thus leading us to the very heart of the U.S. policies of surrender.

The New York Times did not reveal the circumstances under which the paper, officially frowned upon and only privately circulated in the Soviet Union, reached the office of its editor. But, under the title "Outspoken Soviet Scientist," the *Times* presented the highlights of the career of one of the leading physicists of the USSR: "As a member of the scientific and technological élite of Soviet society, and as a man with broad intellectual horizons and range of interests, Dr. Sakharov has not been afraid to speak out, even if his views are in conflict with official policy . . . In recent years Dr. Sakharov . . . has continued to voice his views on public affairs. But instead of being officially sanctioned by publication in *Pravda*, his opinions, often critical of domestic and foreign policy, were circulating in manuscript among friends and associates.

"His latest essay, written last month and now available here, outlines a plan for Soviet-American cooperation and ultimate rapprochement that he views as the only way to save mankind from thermonuclear war, overpopulation and famine and pollution of the environment."

A paper on world affairs, written by a top Soviet scientist, and presenting a plan for the solution of all the main problems of mankind, cannot be dismissed lightly. Especially when *The New York Times* gives it full publicity and warmly recommends it.

And there is another reason for taking Sakharov's move seriously: it is highly improbable that the plan is just a private affair, disapproved by the Soviet authorities. *The New York Times* says that *Pravda* did not print the essay. This proves that it did not want to endorse it officially, nothing else. But if Sakharov was free to circulate it among friends for some time, it means that the Soviet official circles had no serious objections to its ideas, arguments and purpose.

Sakharov's point of departure is that mankind is at this juncture gravely threatened by "a thermonuclear war, catastrophic hunger for most of mankind, stupefaction from the narcotic of 'mass culture' and bureaucratic dogmatism," and finally "degeneration from the unforeseeable consequences of swift changes in the conditions of life on our planet."

The main obstacle to an effective action to surmount these dangers, is the division of mankind, above all the division between the United States and the Soviet Union. The overcoming of that division is a matter of life and death for all mankind.

Sakharov has gone to great lengths to prove that U.S.-Soviet coexistence, collaboration and finally the establishment of a one-world government are not only desirable, but well within our reach.

As far as the USSR is concerned, his main claims are: that there are only two superpowers in the world today and that the USSR is the socialist superpower. Its socialist system has demonstrated its ability, competence and vitality in every way: it has ensured a high standard of living for Soviet citizens; it has done "a great deal for the people materially, socially and culturally. Actually, in regard to productivity, development of productive forces and high standards of living for most of the population, the USSR has "played to a tie" (!) with the United States. As far as scientific research and technological development are concerned, the two countries are engaged in a "ski race," where the great initial advantage of the United States is gradually diminishing. Now and in the future everything will depend on the "relative vitality of the R.R.S. (Russian Revolutionary Sweep) and A.M.E. (American Efficiency)."

Militarily, there is also a situation of a "draw," since the "difference between the technical-economic potentials" of the two countries "is not so great that one of the sides could undertake a "preventive aggression" without an almost inevitable risk of a destructive retaliatory blow."

On top of all that, the USSR possesses the basis for U.S.-Soviet coexistence, collaboration and the salvation of the world—socialism. This is the only conceivable basis for overcoming the division of mankind and saving it from destruction.

Sakharov admits that everything is not perfect in the USSR. The main problem is the problem of Stalinism, dogmatism and bureaucratism, which are preventing the USSR, or rather the Communist Party of the Soviet Union, from becoming the "spiritual leader of mankind." Stalin and Stalinism have "befouled our banner" by their cruelty, ruthless liquidation of party members, dogmatism and betrayal of Leninist ideals. And today bureaucratism is standing in the way of intellectual freedom, without which there is no progress and no true coexistence and collaboration. "Is that not a disgrace?" exclaims comrade Sakharov.

But the USSR "has started on the path of cleansing away the foulness of Stalinism." All that it needs to do, is "to persevere on that path of strengthening human values." "Any attempts to revive Stalinism in our country . . . would . . . be an awful blow to the attractive force of communist ideas throughout the world." So, what must be done is to restore the "Leninist principle" of democracy. Then communist ideas would recover their lost attractiveness in the eyes of the world, for the good of the USSR, communism and all mankind.

As for the United States, Sakharov in his assessment magnanimously departs from the traditional views of "dogmatic" Marxists who consider "the capitalist mode of production . . . inferior to the socialist mode in labor productivity." In his estimation, "there are certainly no grounds for asserting that capitalism always leads to absolute impoverishment of the working class." "The continuing economic progress being achieved under capitalism should be a fact of great theoretical significance for any undogmatic Marxist."

However, Sakharov stresses that real progress and real improvement of the position of the working people in the United States and other capitalist countries, has been achieved because "the capitalists are actually using the social principle of socialism."

So, today "both capitalism and socialism are capable of long-term development, borrowing positive elements from each other and actually coming closer to each other in a number of essential aspects."

But, even more than that, "the development of modern society in both the Soviet Union and the United States is now following the same course of increasing complexity of structure and of industrial management, giving rise in both countries to managerial groups that are similar in social character."

Therefore, the United States and the Soviet Union should stop "looking upon each other as rivals and opponents." The course to follow is "ever increasing co-existence and collaboration between the two systems and the two super-powers, with a smoothing of contradictions and with mutual assistance," because "on any other course annihilation awaits mankind. There is no other way out."

Now, there *are* grave problems, i.e. grave roadblocks to coexistence, collaboration and world peace in the United States, and these are nationalism, militarism and racism, as well as capitalism itself. The biggest two problems are the problem of American Negroes, who have been exploited for very long and live today under very bad conditions. And the main impediment to the solution of the Negro problem in the United States are the American whites, who "at this time . . . are unwilling to accept even minimum sacrifices to eliminate the unequal economic and cultural position of the country's black citizens."

The other big problem, of course, is U.S. militarism, e.g., in Vietnam, where "the forces of reaction . . . are violating all legal and moral norms and are carrying out flagrant crimes against humanity" and where "an entire people is being sacrificed to the proclaimed goal of stopping the "Communist tide."

Luckily, as opposed to the U.S. internationalists, racists, militarists and unregenerate capitalists, there are quite different, progressive people in the U.S., who not only hold different views, but represent the ruling class. They are interested in peace and in solving the Negro problem, as well as in "convergence," i.e., "in a democratic, peaceful transition to socialism."

So what obviously must be done is to lend a hand to those progressive Americans, to that "reformist part of the (American) bourgeoisie," while at the same time waging a massive campaign for the re-education of the egotistic and reactionary American whites, who are the bearers of intolerance, racism, nationalism and militarism.

Such an alliance of "leftist Leninists" in the Soviet Union and "leftist Westerners" in the United States is unbeatable. The struggle may be arduous, but the victory is theirs.

There would be other important changes to be effectuated in the United States, to facilitate the merger, such as "not only wide social reforms . . . but also substantial changes in the structure of ownership," "an increased public control over the managerial group" and a "serious decline in the United States rate of economic growth." But all that, Sakharov tells us, would be a small sacrifice to save humanity. "The Americans should be willing to do this solely for the sake of lofty and distant goals, for the sake of preserving civilization and mankind on our planet."

So, Sakharov's position is that if the United States continues its advance in the direction of socialism, and the USSR perseveres on its course and preserves its socialist system, the two superpowers will be able to assure full coexistence, proceed to collaboration, solve all problems and assure the happiness of mankind.

And he has set a time-table:

1960–1980 would be the years of "increasing peaceful coexistence, strengthening democracy and expanding economic reforms;

In the second stage (1972–1985) the "leftist reformist wing of the bourgeoisie" would have achieved its victory in the United States and begun "to implement a program of rapprochement (convergence) with socialism . . . on a world scale." This would include a decisive "attack on the forces of racism and militarism."

In the third stage (1972–1990) "the Soviet Union and the

United States, having overcome their alienation, solve the problem of saving the poorer half of the world." At the same time, "disarmament will proceed."

In the fourth stage (1980–2000), "the socialist convergence will reduce differences in social structure, promote intellectual freedom, science and economic progress and lead to the creation of a world government and the smoothing of national contradictions."

In other words, by the year 2000—only 32 years from the publication of Sakharov's Memorandum, which historically speaking, means very soon—the world, by following his plan, would become one happy "single family without divisions into nations other than those in matters of history and traditions."

The Difficulties and Sakharov's Solution

Realizing that his plan implies a true revolution in the "traditional method of international affairs," where every power aims at "maximum improvement" of its own position—"causing maximum unpleasantness to opposing forces, without consideration of common welfare and common interests,"—Sakharov has given much thought to the means of bringing about that revolution.

The "egotistic principle of capital" produces "monstrous relations in human and international affairs . . . when it is not under pressure from socialist and progressive forces."

"Before the advent of socialism, national egotism gave rise to colonial oppression, nationalism and racism." Today Sakharov realizes that "the tragic aspects of the poverty, lack of rights and humiliation of the 22 million American Negroes . . . is . . . primarily . . . a racial problem, involving the racism and egotism of white workers." And, as opposed to the only correct "political strategy of peaceful coexistence" as a means of solving the problem of thermonuclear war, "scientific and militarist circles in the United States" have "worked out . . . the strategic doctrine of escalation," which spells doom for civilization and mankind.

From this, Sakharov draws the logically inescapable conclusion that "it is necessary to change the psychology of the American citizens so that they will voluntarily and generously support their government and world-wide efforts to change the economy, technology and level of living of billions of people." To that end, a

"scientific democratic approach to politics, economics and culture"
must be applied, because that "scientific democratic method" is
simply "required by history."

"International affairs must be completely permeated with scientific methodology and a democratic spirit, with a fearless weighing of all facts, views and theories, with maximum publicity of
ultimate and intermediate goals and with a consistency of principles."

To implement coexistence and collaboration, "scientific methods of international policy will have to be worked out, based on
scientific prediction of the immediate and more distant consequences. Sakharov reminds us that science today is mightier than
ever, that among new sciences the science of cybernetics, founded
by Norbert Wiener, author of the book on the *Human Use of Human Beings—Cybernetics and Society,* is one of the most promising:

> "Modern technology and mass psychology constantly suggest
> new possibilities of managing the norms of behavior, the striv-
> ings and convictions of masses of people. This involves not only
> management through information based on the theory of adver-
> tising and mass psychology, but also more technical methods
> that are widely discussed in the press abroad. Examples are
> biochemical control of the birth rate, biochemical control of
> psychic processes and electronic control of such processes."

The "social progress of the 20th century" has been made possible by the competition of capitalism with socialism and "the
pressure of the working class." "The moral and ethical character
of the advantages of the socialist course of development of human
society," have been clearly established.

With the powerful and wholehearted support and collaboration
of the "ruling group in the United States" which is interested in
solving all the problems indicated because it "supports such a program of convergence," nothing will be impossible. Moreover, it
will be certain to realize "the aim of eliminating painlessly domestic and international difficulties," as well as consolidating the new
order by "preventing a sharpening of international tensions and a
strengthening of the forces of reaction."

In following the unfolding of Sakharov's plan, one cannot help observing that he explicitly rejects not only some well-known and well-established Marxist positions, but practically the whole "science" of Marxism-Leninism, its foundations, its very philosophical premises.

He first rejects the concept of struggle, which has been the cornerstone of communist theory and communist policies ever since the Communist Manifesto. The U.S. and the USSR must demonstrate "a desire to cooperate, not to fight."

Instead of the idea of class struggle, as the key ingredient of world history, on which Marx and Engels built the Communist Manifesto and all their later works, instead of Lenin's thesis about the unbridgeable conflict which separates the capitalist world from the socialist world (*Imperialism, Supreme Stage of Capitalism,* 1916), instead of the basic, pioneer work of Lenin (*What Is to Be Done,* 1902) with its accent on the imperative need to exploit the slightest weaknesses and mistakes of the class enemy, Sakharov's pronouncements sound 100% heretical:

"If mankind is to get away from the brink, it must overcome its divisions." The interests of mankind, in other words, are not identical with those of the communists. They are larger and include even the "class enemy." The division of mankind into the capitalist and the socialist sectors, is apparently surpassed, or at least ought to be. Sakharov is not even resentful against the millionaires!

Asserting that today the U.S. and the USSR are "following the same course of increasing complexity of structure and industrial management," he is scrapping another pillar of Marxism-Leninism: the basic difference in the situation and laws of development of bourgeois and socialist societies.

The two superpowers, the U.S. and the USSR, must stop considering each other "as rivals and opponents." They must understand that they are collaborators in the noble undertaking of saving mankind, and for that purpose they must adopt "unified and general principles," among which the first is that "all people have the right to decide their own fate with a free expression of will."

To remove any possible doubt about his approach to international problems and the conflict which is dividing mankind, Sakharov bluntly rejects dialectics. While "the capitalist world could not help giving birth to the socialist," "the socialist world should not seek to destroy the capitalist world," because "under present conditions, this would be tantamount to the suicide of mankind."

Instead, socialism should "ennoble" the capitalist world and finally "merge with it."

And as if all this were not enough, Sakharov has topped his new approach and outlook with the worst heresy: contempt for the authority and competence of the Communist Party itself. He denounces the official insistence on subordinating the "striving of the intelligentsia . . . to the will and interests of the working class," because "What these demands really mean is subordinating to the will of the party or, even more specifically, to the party's central apparatus and its officials. Who will guarantee that these officials always express the genuine interests of the working class as a whole and the genuine interests of progress rather than their own caste interests?"

In other words, Sakharov makes a shambles of the fundamental dogma of all Marxism-Leninism, that the working class represents mankind (and its true interests), the party represents the working class, and that the party leadership represents the party, the working class and mankind.

Comrade Sakharov, it would seem, is brave and bold as a lion, he is a hero, he almost sounds counter-revolutionary! He is determined to save mankind at any price, including the sacrifice of Stalinism, Marxism, Leninism, hostility toward the West and the U.S., struggle and conquest. His hand is outstretched in sincere cooperation!

In any case, both Sakharov and the official Soviet circles must have been gratified by the response which his Plan elicited at its target, the West. For, starting with *The New York Times,* the Plan has received considerable attention, it has been published in a number of European countries, in several languages, and has on the whole been received with open arms.

The German socialist weekly *Die Zeit* called it "the most exciting document to come from the Soviet Union since the beginning of de-Stalinization, i.e. since Khrushchev's epochal speech at the XXth Congress." A prominent Italian, Pietro Quaroni, presently President of Italian Radio and Television Company, has stated that "Sakharov's Memorandum has given us all a great hope." A British diplomat and educator, William Hayter, has heard "the voice of reason" speaking through the Memorandum.

On this side of the ocean, Louis Fischer, from Princeton, has stressed that Sakharov was "often called the father of the Soviet hydrogen bomb" and estimated that "Andrei Sakharov, the social philosopher, is a valuable gift to the Soviet Union and the whole world." For, after asking whether there were eleven Sakharovs in the USSR, he explained: "What if they were to replace the eleven ossified members of the Politburo? The thousand years old tradition of tyranny in Russia could hamper them. But they could mightily change politics."

But in spite of these and similar assessments, it is clear that Sakharov's Plan, while containing elements which may appear new and heretical, is built around well-known communist attitudes, dialectically combined with his "heretical" positions.

Sakharov, whatever else he may be, is a consummate dialectician! He has subjected communism to devastating criticism, rejected Marxism-Leninism, subordinated mere socialist interests to those of mankind, including capitalism. But he has in the same breath, used communist semantics to turn every position critical of Soviet conditions and reality—and seemingly approving of Western conditions and reality—into its opposite.

He speaks about the evils of the division of the world: "Any preaching of the incompatibility of world ideologies and nations, is madness and a crime." But he passes silently over the basic fact of our era, that the split, the unbridgeable gap and irreconcilable conflict which threaten mankind with destruction, were created and are maintained by the communists. If an end must be put to the division of mankind, the only way would be for the communists to cease and desist, to change fundamentally. But Sakharov recommends exactly the contrary. It is capitalism which must change and disappear, while communism must become more communistic, since "only . . . socialism . . . will preserve civilization."

After his fervent appeal to end the division of mankind and create conditions indispensable for intellectual freedom, he has the temerity to warn the reader that "ideological collaboration cannot apply to those fanatical, sectarian and extremist ideologies that reject all possibility of rapprochement, discussion and compromise, for example the ideologies of fascist, racist, militarist and Maoist demagogy."

To which, two remarks: 1. the most fanatical, sectarian and extremist ideology, least amenable to reason, rapprochement, discussion and compromise, is communism; 2. communist practice has always been to dub anybody who disagrees with them and refuses to be used by them or makes a move against communism, as "fascist, racist, militarist," etc., from Congressman Martin Dies, to James Burnham, to Lasky and Toledano, to Barry Goldwater and Strom Thurmond, Ronald Reagan and John Wayne, Richard Daley and Spiro Agnew, etc. So, who is left to discuss and cooperate for the good of mankind but "us communists"?

Sakharov resolutely pleads, in the interest of world peace, for the rejection of the traditional method of conducting international affairs, which is based on the endeavor to harm other countries and advance one's own interests, but at the same time he proclaims his abiding loyalty to the "revolutionary and national liberation struggle" and stresses that the "extreme cases of reaction, racism and militarism . . . allow no other course than armed struggle." Which means that he fully endorses communist worldwide subversion, with its use of the vehicle of National Liberation Fronts everywhere (Yugoslavia, Algeria, Vietnam, etc.) and the basic Leninist-Stalinist distinction between just and unjust wars.

In other words, freedom, equality, etc., are for everybody *except* those who disagree with socialism, i.e. with the official communist line. That is a standard rule of Leninism-Stalinism, or Maoism for that matter (and its "people's democratic dictatorship").

Sakharov stresses the principle of self-determination ("right to decide their own fate with a free expression of will") and explicitly mentions the movement for the liberalization of Czechoslovakia as a hopeful sign of change for the better. He even makes a categorical statement which would seem to fit the situation: "There are . . . situations where revolution is the only way out. This applies especially to national uprisings."

However, when, less than a month after his essay was published in *The New York Times*, Soviet troops invaded Czechoslovakia, Sakharov's protest was not heard. But only innocents could be surprised. It is not only that protesting at that time was a highly dangerous venture in the USSR, but—more important—Sakharov's essay, as if he had anticipated such an event, contains a full justification of the invasion: "All military and military economic forms of revolution and counter-revolution are illegal and tantamount to aggression." It would seem then that it was the Czechs and Slovaks who in August 1968 committed aggression against the Soviet Union!

So, when the military, in Greece and Indonesia, prevent a communist takeover in their own country by foreigners and foreign agents, that is aggression! But when Soviet troops invade Czechoslovakia to impose their will and dictate its policies, that is peaceful coexistence and "an opportunity to prevent tragic events!"

This is nothing new, of course. Sakharov, who wants to save peace and mankind through coexistence, must know that the world champion of that miraculous principle is none other than Chou En-lai, who formulated the famous "five principles of coexistence," when he signed the pact between Red China and India with the famous nonaligned liberal Jawaharlal Nehru in 1955. And yet that same Chou En-lai was still foreign minister of Red China during the military aggression against India in October-November 1962.

Sakharov does his utmost to appear as an impartial observer and judge of international events and problems. And yet on the subject of the war in Vietnam he is echoing the most rabid anti-American line of official communist propaganda, while on the question of the Middle East, his criticism of Soviet policies, Soviet blatant meddling, subversion and warmongering is toned down to innocuous academic remarks.

He speaks a great deal about democracy and democratic spirit, but he proclaims Lenin, of all people, as a champion of democracy! This should be enough to show his own concept of democracy and his democratic sincerity. For he impudently forgets that the most radical philosopher and ruthless advocate of violence "unrestricted by law" (Lenin's term) in social and international affairs was Vladimir Ilitch Lenin, the most prolific communist writer and the first chief of the Soviet state. It is under him that the bases were laid for the Stalinist terror of the thirties under which more crimes were perpetrated, more people were massacred, more violence used than under any other dictator in modern or ancient times, except in Red China. The monstrous Felix Dzerzinsky was Lenin's first chief of the Cheka (NKVD) and all his crimes were committed while the great democrat Lenin,[86] whom Eugene Ionesco properly called "the great scoundrel of history," [87] was the supreme ruler of the USSR. Stalin did not have to innovate, but simply follow in Lenin's footsteps. He did. The concept of freedom that Sakharov has firmly embraced is obviously the Leninist-Stalinist dialectical concept of freedom from "the fetters of capital."

Sakharov does speak of the crimes under communism. However, while he detects real villainy in the "monstrous relations in human and international affairs brought forth by the egotistic principle of capital," he confines communist crimes to Stalin's time and attributes them simply to short-sightedness and narrowmindedness.

Sakharov denounces inhumanity, racism, nationalism and militarism, the cult of personality. But he forgets to tell us about the racist approach to the Jewish question in the Soviet Union during Stalin and after Stalin. And what about the violent protests of Negro (African) students in Moscow, because of the unaccounted disappearance of one of their fellow-students, who dared intimately to befriend a white Soviet girl? And who ever came to the idea of casting the epithet of "*cherni maimuni*" (black apes) to African students, but the authorities of communist Bulgaria? [88]

And as for slave labor and extermination camps in the Soviet Union, he states himself that they "were in fact prototypes of the fascist death camps." In other words, Hitler did not have to invent them. He had the famous Soviet (Leninist-Stalinist) model to copy.

As for militarism, Sakharov does not tell us anything about the Soviet military aggression against Finland (200 million against 4 million) in 1939–1940; nor about the Soviet active help to North Korea in its aggression against South Korea in 1950–1953, nor today about the decisive Soviet role in the aggression of North Vietnam against South Vietnam; nor about the aggressive Soviet naval presence in the Mediterranean and open support to the Arab "liberation struggle" by Kosygin . . .

Sakharov asserts that "the Daniel-Siniavsky trial . . . has compromised the Communist system." Again, he shows his true color. The trial was a scandalous mockery of justice. But he is suggesting that we should be shocked at the staged trial for two writers, while completely disregarding the killing of "ten to fifteen" million people!

Sakharov gives credit and praise to Khrushchev as the pioneer of de-Stalinization in the USSR. But he toes the same line of deploring only the liquidation of members of the communist party, not any non-members. And while denouncing anti-Ukrainism today, he passes under silence the fact that Khrushchev fully earned his title of "the butcher of the Ukraine" in the thirties. Nor does he say one word about his brutal intervention in Hungary in October/November 1956. And he omits mentioning that in the years following the denunciation of Stalin, Khrushchev publicly and emphatically praised him as a great communist: "When it comes to fighting imperialism, we are all Stalinists!"

Motives? Explanations? Always the same: the interests of communist power as the supreme yardstick for morals, justice, interests of the working class, peace, humanity, etc.

To sum up:

While Sakharov has given the semblance of deep soul-searching and attainment of non-sectarian views and stands, based solely on the interests of mankind, in which capitalism and communism are reconciled, he has actually done no such thing. He has not deviated one iota from the official communist position that "socialism" is the alpha and omega for the solution of social and political problems, for it alone offers the democratic method and contains the correct answer to all questions. It is the way of the future for all mankind.

So, Sakharov is not a politically naive idealist who is following his ideals at the risk of displeasing the dogmatic, neo-Stalinist rulers of his country. Not at all. He is a trained and well-conditioned communist and dialectician, toeing faithfully the general line of communist orthodoxy and—which is more important—fully acquainted with the modern communist strategy for winning the world "peacefully," by engineering its surrender without struggle.

He does not have to insist that "actually the views of the present author are profoundly socialist." That is more than obvious to any attentive reader.

Sakharov has moved strictly within communist dialectics and in accordance with its laws. In his plan, the *thesis* is the Soviet Union, with its present dogmatic and bureacratic rulers; the *antithesis* are the leftist Leninists and their allies, representing the West, the "leftist Westerners"; the *synthesis* is the consolidation of communist rule in the USSR and everywhere, the re-education of the American people and the transformation of its institutions away from capitalism, and thus the creation of proper conditions for the establishment of a one-world order, under communist "highly intelligent world-wide guidance."

The importance of the Sakharov Plan is that, while proceeding along the established lines of communist dialectics, it contains a new ingredient: the explicit invitation to the U.S. to surrender through its leaders ("ruling groups"). That is new. Until now, the communists have, in their struggle for power, counted mainly on their "reserves of the revolution," the colonial peoples and the proletariat of the capitalist countries, i.e. on the oppressed on "the other side." There has also been the shift from revolution to the control of the enemy's mind (after World War II). But Sakharov now, without rejecting the "reserves of the revolution" and without departing from the psychological warfare against our minds, is openly inviting the capitalist class of the United States (or a substantial part of it, the "ruling groups"), to come over to their side. His whole plan revolves around an alliance of "leftist Leninists" in the Soviet Union and "leftist Westerners" in the United States.

At the XXth Congress of the CPSU held in February, 1956, Molotov had explained that the emphasis on coexistence was a consequence of the strengthening of the forces of socialism in the world and of the fact that "we now have an international situation of which we could only have dreamed ten or fifteen years ago." Was Sakharov's bold move an indication that the situation had in the meantime again changed so radically and favorably for them that they could afford to extend an open invitation to the leaders of the United States to surrender?

The communists know that their conquests have been made

possible by our policy of surrender and they want us to play the game to the very end. Our rulers have given half of Europe, China, half of Korea and Cuba to the communists. Now they should give them the United States! They have said "a"; now they should say "b." And since the main hindrance for the realization of that scheme is the American people, the Soviet rulers and the U.S. rulers must join hands, "gang up against" the American people to change their psychology and educate them by modern scientific-technological-biochemical means to behave so as to facilitate the "peaceful transition to socialism."

The exact genesis of Sakharov's Plan is unknown to me, of course. But it is obvious that very minute preparation went into it. And it is in full accord with official Soviet policies.

When Western experts called Sakharov's Plan bold, they were right. The only thing where they were wrong is that it was not a bold move away from communist imperialism, but a thrust forward, a uniquely bold invitation to the U.S. to surrender.

The invasion of Czechoslovakia, only one month (August 21, 1968) after the publication of Sakharov's Plan which was proclaiming the sacred right of "all peoples . . . to decide their own fate with a free expression of will," has certainly affected the credibility of the Soviet line of liberalization and coexistence.

But the communists are never embarrassed to use the carrot of coexistence and the stick of invasion, alternately, or simultaneously. For they know that the eagerness of Western leaders and opinion-makers to detect liberalization and good will in Soviet policies is such that it cannot be dampened by any facts about Soviet invasions and imperialism.

So, if the Sakharov Plan may be shelved momentarily, its basic concepts are still in full operation, regardless of the occupation of Czechoslovakia and the Brezhnev doctrine. Henceforth, as until now, all we can expect from the USSR is not cooperation, but political warfare to destroy us. And since this evident and elementary fact is beyond our Sovietologists and Kremlinologists, an examination of the nature of communism and communist strategy and tactics is needed, for without it, we shall be unable to understand the nature of communist policies and the meaning of their strategic and tactical moves.

PART THREE
Communism

4   The Nature of Communism

Power

War

Hatred

Communism is Power

The very fact that communism has been able to seize power in the largest country in the world (Russia, 1917) and in the meantime has spread to one billion people, indicates that the confrontation of the free world with communism has not been a victory for freedom, but, until now, a successful venture of communism. And the key reason is that the West has failed to understand the nature of communism and to pursue a policy to defeat it.

Today (1972), 124 years have passed since Karl Marx and Friedrich Engels published the Communist Manifesto (1848), 55 years since the communists seized power in Russia, 27 years since they installed their agents in power in half of Europe, 23 years since they came to power in China and 13 years since they installed themselves in power at the doorstep of the United States, in Cuba.

But there are still influential policy-makers and public-opinion makers in the West who know as little about communism and the communists as if it had just appeared on the world scene, and to whom communism remains an inscrutable mystery and the communists people whom we shall never understand.

Western experts have studied communism as an ideology, a new philosophy, a secular religion, as "social science," as a movement of extreme fanatics bent upon radically changing human society and re-making the world, as a blueprint for a more just social order. However, the essence of communism, which can be expressed in three words: power, war, hatred, has not received the attention it deserves.

From the first moment, Marx and Engels made it plain that the communists were not interested in interpreting the world, but in changing it: "All philosophers have sought to explain the world, our business is to change it." The road to change was ". . . the forcible overthrow of all existing social conditions" (*Communist Manifesto*). And the goal was total, unlimited power in the world.

Therefore, when communists write it is not to express their beliefs, but to create the necessary political force to attain their utterly ambitious goal.

This point was unequivocally established from the very beginning: "Communist teaching is not a dogma, but a guide to action." Lenin amplified: "All our theories are programs of action."

"We study Marxism-Leninism not because of its good looks . . . It has neither good looks nor magic, it is only very useful," says Mao Tse-tung. Marxist theory is "an arrow . . . which must be shot with an aim. . . at the target of the Chinese Revolution."

Consequently the Marxist-Leninist concept of truth is totally different from ours. "Marx's theory is the objective truth," wrote Lenin, making it evident that objective truth is that which helps the communists seize and hold power. Conversely, "what does not give power . . . is false." [89]

Striving for power has been one of the mightiest impulses of man throughout history. As he endeavored to control the forces of nature, he strived to influence and use his fellow-men.

But no group, organization or movement in history has been so power-oriented as the communists. With the communists, everything is subordinated to, and shaped and determined by a concern for power: its philosophy, its strategy and tactics, its thought and practice, its economy, literature, and the arts.

So, communism is not an ideology and a political movement to create a new world on some definite principles, following some definite blueprint. It is and has been from the beginning (the *Communist Manifesto*, 1848) an ideology, pseudo-science and political movement to destroy existing society and world order and to install communist dictatorship throughout the whole world. That is the essence of communism. Marx could not have been more explicit: ". . . the main question, *viz.* the question of power." And that has remained so to the present day.

Lenin took good care to define the true and precise nature of communist power: "The scientific concept dictatorship, means neither more nor less than unlimited power resting directly on force, not limited by anything, not restricted by any laws or any absolute rules. Nothing else but that."

The Third World Congress of the Communist International (June-July 1921) stated that the "widest masses of workers . . . are being led by a vanguard, whose real aim is in the conquest of power."

In his speech at the 40th anniversary of the Bolshevik revolution (November 6, 1957) Nikita Khrushchev reminded the communists and the world that "The main and fundamental question of any revolution is the question of power."

And in April 1960 Mao Tse-tung, in an article in the *Peking Review* ("Long Live Leninism") expresses the real faith of all communists: "The fundamental question of all revolutions is the question of power."

To the communists, world conquest and world power are not a beginning, or the means to some (whatever) end. Power is everything. It is the goal, the end itself. *Total global power,* unrestricted by law, for an unlimited time, *is communism.*

The realization of this essence of communism opens the door to an understanding of communist strategy and tactics. The failure to grasp it bars access to an understanding of communist policies.

Communism Is Permanent War

Part of the necessary understanding of the essence of communism is the understanding that such an ambitious goal could not be achieved simply and easily. The total destruction of a society and the seizure and exercise of total power for an indefinite time could obviously be achieved only through a permanent total struggle—war—in all fields, against that society.

That is the logical conclusion which the communists draw from their goal. The birth of the communist movement was a declaration of war on existing society and world order.

As a very thorough student of the classical work *On War* by General Karl von Clausewitz (1830), who defined war as a "continuation of politics by other means," Lenin had come to the conclusion that politics was permanent war, in which only the means changed. And the war which the communists waged to change the world, was total, involving all areas of human life and endeavor. In *"Leftism, Infantile Disease of Communism,"* Lenin wrote:

". . . a war for the overthrow of the bourgeoisie . . . is a hundred times more difficult, prolonged and complicated than the most stubborn of ordinary wars between states . . ."

And once the bourgeoisie is overthrown and the dictatorship of the proletariat is established, the war does not stop, but goes over into a new phase:

"The dictatorship of the proletariat is a stubborn struggle—sanguinary and bloodless, violent and peaceful, military and economic, educational and administrative—against the forces and traditions of the old society."

Stalin stressed these points in his *Foundations of Leninism.*

After 124 years of communist writing, many Western experts have not yet learned the lesson. And yet the communist oracles, starting with Lenin, could not have been more explicit. Liu Chaochi, President of the "People's Republic of China," stressed in his book *How to be a Good Communist* (published in the July-August issue of the revue *Révolution*, Paris, 1964), that Marx's real mission in life was to contribute in every conceivable manner to the overthrow of the "capitalist system," so that "the science of Marxism-Leninism is of no use or almost none to those who are not authentic revolutionaries."

Communist "Science"

The communists realized that an extremely ambitious political goal could never be achieved by traditional means of political struggle.

Marx and Engels had studied the socialist theories and movements of Sismondi, St. Simon, Proudhon, Owen, Fourier, and reached the conclusion that they had failed because of a wrong approach to the problems of the transformation of society. They had appealed to and relied on human intelligence, noble sentiments, love, solidarity, good will, to realize their ideals of equality, wellbeing, justice and freedom through the abolition of private property.

Marx and Engels found such an approach doomed to failure. For it ignored the laws of society, history and human psychology. It lacked emotional appeal (stressing love and virtue, instead of hatred and passion), and it lacked the element of inevitability, appealing to reason and conviction, instead of force).

Taking into account the "positivist" mood of the time, they decided that they should, for the attainment of their goal, power, harness the new wonder weapon, endowed with supernatural, superstitious force and prestige, "science." That is the course on which Marx and Engels embarked. The key idea was to impress the public that, as opposed to all other socialist movements in history, which for their success depended on chance and changing human factors, communism was "scientific," relying on laws independent from and stronger than human will, and thus bound to win.

To "prove" that the advent of communism was inevitable, Marx and Engels formulated the theory of historical materialism. They used Hegel's law of dialectics, about the constant and unavoidable change in human affairs. The development of society follows the laws of dialectics: every existing political and social order (the thesis) produces forces which strive to bring it down (the antithesis). The struggle which ensues never ends in a draw, but in a victory of the revolutionary forces, not, however, without adopting in the new order (synthesis), which is established on the ruins of the old one, some of its elements. That synthesis becomes the new thesis, within which forces hostile to it gradually develop (new antithesis), a new struggle ensues, ending in a new synthesis, and so on.

Substituting for the spiritual factors which moved the world according to Hegel, something simpler and more tangible: the production and distribution of economic goods, Marx and Engels claimed that in our capitalistic epoch society is polarized in two classes, the ruling bourgeoisie and the exploited proletariat. The development of economic forces and social relations will inevitably remove the bourgeoisie and capitalism from the stage of history and bring about the victory of the proletariat. "There can be no immutable social systems." "The capitalist system can be replaced by the socialist system, just as at one time the feudal system was replaced by the capitalist system."

Now, this is very impressive "social science," except that its creators deny its validity as soon as it has performed its assigned task of overthrowing capitalism. For, logically, if the law of dialectics is so powerful that it makes the downfall of capitalism an unavoidable process, above human will, then the downfall of communism, at some later date, is equally unavoidable. And if dialectics is not so powerful, then the downfall of communism may be avoided, but so can the downfall of capitalism. No, say Marx and Engels. The law of dialectics is stronger than the capitalists because they do not know the laws of development of human society. But the communists are stronger than dialectics because they have discovered the laws of social development and therefore can control them.

Which reveals the hidden and absolute law of the dialectic mechanism, the interest of communist power. Anything that favors communist power, is scientific, noble, human. Anything that weakens or threatens communism, is unscientific, inhuman, reactionary and fascist.

However, with their sense for political realities, Marx and Engels could not fail to realize that, useful as it was as a political weapon, the law of historical materialism would never bring about the downfall of "capitalism." If socialism were ever to win, the communists had somehow to introduce into the theory of historical materialism (which promised to destroy capitalism and bring about socialism) conscious human action as the determining factor of human history. And this they did in the same *Communist Manifesto*, which lays the foundations of historical materialism. "Every class struggle is a political struggle," i.e. for power. Marx and Engels chide those who "reject all political, and especially all revolutionary action" and who expect everything from "the miraculous effects of their social science."

Marx and Engels know that all their "science" will be of no avail if the proletariat is not politically organized: ". . . the proletariat must first of all acquire political supremacy," must take political power in its hands.

So, from the very beginning (the *Communist Manifesto*), the communist theory contained two logically and "scientifically" ir-reconcilable basic interpretations of history, the economic and determinist vs. the political and voluntarist, and indicated two different courses to follow, the evolutionary vs. the revolutionary. Such a duality split the Marxist movement in two distinct and often hostile groups, whose raging debates filled the second half of the nineteenth century.

This state of affairs could not be tolerated indefinitely. And it is Lenin who brought it to an end with his book *"What Is To Be Done?"* (1902).

Lenin emphatically rejected reliance on science and the development of economic and social conditions, and put all his accent on political organization and revolutionary action. What mattered was to educate *political agitators,* professional *revolutionaries,* who would intervene "in every sphere and in every question of social and political life, striving to rouse discontent and indignation among the masses," utilize every manifestation of discontent in the existing society and "collect and utilize every grain of every rudimentary protest."

Students who joined the Social-Democratic Party "were not so much interested in Marxism as a theory; they were interested in it because it provided the answers to the question: 'What is to be done?'; because it was *a call to march against the enemy"* (emphasis added).

Revolution would never come spontaneously as a result of economic conditions. It had to be made, by professional revolutionaries, who would act "like an enormous pair of smith's bellows that would blow every spark of class struggle and popular indignation into a general conflagration."

In 1916 Lenin made another fundamental change in Marxist theory. Marx's prediction was that revolution would take place first in industrially developed countries. Lenin rejected that. Capitalism, to save itself, had resorted to imperialist, political means, to insure the world market, and had "grown into a world system of colonial oppression and of the financial strangulation of the overwhelming majority of the people of the world by a handful of 'advanced' countries." Thus what would bring capitalism down, was a concerted revolutionary action of the proletariat of the

"advanced countries" and the "oppressed masses" of the underdeveloped countries. And the revolution would occur not in the
industrially most developed country but in the politically weakest
country, in the country which was the "weakest link in the
imperialist chain."

From a "scientific" point of view, Lenin (and Stalin) differed
strongly from Marx. But from the viewpoint of the communist
goal of "changing the world," there was perfect continuity. As
"science" this was ridiculous. But as a change of revolutionary
strategy it was very effective.*

State and Revolution (1917)

To make clear his two basic points: (1) that communism would
result not from economic developments but from political revolutionary action, and (2) that communism was not a social order,
but a movement to establish communist power in the whole
world, Lenin wrote in 1917 his book, *State and Revolution*.

The state was, according to Lenin, the central question of communism. It was "the focus of all political questions," a "fundamental, basic question of all politics." It is very regrettable that many
Western experts have not carefully read and are not rereading
State and Revolution. Of all Marxist texts this is the one which
expresses most forcefully and succinctly the essence of communist
rule. It clearly and unequivocally brings out that the communist
state: (1) is a machine to destroy all enemies of communism; (2)
only after eliminating all its enemies, will the communist state
start "withering away"; and (3) it will take "hundreds of centuries" for that withering to begin. This is the absolutely decisive

---

* In his comparative study on the Russian (1917) and German (1918/1919)
revolutions, published in installments in the magazine *Der Stern*, Sebastian
Haffner stressed the decisive importance of political preparedness and
organization for the success of the revolution. In Russia, where the "scientific"
requirements for the revolution were not fulfilled, the bolsheviks were thoroughly seasoned and organized power-seekers. In Germany, a country where
all "scientific" conditions for the revolution were fulfilled, there was no necessary political revolutionary force. That is why: "The 'impossible' Russian
revolution succeeded; the 'inevitable' German revolution failed." (*Stern*, November 5, 1967, p. 193).

core of the problem: the "bourgeois" state and society must be forcibly "smashed to bits," but the communist state will wither away by itself!

"For the communists . . . a problem of being overthrown simply does not exist," wrote Mao Tse-tung in 1949.[90]

The concept that communism is permanent war is reflected in all communist policies, official statements, press, propaganda and agitation.

Most explicit has been Nikita Khrushchev with his famous statement: "Whether you like it or not, history is on our side, we shall bury you." (At the reception in the Polish Embassy in Moscow, November 19, 1956.)

Free countries must become communistic, but communist countries must unconditionally remain under communism. No matter what problem, what country, what territory is concerned (Cuba, or Berlin, or Vietnam or Eastern Europe), the unmistakable and immutable communist stand is that what is under communist rule must remain so, and what is free, must become communistic.

To any communist this is plain and irrefutable logic: "What is good for the bourgeois and the imperialists . . . is bad for the working class and, conversely, what is good for the working people is not accepted by the imperialists and bourgeois." [91]

Particularly telling is the communist stand on war and the dangers of nuclear annihilation of the whole globe. With slight individual shadings and just a few occasions where they spoke of general devastation, they always express the same position that in case of a new world war, "what will perish will not be world civilization . . . but that rotten social system with its imperialist basis soaked in blood," (Molotov)[92] or "should a madman make any attack on our state or other Socialist countries, we could literally wipe off the face of the earth the country or countries attacking us" (Soviet Defense Minister Marshal Rodion Malinovsky), or

—"If anyone attacks us again there will be a new Stalingrad, but this Stalingrad will be far away, somewhere in the West." (Marshal Chuikov),[93] or

—"We do not need war . . . but if our enemies impose war on us, we shall smash them." (N. Khrushchev)[94]

Incidentally, two years before the Cuban missile crisis of October-November 1962, Khrushchev had proclaimed the death of the

to have peace, the communists must wage war and the free world must "wage peace," i.e. surrender.[99]

In his speech at the 20th Congress of the C.P.S.U. (February 14, 1956), Khrushchev gave the authentic Leninist-Stalinist line:

> "Leninism teaches that the ruling classes will not surrender their power voluntarily. And the greater or lesser degree of the intensity which the struggle may assume, the use or non-use of violence in the transition to socialism depends on the resistance of the exploiters, on whether the exploiting class itself resorts to violence, rather than on the proletariat."

In other words, communist aggression is historically justified, because it eventually brings peace.

On the other side, the free world being historically doomed, its resistance to communist violence is violence, its resistance to communist total warfare is war, and its policy of peace is actually a policy of war, since it makes more difficult the attainment of communist peace.

That is the communist concept of peace which inspires the Soviet Union's efforts to bring about a "peaceful world."

So, when the communists talk of thermonuclear war as a potential danger, they are deliberately passing under silence the war which is going on and which the Soviet Union and all communists are waging continuously, by all conceivable means, all the time. That war is not potentially dangerous. It is actively fomenting unrest in the world, with the possibilities of revolution and war wide open. It is waged all the time, by their foreign policy of aggression and imperialism, by their "wars of liberation" (Vietnam), by their world-wide subversion, by their instigating riots and rebellion in the United States, especially against the U.S. military action in Vietnam, and in many other ways. The USSR is the main fomenter of division, hatred, aggression, distrust among nations, as well as among various groups within the same nations. It is there, in this insidious, relentless, criminally obsessed instigation to intolerance and total war, that the main danger to mankind and its survival lies, be it through thermonuclear war or without it.

And here we are touching upon another vital and almost completely neglected aspect of communism and its total warfare and of the true meaning of its pretense to make peace with other nations and mankind, *hatred*.

Communism is Hatred

To wage the difficult and complicated permanent war for world power, it was obviously necessary to possess, to be able to draw upon some very powerful and replenishable, explosive emotional fuel, to stoke the furnaces and keep under full steam the revolutionary machine of permanent war for total world power.

The communists have thought of that and they have found the answer: hatred. All the "science" of Marxism-Leninism, all its practice, all its policies are imbued with this powerful passion. It is expressed in the words and tone and style and emphasis and nuance of every communist theory (*i.e.* plan of action), every project, every stand on the most varied issues. A contemporary of Karl Marx, Georg Herwegh (1817–1875), who wrote the well-known verses: *"Wir haben genug geliebt, Wir wollen endlich hassen"* ("We have loved long enough, it is time to hate"), is quoted in Alexander Solzhenitsyn's novel *The Cancer Ward*,[100] as a "philosopher" who is taught in Soviet schools.[101]

And not only in the USSR but in all communist-dominated countries, hatred is the central emotional motive around which all education is built. Wild accusations of exploitation, charges of inhumanity or dishonesty or disregard of elementary human decency, are completely replacing any critical, factual, reasoned examination of facts and logical analysis based on positive knowledge of issues under discussion. Hatred against everything "bourgeois" (which term is used so loosely as to encompass anything and anybody who in whatever way may oppose or obstruct communism), is the perspective under which children are taught to view the world and life. It is especially pronounced in the most populous country in the world, China, which has produced her atomic bomb and is working very hard on her nuclear program.

The public in the West is exposed to less propaganda of hatred against communism in one whole year than the communist powers (from the Soviet Union to Albania) ladle out to their own people and the world in one hour.

Even Bertrand Russell, who by no standard was an anti-communist and who rendered very valuable services to communism by his active participation in various communist-front activities in the whole world, came to the conclusion that humanitarian motives which, he claimed, were present in the origins of communism, have given way to the hatred of opponents. "Marx sanctified the hatred and the strife . . . The fundamental cause of the Communist malady, to my mind, is dogmatism and a complete absence of kindly feeling."

What makes the weapon of hatred especially effective is that it is increasingly used in a "dialectical" manner. In the same way that the communists are for peace but foment and wage all kinds of war which they judge favorable for the spread of communism, in the same way that they are humanists but do not have the slightest compunction against killing, in the same way that they are for freedom but practice slavery, proclaim national self-determination but crush nations and practice imperialism and oppression—they hate because they love so much! It is very simple: they love mankind so much that they must hate with murderous intensity those who have oppressed it for centuries and millenia!

This "dialectical" approach to the problem of hate and love is ingenious indeed. All you have to do to hate without bounds, to the point of smashing and totally annihilating, is to love or pretend to love whatever and whomever may be the likely victim of the wrongdoer. Then the vilest of passions, hatred, appears under the pretense of love, the noblest of virtues.

Today, the New Left, the S.D.S., the Black Power movement, etc. are the outgrowth of the persistent communist propaganda and sowing of the seeds of hatred over a long period of time. Upon closer examination, it can be established that there is no consistent line of reasoning, no rational goal, nothing except the idea of destruction, constantly fed by systematically fomented emotionalism, with the supreme concern of arousing hatred against the United States, communism's main target.* The explosive force of hatred has been put to full use.

The effectiveness of hatred in political action was not lost on Martin Luther King, who did a thorough study of communism

---

* Tom Hayden, one of the leaders of the protest movement, asked about its goals, answered: "I don't know. We shall first make the revolution and then we shall see."

and its methods. He understood that the most efficient way to breed hatred was the indirect way, not by making an outright appeal, but by making extreme emotional statements about grave injustice and outrage, no matter how divorced from reality, factual accuracy or truth, and make them with an air of deep righteous indignation. And if they are accompanied by professions of love and nonviolence, the message of hatred and violence gets more forcefully across. (The chasm between our goodness and the wrongdoer's villainy looms much bigger.) In that manner you prepare and charge with volcanic virulence the mood of the masses for "non-violent" action. For instance, all you have to do is to state that for 300 years the Negroes in America have been so exploited that today even if all the wealth of the United States were to be divided among them, it would not make up for the injustices and injury they have suffered.[102] That is enough. You do not use the word hate, you do not call to rioting and rebellion. All you do is make a "historic" statement, indicating a monumental injustice done by the white to the black. With that you so prepare the ground for violence that you are at freedom to talk all the time about love, universal and unlimited, for everybody—the masses get the message without mistake: Hate, smash!

For when you conjure up the picture of injustices which have been perpetrated for 300 years and have produced detrimental consequences which cannot be corrected even by the complete depletion of the richest country on earth and in history—that country is automatically transformed from a country "with liberty and justice for all" into precisely that which communist propaganda makes it all the time: the land of utter villainy, which calls for one response only: Hate and destroy! And the greater the contrast between fact and claim, the wilder the hatred.

5 Present Communist Strategy for the Conquest of the World

Peace

U.N.

Anti-colonialism

Coexistence

". . . Stalin and Molotov considered at Yalta that by our willingness to accept a general wording of the declaration on Poland and liberated Europe, by our recognition of the need of the Red Army for security behind its lines, and of the predominant interest of Russia in Poland as a friendly neighbor and as a corridor to Germany, we understood and were ready to accept Soviet policies *already known to us.*" (Emphasis added)

AVERELL HARRIMAN

The seeds of all later communist strategy and tactics were contained in the Communist Manifesto: (1) in the clearly stated position that the question of power was the principal question; (2) in the simultaneous use of the "scientific," determinist, economic, evolutionary interpretation of problems, and the accent on voluntarist, revolutionary, political factors; (3) in the explicit indication that Communists would enter into temporary alliances with anybody, any non-communists, who may prove useful for the promotion of communist aims.

With the founding of the Bolshevik Party (1903) in London, the basic communist strategic and tactical principles are clearly enunciated by Lenin, and they can be summed up in two terms: the maximal program and the minimal program.

Lenin was a realist. He knew human nature and he knew how deeply communism ran against the basic noble instincts and higher strivings of man. So, he knew that no amount of preaching, agitation and propaganda, reasoning, convincing and exposure to "scientific socialism" could ever bring people to the acceptance of communism, i.e. create enough force so that the aims of communism could be realized in the predicted, only possible, revolutionary way. The answer was to devise the means to avoid the resistance of the bourgeois enemy and moreover to induce him, or part of the ruling class, to participate (consciously or unwittingly) in its own destruction. That is what Lenin did by formulating the idea of the two different and yet inseparable and complementary programs. The elementary, well known program of world communist dictatorship, he called the maximal program. It was the only real program, unchanged and unchangeable. That was the only program which mattered and which was to serve as a guide and yardstick, but that was the program few people would accept or could be won for.

The dilemma was to be solved by the device of a series of programs which contained democratic reforms, every one of which would be acceptable to many non-communists and even anti-communists, but which would be so formulated as to make possible the gradual realization of the maximal program, i.e. create conditions favorable to its realization. Here is what the Serbian edition of the official History of the C.P.S.U. (b) says about it:

"That program consisted of two parts—the maximal and the minimal program. The maximal program pertained to the main tasks of the working class—the socialist revolution, the overthrow of the capitalist's rule, the establishment of the dictatorship of the proletariat. The minimal program pertained to the most immediate tasks of the party, which had to be realized before the overthrow of the capitalist order, until the establishment of the dictatorship of the proletariat: the overthrow of Czarist absolutism, the creation of a democratic republic, the introduction of the 8 hour working day for workers, the abolishment of all remnants of feudalism in the villages, the restitution to the peasants of all the land ("sectors") which the landlords took away from them." *

* *"History of the All-Union Communist Party* (b), Serbian edition, Moscow, 1938, p. 41/42. This most important detail will not be found in every edition of the History of the C.P.S.U. (b), in every language. Actually, today few contain it, if any. The reason is obvious: not to call attention to a most effective stratagem.

As indicated in this text, a minimal program for Russia was already sketched and it was acceptable to many non-communists and anti-communists who had little political sense or knowledge of communism. But their participation was invaluable in inching Russia toward 1917. When the time and conditions were ripe, Alexander Kerensky, the forerunner and symbol of the modern liberal ("leftist Westerner"), thought that what should be carried out was a nice moderate democratic revolution, a nice "minimal" program of the democratization of Russia. Lenin, of course, knew better, since to the bolsheviks, democratization was only the first step to revolution, since all the "democratic" programs since 1902 were made by the communists, and since the communists had created and controlled the revolutionary mood of the masses.

The result is known. The democratic revolution of Kerensky evaporated in thin air before the onrush of the bolshevik revolution, and Kerensky barely escaped alive. But the point to remember is that without Kerensky, his regime and his policies, Lenin would probably never have seized power in Russia.

Immediately after the establishment of the bolshevik regime, its existence was so precarious, its survival so uncertain and the mobilization of all revolutionary energies so decisive that no room was left for tactics. The survival of the regime required the greatest militancy it could possibly generate, within Russia and in the whole world. So, the strategy of the "minimal program" had to be temporarily shelved. Proponents of a course of immediate world revolution (Trotsky), and advocates of "socialism in one country" (Stalin), were united in working to whip up revolutionary zeal, hatred and intolerance to the highest point.

But in 1935 the old Lenin idea came to full bloom with the project of "popular fronts," proclaimed by Georgi Dimitrov, secretary general of the Communist International, at its Seventh Congress. In the face of the danger of Nazi Germany to world communism, Dimitrov maintained that the survival of mankind, freedom, democracy, were at stake and that the communists were willing to ally themselves and wage a common struggle with bourgeois parties which would fight "fascism"; "Our attitude toward bourgeois democracy is not the same under all conditions . . . Now, . . . the choice is not between proletarian dictatorship and bourgeois democracy but between bourgeois democracy and fascism." And while Dimitrov was not concealing the motivating idea of using the weaker enemy to fight the tougher enemy, he made it clear that the communist-bourgeois collaboration would be strictly on communist terms. The communists, by entering into an alliance of convenience, were not in the least departing from their goals or program.

But the plan worked very efficiently. Not so much before World War II, when the groundwork was being laid, as during World War II, when the patient labor produced its full results. The whole Allied (U.S.-British-Soviet) war effort was a huge "anti-Fascist" operation, i.e. an operation where all the efforts, sacrifices and contributions of all three partners were used by one, the USSR. And the reason was that Stalin, entering into the war alliance with Roosevelt and Churchill did not renounce one iota of his communist plans, ambitions and aims, nor did anybody ask him to. While making only tactical, superficial and perfunctory propaganda concessions to his wartime allies and to the common goals of their struggle against Hitler and Japan, he felt perfectly free to continue the political war, not only against Hitler and Japan, but against his own allies, who had no policy, no aims, no political vision beyond the immediate military aim of defeating the powers of the Axis. "In this war we are pursuing strictly military objectives," declared Dean Acheson. When Churchill, in his famous "Iron Curtain" speech in Fulton, stated that "This is certainly not the liberated Europe we fought to create," he was actually speaking of the inevitable result of the strictly military, i.e. non-political approach to political matters.

For Acheson's statement was, unfortunately and unbelievably, true. And that explains how it was possible that a war in which the United States played the absolutely decisive part in achieving victory,[103] served politically solely and exclusively the interests of Stalin and the Soviet Union. Roosevelt not only did not object to the communization of half of Europe, but pledged himself actively to see to it that no regimes unfriendly to the Soviet Union should be established along its borders. The role of Roosevelt in paving the way to the communization of China is also too well-known to reiterate.

Strategy After World War II

World War II had taught Stalin a number of invaluable lessons and created an entirely new power situation in Europe and in the world. The new situation required a new strategy. He used the lessons to work out the strategy.

On the negative side, the war had demonstrated the deep hatred of the Russian people against the Soviet regime, as well as the enormous economic, industrial and military inferiority of the USSR. Stalin, being aware of this real mood of the people, had organized several years before the war, an intensive campaign of Russian nationalism, through film, literature, arts, school, etc., glorifying not Marx and Engels, or Lenin, but Russian national heroes, Minin and Pozharsky, Ivan the Terrible, Peter the Great, Souvorov, etc. It did not help too much. The "fatherland of the workers" was unable to resist Hitler, because the people, who hated the foreign invader, hated Stalin and communism worse. What turned the tide were three factors: (a) Hitler's policy of ruthless cruelty and inhumanity toward the population, which inevitably made bitter enemies out of potential allies; (b) "General Winter," which stopped Hitler at the outskirts of Moscow; and (c) the decisive factor, U.S. participation in the war and help to the Soviet Union.

But the lesson of the unreliability of "the people" in carrying out the grandiose plans of communism was convincingly documented. And so was the towering economic, industrial, technological and military superiority of the West, especially the U.S. However, all of that helped to bring out and to accentuate the key factor, where Stalin and his accomplices possessed great superiority: political warfare. That superiority of will and purposeful struggle for power was decisive. The United States fought and won the war militarily, but the *only* political winner was the USSR, since 100 million Europeans and 500 million Chinese were subjugated by communism in the aftermath of that war.

And so, the main task of Soviet strategy in the new power situation became to preserve that political superiority that had worked miracles in the dire straits of the recent past. It had overcome the hostility of the people in the USSR, it had offset the economic and military inferiority of the USSR and it had harnessed the power of the West to bring about a solution favorable to communism. The USSR, which was disintegrating in 1941, had—owing to President Roosevelt's pro-Soviet policy—emerged out of World War II as a world power controlling a huge empire.

Control of the Mind

So the path for Soviet strategy imposed itself logically: control of the mind of the West as a means of controlling its policies. This was the more urgent since the United States was (until 1949) the only atomic power and immensely superior to the Soviet Union militarily. To paralyze that might, to bring about the moral and political disarmament of the U.S., while preaching coexistence, became a vital Soviet interest. In view of the World War II experience, what had to be done was to present the consolidation and expansion of Soviet power in the form of a "minimal program," i.e. of the "common interests of all mankind."

Logically the first "interest of all mankind" after that devastating war, was:

1. *Peace.*

Or rather the logical first step for the Soviet Union was to impose the idea that the main danger threatening the very existence of mankind was war (not communism), and therefore that the supreme interest of mankind was to preserve peace at any price (including communism and collaboration with communism).

In World War II, when the USSR needed all the help of the U.S., the ideal of freedom was supreme. The worst conceivable evil was not war, but oppression. Now, it was the reverse: no oppression, no tyranny or dictatorship, was as terrible as war . . .

The Soviet interest in preaching this line of "peace" was obvious: to consolidate its stupendous gains from the war.

Conversely, there was no reason on earth why the U.S. should accept that line. For by accepting it, it was bound to devote all its energies to "waging peace," leaving free hands to the communists to pursue their political warfare and move toward world conquest unopposed. Moreover, the incessant stress on the horrors of nuclear war would certainly produce enough pressure from the American public to induce the U.S. Government to pursue a disarmament policy, in the "interest of mankind."

In other words, the message of Soviet "peace" to the U.S. was that the "common efforts" with the Soviet Union to "save peace" were more important than the concern to defend U.S. national interests.

2. *United Nations*

The second vitally important point was to institutionalize the wartime relationship based on "anti-fascism." The Stalin-Dimitrov concept of anti-fascist "popular fronts," launched in 1935, was built around the idea that mankind had one enemy: "fascism," and thus that anybody opposed to communism was automatically a "fascist." The Western democracies, if they did not want to be identified with fascism, had better help the communists beat the fascists. That is what they, especially the U.S., did in World War II. They beat fascism. However, victory over fascism served not the interests of freedom, but the interests of communism, since freedom shrank in the world and communism spread.

But this course of yielding to communism in the name of preserving world peace, was precisely the course on which the West had to be kept.

The safest and most efficient way to realize this truly fantastic project of having the U.S. wage peace while the USSR continued to wage political war, was to create a prestigious international organization to serve as an instrument for its implementation. The anti-fascist United Nations Organization was made to order for the purpose.

The instruments and safeguards were created immediately; the USSR received three votes in the U.N. General Assembly, while every other country, including the U.S., received one; there was from the first moment, according to Trygve Lie, the first U.N. Secretary General, a "gentleman's agreement" between the U.S. and the USSR, that the Undersecretary for military affairs of the Secretariat would always be a man of full Soviet trust; and the vote in the Security Council was subjected to the veto of any of the five big powers. In view of communist political superiority and Western political inferiority, the veto was to be a mighty lever of influence in communist hands.

So, the acceptance of the Soviet concept of the U.N. by the U.S. meant that U.S. national interests were not supreme; there were higher interests, those of mankind, "the world," the U.N. (including the USSR). The U.N. would thus be above any individual country, especially the U.S., but would be subordinated to the interests of the Soviet Union, as Nikita Khrushchev emphatically declared. (See page 345)

3. Anti-Colonialism

Anti-colonialism, which had always been an important plank in the communist program of world conquest, acquired additional importance in and after World War II, owing to President Roosevelt's strongly anti-colonialist stand. Anti-colonialism had become a perfectly legitimate concern, a major point in building a new, democratic world of national independence, self-determination and progress.

The convenience of this vehicle was fabulous: the West, weighted down by its political inferiority complex in relation to the communists and by its "anti-fascist" solidarity, was sure to refrain from any serious talk of communist colonialism which had just announced itself in a most spectacular manner, by creating a Soviet empire in the heart of Europe (10 countries with some 100 million people). But the USSR was free to continue to step up its anti-colonial attacks on the West and denounce it untiringly as the "arch-aggressor" of history, while at the same time filling the power vacuum being created by the withdrawal of British, Dutch, French, Belgian power from Asia, Africa, the Middle East and other parts of the world. Until World War II the West defended its colonies from communist subversion. After World War II it set out to liquidate them, thus facilitating the implementation of the communist program.

The message of the Soviet "anti-colonialist" line to the U.S. was thus that we must subordinate our conduct of international affairs to moral considerations. We should especially respect the aspirations of peoples until now deprived of independent nationhood, to national self-determination and independence. At the same time we should, in the interest of world peace, ignore Soviet aggression and imperialism and refrain from any hostile action regarding the huge communist colonial empire created in the wake of World War II, which imposed anti-colonial restraint and self-divestment on Western powers.

The fourth point of new communist strategy was:

4. Co-existence

with the capitalist world, i.e. the admission of the possibility of the simultaneous existence of capitalist and communist worlds, replacing the old theory about the incompatibility of the two systems, which could be resolved only by armed conflict. Communism was no longer confined to one country encircled by capitalist powers. The USSR, center of world communism, had along its western borders ten countries with communist regimes, just what Franklin Roosevelt had vowed to secure for the safety of his friend Joseph's empire. And the most populous country in the world, China, was on its sure way to communism, owing to Roosevelt's policy, carried out by General George C. Marshall who systematically sapped the foundations of Chiang Kai-shek's government and favored the Chinese "agrarian reformers."

With the vastly changed relationship of forces between the capitalist world and the communist forces, in favor of communism, and with nuclear arms on both sides, coexistence sounded reasonable, since the "balance of terror" made victory on either side unlikely and mutual annihilation almost a certainty.

Actually, coexistence was the only possible logical conclusion from the foregoing three basic propositions, especially the first one, that the main danger to everybody was war, that everybody's main interest was peace, and that peace could be secured only together with the Soviet Union, not against it.

The "dialectical" catch in the device of coexistence, which the West sedulously ignored, although the communists never concealed it, was that it concerned military war, but not political warfare, not subversion. So, it pledged the free world to coexist with communism, which meant to accept its existence as a final, unalterable fact of international life, but it did not pledge communism to coexist with the free world!

It is evident, then, how well chosen these four points were and how well they took care of Soviet interests. It is equally evident how spurious their arguments were as guidelines for the safeguarding of the general interests of mankind. It is nothing short of fantastic that the U.S. considered this communist "minimal" program as perfectly acceptable.

And yet, the four-point scheme, bold beyond words, worked, as everybody knows. The new communist minimal program, with its goal of winning the battle for communist conquest of the globe, was to become the U.S. foreign policy program to stop communism and save freedom in the world!

But before the scheme could work, one key element in the U.S. mind had to be changed: the awareness of the American people that Americanism and communism were incompatible. For, clearly, as long as Americans were sure of this, there could be no lasting accommodation, nor reconciliation. But once Americans started doubting this, or rejected the proposition, there was nothing to stop the communist strategy of deceit to unfold and bring enormous dividends.

Ambitious as it was, the task proved rather easy for the masters of deceit and of political warfare, after their experience of World War II.

6 The Psychological and Moral Disarmament of the U.S.

"We must not forget that the aims of communism have always been . . . : to divide . . . us among ourselves as the strongest nation of the free world, and by dividing, to confuse and eventually to conquer, to attain through those means their announced aim of world domination."

PRESIDENT EISENHOWER
at his press conference of December 2, 1954.
(Quoted in *Eisenhower The President*, by Merlo J. Pusey
Macmillan, New York, 1956, p. 126)

". . . This war has two areas of combat . . . One in Vietnam where the enemy attacks with bullets—and another right here in this country, where his allies attack with words. The enemy has never achieved a meaningful gain on the battleground in Viet Nam. But he has scored heavily here in this country."

GEN. LEONARD F. CHAPMAN, JR.
commandant of the Marine Corps.
(*Chicago Tribune*, September 21, 1969)

"These are years of great national confusion . . . Much of it is contrived confusion brought about by a clever, sustained assault on America's system and institutions."

VICE-PRESIDENT SPIRO T. AGNEW
(*Chicago Tribune*, June 4, 1970)

The idea was not new. It was as old as the world, or at least as old as the teachings of Sun-Tzu 2500 years ago: the secret of victory was to know the enemy and break his spirit without (armed) struggle. From the moment they decided that theirs was to change the world, the communists knew that the success or failure of that undertaking depended on spiritual factors: how strongly they would be able to shake the spiritual foundations of the "bourgeois" world and how strongly to inspire their own ranks with the spirit of aggressiveness and victory, to convince the world that they were inevitably going to win.

The very simple and very effective technique of communist

propaganda and agitation was from the beginning based on three main themes:

1. You (the bourgeois) are vile and dishonest; we (the communists) are good and honest;

2. You are weak—we are strong;

3. You belong irretrievably to the past; the future belongs unquestionably to us (we are the wave of the future).

All three themes had been used with great effect over decades. But after World War II the conditions for their effectiveness were vastly improved: (a) the target had become more concrete: instead of "the bourgeois world," the United States, and (b) the target, besides being the strongest country in the world, was also the least political, thus the most vulnerable.

The communists made the most of this situation, where the U.S. was totally unprepared and disarmed against the communist psychological offensive, which derived its strength and virulence directly from its triumphs in World War II, but indirectly and more substantially from the West's political weakness that made the communist political triumph possible.

The political outcome of World War II was the result of a gigantic confusion of the West's mind and an abdication of its standards. Stalin and comrades were not confronted with any new elements in the political world picture, except that the political weakness of the West surpassed their boldest dreams.

Franklin Roosevelt's philosophy was that in fighting against Hitler, the Soviet Union was fighting for freedom; that the Soviet regime was a (new kind of) democracy; that, therefore, the U.S. should give the USSR all support in every respect, without asking for anything in return. His statement that he hoped to bring Stalin to the acceptance of democratic and Christian principles, was the measure of his alienation from reality.

In Teheran and Yalta the U.S. had accepted, consciously or unwittingly, the Soviet concept of modern politics as a corrector of history and historic injustice. The USSR, the first country of communism, was—in the politically confused mind of F. D. Roosevelt, his main advisors and many associates—the historical victim, and thus entitled to receive all guarantees that it would no longer be wronged and victimized.

To that end Roosevelt vowed to make Soviet western frontiers safe and he made them by imposing communist rule on half of Europe. The Soviet eastern frontiers were also made safe by rejecting the Kuomintang and favoring the Chinese communists.

What Roosevelt did not understand was that once the U.S. adopted the theory of history-as-exploitation-and-injustice, there was no way to moderate and confine it to some reasonable limits and to exempt the U.S. from it. The theory carried only one meaning for any capitalistic country: to disappear from the stage of the world. And Roosevelt's policy had prepared the ground for further communist action. Success in history was synonymous with exploitation. Wasn't the U.S. the most successful country in history? Then, obviously, it had to be the most unjust, most exploitatory, most oppressive and thus most deserving of historical supreme punishment, liquidation.

But more important than Roosevelt's motives were the unavoidable consequences of this policy. That is the crux of the question.

At the Twentieth Congress of the C.P.S.U. (1956) Dmitr Shepilov, while singing in the chorus of coexistence with Khrushchev, Molotov, Mikoyan, Suslov, and company, did not fail to emphasize that "the capitalist and socialist outlooks cannot be reconciled." [104] But we acted all the time as if they were perfectly compatible. And the worst part is that the communists knew all the time that what we lacked was not information or understanding, but political will.* And once we were reconciled to the idea that *we must accept those who do not accept us,* the barriers to enemy penetration were down and our resistance crumbling.

Since 1917 we have lived in an age of communist total aggression, where everything that constitutes the nation, not only its economic and military strength, its state secrets and institutions, but beliefs, traditions, customs, values, whatever shapes the souls and minds of men—is a permanent battlefield, a field of enemy

* The telegram which the then U.S. Ambassador to Moscow, Averell Harriman sent to the State Department on April 6, 1945, is a unique document on the matter: "It may be difficult for us to believe, but it still may be true that Stalin and Molotov considered at Yalta that by our willingness to accept a general wording of the declaration on Poland and liberated Europe, by our recognition of the need of the Red Army for security behind its lines, and of the predominant interest of Russia in Poland as a friendly neighbor and as a corridor to Germany, we understood and were ready to accept Soviet policies *already known to us.* (*The Forrestal Diaries,* The Viking Press, 1951, p. 40)

operations, hostile influences and actions, propaganda and subversion. The difference between peace and war have been blurred and there is no more sharp dividing line between belligerents (active soldiers) and civilians. We live in a condition of permanent war, and everybody is, if not an active soldier, certainly, whether he knows it or not—a target of some kind for the warfare of the enemy.

Therefore, the 19th century concept of politics and international relations, valid until 1917, is outdated. Today, U.S.-Soviet relations include as vital ingredients, beside diplomacy and espionage, the whole range of Soviet warfare (propaganda, subversion, agitation, political war, psychological war, etc.) in all fields, not only politics and public opinion, but in education, philosophy, mass communications media, religion, sports, arts, literature—particularly paperbacks and "best-sellers"—and everything in every area which affects our total material and moral strength as a nation and our positions (political, economic, military, prestige) in all countries and in all parts of the globe.

The Nation and the Government

What requires special emphasis is that the political interests of a nation are the sum of all its interests. In defending its political interests and strength, a nation is defending the basis of its whole national life. Conversely, in surrendering politically, it is committing suicide.

In 1956 Admiral Radford made the statement that "Our greatest security lies, as it always has, in the hearts and minds of the American people."

And one of the most important factors which determine the hearts and minds of the people are the policies of their leaders, the example they set, the standards they uphold.

No matter how much we criticize the Government or pretend to consider it an unproductive institution and burden on our private resources, it does play a crucial role in our lives. For it makes and enforces the law and thus determines not only the framework of our individual lives and the rules for our activities, but sets the standards we follow, consciously or subconsciously.

But Government is not only a system of rules, it comprises a body of values, it is a center of strength and identification. The individual needs something beyond himself to identify with, and this is what the Government, representing the country, must preserve and defend. To speak with President Nixon (Inaugural Address): "Until he has been part of a larger cause than himself, no man is truly whole." For Americans, that cause larger than every one of them individually, is the United States of America.

The U.S. is not merely a system of power, it is not a bureaucratic machine put together by a handful of power- and wealth-seeking individuals. It is the sum of all that the Founding Fathers believed in, fought for and accomplished in the seventies and eighties of the eighteenth century, and of all that their descendants, all Americans since then, contributed in toil, sacrifice, good will, decency, generosity, ingenuity, patriotism and dedication, to keep alive and affirm the values upon which the nation was built. Americans of every generation must revere the accomplishments of their predecessors and be faithful to the national heritage. Otherwise the nation cannot live.

The Government's foremost duty is to uphold the values and standards of the nation, upon which power was established. "Our Government is the potent, omnipresent teacher. For good or ill it teaches our whole people by its example." [105]

Our Founding Fathers fully realized that a nation lives not through its tactics, but through its principles, and that true politics are essentially self-assertion, not self-betrayal. A nation's absolute values and interests preclude compromise and cannot be sacrificed or rejected without destroying itself.

That is the fundamental truth which has been lost on our policy-makers. They do not understand that communism is not only a ruthless enterprise of world conquest, but a denial of all our values and principles. And the communists base their policy of permanent aggressive political warfare on the tenet that, as Stalin put it, "principles triumph, they do not become reconciled." [106]

Therefore, to defend the U.S. means above all to defend our moral, spiritual, cultural values and heritage. The true strength of a nation is expressed not in statistics, but in the determination with which it defends its identity, its essence. Our actions bear unmistakable testimony to our true beliefs. Racine was so right when, three hundred years ago, he warned that faith which does not act, is not sincere. (*"La foi qui n'agit point, est-ce une foi sincère"?*). If our values, principles and standards are right, we must defend them. If we do not defend them, but reconcile with communism, we automatically discredit them, we indicate that they are not worth living and dying for, and that the enemy is right.* We betray ourselves.

The importance of tactics in any governmental policy is evident. But if a nation has only tactics, but no strategy to defend its values and realize its political objectives, it cannot live. A balance of power with hostile countries is possible. But a balance of ideology, of basic beliefs, of absolutes, with a power which has made the destruction of the U.S. the chief goal of its policies and which in its core is opposed to everything we are and believe in—is impossible.

In yielding to the USSR, we are not only changing our type of society, our social and economic system, we are committing suicide.

So that is where we must seek the source of all our troubles. That is where all the confusion, demoralization, disorientation, loss of meaning, emptiness, stem from: from the estrangement of U.S. liberal leaders from America.**

* A few years after the war (1952) I had occasion to hear a well-known American intellectual explain to a group of political emigres from communist-enslaved European countries (in New York) that they must understand the nature of American Titoism: Americans (American intellectuals, to be precise) have lost their faith in America and the validity of American principles (of 1776). On the other hand, they cannot reconcile with communism and its repugnant methods. So Titoism, which they conceive as some nice, liberal, national, democratic communism, would just about be that happy middle ground between traditional Americanism, and its adaptation to changed world conditions, dominated by communist aggression.

** Henry J. Taylor puts it thus: "The decay in any nation's strength is the loss of morals in government bodies. Nations may stand the strains of economic ills, and even of wars, but they cannot stand the loss of governmental moral fibre." ("Congressmen Take Good Care of Selves," *St. Louis Globe-Democrat*, August 18, 1970).

The Opening of the Floodgates

Our surrender to communism in the area of foreign policy opened the gates to their psychological and political offensive in all other fields and areas.

The essence of the communist task was to break U.S. strength. And to break the strength of a nation means to destroy the spiritual foundations of its existence, to undermine its morale, destroy its values, confuse its thinking. Nobody knows better the supreme importance of moral and psychological factors and spiritual strength (love of country, dedication to its values and interests, discipline, order, hierarchy, effort, sacrifice, struggle) than the communists, in spite of all their materialistic philosophy and economic determinism.

Whenever the subject of communist moral and psychological subversion is discussed, the communists and liberals come with the ready retort that the conservatives, the "right-wing extremists" see communists under every bed and thus attribute to some imaginary communist plots and machinations, events which have no connection with communism, and would have happened anyway.

The retort is patently invalid and vapid. The first and most important fact which the communists and liberals deliberately ignore is that the communist world movement was created to "change the world." And that, after World War II, came to mean above all to destroy the U.S. So, the alleged invention or paranoic delusion of the right-wingers is nothing of the kind, but is in reality a fundamental and openly proclaimed communist basic plan.

The other standard maneuver of the communists and liberals in discussing communist infiltration in Government, press, education, movies, television, radio, is to deny it by saying that such and such book or film, article or speech, address or statement does not say anything about Marxism-Leninism or communism, nor does it advocate the forcible overthrow of the U.S. Government and social order, and, therefore, it is ridiculous to speak of communist influences and tendencies.

But what those experts do not know (or pretend not to) is that, to work for communism—a book, a film, an article, a speech—one does not have to use the word communism, or propagate the theories of Marx, Engels, Lenin or Stalin.

Stalin had instructed Benjamin Gitlow, who in 1926 was secretary of the Communist Party of the U.S.A.: "There is one word you must never use in your work in America—communism. Because it is a scare word there. But behind the screen of democracy, freedom, humanity, civil rights, progress, etc., you can go very far." [107]

That is precisely, as we have seen, why Lenin established his basic principle for all communist strategy and tactics, the minimal program: to enable the party to use the shield of democratic dissent to promote communist ends and to harness non-communists to do communist work: "We need only one thing to march to victory with more confidence and firmness, and that is the awareness . . . which all communists in all countries must possess, of the need to attain the maximum of *flexibility* in their tactics." [108]

The communists know the most effective way to achieve communist ends is not to preach communism, communist "science," or concepts of some ideal society, but to destroy the moral foundations of a society. To do communist work, you do not have to be a registered member of the party. You do not have to say one word about communism. You do not have to believe in the collective ownership of the means of production, or dialectical materialism, or the pauperization theory, or the surplus value theory, or the withering of the state, or the rest. All you have to do is to contribute to the destruction of free society. The very emptiness you create by tearing down everything and calling everything in question, casting doubts on every value, is enough to create ground receptive to communism, which has a ready answer to every problem. The communists themselves do not believe in their theoretical nonsense, except strictly insofar as it is politically effective. And the political effectiveness of communist theory is precisely measured by the extent to which we have adopted their inanities as beliefs, which will erode us from the inside.

The Magic Word: Change

As indicated before, all communist strategy has been based on the fact that our World War II policy accepted the necessary premises for their conclusions: that communism absolutely must remain and that the U.S. absolutely must change fundamentally. To bring about the consequences of that premise, all that was necessary was to create a state of mind, an atmosphere, a guilt complex, to put the U.S. permanently and on every issue on the bench of the accused. They did not need anything more. If that were achieved, the Soviet Union could not fail to win.

The communist method was thoroughly researched and astoundingly simple. The first step was to question everything, to open to discussion all values, all principles, all absolutes. Nothing was to remain sacred before the onrush of "scientific" investigation, and especially the search of "social science" for "objective truth."

Once that process was under way, it was very easy for the "researchers" to magnify every trouble, every conceivable ill, personal or social, rooted in unchangeable categories of human existence, independent of social conditions and the existing political order—and attribute it to the political and social system of capitalist America.

From there the next step, logical, crucial and imperceptible, was to respect nothing. Constant, unending change of everything was the fundamental law of social life and development. Nothing was permanent and lasting. Consequently nothing was valid beyond doubt and beyond certain changing social conditions. All and any values and standards of morality and behavior must be constantly questioned, doubted, destroyed, replaced, revolutionized. Whittaker Chambers, in his fundamental book, *Witness,* says with deep insight that amid all the most heterogeneous elements and factors which drive people to communism, there was one which could be considered a common denominator and that was the belief in the absolute need for change, unconditional and radical. That was the "scientific" premise. Anybody could draw the evident revolutionary conclusions.

For if everything must be questioned, nothing respected, everything changed, then at the end of the process a conclusion was bound to emerge as evident: a society which has nothing valid, which holds nothing sacred, where everything must be changed, is rotten, and there is no solution for its problems save one: destroy it and start from scratch!

It is impossible to draw a sharp dividing line between the four stages: doubt, disrespect, change, destruction. But the communists and their liberal helpers have left nothing sacred, nothing unquestioned, nothing beyond discussion.

The main points of their psychological offensive were chosen carefully so that, once accepted, they would act as corroding, disintegrating agents in our national life. That is evident in the fundamental proposition that "God is dead." *

"God Is Dead"

The general line of the argument about "God's death" is that God was all right for simpler, less sophisticated times, when man was ignorant and powerless, and sought reassurance in superstition and religion. But today, owing to the progress of science and technology, man is, for the first time in history, in a position to control the forces which shape events and to determine his own future. So, who needs God? !

The shallowness and fatuity of this line is best demonstrated by the fact that the rejection of God has not enabled man the better to solve his problems. The contrast between man's technological almightiness and his helplessness in the face of human problems, is notoriously the key paradox of modern man and modern society. He now has the technological means to destroy himself, but not the wisdom and means to save himself by solving his real problems, which are problems of human relations, of values, principles, truth, absolutes, meaning.

Man is fundamentally, to the core of his being, a God-seeker. He cannot live without relating himself to the Universe and trying to live in harmony with the forces and laws which govern it. He cannot live without seeking and finding meaning to his life. When he speaks of God's death, man actually proclaims his own.

If God is dead, then the certainty of a natural moral order is destroyed.

The qualities which make man: human dignity (which is the

* The German theologian Dietrich Bonhoeffer apparently thought that "what we call God is being more and more edged out of life, losing more and more ground." He suggested "religionless Christianity" as a valid substitute. ("An American Bishop's Search For a Space Age God," by Christopher Wren, *Look*, February 22, 1966).

striving to keep alive the divine spark in man), duty, courage, effort, responsibility, love, charity, hierarchy, sacrifice, become empty words. And the whole moral structure of America must collapse.

That is precisely why so much attention has been paid to the campaign of spreading the word about God's death. And there can be little doubt that the campaign has achieved considerable success.

The head of the Jesuit Order, Pedro Arrupe, is reported to have insisted in 1966, when he rose to his position, that "there is in the world a vast conspiracy to propagate atheism . . . which exerts a powerful influence in international organizations, financial circles, as well as those of information, television and the movie industry . . . That mentality has slipped insidiously . . . up to the spirit of the believers, the priests and the members of the religious orders. The results of this infection are, in the Church, naturalism, distrust and rebellion." [109]

It is noteworthy, however, that the communist campaign about the death of God has achieved much more success at the top, in the ranks of those who represent and make the Church; much less among the faithful, who have not lost faith in God, but have been disappointed and repelled from the Church by the dismal instances of self-betrayal. Anonymous believers put several years ago signs on the bumpers of their cars: "Our God is not dead; sorry about yours!"

But priests, low and high, have betrayed the Church and followed not Christ, but Judas. They have rejected the true mission of the Church and endeavored to turn it into an effective "instrument for social change," i.e. an instrument of communist policy. Those who may be in doubt about this, should read the article about the World Council of Churches in the *Reader's Digest* for October 1971.

Extremism

The issue of extremism has been for years the subject of most heated debates. The communists know that those who have convictions, beliefs and ideals, do not yield easily, but defend them with every ounce of their strength and energy, and make supreme efforts to win. Those are the extremists. That is why the communists—the most rabid and intolerant fanatics and extremists in history—do not like anybody outside of the communist party to be an extremist, especially if he is against communism.

That is the secret of their hysterical campaign against "extremism." If they deter extremism in our ranks, the road to world conquest is open for them. Senator Barry Goldwater was right when he stated in his acceptance speech in 1964, that "extremism in the pursuit of liberty is no vice." It is a pity that "extremism" was absent from his presidential campaign.

The communists also know that those who have no real beliefs, are lukewarm and will defend no value, no right, no interest with determination. That is the kind of "adversaries" they like.

So, the communists have worked on the mind of the West to accept the double standard that they, being revolutionaries, are entitled to the wildest extremism, whereas those who oppose communist subversion and treason must be bound by the rules of utter tolerance, moderation and conciliation. Only the destroyers, the protesters, the rebels are supposed to get angry. Their anger should also demonstrate their sincerity, their "high motivation" and the validity of their "cause." The wilder the better. They are free to organize riots, defile the American flag, vandalize universities, threaten and beat people, kill and bomb, flaunt weapons, use the foulest language publicly to insult humans, disrupt court proceedings and destroy the dignity of U.S. courts of justice.

But the rest of us? No! All we can do is state what we think, formulate our views and opinions, the more academically the better, and then we must go home, be nice boys and leave the streets and the public place to the angry rioters and destroyers of America. Anybody refusing to comply with this double-standard treatment, is ruthlessly smeared as an "extremist," right-wing, of course.

To the great disgrace of the free world, the communist campaign against extremism has been successful. By wielding their weapon of anti-extremist intimidation long and boldly enough, they have imposed self-restraint in the ranks of anti-communists, while keeping their own subversive, extremist hands free. Too many Americans have lost the capacity to get angry. We have become punch-pullers. Like the children in Aldous Huxley's

Brave New World, who are conditioned by electrical shock waves, we have been conditioned into self-paralysis by the blackmail of the communist-liberal anti "extremist" smear campaign. Anything, anything at all, is preferable to being accused of right-wing extremism. For that, "as we all know," is the one thing which must not be tolerated.

The communists can be content: if anti-communism is extremism, and if extremism is absolutely unacceptable, communism is safe and America will not be defended.

It goes without saying that, next to the attack on God, the attack on America, on patriotism, on the most elementary feeling of loyalty to one's country, has been at the top of the list of the anti-American campaign.

It has taken many forms, from re-interpreting America as loyalty to "social" and "human" values (as if America were unsocial and inhuman) to substituting loyalty to the U.S. by loyalty to the world, or simply denying the loyalty to country under whatever excuse. To give a few examples:

The Liberal Papers, published in March 1962, were utterly and defyingly defeatist: ". . . as the cold war continues, it becomes increasingly difficult for decent Americans, humane enough to prefer peace to an egocentric national honor, to be outspokenly and genuinely anti-Communist" (Article by David Riesman and Marshall MacCoby).

The Saturday Review rated loyalty to all mankind above loyalty to the U.S.: ". . . It is the world, and not just a nation, that is now the arena which needs to be shaped and protected . . . Patriotism, to be truly American, begins with the human allegiance." [110]

And an educator, Edgar Z. Friedenberg, posed the direct question: "Does the preservation of the United States contribute to the general welfare?",[111] which answers itself.

The champions of social change make a mockery of the institution of marriage. Sacred? Ha! Don't you know the statistics of divorce, pre-marital and extra-marital sexual activities of both men and women, or group sex, etc. Have you never heard of the tremendous scientific work of Dr. Kinsey and, even more scientific, of Drs. Masters and Johnson? !

And then, as modern people, living in the nuclear age, we cannot ignore what "science" says. And science (psychoanalysis, the new psychology and the new sociology) has apparently reached the conclusion that some marital infidelity is not bad, but good for both husband and wife. Instead of destroying the bonds of marriage, extra-marital affairs can consolidate them!

As early as 1962, Msgr. George A. Kelly, director of the Family Life Bureau of the Roman Catholic Archdiocese of New York, took a typically "situation-ethics" view of marital infidelity: "We can't say that people commit adultery because there is something wrong with their marriage. Many people are perfectly content with their marriage and just fall into a situation where they misbehave." [112]

In May 1970, the United Presbyterian Church published a study of its council on church and society, which for three years had studied the problems of "abortion, adultery and homosexual behavior." It approved adultery in certain situations which "provide socially meaningful relationships." [113]

Is love the proper basis for marriage? A Salt Lake City psychologist, Dr. William H. Brown, ventured the expert opinion that love is a "lousy basis for marrage" and added the explanation (!) that "Probably the ideal marriage would be two people who do not need each other"! [114]

What about motherhood? Isn't the desire to have children "something that all normal women instinctively want and need?" No! "Women don't need to be mothers any more than they need spaghetti," is the verdict of Dr. Richard Rabkin, a New York psychiatrist, quoted by Betty Rollin, senior editor of *Look* magazine, in her article about "what may be history's biggest fallacy: The Motherhood Myth." [115]

The notion of marriage limited to persons of different sex is apparently also a remnant of the past. There are already "marriages" performed by "priests" between persons of the same sex. It started apparently in Holland (where the reaction among the people of the cloth never elicited revulsion and condemnation, but went from approval to no comment to strictly academic disapproval), and spread to the U.S. Rita Hauser, a lawyer by profession and U.S. representative to the U.N. Commission on Human Rights, advocates marriage between people of the same sex. First in the name of justice and equality (?!) between the sexes, and second, for the sake of stopping most effectively the population explosion, which it undeniably would.

What about the need to train children in discipline and self-discipline? Wrong again. Self-discipline is destructive of self-expression and it is the surest way to personal unhappiness. People must not repress, but express whatever is stirring within them. So, down with self-discipline! As for discipline, it is the strict parents who, by trying to impose certain patterns of behavior and a system of do's and don'ts, frustrate their children and provoke resistance and rebellion.

What about sin? Well, "as we all know," there is no such thing. Only reactionary people, with outdated concepts, entertain such concepts, while individuals enlightened by the new morality, know that the only sin is just inhumanity of man to man, and above all war (the war in Vietnam, to be sure, not World War II). As for sin in the conventional sense, it is only an invention of a repressive society which is trying to preserve itself against the trends of the times. People strive to exercise their natural urges and express themselves. Those tendencies are called sin by oppressive societies.

As for crime, that again is a misnomer. For modern science, combined with the new morality, tells us that the root of all evil is in social conditions which breed anti-social behavior. Eliminate those conditions (the cause), change society toward more "social" concepts, and there will be no crime! But even now, right now, punishment is wrong. Hasn't one of the top psychiatrists in the nation, Dr. Karl Menninger, entitled his book on the subject: *The Crime of Punishment?*

As for morals, we know (don't we?) ever since the Communist Manifesto (1848) that morals are not a matter of rules valid for all times and all societies, but strictly a reflection of social and political conditions and interests (vested). So, what is moral and immoral, ethical or unethical, depends on circumstances.

As far as women and their conduct is concerned, modern society is so oppressive and hypocritical, that Ti-Grace Atkinson, "who might be termed the Trotsky of the Women's Lib," claims that the prostitute is "the only honest woman left in America." And this view is apparently deduced from the Women's Liberation Movement's philosophy that "it's braver to sell your body by the hour than to submit to a marriage contract which forces a woman to work for a lifetime without pay." [116]

And the red thread which connects all these seemingly unconnected theses pertaining to diverse subjects, is that for all conceivable ills and troubles, personal or social, "society" was guilty, i.e. America, with its social and political system. It is owing to this powerful, brazen and persistent offensive, based on moral blackmail and couched in terms of "scientific" scrutiny of all its evils and wrongs, that the communists have succeeded in creating a widespread image of America, which consists of a composite picture where every real trait has been distorted.

The Founding Fathers, after all, were not the pure idealists that we have learned to know, but rich landowners, representatives of the higher classes and moneyed interests.

The economic development of America was due not so much to free enterprise and individual effort under conditions of freedom, as to exploitation of the weak by the strong and ruthless.

The American principle of liberty and justice for all was a bold hypocrisy, since the Negroes in America were underprivileged, as were a number of other groups.

The U.S. uniquely high standard of living for the broadest masses of people was a sham, since there were millions of Americans suffering from malnutrition and going to bed hungry every night. Besides, the reverse side of the shining medal of general affluence in the U.S. was crass materialism, which confined the interest of individuals to the "almighty dollar" and rendered them callous to the ills, misery, disease and ignorance prevalent in most of the world.

And then, of course, there was "dollar imperialism" which made the U.S. rich by making other countries, especially those of Latin America, poor through ruthless exploitation.[117]

U.S. traditional high morality was nothing to be proud of, since the Puritan ethic on which it was essentially based had wrought havoc with the American soul, by repressing the natural instincts, urges and passions of individuals, thus frustrating them, making them unhappy and psychologically maiming them for life.

The unique achievements and level of U.S. technology were not a ground for pride, but a ground for indictment, since they were robbing the individual of the finer pleasures of life and transforming him into a robot.

And so on, and so on.

To know that the above outline reflects a powerful trend in current public opinion, it is not necessary to do any special research. Modern mass communications media and means of influencing people are so ubiquitous and all-pervading, that nobody can escape them. Exposure to their influence is a matter of daily experience for practically everybody.

While its full impact is not immediate, it is cumulative and deadly. All of a sudden we find that our values have been invalidated, that we no longer believe in what we used to believe, we are no longer sure of anything, we find nothing worth fighting for, we no longer see meaning in anything that makes the nation. And we are becoming more receptive to concepts and standards which until recently we used to despise and spontaneously reject. We are, as individuals and as a nation, changing, and by adopting alien values, yardsticks and logic, we are moving in the direction in which the enemy is propelling us.

A few years ago (1962) Gus Hall was able to brag about the great success of the Communist Party of America in creating a number of "state-of-mind" communists, i.e. non-communists who do communist work. These people are not members of the party, many are in disagreement and strongly opposed to communism, but they have been conditioned, unbeknownst to themselves, to think and react on various problems and in various situations, like trained communists.

The constant exposure to the communist offensive against the American mind could not fail to produce effects. The re-education of policy-makers and public opinion-makers gradually produced a climate of public opinion intolerant of real anti-communism and favorable to the realization of communist objectives.[118]

It can never be overemphasized that the factor which made the difference between the public's rejection and its acceptance of communist propaganda was the U.S. policy of reconciliation with communism, manifested not only in the fraternization of World War II, but in our whole policy of coexistence.

For no matter how the policy of surrender is explained, or concealed or rationalized, its inevitable consequence is an erosion of faith in the nation and its values.

When communism is accepted as a whole, then no single communist attack on any U.S. value seems unacceptable in the long run. For people ("ordinary people") will always reason that the men in Washington know what they are doing and they know better than the average citizen what it is all about. So, since we are co-existing and collaborating with communism, it cannot be that bad, after all. If President Eisenhower was so impressed by Soviet Marshal Zhukov's arguments about the superiority of communism (the Soviet system) over democracy (the American system), that "he left me breathless," how can we expect the "ordinary citizen" to stand fast under the unceasing attacks against our basic values through all conceivable avenues, means and media?

To achieve their ends, the communists have made use of all channels and vehicles available: the press, radio, television, the movies, textbooks, literature —all the means which most effectively affect and influence the mind, spirit, morals, thinking, as well as the emotions and spontaneous ("conditioned") reactions of the American people. Special attention was paid to textbooks, to mould the mind of youth.[119]

The importance of the press and the printed word in general in shaping the minds of people has been clear to the communists from the first moment. In 1905 Lenin stressed that "the writings of the socialist proletariat are not . . . a private matter independent from the general cause of the proletariat." "The newspaper is not only a collective propagandist, and collective agitation, but also a collective organizer."

This is a basic stand where no real exception or arbitrary deviation is permitted to develop. In 1962 when some people in the Soviet Union tried to take advantage of the "liberalization" in literature and arts, Nikita Khrushchev sounded the warning: "The press, radio, literature, music, the cinema and the theatre are a sharp ideological weapon of our Party," which must at all times hit "the enemy without fail." (See page 207)

In May 1969, on the "Day of the Press" in the USSR, the Government paper *Izvestia* forcefully restated the Leninist-Khrushchevist line on the role of the Soviet press.[120]

The Vehicle of Literature

The fact that literature powerfully influences people's emotions and thoughts has not been adequately appreciated in the free world.

In his article on the 50th anniversary of the "October Revolution," published in *Esquire* magazine of May 1967, C. P. Snow pointed to the practically unnoticed fact that the communists in general, and especially Soviet leaders, pay the greatest attention to literature, because they understand its importance as an expression and indication of the mood of the people, and its influence in shaping their minds. In the West, however, literature is more a matter of general education and culture, but Western leaders are practically unaware of its crucial importance as a psychological factor and force. The communist leaders know how decisive the writings of the Encyclopedists were in preparing the ground for the French Revolution of 1789, as well as how decisive the influence of Russian literature in the 19th and beginning of the 20th centuries was in preparing the ground for the Revolution of 1917. The bolsheviks have always idolized Tolstoy and hated and denounced Dostoyevsky. Why? Because Tolstoy's philosophy contributed to the disintegration of Russian society, whereas Dostoyevsky's novels and essays worked against the revolution, since they exposed the spuriousness of communist "progressive" ideas and the misery of their premises about man, society and human affairs.

Between the two world wars the communists used literature as their mightiest weapon. In the Soviet Union its task was to glorify communism and consolidate communist power. (Mikhail Sholokhov defines "socialist realism" as that which "stands for Soviet power.") In the West its assignment was to present a picture of evil, hypocrisy, injustice, rot permeating Western society in all its aspects. The aggregate effect of this powerful psychological offensive contributed to the formation of communist cadres everywhere and prepared the mood and pro-Soviet climate of public opinion in the West, without which Stalin could not have won the war and enslaved half of Europe.

The effectiveness of communist propaganda is rooted in the fact that communist literature of any kind ("scientific," fiction, popular, agitation) is an integral part of the communist movement.

Every communist book or writing is an act of war, to tear down our values, destroy our self-confidence and institutions, create doubts in our philosophy and way of life, bring about confusion and vacillation, paralyze our efforts and will, and promote communism.

It is because communist writers have functioned as the press secretariat of a well-organized political army in action, that they have been able to penetrate and influence the political thought of the West. The line dividing strictly communist theses from positions supposed to express Western interests has been blurred.

The Movies

As might be expected from seasoned political warriors and aggressors, the communists immediately realized the fabulous possibilities of the movies as a weapon to promote their goals. Stalin fully understood the importance and potentialities of the medium of the cinema as a miraculously effective and potent means of influencing and shaping the minds of people. He is unlikely to have expressed his evaluation in the actual words attributed to him by *Life* magazine (December 20, 1963): "If I could control the medium of American motion picture industry, I would need nothing else in order to convert the entire world to Communism." For the communists are not interested in converting anybody to alleged communist beliefs, but in conditioning as many people as possible to accepting the imminence of communism, and to rejecting any idea of resisting its victorious march to world conquest.

However, the quote in *Life* magazine does point to Stalin's keen awareness of the movie medium as a uniquely effective political weapon.* He understood that in the film age, Hollywood was mightier than Washington, D.C.

---

* At the Moscow Film Festival of July 1963 the Soviet representatives openly "argued that films are a means of actively invading life in order to improve the world." (*Chicago Tribune*, July 23, 1963).

And Peter Weiss, the German playwright who won fame by blending revolution, insanity and sadism in his play "Marat" (1962), after which he espoused, openly and without reserve, communism, stated in an interview:

Again, according to *Life* magazine, Cecil B. DeMille once said that "the highest officials of Egypt and Burma" had told him "that as boys they derived their conceptions of the world, their ideal of right and wrong, from American motion pictures." [121] Evidently, the laws, statements, addresses, speeches, pronouncements of Governments are infinitely less powerful in influencing the minds of people than what people "see for themselves" on the film screen. The former is theory, abstraction, preaching, sermonizing. The latter is life, palpable evidence—truth! The beauty of it, from the viewpoint of propaganda and brainwashing, is that many people, unaware of it, experience the medium of the movies as witnesses, so that they feel they can practically say, "I saw it happen!," whether it is a contemporary war, or a social problem or events of decades or centuries ago.

Considering the contribution of the movies in the total havoc which the communist offensive against the mind of the West has wrought, Stalin can be satisfied with the work of his divisions of the film front in the total struggle against the free world. They followed the first principle of all communist policy and propaganda: strengthen the USSR and weaken the West. Communists and their liberal minions produce in the West films replete with moral corruption, bad taste, degeneracy, sex, cynicism, and materialism—while Soviet critics assail Western movie-makers for making these very films.[122]

So, we are exposed to the "one-two" treatment. On the one hand our left wing extremists are swamping us with morally, artistically and patriotically sick films ("Patton," as an exception, serves to underscore the rule). And on the other hand critics from communist countries point to Western movies as a sign of Western degeneracy!

Film makers in the Soviet Union and Red China do not give sex and "dolce vita" to their viewers. They show the "glories" and "virtues" of communism and extol all the things that are needed to strengthen it (war, patriotism, duty, loyalty, the joy of life, effort, personal responsibility).

Commenting on the film "Dr. Strangelove," *Life* quoted the

"It is necessary to write with the intention of influencing or changing society." (*La Stampa*, Torino, October 20, 1965).

opinion of a Western observer: "No Communist could dream of a more effective anti-American film to spread abroad . . . United States officials, including the President, had better take a look at this one to see its effect on the national interest." [123]

In 1970 the thoroughly pro-communist film "Z" was awarded several first prizes at the annual "Oscar" festivities in Hollywood. The runner-up was the internationally produced film of ignominious pro-Tito propaganda, "The Battle of Neretva."

Incidentally, since 1917, there has never been any film about the horrors of the Soviet regime in Russia. Nor has there been one film about the crimes of Tito's regime in Yugoslavia or any communist regime in Eastern Europe. Nor has anybody (since 1949) made a film about the murder regime of Red China which massacred in cold blood some 36 million Chinese.

Stalin can sleep peacefully.*

The impact of television is, of course, a hundredfold stronger. For the influence of the movies is limited to those who take the time to go to a movie theater, whereas TV has invaded our homes. It is permanent, instant cinema at home, around the clock and on all topics: education, social problems, civil rights, current events, history, religion, politics, sports, whatever.

It is most likely that Stalin, had he not died in the mere infancy of television, would have been delighted with its accomplishments.

The Liberal Contribution

However, the communists would never have been able to achieve their success without the crucial help of the liberals, both

* The film "The Confession" (L'Aveu) made by the producer of "Z," Kosta Gavras, is a special case, an exception confirming the rule. If Gavras, who made a pro-communist film, also made an anti-communist film, it is because he is no real communist and does not understand what communism is all about. He thinks it is about social justice and humanity and equality of opportunity, while it is about ruthless power, oppression and utter inhumanity.

Because he is unaware of this, Gavras produced a film like "The Confession." Subsequently, he has received notice from the communists that he committed the unforgivable crime of equating Stalinism with communism. What remains to be seen, is whether Gavras will remain an artist in search of truth and justice, or turn communist propagandist toeing the party line on the movie screen.

in policy-making (the experts) and public opinion-making positions (mass communications media). It is this help from the liberals and the conditions of mass society which have made it possible for the communists to accomplish their task.

Mass society tends to reduce the size and importance of the individual, and thus his freedom. It is a society of the leveling down of all standards (of behavior, morality, performance and, especially, of responsibility). The interest of the individual for public affairs is diminished in direct ratio to the diminution of his power and importance as an individual.

The natural consequence of this is the abdication of individual responsibility and the transfer of the attributes and rights of the "average citizen" to a small number of citizens, the experts. The "massification" of our society has produced such division of labor and specialization in professions, skills and trades, that there is practically no problem which is not being solved without some kind of expert, whether we want him or not. As far as public affairs are concerned, this has brought the individual to the point where, feeling confused and powerless to influence the course of events, he seems willing to leave the analysis and appraisal of political problems and the making of his opinion on American and world affairs, to the experts (many of whom he never sees, nor elects, nor even knows anything about).

This generally means a transfer of authority and power from all citizens to a small number of specialists. The individual citizen becomes powerless, the expert very powerful. To accentuate the process, a very considerable transfer of power also takes place from the politicians to the experts. Our age is the age of expertocracy. They "exert . . . an enormous influence on the laws and policies of the United States," and form "the most powerful community in our society," according to Theodore H. White.[124]

That is the problem of mass society. The new "élite" of experts can take one of two courses: make every effort to protect the freedom of the individual as an irreplaceable moral and social value, or swim with the current, yield to the temptations of power, (with the inevitable consequences predicted by Lord Acton: "Power corrupts, and absolute power corrupts absolutely"). In this case, the experts tend to supply not objective information with choices of possible interpretation; they supply the public with the news, and at the same time the only "correct" interpretation of that news.*

The uproar following the two speeches of Vice-President Agnew in November 1969 on the modern mass communications media, is understandable, for they went to the heart of the matter, raising fundamental questions and expressing the strong feelings of a great part of the public. The rebuttal that reporters do not make news, but only report, is incorrect and untenably naive. For while we may quibble about the line which separates power from influence, it is evident that opinions expressed about news not only can decisively color news, but can make it or kill it, and can greatly influence events, decisions and the shaping of power and politics.[125]

The variety of trends and philosophies among the experts is a safety valve, since conflicting views tend to preserve a balance in the interpretation of the news. But if most of the experts are of one hue, one philosophy, one trend, the danger to a free society becomes imminent, for we move from unbiased reporting to the conditioning and finally control of public opinion. And this is exactly the trend prevailing in many countries of the free world where the liberals hold a position of monopoly. Howard K. Smith, well-known television commentator and widely considered a lib-

---

* Theodore H. White's novel, *The View from the Fortieth Floor,* William Sloane Assoc., 1962, which deals with the life and problems of a mass circulation magazine in Manhattan, presents a very succinct picture of the liberal monopoly of opinion-making: ". . . You put the point of a compass down where this building is and swing it a mile around it. All the radio nets and all the TV nets are in the circle. All the syndicates and all the press agencies. Every advertising agency and world packager is here . . . They decide what movies Hollywood is going to make from here. They publish 90% of the books of the country here. The magazines are all here, or almost all of us. And we're all guessing what makes them angry, what makes them cry, what makes them laugh. We sell them dreams, and ideas, and news. They couldn't live without the stuff, but they don't know it themselves. In Russia, the Kremlin decides what they need to know and dream, but here, we do it . . . The first time somebody sat in this kind of office in New York and started to play with the mind of the country, things started to happen . . . Think of it! . . . The whole country racing and changing all around us, everybody pushed along into tomorrow or wherever the hell we're going. But when you sit here in this office, you're not being swept along—you're making the changes happen."

eral himself, sharply characterized in a statement which does him credit, the role of liberals in television and other news media by saying:

"They have a strong leftward bias . . . They have a set of automatic reactions. They react with . . . oversimplification.

"They're conventional. They're conformists. They're pleasing Walter Lippmann, they're pleasing the *Washington Post,* they're pleasing the editors of *The New York Times,* and they're pleasing one another." [126]

Why the liberals have so utterly forsaken liberty, will be discussed more fully later. What must be said at this point is that the main impetus was provided by the combined influences of the Depression (1929) and communism. The Depression did more than disrupt America's economy and revolutionize economic thinking in the direction of Keynesian categories. It deeply shook the confidence of Americans in their system, their political philosophy and their institutions. For the liberals, who, by definition and in spite of very trying times and experience, should have been the staunchest defenders of freedom and searchers for new ways of preserving it under new conditions, the Depression was a turning point, a good-bye to "old" concepts. Ever since, the liberals have been afflicted with a loss of faith in freedom and the American way, and with a belief in the future of communism and the USSR. For in their minds the two were linked as closely as the problem (Depression) and the answer (Socialism). Anyway, even in the early days and then incessantly and increasingly, communism has not been considered the enemy to be destroyed, but a "fact of life" with which we must learn to live, while at the same time trying to blunt its edges, tame it, make it accept some "capitalist" ideas, traits and usages, as we introduce more socialism in our ways.

That is apparently the conclusion to which the liberals were led, faced with the complexities of mass society and the challenge of communism.

Liberal Control

Armed with the tremendous power of modern means of public opinion-making, the liberals wasted no time and left no avenue of possible influence unused.

They worked in two main directions: to determine our field of vision and to determine our vision itself, by impairing our capacity of rationally evaluating facts. By doing this over a period of years they have narrowed and limited our choice of factual evidence and presented us with false pictures of the world and its problems. They have torn down traditional values—starting at the same time "little insurrections in the realm of readers' convictions," as *The New Republic* put it in a subscription circular of a few years ago—and left us with a vacuum, or imposed on us values and yardsticks which necessarily led away from the principles upon which the Founding Fathers built the nation.[127]

These liberals have been in power for over forty years and they are responsible for the situation in which the U.S. and the world find themselves today. It is of those people (whom he protectingly and euphemistically calls the Micawbers, headed by Walter Lippmann), that John K. Jessup, chief editorial writer of *Life* magazine, has said that they have played a decisive role in formulating our policies:

> ". . . The fact remains that they have also . . . mainly called the tune of Western policy during the 16 years of the Cold War to date; that during this period the Communists have greatly increased their strength, territory and self-confidence, while in the West . . . what was for so long the debate over liberation or containment has been deteriorating into the debate over containment or surrender." [128]

Unable to change either their policies—which would entail the loss of their unique positions of total power and total irresponsibility—or reality, they opted for the line of "investment in error," which meant to continue on their course and use their power to change our minds or reduce us to silence.

"We All Know"

This was to be achieved through the intensified use of the mechanism of the "we-all-know" device and by the intimidation of the dissenters.

The Founding Fathers had proclaimed some self-evident truths in which the whole nation believed. The liberals found a substitute in the things which "we all know." Those things are selected and presented in so many different ways, in so many forms, through so many media (including comic strips and crossword puzzles),[129] that man's conscious and subconscious mind will be saturated, bent, conquered and won. The public must simply be brainwashed into believing that there is no thinking except liberal thinking and no interpretations except liberal ones.[130]

And the moment the liberal slant is firmly implanted in the minds of the citizens, any other viewpoint simply "isn't knowledge," but belongs to the realm of phantasy.*

It is a matter of everyday observation that there are some important positions which "we all know," such as

—that communism has undergone deep changes and is in the process of even more radical change;

—that the concept of communist world conspiracy no longer corresponds to the present-day reality of communism;

—that the Russians love peace as we do and hate war as we do;

—that American Whites have ruthlessly exploited American Negroes for 300 years;**

---

* Commenting on the fact that the three infamous British diplomat-spies: Burgess, MacLean and Philby were able to operate freely although it was almost a public secret that they were communists, Rebecca West says in her book, *The New Meaning of Treason:* "Everyone knew they were communists . . . It also, very unfortunately, happens that the communist conspiracy repeats a pattern which was exploited by writers at a time when the corresponding reality was only faintly discerned by observers of society . . . Thus it happened that international conspiracy was established in the common mind as a feature of a vulgar district in the world of fancy, and it seems quite ridiculous to think of it as a real threat."

** The Foreword to the Report of the National Advisory Commission on Civil Disorders of February 1968 quotes the words of President Johnson from his Executive Order of July 29, 1967, establishing the Commission: "Let your

—that the organized Church must adapt itself to the changes and trends of our modern industrial society;

—that old concepts, tabus and limitations in sexual freedom must be rejected;

—that family relations have undergone revolutionary changes with the dissolution of old and the creation of new social relationships and forms;

—that the state (Federal Government) must not limit itself to protecting the country from foreign aggression, and maintaining internal law and order, but must expand its responsibility to the vital job of social engineering.

And much more.

Now, it does not matter how much factual accuracy, truth and common sense the various formulas of what "we all know" contain. The important thing is to impose them on the public officials and the public. Once this is done, the situation is under control: for, obviously, if some people do not know what "everybody" knows, and refuse to recognize as valid what "everybody" does— who would want to carry on a discussion with such people or take their opinions seriously?

The intolerance of the liberals is proverbial. If you disagree with them, if you question the veracity of their reporting, the validity of their premises, the factual adequacy of their analyses and interpretations, you must be a reactionary, a right-wing extremist, racist, fascist, bloodthirsty warmonger,* and, yes, even possibly mentally unbalanced. The examination of facts, reasons, argu-

---

search be free . . . As best you can, find the truth and express it in your report." But one page before quotes President Johnson's words from his Address to the Nation of two days earlier (July 27, 1967): "All of us know what those conditions (i.e. breeding despair and violence) are: ignorance, discrimination, slums, poverty, disease, not enough jobs . . . We should attack these conditions . . . because there is simply no other way to achieve a decent and orderly society in America."

So, the "we-all-know" formula has reached as far as the President's office, and thus the diagnosis and therapy are pronounced before the examination has begun.

* The TV advertisement of the political opponents of Barry Goldwater about the little girl with a flower in her fragile hand, blown to pieces by an H-bomb, ruthlessly used by a warmongering U.S. President, is a typical example of a liberal concept of political fairness.

ments and rational analysis has been discarded in favor of an attack on the disagreeing critic, who must be discredited first, before he is refuted, or without being refuted.

The liberals have succeeded in creating such a gap between reality and the interpretations of reality to which we are subjected, that often, when we hear official pronouncements and statements, or listen to the mass communications media commenting on problems of the modern world, we feel as if we were hearing fairy tales from some imaginary world unrelated to our own world, or reports from enemy sources.* As a consequence, confusion and bewilderment have increased. People no longer know what is true, whom to believe and how to eliminate the enemy's lies from the truth.

Behind most of our policies there are the inevitable liberal experts who are determined to impose their opinions on our policymakers and on all of us. One of the most glaring examples of the liberal contribution to the moral and political disarmament of America, is certainly the article of Congressman John Brademas, dealing with the responsibility of U.S. colleges and universities to turn out the future leaders of America.

The trouble, according to Mr. Brademas, was that too many of the young men and women had a "highly moralistic approach" to issues and were inclined to take "a simple, ethically uncomplicated position." The Brademas advice was that, instead, "they must learn adjustment, negotiation and compromise." To make himself perfectly clear, Mr. Brademas quoted from an "excellent little book" by Charles Burton Marshall the following message to the 1962 generation of college students:

> "We Americans tend to make these things too simple. We admire Davy Crockett's terse formula: 'Be sure you're right; then go ahead.' That is much too facile for purposes of world politics. The best we can expect is some such paraphrase as this: Be

* Testifying before the House Committee on Un-American Activities on August 10, 1967, the Rev. Richard Wurmbrand, who spent 14 years in jail in communist Rumania, said that officials of the National Council of Churches in New York told him: "Don't speak against communism because this will make men hate communism and the Russians." And he asked them in return: "How is it possible that you give me the same advice as the communist secret police gave me?" (*Chicago Tribune*, August 11, 1967).

as sure as you reasonably can of the rightness of your premises. Take care the best you can to see that the conclusions which you draw from them are tolerably right. Take adequate account of the legitimate interests and viewpoints of others. After you have done your best to meet these obligations, go ahead as far as the circumstances taken as a whole warrant, getting others to go along as far as you can." [131]

It is difficult to imagine that Moscow or Peking mind-conditioners, even in their most sardonic anti-American mood, could formulate more contemptuous and insulting recommendations to U.S. youth. Mr. Brademas, however, seemed to regret that "few students look at politics that way."

But regardless of Mr. Brademas' attitude, the simple truth is that if Americans accept enemy propaganda about their society, history, values and accomplishments as valid criticism, they cannot survive.

A nation which is willing to sit all the time on the bench of the accused before history and before the world, can never be right, never justify itself, never solve any problems. Its life is reduced to gradual self-liquidation.

In 1968 both President Johnson and President Nixon, speaking on Vietnam, expressed their most serious concern about the disunity among Americans, which had never been so deep. But this is the inevitable result of the process of the destruction of values and erosion of faith, which we have allowed to take place.

Without absolutes, without unquestionable values and principles, without faith and self-esteem, there is nothing to bind individuals together into a nation nor to give meaning to their lives. And when there is nothing sacred left in a nation, nothing which everybody must respect, neither the basic national interests, not the achievements and heritage of the forefathers, not the sacrifices of the fighting men, nor the search for truth, nor law and order, nor common decency and human dignity—what can unite its members? Our disunity has resulted from the rejection of the values of the nation.

Our surrender in the field of reason and the communist success in implanting in us a paramount guilt complex account for their almost miraculous success in turning the tables on us—in the U.S. and in the whole world—on the issues of poverty, civil rights and Vietnam.

The U.S., the wealthiest country in the world, with the highest standard of living for the broadest masses in history, has accepted the problem of poverty as its own crucial problem, allegedly indicative of American social injustice, callous social conscience and lack of human consideration.

The problem of civil rights, i.e. equal rights for the American Negroes, has been built up as a problem of racial injustice in a country which has endeavored to guarantee liberty and justice for all, where the Negroes have attained a standard of living higher than Negroes anywhere else in the world and higher than the standard of many Whites in many countries, and where they are daily making big strides toward full equality. Nevertheless, the Negro problem has been made into an international weapon of calumny and political warfare against the United States.

And the communists, who have the most sinister record of all time in aggression, killing and inhumanity, have put the U.S., whose troops are defending a small Asian country from concerted communist aggression, on the bench of the accused before "the court of world opinion" as the "arch-aggressor" of history, to use the words of Martin Luther King.

(And in spite of all that, we have actually appealed to the USSR, without whose instigation and influence there would have been no Korean war nor any communist aggression in South Vietnam, to help us save peace in the *Pueblo* incident and the shooting of our EC121 plane in Korea and to stem the communist aggression in South Vietnam, and that immediately after the Soviet re-invasion of Czechoslovakia!)

But nothing illustrates the measure of the inroads which the communist psychological and political offensive has made, better than the My Lai case.

My Lai

The whole My Lai affair indicates a pernicious level of our inability to perceive enemy actions and interests, as opposed to U.S.

interests. It is a matter of record that all communists and most liberal newsmen and commentators have indulged in an orgy of denunciation of U.S. "inhumanity." *

That alone should have opened the eyes of the public as to the true nature of the My Lai affair. Instead, even some conservative writers were unable to resist the pressure of conditioned "public opinion" and strewed their heads with ashes of American guilt!

The fact is however, that in all the publicity about the horrors of My Lai there was not the slighest concern for truth and humanity. None of those allegedly outraged by My Lai was ever outraged by any communist crime anywhere, especially not in Vietnam.

In the Montagnard village of Dak Son the Vietcong killed on December 5, 1967, 200 persons, mostly women and children, and abducted four hundred. In Kon Horing, on February 23, 1969, the North Vietnamese killed and burned to death 278 persons. In Hue in April 1968, the Vietcong and North Vietnamese jointly massacred some 3500 people. But there was not a ripple on the liberal conscience, nor was any liberal voice raised. The liberal conscience follows the communist conscience. It stirs only when an action can be utilized to hit the U.S. and its "callous inhumanity"!

The whole case of My Lai and the publicity about it indicate how badly communist propaganda and mind-conditioning have maimed our mental alertness and psychological defenses. For except for the spontaneous explosion of popular indignation at the sentencing of Lt. Calley, there have hardly been efforts to put the whole thing in proper light by stressing the following:

A. If war is absolutely immoral and intolerable, to the point of being unacceptable under any circumstances, then we simply should not wage war ever.

We should not have waged war in 1776–1783, in 1812, in 1861–1865, in 1898, in 1916, in 1917–1918, in 1941–1945, in 1950–1953.

However, we must consider the consequences. Without war we might still be a British colony, or a Hitler colony. And if we refuse

---

* Cartoonists did their share. In one of William Mauldin's cartoons, a young GI, bearing the inscription "Pinkville," is entering a pool of blood where an ignominiously grinning Nazi is standing chest-deep, with the inscription "Lidice." One wonders what such American cartoonists leave for their counterparts in Hanoi, Moscow and Peking!

any war action now, we shall be enslaved by communism. Is that what the enemies of war at any price desire? ("Rather slavery than war.") If not, they cannot oppose war unconditionally.

Those who oppose only some wars, especially the war in Vietnam, but were very much in favor of World War II and today favor the communist-instigated "wars of national liberation," are not against war. They are against the United States and for communism.

So, we cannot have it both ways. If no war is admissible, we should surrender and accept slavery. If, however, freedom and national independence are worth fighting for, then we must decide whether a given situation calls for war action and if it does, we must wage it with all our might and give all the support to our fighting men.

B. The conditions of the war in Vietnam are exceptionally difficult and taxing,

1. because it is a most unusual combination of foreign aggression and civil war;

2. because the distinction between combatants and civilians has been obliterated, and women and children, down to the tenderest age, have been ruthlessly used to kill Americans (as well as South Vietnamese, of course); 3. because of our policy of non-victory which proclaims that it is perfectly acceptable for Americans to be killed by communists in Vietnam, but absolutely unacceptable for Americans to strive to win over communism in North Vietnam;

C. The war in Vietnam being unlike any previous war, it stands to reason that it is impossible to apply the rules of "normal" warfare, where both sides abide by some elementary standards of decency and morality. If the "winds of change" which are changing the world, are irresistible and entitled to wreak havoc with American traditions and interests, how come they have not upset the same old rules of civilized warfare at a time when the U.S. is engaged in Vietnam in a merciless war against the most uncivilized and ruthless power in history, world communism!?

D. Thus we have accepted the double standard that the communists can wage war without any moral restrictions, while we are bound by moral scruples of the most delicate kind.

E. By accepting this double standard of morality, we have not only marked Lt. Calley as a war criminal, but the U.S. as well. For if we decry and condemn Lt. Calley as a premeditated murderer, nobody above him who is responsible for the war in Vietnam and the conditions under which it is fought can be exempt.

Lt. Calley did not go to Vietnam for fun. Nor did he have any personal accounts to settle with the Vietcong and North Vietnamese. He went as a soldier, to whom his country, America, gave professional military training, and weapons, and sent him overseas, to fight, kill the enemy, at the daily risk of being killed himself. He did not write the rules of war, nor determine the conditions decided by others and as any other soldier, had to obey the orders of his superiors.

But to organize an army, train fighters, send them to Vietnam to be killed, and then forbid them to win, and finally indict and court-martial them and condemn them as premeditated killers, that is a unique victory of evil, of the enemy's interests above U.S. interests, a monstrous perversion of ethics, justice and reason.

If a man called to carry arms for his country, kill its enemies and be exposed to being killed himself by the utterly inhuman and ruthless communist enemy, must always observe peacetime morality, how can he fight? If he runs the risk of being considered a criminal and not a soldier, not only by enemy propaganda but by his own fellow-Americans and public opinion, who will carry arms and how can there be a U.S. Army? And how can there be any army if at every moment every soldier, from private to General, can question his orders and set his conscience as the supreme judge, while on the communist side the question of conscience does not even exist, but only the fierce fanaticism of the leaders to win and the most absolute obedience of the soldiers?

If every citizen is a conscientious objector (or may at any moment turn into one), then there can be no Army.

The possible crime at My Lai cannot be excused by the infinitely worse and positively committed crimes of the communists. But, if we raise the question of My Lai, then we must raise a million times more the question of communist crimes. Only then can justice and civilization prevail.

However, if we court-martial Lieutenant Calley, but do not brand as war criminals the Soviet and Red Chinese leaders, and the leaders of North Vietnam, Tran Van Dong, General Giap and others, and all those who unconditionally obey them, down to the level of North Vietnamese lieutenants—we are not serving the cause of justice, humanity and civilization, but of injustice, communism and barbarity.

Instead of taking action against the real criminals, those who masterminded the whole My Lai case and its publicity, we condemned Lt. Calley and demoted Generals Samuel W. Koster and George H. Young, which in itself was a clear admission of U.S. war crime guilt before the enemy and the world.

And the communists lost no time in putting President Nixon on the same level with Hitler and all those who at Nuremberg were condemned as war criminals.

This is the end result of Nuremberg, where we accepted the arch-criminals of history, the communists, as equal partners of Western allies, fully qualified to dispense justice. With one stroke all communist crimes were erased and the criminals were elevated to judges.

The unavoidable result of our lack of vision and courage to put the communist criminals of Katyn on the bench of the accused, next to the Nazi criminals, or at least deny them the right to dispense justice, was that twenty-five years later they put the U.S. on the bench of the accused before the whole world, equating U.S. soldiers tagged with "My Lai," with the Nazi executioners of Dachau, Mauthausen and other concentration camps.

My Lai is not only self-inflicted and self-advertised disgrace, nor is it merely suicide; it is both.

Only the victory of treason and the decline of American spirit and vitality can account for it.

If Lt. Calley was really guilty of crimes attributed to him, he could and should have been tried and condemned without any publicity at all. But publicity, not justice, was precisely what the communists were interested in.

Instead of the U.S. Government and the whole nation standing behind our fighting men in Vietnam, we have stabbed them in the back.

The Pentagon Papers

The trial of Lt. Calley and the publicity surrounding it, which can be called a miniature Nuremberg, cannot be separated from the scandal of *The Pentagon Papers*. It took only a traitorous thief and a big newspaper without conscience and responsibility to complete the job of My Lai.

For My Lai had allegedly demonstrated the villainy of U.S. soldiers "exposed" as common murderers. *The Pentagon Papers* "proved" that the real culprit in Vietnam was not North Vietnam or the Vietcong, or the Soviet Union or Red China, but the United States and its supreme civilian and military leaders.

The communists never consider any communist, but only enemies to be war criminals. The U.S. has branded Nazis as war criminals, now also an American, yet never a communist! By meekly adopting communist logic and the double standard, we put the stamp of war criminal on the U.S. Army and national leadership, while absolving the communist criminals from their crimes and making them appear, in comparison, as idealistic fighters for a better world.

My Lai may, in the long run, turn out to be a much worse calamity than Pearl Harbor.

The Loyalty Must Be Mutual

What has been overlooked in the tangle of moral erosion and intellectual confusion produced by our policy of reconciliation with communism, is the elementary fact that the relationship between the citizens of a country and its Government is made not of unilateral, but reciprocal obligations and loyalty.

The individual citizen, who owes his country full loyalty and readiness to defend its interests with all means including the sacrifice of his life, must also be sure that the nation is behind him. He must be able to count on his Government, representing him and his fellow-countrymen, to reciprocate his loyalty to the nation by its full support for him when he is in need. He must always be sure that he can identify with his nation.

But how can a man identify with his nation if the nation does not defend its identity? How can he fight the nation's enemies, if the nation itself reconciles and coexists with them?

The essence of the relationship between citizen and state was expressed long ago in the saying "Civis Romanus Sum" (I am a citizen of Rome). It was more than the secure feeling of being part of a mighty state. It was the pride of being able to identify with it, its institutions and achievements and the certainty that Rome cared and gave protection to everybody who could claim to be a citizen.

With all historical differences involved, this is the situation which for a long time existed between the United States and U.S. citizens, even in cases where individuals had not yet attained full-fledged citizen status, but only applied for citizenship and in possession of their "first papers." The case of Perdicaris, kidnapped by a Tunisian brigand and Theodore Roosevelt's intervention as President of the United States to have him immediately released at the risk of U.S. armed action, is a shining example of the ideal relationship between Government and citizens, which had evolved in the U.S.

However, that relationship has unfortunately changed to an unbelievable and most perilous extent.

The war in Korea has been the subject of many books, articles and studies, especially the poor resistance to pressure and brainwashing of many G.I.'s in Korean communist captivity. This has been a matter of attention and justified grave concern. The gist of the whole thing is this: if the Korean war was the first war in U.S. history which the U.S. was unable to win, it is because it was not fought under the U.S. flag and for the U.S. The vital link between the nation and its fighting men was cut. American G.I.'s were not *cives americani*! They were fighting under the spider flag of the U.N., whose leading member, the USSR, was inspiring and directing the operations on the other side of the firing line! And those who were captured were left virtually alone, bereft of any feeling of identity with their country and with the cause it was defending. Those who behaved in true American tradition, bore witness to the strength of the national character. But those whose resistance collapsed under communist pressure, were a crushing indictment of the weakening of U.S. self-respect and identity in the face of the mortal enemy. James Burnham, speaking of the Koje Island affair, where unarmed communist prisoners practically achieved control of the situation over fully armed G.I.'s, and which he called "one of the most disgraceful in American history," con-

cluded that "On the American side, there were only brave soldiers, uninformed of the nature of the enemy, and castrated by a
disastrous policy and an irresolute political leadership." Instead of
standing behind its brave soldiers, the country had dissociated itself from them and delivered them to the U.N.! They could not
help feeling empty and forsaken, betrayed.

The failure of the Government to defend the nation's identity
has reached its lowest level in Vietnam. The criminal anti-
Vietnam agitation, in the U.S. and in the world, which is the work
of professional communist agitators, assisted by the widest as-
sortment of innocents, is inexcusable.

But it would be utter folly and utter injustice to stamp all those
who oppose the war in Vietnam as traitors. That simply is not
true. The refusal to bear arms for a country, which gives all the
vital protection and safety and makes possible for an individual to
live like a human being, is inadmissible. But conscience and reason must rebel at the horrible unreason in the conduct of the war
in Vietnam, which provides the ground on which the communist
propaganda of ". . . no, no, we won't go" thrives.

The official policy of the Government, of asking its youth to go
to Vietnam to shed their blood and give their lives to stop communism, and at the same time proclaiming that our aim in Vietnam is *not* to defeat communism, to win, is more immoral and a
deeper sin than the refusal to bear arms.

The only justification for sacrificing the youth of a nation, its
most precious asset, is to strive for victory. That is the permanent
and binding understanding between the troops and the Government. How could U.S. troops in Vietnam know, how could they
even conceive, that this was no longer so?

And once they became aware of the "new morality" of warfare,
how could they possibly be expected to reconcile with it?

But the senselessness of the war, the feeling of futility, of being
let down by the Government, are growing and becoming a factor
of increasing strength and influence in the climate of public opinion of today and tomorrow.

As for the *Pueblo* affair, which President Nixon called "the ultimate insult" in his acceptance speech at the Republican Convention of 1968, its consequences will be felt for a long time and its
problems are yet to be tackled and solved. But its essential point is

again that U.S. fighting men were let down by the nation they were to protect, fight and die for.*

The action of the U.S. Government in the Perdicaris case, made history. But what history will our policy regarding our POWs in Korea and Vietnam make?

There are two statements, by two U.S. Presidents, which sum up the situation and bear out the main lines of this presentation of the communist offensive against the U.S. mind and our sorely inadequate response to the challenge.

The communists have done their utmost to control our thinking. But the minds of our policy-makers did not even register the communist offensive. Their chief preoccupation was winning elections and, in that perspective, the material needs, production figures and material welfare of modern mass man.

It was President Johnson, the exponent of the "bigger-bowl-of-rice" philosophy for solving the problems of Asia, who formulated the most cogent and devastating refutal of the materialistic (economistic) approach to political and social problems, when he said:

"The most prosperous, the best housed, the best fed, the best read, the most intelligent and the most secure generation in our history, or all history, is discontented." [132]

Without knowing it, he had put the finger on the sore spot. There was the gist of the whole problem of the dissatisfaction of modern man, and the key to the understanding of the relationship between the Government and the governed. It is in leadership

---

* According to a UPI dispatch of March 1, 1969, Communications Technician 1 C Don E. Bailey, 39, of Portland, Ind., said: "The beatings didn't hurt half as much as the fact that we got no help from the greatest country in the world."

A few days later, on March 5, 1969, a UPI dispatch reported that the most severe beating was administered to Communications Technician 2 C Earl M. Kisler, 22, of St. Louis, for refusing to "sign a letter to *Newsweek* magazine asking that the United States apologize for the Pueblo affair." "The sight of Kisler after his torture frightened . . . (several Pueblo sailors) into writing propaganda statements for the North Koreans." But Kisler was undaunted: "It was my own decision . . . Here was a rinky dink country with people that were less than people telling the strongest country on earth what to do. I'd had it."

and the failure thereof that we must look for the secret of the dissatisfaction, turmoil, dissent and disunity in America, as well as in Asia and the whole world—not in a "bigger bowl of rice."

And then there is President Nixon's statement in his Inaugural Address, indicating that the nature of the U.S. crisis was not alien to him. He spoke of the "long night of the American spirit," and stressed the contrast between material wealth and spiritual emptiness and incertitude: "We find ourselves rich in goods, but ragged in spirit, reaching with magnificent precision for the moon, but falling into raucous discord on Earth . . . We are torn by divisions, wanting unity. We see around us empty lives, wanting fulfillment . . . To a crisis of the spirit, we need an answer of the spirit."

The answer is still wanting.

The first requirement for finding it is to take a mercilessly candid comparative look at the U.S. and the Soviet Union at this stage of the struggle for the world.

The U.S. and the USSR

The communists have an aim. They have a policy. Their goal is evil, but they have laws and standards, by which to live and conquer. Being ruthless plotters, they think all the time about all problems, seeking ways and methods to be more effective in the pursuit of their goal. They strive not for compromise or coexistence, but for victory. Their policies are based on world realities and guided by the interest of preserving their power. They never allow any problem to stand in the path of that supreme objective and interest. The interest of the communist party, the "science" of Marxism-Leninism which serves it, the world-wide victory of communism, are their absolutes.

They, and all of them without a single exception, Stalinists and "liberals," Trotskyists and Titoists, Maoists and Brezhnevists, Husakists and Dubcekists, Gomulkists and Gierekists, Kadarists and Ceausescuists, etc., all the bureaucrats and dogmatists and all the heretics and self-critics—consider communist power as the absolute value, absolute yardstick and absolute point of orientation. All social reforms and all measures to bring about "humane socialism" can be taken only and exclusively within the framework of communist power and are subordinated to it.

As for us, we are in the clouds. In the utterly political world of today, we have no political aim. We lack the courage to face the facts of international life and to confront the truth of communist implacable hostility. "We have known what was in the mind of the Soviet for thirty years and we do not want to look at it . . . it is the extension of the Soviet system to the entire world," says Salvador de Madariaga.[133]

Our policies are based on ideas divorced from reality and contrary to our national interests. The four points of our foreign policy (peace, U.N., anti-colonialism and coexistence) are the present communist minimal program for the conquest of the world. And all the objectives which are presented as goals of U.S. foreign policy (the basic G. C. Marshall formula of eradicating poverty, ignorance, desperation and chaos in the world) are vague, non-political commonplaces, which are all encased in the above four points.

Because we have no aim and because we have failed to grasp the nature of communist aims and policies, the communists have, in waging their political war against us, been able to evolve a double-standard strategy and bring about a double-standard situation, which spell our undoing, since the laws of life and victory apply to them, and the laws of defeat and suicide are for us.

That double-standard strategy is based on the proposition that:

They (the communists) want the world. Being revolutionaries, they have the right to be as ruthless and machiavellistic as they please. They are bound only and exclusively by the rules of political realism. Anything goes. They are entitled to the foulest means and methods. Their aggression is respect for national independence and non-interference in the affairs of other nations; their war is peace; their violence is love and their violence is justice; their terror is freedom; their hegemony is self-determination.

We, however (the West, and particularly the United States), are irrevocably doomed by history. Being people of decency, democratic convictions and lofty principles, (as well as philistine limitations), we are bound by rules of absolute honesty and morality. For the U.S., only strictly non-political yardsticks apply in politics. Since the U.S. is not without blemish, it has no right to defend itself, to criticize, be hostile, fight, oppose anybody. So, we have no choice but to go down, the more quietly the better. Every resistance to communism is resistance to inexorable history and its winds of change. Whatever we do to uphold and defend the basic values of Western civilization and free society, is automatically provocation, fascism, aggression, oppression. The only thing the U.S. can and must do is to cooperate with all the regimes of the world (particularly the communist ones) to eradicate the non-political ills of mankind (George C. Marshall concept).

The Soviet Union is free to commit any crime and villainy without having to account before any court of world opinion. The U.S. is obligated to perform in accordance with the highest standards of moral perfection, and anything short of that calls for the most drastic, world-wide, merciless condemnation of the U.S. as the main force of evil in the world.

The only attitude which they allow us, is compliance with their revolutionary action, their "social change." They create tensions. We must "ease tensions." Our slightest opposition is "overreaction." And while they wage civil war unhindered, they—in advance—decry "right-wing repression."

If a Chicago policeman, facing a criminal who is hurling rocks or human excrement at him or using a nail-studded baseball bat to maim him, uses his stick, that is the end of democracy in America!

But when the communists (The Soviet Union, Red China, etc.), using the most inhuman and degrading methods in history, kill, torture, starve to death dozens of millions of human beings,—there is no upsurge of the Western liberal conscience. For that is the inexorable march of history!

And the most scandalous thing about the logic and ethics of this double standard against us, which indicates the degree of our mental subjugation, is that, instead of fighting back, we are meekly adapting ourselves to it. We accept the existence of the Soviet Union, *as is,* as a final and unchangeable fact of life. But we also accept as justified, criticism of U.S. shortcomings—unilateral criticism, which aims at destroying us.

The communists, being revolutionaries, have the right to smash us to bits. But we, being dedicated to peace and humanity, have no right to smash anybody, but must guarantee all rights to the enemy, including their right to smash us to bits.

The great advantage of this double-standard technique is that they do not have to lie all the time about everything. They can afford to present facts about the U.S., statistics, figures, etc., which can be corroborated by objective observation. However, the villainy of this "truthful" procedure is that, whatever the real ills of the U.S., they are actually being distorted and misrepresented as long as silence reigns about the infinitely, incomparably worse ills, injustices, wrongs and sores of the communist world.

To this, the favorite liberal rejoinder is that "two wrongs do not make a right," i.e. that if the Soviet Union is bad and because it is bad, that does not mean that the U.S. is blameless. The ills of the U.S., runs the theory, are objective and cannot be undone or made or considered nonexistent by the fact that the same or worse evils exist in the Soviet Union.

This reasoning, which at first approach looks plausible, is thoroughly fallacious. First of all, there is such an immense difference in quality and quantity between wrongs in the U.S. and communist wrongs, that they cannot be put in the same category. Basic is that the foundations of the U.S. are sound and good, and the imperfections of the U.S. are mainly derived from the imperfections of human nature. However, communist foundations, in the USSR and everywhere else (China, Yugoslavia), are intentionally, in their very essence, evil, upside-down, deliberately formulated so as to enslave, debase, humiliate and destroy men and civilization.

Second, international life has never been a realm of objective, dispassionate observation, strict fairness and absolute ethics, but rather, an outspoken realm of conflict, intrigue and merciless struggle. Today, when our country is engaged in a total war where no value is respected and the enemy aims at our total annihilation as a nation—no one has the right to be "objective," to pose as an "impartial" arbiter between the U.S. and communism, standing "above the melée." Such objectivity is treason. It was treason in 1776, as it was in World War I and World War II. Today it is treason more than ever.

And yet we reconcile with that situation as a basis for our policies.

The USSR maintains that it is fighting for communism, and it is. We maintain that we are fighting for freedom and democracy, but we are doing nothing of the kind, since we are surrendering, not fighting. We started by betraying our most faithful allies of World War II (Draza Mihailovich and the Polish resistance fighters), and we are now (in Vietnam) doing everything not to win. The communists use all their energies to destroy us. We use all our energies to be friends with them.

To them, political aims are supreme. To attain them, they are willing to destroy any conceivable number of human lives. To us, human lives are most important. To save them, we are willing to make all political concessions, including surrender.

The Soviet Union has constantly done everything in its power to assert its identity, distinct and at sharpest variance with the West, particularly the U.S. However, U.S. policies since 1933 have blurred, renounced, confused U.S. national identity, and thus tended to discourage Americans from relying on and identifying with the U.S. The accent, instead, has been on interdependence and a gradual merger with everybody, including the Soviet Union, in a supranational "democratic" identity of the "human race."

The net result of Soviet and of U.S. policies has been to weaken U.S. identity and prestige and strengthen Soviet (and, generally, communist) identity and prestige. The urge to identify with the U.S. has declined and the inclination to identify with communism has been correspondingly reinforced.

While the communists are busy conquering the world, the U.S. is neglecting its vital interests and investing its efforts and resources in the realization of objectives for the improvement of mankind, the creation of an ideal society, global equality and happiness. Everybody must be absolutely satisfied with life and happy, everybody intelligent and well-educated, all ills and suffering in the world eliminated, ignorance and disease abolished, war outlawed and peace reigning supreme. Final solutions must be found for all problems (war, youth, civil rights, poverty).

And those final solutions for all the problems which mankind has been unable to solve in some 7000 years of its recorded history, must be found and realized without delay, now, right now! Since in our society, it is always "society" which is guilty, never the individual, the U.S. must fulfill all expectations, or else be destroyed.

In the Soviet Union, "society," i.e. the communist regime, is always right. The whole social and political system is geared to implant in its citizens the concept of duty, obligation, service, devotion to the common good, to communism, to the state, to Soviet society. The individual's concern must be not how he can best advance his own interests, but what he can contribute to making the Soviet state mighty and Soviet society functioning smoothly. For all accomplishments he must be grateful to the "glorious" party, state and system under which he lives. For all personal troubles and misfortunes he can blame only himself, not society, nor the system.[134] The Soviet citizens' relationship to the regime is made of obligations, among which stands out the obligation of unconditional support and obedience to the regime. All existing or potential immense dissatisfaction is channelled exclusively against the "capitalists," i.e. against foreign countries, particularly the United States.* No matter what we may think of this arrangement, it is hardly doubtful that it tends to make the state strong and thus better equipped to survive in international competition.

The communists not only wage political war, agitate and subvert the United States, but they adduce the resulting troubles, such as protests, riots, and demonstrations in the U.S. and in the world as a proof that America is bad and corrupt, since everybody is protesting and rebelling against everything, especially youth, while in the USSR, nobody protests and rebels against anything.**

* ". . . Soviet students . . . are weary of official propaganda, hypocrisy, self-celebration, bombast, evasions and lies. Their "ferment," however, is not rebellion against the major principles of Marxism-Leninism, but a longing to make them work." (George Feifer, author of *Justice in Moscow,* in his review of William Taubman's *The View From Lenin's Hills, Soviet Youth in Ferment,* in the *New York Times Book Review,* November 2, 1967).

** When, in 1968, New York Mayor John Lindsay asked his Moscow counterpart, Vladimir F. Promyslow what measures were taken when city employees in Moscow went on strike for higher wages, Promyslow laughingly replied, "in 50 years of Soviet power it has not happened once." (*Chicago Tribune* May 18, 1968). The implied logic was disarming: people go on strike when they are dissatisfied. Since Americans strike, they are dissatisfied. And since Soviet citizens do not strike, they obviously are satisfied with their regime!

The communist strategy is to create continually all sorts of domestic problems for us to occupy our attention and strength. In that manner we spend our energies fighting among ourselves, which leaves no time or energy for fighting the enemy of all Americans, the communists.

The communist offensive against our minds has been successful precisely because we have succumbed to the blandishments of the *Communist Manifesto* and the view of history contained in it, i.e. that the whole of history has been a big blunder and crime and that man's job now is to destroy everything in existence and create a new world on entirely new foundations. As explained in the chapter on Liberalism, the idea of correcting all ills of history and creating a perfect world, has been accepted only in the West as a proper object of statesmanship, while the communists, the promoters of the idea of final solutions, are steering clearly away from any such nonsense. It is the West which is afflicted with the poisons of the *Communist Manifesto* "science." The communists are not. That theory is for us. It is the political LSD which the communists peddle to the West, but they never touch the stuff themselves. They just use it against us. They talk a great deal about lofty aims and ideals, their propaganda is replete with concern for the welfare of mankind, but their policies are as realistic as their aims and methods are reprehensible. They use their energies and resources *not* to create ideal conditions in the world, but to brainwash the West and induce it to take that path, so as to facilitate their conquest of the globe.

To make the paradox worse, they have at the same time, while convincing us that they were irresistible and the wave of the future, also convinced us that communism simply does not exist. It is a non-problem, a figment of the paranoid imagination of rabid anti-communists, "McCarthyites," right-wing extremists. Evidently: if communism does not exist, then all anti-communism is senseless, and the cold war is equally nonsense. As we have seen, this is the view which unfortunately permeates our official estimate of the international situation, of communism and of the position, tasks and responsibilities of the U.S. in the next decade. In this manner, our moral and political disarmament is induced from two opposite directions: because the communists are so strong that there is no point in resisting them, and because they have changed so thoroughly that they practically do not exist!

It should be obvious that this situation has not just come about, but has resulted from the political warfare waged against the United States by the Soviet Union and all world communists, and that this warfare has been very successful.

7   The Death of the Communist Dream

"The dream of socialism has become the nightmare of totalitarianism."
RAYMOND ARON

The preceding presentation of the communist offensive strategy to destroy the values and control the mind of the West, would be incomplete without a presentation of the communist defensive strategy, and its wonder tool, self-criticism.

Communist penetration in the West is a matter of record, if not of adequate evaluation. But at the same time and partly as a price for that penetration, there has been a tremendous disintegration in communist ranks. This, to a great extent, is due to the permanent presence and tireless activity of the "non-communist fifth column within" every communist.[135] For all its intensity, drive, fanaticism, aggressiveness, power of penetration and conquest, communism is at its very core, incurably contrary to human nature, its elementary strivings, its basic decency. This is communism's main problem, especially today.

While communism was only a dream, it had the power of a dream: to move mountains and men's souls and minds, exact sacrifices, nourish hopes, make all existing ugliness nonexistent or irrelevant, and all Fata Morganas real and alive.

But communism has now been realized, put into practice. The capitalists have been expropriated, the "state of the workers and peasants" has taken over the factories; millions of bourgeois, kulaks, "remnants of the old society," have been killed, the whole gigantic propaganda, indoctrination and brainwashing apparatus of the new society has been working full steam ever since 1917 to convince its citizens that they never had it so good, to urge them to work more and sacrifice more, to beware of the enemies of socialism and of foreign agents lurking behind every corner; a whole new literature of "socialist realism," and a film industry, have been brought into being to sing the glory of the regime, to consolidate it and to urge citizens to feel deliriously happy . . .

And the more communism became reality, the more the communists by their actions and policies showed what communism really meant, the more surely the communist dream began to die. Finally, the inevitable happened: the reality killed the dream. "Whatever the Communist Party once was, today it is a prison for man's best and boldest dreams," wrote former communist Howard Fast in the conclusion of his book *The Naked God.* [136]

All the efforts of deceit and propaganda, all the Pavlovian brainwashing and conditioning of reflexes, has been powerless to prevent the transition from dream to ugly reality. "The dream of socialism has become the nightmare of totalitarianism," in the words of Raymond Aron.[137]

We are not concerned here with the economic failure of the communist economic system, spectacular as it is. Between the two world wars, industry in the USSR was kept alive by capitalist investments and know-how. How wise that policy was politically, is something else. But the fact is there, and it weighs heavily in the appraisal of the achievements of communism.

In World War II the Soviet Union received some $11 billion lend-lease aid, containing beside war material, many millions of non-strategic goods such as clothing.

The industrial dismantling of Germany allowed the Soviet Union to strengthen its economy with German plants, experts and scientists. Soviet atomic development was made possible not only by U.S. traitors, such as the Rosenbergs, but by the official policy of sharing every secret with our "wartime ally."

As Werner Keller has convincingly and copiously demonstrated in his book *East Minus West = Zero,* there would be no Soviet industry today, if all the contributions of capitalist economies were taken away.

Despite all that help, the Soviet economy has been and is afflicted with the endemic disease of socialist inefficiency, bureaucratism, corruption and lack of incentive. Scholarly and thorough studies by Professor Warren Nutter have demonstrated this. And Eugene Lyons, a one-time believer in the communist Utopia, has drawn a revealing picture of the achievements of the USSR in fifty years, in his book *Workers' Paradise Lost.*

Maybe the most telling fact of the Soviet economic record is that after a half a century, with its immense spaces of agricultural land, it cannot feed its population, and must import wheat from the United States and Canada (and other capitalist countries). And, for all its great natural resources, the USSR cannot hope to catch up with the free world, especially the United States, in industry and technology.

Equally unconcerned are the communists about that failure to correct the social injustice and other ills of the old society, to make human relations more brotherly, to bring about a society superior to the one they destroyed in 1917. The fact that communist society is from a moral standpoint the worst known to men, that under it human dignity is at its lowest point, does not unduly upset the communists. For the creation of a better society was *never* their aim.

What worries the communists is that the hoax has been exposed, the hoax of communist idealism, humanitarism and love for mankind, for the common man, the workers and peasants, for oppressed and suffering humanity. And their promises to remove all ills and create a society of justice and equality, brotherhood and decency, joy and creative progress, have been exposed for the cynical lies they are.

"So that there should be no more prisons, we built new prisons; so that not one drop of blood should be shed, we killed and killed and killed." [138]

"In the name of the ultimate goal, we resorted to methods used by our enemies . . . We introduced torture and epaulettes . . . we placed a new Czar on the empty throne . . . It seemed at times as if for the sake of a complete victory of Communism, all we had to do was to give up the idea of Communism." [139]

Communism had shown its face, in Europe, in Asia, especially in China, everywhere. And the world did not like that face. The old warning of Lenin that the fate of communism depended on its ability to keep the faith and confidence of the masses of the world, especially in Asia, had become a threatening actuality. The communist empire had grown fabulously as a result of World War II, but confidence in the peaceful, humanistic, democratic, truly progressive intent of the communists had shrunk correspondingly.

And that is no trifle. For the communists know what most

Westerners have forgotten, that the deepest foundations of power
are spiritual. The communist movement grew because people believed in it, and the main pillar of strength of the bolshevik regime
after 1917 was that many people believed that its representatives
meant what they said, that they were determined to create a better society and that they would create it. It is only by relying on
that popular belief and taking advantage of it, that Stalin was
able to kill several million kulaks, carry out his purges which liquidated most of the old bolshevik guard and the pick of the offi-
cers' corps of the Red Army and institute a reign of terror never
known before.

But there are limits to man's gullibility, naiveté and idealism.

The poignant and expressive summary of Arthur Koestler about
what happened in his mind and soul when he joined the communist party and when he left it, is not only a personal experience. It
expresses, in words others cannot find, the experience of millions
of former (and active) members of the CPSU and all communist
parties. It is a disillusionment which goes to the very depths of
one's mind and heart, to the inner springs which form our conscience and determine our most important choices and actions:

"I went to Communism as one goes to a spring of fresh water,
and I left Communism as one clambers out of a poisoned river
strewn with the wreckage of flooded cities and the corpses of
the drowned." [140]

Mikhail Soloviev, a Russian, who was a boy in 1917, and absorbed communist theory as he lived communist life, wrote after
World War II a remarkable novel, *When the Gods Are Silent,*
where he told in a most impressive and direct manner the story of
the death of the communist dream, of the communist idea.

The hero of the novel, Mark Surov, grew up under communism
and received the strictest communist education. He was thoroughly trained to meet and dismiss dialectically the voice of his
conscience rebelling against communist reality and communist
policies. No matter what happened and what crimes were committed in the name of the "cause," he tried to find an excuse to
remain loyal and to convince others to follow the same path: "We
must smash the past that is part of us and everything around us.

That's harsh . . . but we do it in the name of the future . . . You can't chop wood without making splinters . . . History will understand us, and it will not condemn us because of the splinters we're making in our great work of construction . . . We've got to build and we must sweep aside all who interfere."

Even after coming to the conclusion that "all the blood was shed in vain," Surov invokes Dzerzinsky's famous dialectics of freedom-through-slavery: "We shall come to power over the system through subjection to the system. That one simply must believe, and never dare to doubt." To a "real Stalinist the groans of human beings . . . are his 'symphony of construction'" since "without violence you cannot open the door into the future."

But finally the strain of communist dialectics is too much for Surov. His conscience, his sense of justice and elementary humanity as well as the pressure of plain facts and overwhelming evidence liberate him: "I used to believe that when you chop wood splinters fly. But now I see so many splinters that nothing is left of the communist forest . . . We know that our idea has been killed and that the idea itself is defective and false."

Among political writers and former communists, no one has more emphatically and clearly linked communist practice directly with communist idea than Max Eastman (*Reflections on the Failure of Socialism*, 1958). The gist of the matter being that the evils of communism were derived not from the imperfections of its fulfillers, but from the idea itself. Life under communism was monstrous because the communist idea was monstrous.

Consequently, the erosion and disappearance of communist faith is not the result of alleged Western subversion, but of the people's discontent with communism, in spite of Western collaboration with communism and ample help to communism.

The essence of the present situation is expressed in the masterful estimate of two young Polish intellectuals, Kuron and Modzelevski:

"The walls of the jails, barracks and arsenals are so strong not because they are built of solid material, but because they are protected by the hegemony of the ruling class, by the authority of power, by fear, by the acceptance of the existing social relations. The existence of these mental walls permits the powerholders to feel secure behind the brick walls. The growing social crisis deprives them of their hegemony, their authority; they are opposed by the overwhelming majority of society; social conditions themselves finally force the working class and its allied social forces to rise against the ruling monopolistic bureaucracy . . . a revolutionary situation shatters the mental walls; then the walls themselves are no longer an obstacle." [141]

The crumbling of the walls has started. To be sure, the picture looks confused and there are all sorts of elements striving hard to attain ends which they either only dimly perceive or which are incompatible with one another. (At the student demonstrations in Belgrade in June 1968, the participants included everybody, from the purest freedom fighters, to "democratic socialists", Maoists, Guevarists and stooges of Tito's regime, against which the demonstrations were organized).

But that is not the main point.

The main point is that the spell of communism has been broken and that the search for an alternative has begun.

The sources and goals of dissatisfaction, dissent, opposition and revolt against communism in communist countries are diverse. They can, however, be grouped into three basic categories (each with a number of sub-groups).

1. Those who believe that communism is basically good. It is the practice of bureaucratism and dogmatism that has led communism astray from its original intents. Unable emotionally to face up to the failure of communism, they would like somehow to bring about a rebirth of the original drive, zeal and faith—all of which have vanished long ago. They cling to the simplest explanation that the degeneration of communism into bureaucratism and dogmatism has resulted from the very harsh historical conditions under which the communists had to struggle to save the revolution!

Now that communist power has been consolidated and communism become a decisive factor in world politics, the humanitarian promises must be fulfilled. To that end, of realizing a communism "with a human face," a liberal, democratic communism, a process of democratization must be initiated. For "true communism" calls for a free exchange of ideas, an exploration of new possibilities, the tracing of new roads. (Milovan Djilas, Andrei Sakharov, Piotr Kapitsa belong unequivocally in this group). But, no matter how much they criticize communism and want to "improve" it, they do not attack or wish to destroy communist power. To them, it is a "historically settled question." Communism is here to stay.

This group then is made up of true "self-critics" of communism, who know that freedom and communism are incompatible, and have clearly opted for communism. Their plea for "freedom" is strictly a means to the end of protecting communism from an explosion of popular discontent which may blast it to pieces. As long as communist power is preserved, they estimate that some relaxation of terror should be permitted, enough to serve as a vent for popular discontent. Among others, here also belong opportunists like Yevgeny Yevtushenko or Vladimir Dudintsev (author of *Not By Bread Alone*), who criticize Soviet society, but only within the bounds indicated by Soviet power.[142]

2. The second group is made up of those who recognize communist power as a temporary fact of life, but accept it only conditionally, provided the communist powerholders make possible increasing and expanding cultural, spiritual freedom. Their main thrust is directed not against communist power, but in favor of some elementary freedom, to redeem the dignity of man, which is smothered under communism. So, they insist on the principles enunciated in the Soviet (or any other communist) Constitution (freedom of thought, and expression, human rights, legal protection of all citizens, etc.).

It is impossible to say whether they realize that the written law in communist countries can be interpreted only dialectically, i.e., strictly as a function of the supreme power interest of the regime. It is most likely that there are among them both naive believers in the legality of communism, and those who are aware of the hoax, but consider that the invocation of the law is nevertheless a weapon in the struggle against oppression and obscurantism, for it arouses public opinion and makes it more difficult for the powerholders to maintain their oppression. So, the protestation of communist loyalty of the members of this group may express the fact that they have not (yet) rejected communism as an "ideal," or they may simply be tactics of self-protection. They may count that if some measure of "liberal" communism is allowed, it may gradually or suddenly gain uncontrollable momentum, and destroy the framework of communist power. It is this feeling of moral and spiritual suffocation under communism which drives men like Siniavsky and Daniel in the USSR, or Kuron and Modzelewski in Poland, to speak up. They can no longer live smothered by lies, dishonesty and oppression, surrendering their intellectual honesty and human integrity to the commands of a regime which has only the deepest contempt for man. The gates of the jail must be opened somehow, but they must be opened (Kuznetsov).

Related to this group is a sub-group made by those who simply know that man can never stop (or be stopped) thinking about new problems as well as re-thinking old ones, especially the eternal ones (Felix Gardavsky, a Czech philosophy professor, author of the book *God Is Not Quite Dead* is a representative of this group).

The official thinkers "think" with the sole purpose of making sure that everything fits neatly into prefabricated Marxist-Leninist patterns of thought. But others feel no such obligation, only the human obligation of thinking problems through, wherever the chips may fall.

3. The third group is made up of those who realize that communism is inherently evil. They know not only that communism excludes freedom, but also that communist power today rests on very shaky grounds, and that the only road to freedom is to destroy communism, which is strangling it.

Here belong, among others, Mikhail Soloviev, Valeri Tarsis, Galanskov and Ginsburg of the Leningrad group (tried in 1967/68), who have no illusions left about the gigantic enterprise of deceit called communism and who consider the destruction of that enterprise as the only way to fulfill their duty as patriots, citizens and human beings.

Those of the younger generation have never known from personal experience anything but communism, so that they have no basis for comparison. But the indestructible basic decency and humanity in man not only rebels against communism (theory and practice), but is proving stronger than all its propaganda and brainwashing. "I am against the system from organic revulsion, I cannot listen to the Soviet radio, I cannot read *Pravda*. It is crude, stupid and full of lies," says Andrei Amalrik.[143] They may know little about politics and dialectics, but they are sure that all the talk about spiritual freedom is idle as long as there is no political freedom.

. . . And then there is Alexandr Solzhenitsyn, who stands in a separate class quite by himself.

The Western literary critics and opinion-makers liked his first book, *One Day in the Life of Ivan Denisovich* and hailed it as a great work of art. It was quite to their taste: passive suffering, resignation, no revolt, acceptance of the Vorkuta dimensions of human life, building of a wall in the jail as fulfillment, no conclusions against communism.

They thought that that was all of Alexandr Solzhenitsyn. They had read the book. They did not know the man. So they got the shock of their lives when *The Cancer Ward* came. Solzhenitsyn was showing his true color. He was not a weak, trembling Vorkuta inmate, passively reminiscing on his sufferings. He was a man, unbroken by Vorkuta, by terror, by cancer, by torture, and indicting his jailers, to the top of the pyramid.

And then came *The First Circle,* in which Solzhenitsyn raises crucial issues which cannot be ignored and tells the truth about communist morals, lies, hypocrisy, the whole system, in such an unambiguous manner and tone that it hits the conscience like a pile-driver and leads to the evident conclusion that there can be no coexistence and no compromise. (Tibor Dery, the Hungarian rebel writer, turned "self-critic," liked *One Day.* He reserved his opinion on *Cancer* and *The First Circle.*)

Alexandr Solzhenitsyn is a most obnoxious and dangerous man. He is asking questions which the communists cannot answer, and he is unremittingly knocking at the conscience of his fellow-citizens, giving them no rest and forcing them to make a decision.

There is a world of difference between him and Boris Pasternak. Pasternak never rebelled against the Soviet regime. On the contrary, when the author of *Dr. Zhivago* states that all he is interested in is "life, birth, love, nature, and the blooming of flowers and trees," and not at all in the "trifle" of making the revolution and changing and ruling the world—which he is leaving to the communists—they could not agree more. Pasternak is making room for them, he is a consolidator of communism.

But Solzhenitsyn knows that who is not free as a man and citizen, cannot be free as a writer. So, he will not leave the "trifle" of changing and ruling the world to the communists. He insists that he be heard on the matter.

In *The First Circle,* Solzhenitsyn says that those are strongest from whom everything has been taken away. Solzhenitsyn is unconquerable because they have taken away from him that which makes life worth living: freedom, truth, justice. He cannot be bribed, he cannot be intimidated, he cannot be coaxed, he cannot be blackmailed, he cannot be deceived. He is a most dangerous man, for he speaks not of guns, rifles, grenades and explosives, but of the absolutely unbreakable strength of the human spirit, stronger than communism. Accused of the crime of publishing his books abroad instead of in the Soviet Union, Solzhenitsyn silenced his accusers with one blow: "Why didn't you let me publish them in this country?"

Member of the Union of Soviet Writers or expelled from it, alive or dead, he is an inexhaustible source of strength. And, without ever mentioning the term anti-communism, he is a most efficient anti-communist. Before such men, communism and communist self-criticism are powerless.

For all its diversity and heterogeneity, the opposition is not made of the "remnants of the bourgeoisie," sons of "capitalists" seeking revenge upon a regime which has dispossessed them, and trying to revive a dead past. On the contrary, it is made of people who grew up under communism or were born after 1917.

So, the explanation that the dismantling of the walls is the work of "foreign agents" (Wall Street, the C.I.A., etc.) or of the remnants of the capitalist system, is ludicrous and, what is worse, nobody believes it.

This is not saying that communist power is about to collapse. It may take some time. But the foundations of power, the belief, the fears, the helpless and resigned acceptance of communism as a *fait accompli* of history, *that* is disintegrating.

Ortega y Gasset has made the remark (in *The Revolt of the Masses*) that nobody, no regime, ever ruled exclusively by brute force. There are always other important elements present, such as fear, intimidation, discouragement of the people, propaganda, a strong sense of purpose by the rulers, which weaken the resistance of the governed and enhance the prestige of those in power.

Ortega y Gasset is absolutely right. As long as the citizens are afraid of the Government, or are impressed by its strength, as long as they believe that the rulers know where they are going and are in control of the situation and its developments—the Government is safe.

But once a political regime evinces the inability to solve the elementary problems of government, when it falls short of the people's natural expectations, when the citizens gather the impression that their rulers have no other concern but power for power's sake—then the psychological basis of power starts disintegrating. The citizens, who until then may have resented or hated the regime, but had nevertheless been willing to identify with it, begin to disassociate. Then the regime is in serious trouble, for the increasing resort to brute force does not suffice.

As for the "reserves of the revolution" in the working class of Western democracies, they have felt the full impact of the betrayal by communism. They may still be opposed to the "bourgeois" governments of their countries and still vote against them, but the faith in the revolution and the promise of communism is gone.

A poll organized not long ago by the French Federation of Democratic and Socialist Left yielded the following results, catastrophic for the French Communist Party:

> ". . . only 25% of the voters for the Communist Party would like to see it run the government; only 18% are in favor of the establishment of a communist regime in France; only 10% are against inheritance and private property and 75% accept as their own the position expressed in the following points: 'There are things, which must not be ridiculed, such as religion, love for country and the authority of the father.' " [144]

That these findings are not arbitrary, but express the real state of affairs, was borne out by the June 23, 1968 elections in France, when the French people, especially in the traditionally "red belt" around Paris, gave an overwhelming vote of confidence to De Gaulle, which was a vote of resolute rejection of communist and anarchist agitation, subversion and disruption.

These fundamental developments, which have hardly been noticed or properly understood in the West, have been on the mind of the communist leaders for quite some time.

While the dream lasted, it was easy for them to rule. People had hopes, they were willing to accept all sorts of privations, and they were not in a mood of rebellion. But now the dream is dead, the faith gone. Communists are still willing to kill for communism, but are not ready to die for communism. And that makes all the difference in the world. It does not suffice to rule.

And the communist leaders, masters of politics and political psychology, realize the inherent mortal danger. This concern is evident in the Sakharov Memorandum:

> "The prospects of socialism now depend on whether socialism can be made attractive, whether the moral attractiveness of the ideas of socialism and the glorification of labor, compared with the egotistical ideas of private ownership and the glorification of capital, will be the decisive factors that people will bear in mind when comparing socialism and capitalism, or whether people will mainly remember the limitations of intellectual freedom under socialism or, even worse, the fascistic regime of the cult of personality."

Aside from the somewhat sensational revelation that Stalin was a fascist, here is the essence of the troubled Soviet peace of mind. But that is nothing new or exceptional. Fifteen years before Sakharov, Milovan Djilas, that "heretic of heretics," driven to despair by the failure of communism in Yugoslavia, exploded in an identical Jeremiad: "If only one revolution—ours—ends in the splendor of the new democracy, that will give a brilliant lustre to the intoxicating idea of the revolution . . . the faith in the new world, in socialism, becomes reality."

But how can communism end in democracy? Dialectically, of course, there is no problem, since, "as we all know," communism *is* democracy! But how do you transform communist reality so that it becomes democratic reality? People, no longer believing in the bright promises of communism for the future, want substantial improvement *now*.

It is easy for a poet and (moderately) heretic communist, Joseph Biermann (East Germany) to exclaim: "Create in reality more happiness, and no longer will you need the ersatz of my words." [145] But the "bureaucrats" are free from such political naiveté. They know that they cannot change reality without renouncing communism, i.e. communist power. And that, of course, is out.

So, the only alternative left is to revive the dream, to divorce communist reality from communism, to exonerate communism from any responsibility for producing communist reality. The failure of communism must thus be attributed to definite historical circumstances, which are now changing. What also must be changed is the West's perception of reality. We must be led to believe that if communism has failed, deceived and betrayed the expectations and trust of mankind, it will nevertheless fulfill its promises in the future.

In any case, the communists must unconditionally keep power in their hands, and the revival of the communist dream must be realized not by destroying communist power, but while preserving it.

8   The Answer to
the Problem: Self-Criticism

Self-criticism is "a mighty instrument in the hands of the party."
ANDREI ZHDANOV

It is in this direction that Stalin, who realized the danger more keenly than anyone else, looked for a solution. Unable to change Soviet policies, he set out to change the West's awareness of Soviet policies and its ideas about world reality. To that effect he needed: (a) an offensive strategy to destroy the West by destroying its values, principles and confusing its thinking, and (b) a defensive (or rather offensive-defensive) strategy to defend the USSR by self-criticism based on the pretense of change in communism. The skillful use and combination of these two strategies could not fail to confuse and politically disarm the West.

Which leads us straight to the communist device of self-criticism, which is at the core of the present communist world strategy. And the most remarkable thing about it is that, to the knowledge of this author, its existence has never even been acknowledged in the West, much less studied, weighed and considered in appraising communist policies and their effects.

The communists use theories that they do not believe in. So, they realized that no amount of dialectic juggling could stop hostility to communism, be it on the part of the newly enslaved (1945), who never wanted it and actively resisted it, or on the part of those who grew up under it and changed their minds after living under it. Any regime, any social and political order, must bring about opposition, criticism, hostility. Communism is no exception. World War II had shown the deep hatred of the Russian people against the communist regime. And then 100 million more people were put under communist rule, which augmented the mass of the dissatisfied and the fuel for "counter-revolution."

Communists have always been afraid of those dialectics which irresistibly make them think of the devil's apprentice who could not stop the forces he conjured up and set in motion. Rosa Luxemburg had from the beginning pointed to the danger that the kind of "criticism" which brought down Tsarist Russia, must stop and be replaced by "criticism" from inside the revolution, by friends of the revolution.

However, the problem was much more acute in 1948 than in 1917. Criticism became the supreme bugaboo: counterrevolution! That is where Stalin put his ingenuity to work. The result was presented in his article: "Criticism and Self-Criticism, Principle of Development of Soviet Society," published under the pseudonym M. Leonov, in the magazine *Bolshevik* of March 15, 1948:

> The Soviet society is a society which is developing under the knowledgeable leadership of the bolshevik party and the Soviet state. Armed with the ability to foresee the course of events, and the ability to follow the line of progress of the general development, the party simultaneously discovers the contradictions which are arising and makes conscious efforts to overcome the opposites, and organizes a determined struggle against everything which tends to hinder our successful advance . . .

> In 1928, in the report to the Central Committee, comrade Stalin said: "We expect . . . from self-criticism . . . to prevent anything 'unforeseeable' in the building of our society . . ."

> The leadership that knows the laws of social development is saving our society from the danger of the spontaneous rise of opposites . . . Criticism and self-criticism is a form of controlling the opposites in the Soviet society, which is implemented through the organizational activity of the party and the state.

> Soviet patriotism could be defined as follows: ". . . keep increasing the power of the Soviet society."

> In the USSR criticism is a force to strengthen society; in capitalism it destroys it.

> In the USSR, the liquidation of antagonistic classes has removed the necessity of criticism by weapons, and the weapon of criticism and self-criticism has acquired greater importance and become the moving force of the development of the Soviet society.

One thing must be said for Stalin's presentation of his "new dialectical principle": there is no ambiguity about it. Under capitalism the enemies of the existing order, the communists, criticize it to destroy it. The "old" must be destroyed, so as to make room for the "new." Under communism, however, the enemies of the existing order must be silenced and made inoffensive at any price. Criticism must be reserved for communists who will practice it so as to preserve the regime, not destroy it. The "old" (communism) now must win the battle against the "new" (anti-communism).

The communists, being future- and progress-oriented, are perennial critics, under capitalism and under communism. What changes is just the nature and function of their criticism. Under capitalism, criticism requires that you destroy your country. Under communism, criticism requires that you strengthen the regime! The communists rule, they criticize themselves; and they consolidate their power.

Whatever the shortcomings and evils of communism, it is here to stay, for there is no alternative to it. Capitalism must be destroyed at all costs, communism must be preserved at all costs. That is the essence of self-criticism. What makes this preposterous thesis so effective, is the fact that it represents not only the official Stalinist line, but also the stand which many Western liberals, "leftist Westerners," have, disgracefully and suicidally, made their own.

The General Line of Communist Self-Criticism

Non-communists may find it difficult to determine what is hostile, destructive criticism and what is benevolent and helpful criticism.

For the communists, masters of deceit and of psychological warfare, the rules of the game of self-criticism were not too difficult to establish.

In the same way as the literature of "socialist realism" has one clear and all-encompassing yardstick: to consolidate Soviet power —communist self-criticism must operate so as to lead to the strengthening of communist power. Communist criticism must make it stronger. In the course of time, some elementary rules have naturally evolved:

1. Communism (socialism) is good, essentially, unalterably;
2. All the evils and troubles of communism stem not from com-

munism but from developments extraneous to communism, which have distorted its true character.

3. The most important thing is that communist *power* must be *preserved* at all costs. All criticism must unconditionally move within this requirement and aim at fulfilling it.

4. Only within the unconditional maintenance of communist power, can the aim of realizing the human content of communism, democratic communism, the merger of communism and freedom, be pursued.

The first point is, of course, basic. We can criticize and condemn Stalinism, Kremlinism, "Iron-Curtainism" (the Overstreets), bureaucratism, dogmatism, the Soviet invasion of Czechoslovakia, etc.,—but never communism, "the Revolution."

In his very enlightening book *I Was an N.K.V.D. Agent*,[146] Anatoli Granovsky tells about the instructions he received from his superiors before being dropped by parachute as a spy: "When you talk publicly against the Soviet Union, . . . follow the harmless line . . . Talk of purges, prisons and the Cheka. But do not draw political conclusions opposed to the Marxist-Leninist philosophy." "I learned," says Granovsky, "that I must convey the impression that the members of the Politburo were unaware of the extreme misery of some of their subjects, that Stalin and his People's Commissars were theorists and idealists whose projects were only imperfectly put in practice and that it is the lesser leaders who abused their power for their own advantage." (p. 184)

Khrushchev's famous "anti-Stalin" speech of February 24–25, 1956 (super-secretly smuggled out of the Soviet Union to be published in full in *The New York Times* of June 5, 1956), was also a typical piece of communist self-criticism: it was not directed agaist communism; on the contrary, Stalin was castigated only insofar as he had hurt communism by the excesses of his zeal and personal ruthlessness, not however on the grounds of humanity, or democracy or from the viewpoint of the people's welfare.

The communist "rebel" and "heretic" Lescek Kolakovski, former professor of philosophy at the University in Warsaw (until 1966), is anything but an innocent in matters of communist dialectics and self-criticism. When his book, *The Man Without Alternative*, (about the possibility and impossibility of being a Marxist) came

out in 1960, he was praised and lionized for his tremendous courage by the usual pro-communist (leftist Western) circles. And yet
the whole book and all Kolakovski's philosophy and criticism is
that of Stalinist self-criticism. "The possibility of a socialist criticism is the necessary condition for a successful refutation of
counter revolutionary criticism." (p. 81).

After publishing the first part of Mihajlo Mihajlov's *Moscow,
Summer 1964,* the editorial board of the Yugoslav magazine
Delo issued (in March 1965) a public recantation following the
standard line of communist self-criticism:

> "The criticism of Stalinism, which we consider inevitable,
> should never be perverted into its opposite. *Stalinism is not the
> logical consequence of the Revolution* but rather something
> which deeply and tragically threatened its noble and historical
> meaning." (Emphasis added)

Even before the Soviet invasion of Czechoslovakia, the line of
communist self-criticism was evident in the approach to problems
both by communists and their liberal helpers, as for instance in a
correspondence between Pavel Kohout, the Czech "liberal" communist, and Günther Grass, the German high-publicity socialist
writer.[147] Kohout was supposed to defend the communist side,
Günther Grass the side of the West. They both followed the line
of communist self-criticism. Kohout, speaking of the evils in communist practice, exonerated communism and accused "police bureaucracy." Günther Grass, claiming that the crisis of democracy
is world-wide ("I too live in a land which knows terror"—Grass
lives in Western Germany), refused to write "from the pedestal of
anti-communism." He denounces anti-communists such as Willi
Schlamm, who is Jewish, as "Nazi remnants." As for the negative
things under communism, it is not "the party" that is responsible,
but "concrete persons."

According to Kohout, the difficulty for all those who want to
"liberate socialism from its Stalinist deformation," is "not to
throw out the child with the bath." The only solution consists in a
"process of an inner renewal of socialism . . . which must begin
in the communist party itself" (p. 85).

The Soviet invasion of Czechoslovakia (August 21, 1968) pro-

duced a massive exercise of communist self-criticism by its communist and liberal critics. Holding a manifestation in Basel
(Switzerland) on September 8, 1968, eighteen days after the invasion, an assorted group of leading European "leftist Westerners" (Friedrich Dürrenmatt, Heinrich Böll, Max Frisch, Günther
Grass, Peter Bichsel, Kurt Marti, etc.) followed, with slight individual differences in emphasis and style, the general line of communist self-criticism in analyzing the invasion and drawing the
necessary conclusions: the liberalization of Czechoslovakia was a
great democratic thing; the Soviet intervention was criminal, undemocratic and unmarxist. Therefore (!) in the interest of democracy we must not fight Soviet communism, but must steer communism in the direction of true Marxism under the guidance of true
Marxists and be alert against the cold warriors, enemies of communism!

A well- known former (?) communist, Wolfgang Leonhard, also
rushed into the fray to save communism after August 21, 1968. He
spoke of Moscow's "police communism" [148] as opposed to "human
communism." In any case there was no room for any struggle
against communism:

> "The lessons from the events in Czechoslovakia are not in a
> revival of the cold war between West and East, or in an indis-
> criminate struggle against communism, but in a clear and un-
> ambiguous differentiation between those communists who have
> committed the crime against Czechoslovakia and those commu-
> nists, who condemn it."

But the first prize for "self-critical" confusion, despair, inconsistency and outright nonsense, goes undoubtedly to the Slovak
writer Ladislav Mnačko,[149] a well-known communist liberal
"rebel" (author of La Septième Nuit, Paris, 1968). After criticizing
the practice of communist Czechoslovakia and the invasion in the
most violent terms, Mnačko concludes that he still believes in
communism and remains faithful to it (p. 229). For the "shame-
ful things" which have happened, the "ignominies," result not from
communism, but from a betrayal of communism: "Force, in any
form, is anti-Marxist, anti-socialist" (p. 246). "There is nothing in
Marx or Lenin to justify the occupation of Czechoslovakia" (p.
243). "The Soviet Union has taken the adventurous path of con-

quest . . ." (p. 235) ". . . which no socialist power can allow itself if it wants to be and remain socialist" (p. 243).

If Lenin, the author of *Leftism, the Infantile Disease of Communism,* were alive today, he would die laughing at the incorrigibility of some communist "idealists."

And Joseph Stalin, the inventor of communist "self-criticism," would be delighted with the workings of his brainchild, operating strictly along the lines of the interests of the preservation of communist power, against all evidence and logic, and in defiance of intellectual probity and moral courage.

In any case, it is not too difficult to tell a communist "self-critic" in action. He will criticize the unimportant, the secondary, the non-essential, or the deficiency of minor officials, their ineptitude, corruption, bureaucraticism and dogmatism, not communism itself and the communist leadership. He will discuss communist philosophical and "scientific" errors, the ills of communist practice, their inconsistency, lack of prophetic accuracy, etc. But the absolute which must be respected at all costs, is communist power. Communism must be "improved" and consolidated, not destroyed. What must be destroyed is the free world.

It should be noted that, like all communist strategic and tactical devices, self-criticism works mainly because the West ignores it. Actually, its chief arguments are very vulnerable. For instance, when they, like Andrei Sakharov, glorify Lenin as the paragon of democracy, tolerance and peace, they unmistakably prove that the communist meaning of those words is dictatorship, intolerance and war, and thus that "humane communism" is in fact "police communism."

For, to speak of "Leninist democracy" is as senseless and brazen as to speak of "Jeffersonian fascism." Lenin's lifework was not to bring about democracy but to make revolution and install communist power as dictatorship "unrestricted by law." To that purpose he never tired of emphasizing (especially in *What Is To Be Done* (1902) and *Leftism* (1919) "the rights and power of the central body against the parts," [150] i.e. military organization, centralism and bureaucratism against democracy.

So, the emergence and rule of Stalin and Stalinism was no "irony of history," but the natural, authentic expression of communism in action. If Stalin "fooled the working class," he did it not by departing from communism, but by implementing it. "Stalin made Lenin's metaphors come true," as Sinyavsky put it.[151]

Is Communism Changing?

All this leads to a crucial question for Western policy-making. It is the problem of the change of communism. The whole (pro-communist) policy of the West has been based on that premise, from the days when Joseph Stalin radically "changed" in 1943 by abolishing the Comintern and permitting "religious freedom" in the Soviet Union, to the present day.

The theory of the change of communism can be reduced to the following proposition: Communism is an international movement, whose strength resides in its monolithism, i.e. the uniformity of its traits in all countries, the adherence to dogma in the approach to all problems, and in the unconditional solidarity of all communists. That has been changed out of recognition. Communism has been broken by the nationalism of the countries where it has been introduced; dogmatism has yielded to pragmatism, and communist solidarity has been replaced by strong trends of national independence, as well as by inter-communist rivalry and serious conflicts. So the theory goes.

On these utterly shallow claims, our policy-makers have based our pro-Tito policy, our pro-Gomulka policy, all of the coexistence policy with the Soviet Union and Red China; our policy of building bridges of trade and culture with the communists, and our policy of rejecting confrontation in favor of negotiation.

First, as everyone knows, everything changes all the time. Twenty-five centuries ago Heraclitus proclaimed that the only thing that does not change is permanent change. So, in that sense, that all existing things change all the time, communism has certainly changed enormously since 1917. (Its most conspicuous change is its fantastic growth. That is the change which most Western experts never see, or consider, in their musings about communism.)

But that is not the issue. The issue is: has communism changed in its essence, has it renounced its aim of world conquest, has it renounced its criminal methods and become civilized, has it from

a movement bound by solidarity, become a polycentric movement, where every regime pursues its own policy (the Djilas-
Rostow thesis), has it moved from dogmatism to pragmatism
and from implacable hostility toward the West to genuine coexistence? Has, finally, the principle of national independence in the
communist world won over the principle of communist internationalism?

To answer these questions, let us first clearly establish the true
character of the communist starting positions. For, obviously, we
can speak of change only if the classics of Marxism-Leninism-
Stalinism had denied any thought of national adaptations of communism, any possibility or acceptability of national diversity, or if
they had proclaimed that the right to national self-determination
was an absolute right. Only in such case, can the present situation
possibly be interpreted as a fundamental change, an unexpected
deviation from communist orthodoxy, a denial of original communist positions, which communists cannot accept and against which
they must rebel and do rebel.

When we turn to the basic teachings of Marxism-Leninism we
can ascertain that the thesis of communist change is clearly and
unequivocally opposed to the very core of communist theory. For
the communist positions on the problems in question have been
established with utter precision:

In 1917 Lenin stated that "all nations will come to socialism,
that is inevitable, but all will not come in the same manner, each
will introduce its own peculiarity into one or another form of democracy, into one or another variety of the dictatorship of the
proletariat." [152]

In *Leftism, the Infantile Disorder of Communism* (1919),
Lenin clearly stated that:

". . . the unity of the communist workers' movement of all
countries will require not the erasing of all diversity, not the
suppression of national particularities . . . but the application
of *fundamental* principles of communism (Soviet power and
the dictatorship of the proletariat), which modifies the details,
adapts them and adjusts them to the national particularities and
those of each country."

Twenty years later, in his report to the Thirteenth Party Congress, Stalin deemed it necessary to return to the theme and quote Lenin:

> "We do not view Marx's theory as something final and unchallengeable; on the contrary, we are convinced that this theory has only laid the cornerstone of this science, which socialists *must* develop further in every direction, if they are not to lag behind life . . . This theory gives only the *general* premises and directives, which are concretely to be applied differently in France than in Germany, and in Germany differently than in Russia."

Communist theory is as unambiguous in regard to the principle of self-determination. In *Marxism and the National and Colonial Question*, which is considered to be the most authoritative work on the subject, Stalin wrote:

> "It should be borne in mind that besides the right of nations to self-determination there is also the right of the working class to consolidate its power, and to the latter right the right to self-determination is subordinate. There are occasions when the right of self-determination conflicts with the other, the higher right—the right of the working class that has assumed power to consolidate its power. In such cases—this must be said bluntly —the right to self-determination cannot and must not serve as an obstacle to the exercise by the working class of its right to dictatorship. The former must give way to the latter."

So, as opposed to the thoroughly gratuitous fable of national communism and the thorough change of communism as a consequence, the simple facts of the situation are that:

Marxism-Leninism never vetoed national differences, but considered the adaptation to national conditions indispensable for the success of communism. So, by adapting communism to national conditions, nobody broke any Marxist-Leninist tenet, nor monolithism. (Communist monolithism is discussed further in the chapter on the Kissinger Plan).

Marxism-Leninism never promoted self-determination as an absolute principle. On the contrary, it subordinated it completely to the interests of the international communist movement. So, it is ridiculous to speak of the violation of the principle of self-determination of communist countries by Moscow. That principle was violated when communist rule was imposed on those nations, jointly by Moscow and the local Czech, Slovak, Polish, Yugoslav, and other communists.

Tito and Djilas (Most Heretical Heretics)

But the whole hoax of the theory of communist "change" can best be evidenced in the examples of Tito and Djilas.

Tito and Titoism

Western liberals have always (since 1941) considered and hailed Tito as a "different" communist. After his expulsion from the Cominform (1948) he became even more "different." The liberalization of communism, with its two components of internal democratization and increased national independence (from Moscow) in international relations, has become the cornerstone of U.S. foreign policy. And communist Yugoslavia has been proclaimed the world champion of communist liberalization (domestic and international), and that with double emphasis.

Joseph Broz-Tito symbolized the emergence of "good," independent, national, democratic, liberal communism. (Former Brigadier Fitzroy McLean wrote a book about him under the title *The Heretic*). And another Yugoslav communist, Milovan Djilas, was the communist heretic of heretics! (C. Sulzberger of *The New York Times* calls him "the chief heretic within Communism's most successful heresy.")

Tito had, by his alleged defense of Yugoslav national interests, defied Stalin, broken up communist monolithism and started a world-wide trend of the development and affirmation of national independence of communist satellite states. As champion of national independence, a communist rebel, he was so different from the communists in Moscow, that he had created a new type of communism, with which we can and must coexist and which we must wholeheartedly support.

On the other end, Djilas was, by his allegedly bold criticism, upturning all communist values and breaking all idols, starting a real revolution within the world communist system. These two heresies, combined and in dialectical conflict, may, regardless of and against the intentions and repression of those in power (the bureaucrats) bring about changes which will produce a communism thoroughly different from the bureaucratic version we have known so far, a communism genuinely democratic, liberal, humanistic—while remaining communist!

There is no need within this study to examine at any great length the facts about Tito, his record (domestic and international), his real policies and place in the world.[153] The simple truth is that Tito, for all the praise that has been lavished upon him, all the help which he has been given, all the disregard for truth and U.S. interests with which he has been propagandized and glorified, has never basically changed. Here are a few highlights of his record:

In 1955 Tito visited Asia. Upon his return, he was interviewed about Yugoslavia's "new" policy. His answer was that it was "the same as six, or seven or eight years ago," i.e. before the break with Stalin.

In June 1956 Tito had, for the first time after being expelled from the Cominform, visited the Soviet Union. One of the main events of the visit was a ceremony in Stalingrad, commemorating the victory of Soviet arms over the troops of Nazi Germany. It is on this occasion that Tito made his famous pledge of unconditional solidarity with the USSR: "Yugoslavia, in time of war as in time of peace, marches shoulder to shoulder with the Soviet people towards the same goal—the victory of socialism." Those words and the report about the ceremony in Stalingrad and Tito's speech were published on the first pages of the main Yugoslav daily newspapers.

However, this went against the liberal theory of Tito's change. So, a well-known and prestigious magazine, *The Reporter,* published an article asserting that the words about Soviet-Yugoslav solidarity were uttered by Marshal Zhukov, and they went so strongly against Tito's sentiments, that "Tito's face was black when he left the platform; and while the Western press gave the Zhukov talk big headlines, the Yugoslavs didn't print a word of it!" [154] Needless to say, the magazine never printed a correction. It continued, supported by public endorsements and recommendations from some leading liberal politicians, to misinform the public and misshape its opinion.

After the uprising in Budapest was crushed, Tito made his famous speech of November 16, 1956, which the liberal mind-conditioners in the West hailed as evidence of his staunch opposition to Soviet interference in the affairs of other countries. The plain truth, however, is that the whole speech is a full endorsement of the Soviet intervention. Tito condemned the West for instigating unrest in Hungary, condemned the government of Imre Nagy for not crushing the revolution with enough determination, praised the Soviet quisling Janos Kadar and comrades as "that which is most honest in Hungary," and concluded that—although he was on principle against foreign intervention—"Soviet intervention was necessary," for it saved communism in Hungary.

Twelve years later, when Tito visited Czechoslovakia, only a few days before the Soviet invasion, again our brains were washed by the liberal opinion-makers. Tito was hailed for going to Prague to, allegedly, put some starch in the spine of liberal communist Dubcek, so that they would oppose the Soviets. Tito himself belied this story by stating, upon his return from Prague: "I did not go to Prague to arouse the Czechoslovaks." He had gone to talk with Dubcek and comrades about the existence of "reactionary and counter-revolutionary elements in Czechoslovakia" and the need "to take a more energetic attitude toward them." [155]

These statements constitute the authentic and incontrovertible outlines of Tito's alleged heresy of national independence and "national communism." Refuting the assertion that Titoism was a new doctrine, Tito had stated as early as 1954: "To put it as an ideology would be stupid. I do not say that out of modesty. It is simply that we have added nothing to Marxist-Leninist doctrine. We have only applied that doctrine in consonance with our situation . . ."

And there is nothing in the whole record of Tito, not one single case that he would in any issue of importance (Korea, Vietnam, disarmament, Germany, colonialism, Cuba, etc.) take a stand different from the Soviet Union and other communists.

As for Tito's receiving over $7 billion in loans and outright gifts from the West,[156] there was certainly nothing heretical about that.

As Anastas Mikoyan, asked to voice his opinion, stated during his visit to the U.S. in 1959: "It is always a very good thing when capitalists give money to communists."

What the West is doing and saying to help and glorify Tito as an independent, "national" communist, does not explain anything about Tito's real policies. But it speaks volumes about those who help him, in defiance of all facts, all evidence and all truth.

Milovan Djilas

As for super-heretic Milovan Djilas, who, according to his Western adulators, should be the most dangerous man in the communist world, threatening both its ideological and political stability and "peace of mind,"—the contrast between liberal propaganda and the truth is as glaring as in the case of Tito.

From 1953, when he published his article "The Beginning of the End and of The Beginning" (in the periodical *Nova Misao* (New Thought) of August 1953), where he denounced Stalinism and bureaucratism but glorified Malenkovism as the beginning of democracy under communism—up to the present day, i.e. his book *The Unperfect Society* (1969), Djilas has, in spite of all his confusion and muddled thinking, never wavered from the positions of pure Stalinist "self-criticism." He has always and without exception "criticized" communism to protect and strengthen it, never to hurt it or destroy it.

As he explicitly stated in *The New Class*, he criticized neither the socialist idea nor did he in any way question communist power. As opposed to the publicity which presented him as a martyr who spent years in a communist jail for his heresies, he enjoyed highly privileged status in jail, which is also evidenced by the fact that he was able freely to write books (which nobody else could dream of doing) and "smuggle" them out to his American publishers!

But, in jail or out of jail, in his articles or interviews, and regardless of the sensational titles and subtitles under which they appeared to make him look as a prophet of the doom of communism and the advent of democracy, the absolutely decisive concern: to preserve communist power is dominant everywhere, without fail and without exception. It is the red thread which binds all Djilas' activity and gives it consistency.

His latest book, *The Unperfect Society* (Beyond the New Class), Harcourt, Brace and World, 1969, is a most resolute defense of communism, for all its spurious anti-communist sensationalism (disintegration of international communism into national states and parties; "Lenin . . . dogma . . . is unacceptable today"; Tito's "acme of callousness and duplicity," the fetters which communist "party monopoly" has imposed on the production forces, etc.).

Djilas pays tribute to "those Marxist achievements that . . . have become part of modern social science and modern thinking." Communism, which he calls a "unique scientific philosophy" has wrought in human society "transformations unparalleled in human history." And the world, after and in spite of all failure of Lenin and the terror of Stalin's rule, is "if not a better place . . . not a worse one." Which, obviously, is the reason that Djilas stresses "Communism's idealistic objectives and . . . the good intentions and qualities of its leaders."

Djilas explicitly exonerates communism for communist ills and troubles. Finally, Djilas disclaims any conceivable anti-communism, although Western liberals have built him into a fighter for freedom and even given him the Freedom House award in New York (November 1968), which might as well have been given to Adolf Eichmann. "I have never considered myself to be an anti-Communist." "This book is not intended . . . as a refutation of Marxism."

All that Djilas wants to accomplish is to abolish "the party bureaucracy's monopoly." But the supreme concern is that no revolutionary action should be taken against communism at any price: "I am opposed to revolutionary means and the use of force in the struggle against Communism."

To believe Djilas, communism is today in the midst of a process of self-democratization. "Communist parties are . . . becoming . . . more democratic." And the Soviet Union is apparently leading. As for Yugoslavia, "Freedom is also radiating from the Communist party . . . from its ranks of honest and thoughtful men."

Djilas says that after being ousted from the party, he "continued to feel that I was a Communist . . . that I was bound body and soul to the Communist Party."

That Djilas still is, and *The Unperfect Society* proves it.

The incontrovertible truth about Djilas is that the alleged heretic is not innovating anything, nor rebelling against communism, nor changing it. He is simply, as a thoroughly trained and conditioned communist, practicing communist self-criticism, i.e. always applying the same Marxist-Leninist guidelines in accordance with the changing power situations in the world.

Instead of changing communism, he is changing the West's mind about communism, playing along with the pet liberal theory of communist change, which allows the communists to remain what they are and the liberals to practice pro-communist policies, based on the claim of communist change.

In discussing communist Yugoslavia's role in championing communist national independence, we must never lose sight of an attitude unprecedented in the history of international relations, which Western liberals never mention. And that is that on June 5, 1945, in a talk with the Soviet Ambassador Sadchikov, the Vice-President of communist Yugoslavia, Edvard Kardelj, invited Soviet occupation:

> "We would like the Soviet Union to consider us as representatives of one of the future Soviet republics and not as representatives of a foreign state, able to solve its problems independently, and that it consider the Yugoslav Communist Party as a part of the All Union Communist Party (b), that is, that our mutual relations be based on the perspective that Yugoslavia will in the future become a component part of the Soviet Union."

After the break between Yugoslavia and the Soviet Union, in June 1948, Kardelj was not liquidated, but remained for almost 25 years first Vice-President of communist "independent" Yugoslavia.

So, clearly, to grasp the truth about the change of communism, we should look not to the communist world, but to the Western liberal mind.

It is amazing that those who readily accept the tale of Titoism as a new trend away from Moscow and toward the U.S., never happened to ask themselves a simple question: who has over the years cheered the "breakup of the communist world empire," of communist monolithism through Titoism, i.e. alleged "national communism"? Conservatives, right-wingers, anti-communists? By no means. The main cheerleaders, the apologists, the ideologues of the so-called decline and disintegration of world communism through Titoism, were and are leftist Westerners, the same ones who spearheaded World War II fraternization with Stalin, made propaganda for him, glorified Tito and justified the murder of Mihailovich. So, how can Titoism and the whole Titoist concept be detrimental to communism and beneficial to the United States?

In 1956 the Titoist strategy was applied in Poland. It worked. Of course, the leftist Western press spoke about a revolution, about the victory of national communist Gomulka over his Stalinist competitors, and similar nonsense. Gomulka only several days after being hailed as the revolutionary national communist, a "Polish patriot of the highest order," showed his true color during the Budapest uprising, when he sent a stern "hands off!" message— not to Nikita Khrushchev and the Soviet Union, which was using its military might to quell the uprising—but to President Eisenhower! Which did not prevent U.S. foreign policy experts of leftist persuasion from promoting "national communism" in Poland as they had in Yugoslavia. Poland was put on the list for foreign aid and in a few years reached the sum of $1 billion. The net result is that on August 20, 1968 Polish "nationalist" communist troops, marched along with Soviet troops to occupy Czechoslovakia.

In the Budapest uprising of October 23, 1956, it was initially the Premier and later "martyr" Imre Nagy, who first issued the order to the regime's police and troops to shoot at the rebels, while Janos Kadar was on the side of the rebels, grinning into the TV cameras. But when Kadar realized that the rebels were going to be the losing side, because the Soviet troops would receive substantial reinforcements and crush the "class enemy," he became the Hungarian champion of the Soviet pacification and normalization of Hungary, and that under the explicit banner of "national independence"! For while Soviet Mongolian troops were installing him in power, this unabashed communist quisling stated that the basis of all his policy would be the "unconditional insurance of the national independence and sovereignty of our country." [157]

In this connection, it should never be forgotten that the first "independent" communist, Tito, was installed in power in Belgrade (October 1944) by Soviet troops under the command of Marshal Tolbukhin.

As for Czechoslovakia, the basic fact about its "liberalization," without which no proper understanding of the events is possible, has been almost totally ignored by the West. And that fact is that the experiment of communist liberalization of January 1968, was launched not to satisfy the demands of the people, but with the consent and blessings of Moscow. Antonin Novotny, the old Stalinist, was ousted and Alexander Dubcek, the liberal, took over, because the first was incompetent and incapable of playing the game of liberalization, and the other was much more flexible. But both were communists, and it was Dubcek who had received thorough training, indoctrination and conditioning for many years, in the Soviet Union itself. In any case, Moscow trusted Dubcek as it trusted Novotny.

There was no misunderstanding between Dubcek and Moscow. The misunderstanding was between Dubcek—and Moscow—and the people of Czechoslovakia. For while he meant communist liberalization, the people meant liberty. And since every tyrant, dictator and oppressor dreams of being popular and adored by the masses which he oppresses, Dubcek could not resist the heady situation which was developing, where he was being both a communist supported by Moscow and a popular liberal democratic leader, supported by the people. He lost control of the situation because he allowed popular demand for freedom to outpace his "liberalization." The Soviets properly felt that communist power in Czechoslovakia was being jeopardized. They intervened, against the will of the people, as they did in 1948 when they were instrumental in killing Jan Masaryk and taking over the government completely.

Which does not make Dubcek an enemy of the Soviet Union, to which he owes everything,* much less a fighter for freedom and for the national independence of Czechoslovakia.

* Which, incidentally, is a fact that Tito did not hesitate to admit at the height of his clash with the Kremlin: "I owe to our Party every achievement

This reality of the polarization of all communists (Stalinist and liberal) on one side and the people on the other side, has asserted itself increasingly. Jan Palach, the young Czech student who on January 18, 1969 burned himself in protest against the Soviet occupation of his country, made it clear that the protest was also directed against Dubcek and the whole liberal clique collaborating with the invader.

The most eloquent (and disgraceful, from the viewpoint of the defense of freedom) testimony of the true character of communist liberals and heretics, is the interview of Pavel Kohout, the leading Czech liberal writer, given during his sojourn in Italy a few days after the Soviet invasion of Czechoslovakia. It speaks volumes and does not need comment in this context:

". . . In my opinion, the worst consequence of the occupation is that the cold warriors will prove that the policy of easing of tensions has failed. I am deeply convinced that this is no proper proof, and if the cold warriors find again people to listen to them, that will . . . it is not easy for me to say it, because I am so unhappy over the situation in Czechoslovakia, but that would be more dangerous than the occupation itself." [158]

To eliminate any doubt about bureaucratic-heretic ("conservative"-"liberal") unity among communists, Gustav Husak, the new champion among the communist satellite leaders, stated in August 1969, talking of the "entry of Soviet troops in Czechoslovakia," that "Czechoslovakia is a fully sovereign, independent state, politically, economically, and militarily." [159]

The Risks and the Rewards

The principle of Titoism, i.e., independent, democratic, liberal communism, has been and remains the key operation of modern Soviet strategy. The game is not without risks. For "heresies" and "deviations" like Tito's, create in communist ranks some confusion and disorientation. They also give to the oppressed hopes of liber-

---

I have made. I was an ignorant young man and the Party took me, educated me, made me a man. I owe it everything." (Tito's official biography by Vladimir Dedijer: *Tito*, Simon & Schuster, New York, 1953, p. 418).

ation and thus produce "counterrevolutionary" thoughts, trends and currents.

So, the communists may have some trouble with the people, as they did in Czechoslovakia. But they take care of those growing pains of communist liberalization by an immediate use of old-fashioned Stalinist force and invasion, without suffering the slightest embarrassment or difficulty from the West. The West usually sends a diplomatic note (serious, of course), expresses regret and sympathy for the victims of Soviet intervention, and voices hopes that some day the oppressed will be free. And that does not unduly upset the Soviet invaders.

So, under present conditions, the rewards of "liberalization" outweigh by far its risks. In the communist camp everybody remains communist, with the same aim, methods and attitude towards the free world and towards the maximal program of communist world conquest. In the West and among the enslaved every new surge of hope is beaten down and betrayed by a new display of Western lack of political intelligence, wisdom and courage. And that is the nub of the whole question. As long as the communists are sure that there is one thing which the West will *not* do—take advantage of the troubles of the USSR and world communism—the strategy of Titoism, derived from the Stalinist principle of self-criticism, will function perfectly, changing our muddled minds and consolidating communist power.

Communist change is but an operation of communist strategy and its ultimate weapon, self-criticism, derived from the communist principle of dialectics. The logic is to assume all roles on the world scene:

—they are the champions of the most ruthless imperialism, but it is a communist, Tito, who is the champion of national independence in the world;

—they are the champions of total dictatorship, unrestricted by law, but then a communist, Djilas, is the world champion of freedom (under communism);

—they are ruthless murderers and violators of freedom, but then a communist, Imre Nagy, stands out as a martyr for freedom!

—their concept of man as well as the concept of spiritual freedom are summed up in the notion of "socialist realism" in literature, which has only one yardstick, to serve communist power, but a man from the Soviet Union, Boris Pasternak, has been hailed as the champion of humanism in our inhuman world.

In other words, they stand for their interests and viewpoints, opposed to ours, and they also stand for ours! How then can they lose? ! And how can we possibly win, when all the roles on the world stage have been taken over by the communists? The only thing left for us is to depart from the stage. That is the necessary conclusion from the application of the communist principle of self-criticism and that is what the policy of coexistence is accomplishing with our full acquiescence.

It is not enough to note that communism has not changed, but it is even more important to bear in mind that as long as the policy of the West is one of accommodation with communism at any price, there is no chance for a substantial change of Soviet policy, nor is there any reason for it. The communists have been so fantastically successful in pursuing their goal of destroying the West and expanding communist power, that any man with a sane mind must ask: why should *they* change?

The communists have one paramount goal: global power. All theories and principles derive from that basic goal, and all changes of their principles and theories derive from the application of the unchangeable yardstick of communist power to changing international power situations.

The inaugurator of the first Soviet "change" (the "popular fronts" in 1935) was kindly "Uncle Joe" Stalin. He was not departing from the maximal program. He was using appropriate minimal tactics dictated by the needs of the situation.

That is what the whole Soviet policy of World War II was about. Stalin had not decided all of a sudden to change everything and become a friend of the West. He simply needed the West so badly, especially the United States, as allies against Hitler and Japan, that his fate depended on it. That is why he had to play the game of alliance, world brotherhood, world democracy, etc. That is why he ostensibly abolished the Comintern and re-established "religious liberty" in the Soviet Union. All this was perfectly spurious and had no practical value whatsoever. Former President Herbert Hoover said very appropriately that "the war-

time alliance with Stalin served only to spread communism and
. . . resulted in "one of the most gargantuan jokes of all history." [160] We cannot blame Stalin for this.

So when Stalin occupied half of Europe in 1945, he was not departing from any previous basic course. He was simply acting as a communist only could and should in pursuance of the maximal program.

When (in 1956) Khrushchev denounced Stalin, he was not deviating or changing. He was doing what any well-trained communist would have done, what Stalin would have done in his place: "criticize" communism to save its face, reestablish its prestige and credibility and disarm the West. Nor was there any change when the kindly grandfather, peaceful coexistentialist and anti-Stalinist, Nikita Khrushchev sent Soviet troops to Budapest. He was simply protecting communist power in that country.

And there was no change in all the years since Khrushchev's removal from power. There was simply adaptation to the changing world situation. If the United States was accepting as compatible with the principle of coexistence the fact that the Soviet Union was stoking the furnace of war in Vietnam (where thousands of Americans have been killed), and at the same time playing the game of nuclear collaboration and building of bridges of trade, mutual understanding and peace—why should Alexei Kosygin or Leonid Brezhnev object?

There was no change of Soviet policy when the USSR let Dubcek dump Antonin Novotny. Just a somewhat bold plunge in the direction of communist liberalization.

In his examination of Soviet foreign policy ("Has Russia Changed?", *Foreign Affairs,* April 1960), Leonard Shapiro concluded that:

"The conduct of foreign policy remains a bold game of political warfare, aimed not at compromise, agreement, equilibrium and relaxation of tensions, but at gaining, more skillfully than ever before, a succession of points on the long road to "world communism."

This is as true and elementary today as it was in 1960.

It is worth concluding this brief analysis of the theory about changing communism by quoting Roger Garaudy, one of the chief ideologues and leaders of the French Communist Party, hailed in the late sixties as a conspicuous dissenter from the official line and apostle of the change of communism into "democratic socialism":

> "Our cause is just, our objectives will be achieved—all the more quickly when our methods have been profoundly changed." [161]

What comrade Garaudy is actually saying is that there is no deviation from the "cause" of communism, nor from the purpose of establishing power "unrestricted by law" in the whole world. What he wants, is only improved methods. And that, the untiring search for new, effective methods to implement the unchanged purpose of communism, is the core of Lenin's maximal—minimal tactics, as it is of Stalin's "self-criticism."

However, if all the tactical and strategic zig-zags of Soviet policy, instead of helping us realize the full continuity and consistency of communist pursuit of world conquest, confuse us and lead us astray to conclusions totally unrelated to what is happening before our eyes—we should not blame Lenin, Stalin, Khrushchev, Brezhnev or any other communist.

The "Breakup of Communist Monolithism"

Against this background, it should not be difficult to see in true perspective the famous slogan-theory about the breakup of communist monolithism, which has become a liberal favorite. This theory unfortunately has been fully accepted in the Kissinger plan and made one of its main pillars. The theory asserts that the strength of communism which consisted in full global unity, was broken by the development of the forces of nationalism in communist countries. Therefore, since unity (monolithism) is strength, and disunity is weakness, communism is weaker today than when it was united and monolithic.

Thus, the theory can be reduced to two chief claims: (1) that power in the communist world is no longer directed from one center, Moscow, but emanates from many centers, and (2) that there is no longer communist international solidarity as it once existed.

Both claims stem from a gross failure of logic or deliberate oversight. The advocates of the theory conveniently forget that as a result of the war, communism had made huge, decisive steps forward, spreading from one country to a dozen countries. Instead of one single communist government in the world, which then automatically must control and direct the work of the communist parties in countries where they are not in power—World War II produced a number of communist governments in half of Europe and in China. By that very fact, it is inevitable that Moscow's control must become less direct. The "breakup of communist monolithism," including open intra-communist disagreements, is a result of the growth of communism, not of its decline.

When we discard the vagaries of the liberal mind and consider the hard facts and evidence about communism and communist policies, we cannot fail to see that, as opposed to the phantasy of communist "change," reality presents the following features:

1. All communists in the world, regardless of their internal feuds, conflicts, divergences, mutual strife and verbal wars, pay tribute to and are led by the same ideology of Marxism-Leninism; which means that

2. All communists in the world do not have as their aim any conceivable compromise or lasting coexistence with the free world, but the destruction of the free world, on the ruins of which, a "better," i.e. communist world (ruthless dictatorship "unrestricted by law," according to Lenin),—is to be erected.

3. Despite all conflicts and divergences of opinion, interpretation and tactics, all communists in the world prefer one another to any non-communist and anti-communist government which could be established in the countries they now rule. No matter how much they may feud, they will protect communist power anywhere against any anti-communist action of the people.

4. Internally the communist regimes have changed only their tactics and appearances (in precisely the measure of the despair and apathy of the masses, let down, betrayed and systematically rejected by the West). But the police system invented and established by Lenin and his bloody hangman Dzerzinsky fifty years ago, has remained the same. The North Vietnamese and the Vietcong today are faithful disciples and followers of the most ruthless

concepts of violence and terror as the best way of ruling the masses. The trials of the Russian writers of the last few years (Sinyavsky and Daniel, Galanskov, Ginzburg, et al.) as well as the defection of Anatol Kuznetsov, and the treatment to which they are subjected, prove to everybody save those determined not to be "swayed by the evidence," that communism has not changed in its attitude toward democracy, human rights and political freedoms.

5. Communist imperialism has not changed either. It seems that every few years, the Soviets themselves must undertake some action to shock us out of our utterly irresponsible pro-communist, coexistentialist euphoria, to show us their true and unchanged Leninist-Stalinist face. In 1956 they invaded and brutally crushed the Budapest uprising. Twelve years later, in August 1968, they invaded Czechoslovakia. The trouble is that the West never learns.

6. The theory of the breakup of communist monolithism and the alleged re-orientation of communist satellites toward the West, is equally ill-founded. Tito's record speaks for itself. As for the newest champion of national independence among the communist satellite leaders, Nicolae Ceausescu, of Rumania, it is noteworthy that in September 1969, after he had been proclaimed and hailed by the West as the greatest living communist heretic, overshadowing Tito himself, the two met at the Roumanian-Yugoslav border and issued a joint statement proclaiming again their unconditional loyalty to international communism and castigating the bourgeois press for its persistent propaganda about some non-existing national communism.

7. The theory about the rise and prevalence of national sentiments and independence among communists in all countries has recently been belied by the purge of some leaders (Dorothy Healy, California, and Gilbert Green, New York) among others, of the Communist Party of the U.S.A., "who have disagreed with recent policies and actions of the Soviet Government." [162]

The communists have no compunction whatever in using any sentiment, any value, any idea or ideal—no matter how abhorrent it may be to them—to promote the cause of communist power. As we mentioned before, Stalin was, in the years preceding World War II, an outspoken Russian "nationalist," since he knew that he could not rely on the loyalty of the masses of Soviet citizens to communism.

At the same time, communists use national sentiments to undermine and destroy anti-communist governments and to install "anti-colonial" regimes.

However, this does not affect one iota the fundamental Stalinist principle that "proletarian internationalism," i.e. "the right of the working class to consolidate its power" is always superior to the national "right to self-determination." That is what the whole Brezhnev doctrine is about and what all communists understand and accept.

This was clearly evidenced as recently as the 24th Congress of the C.P.S.U., in Moscow, March-April 1971. While Gustav Husak's sycophantism was the most reprehensible, since he thanked the Soviet Union for invading his country, his attitude: ("This international help saved our country from civil war and counter-revolution and helped to defend the gains of Socialism." [163]) is 100% Stalinist, as well as Khrushchevist. (Janos Kadar glorified the arrival of Soviet tanks and Mongolian troops on November 5, 1956, as the victory of national independence in Hungary!)

More important for the purpose of the point under discussion is what the two "dissenters" at the 24th Congress had to say. Nicolae Ceausescu of Rumania stated:

"Our party declares against any interference in the internal affairs of other parties, which leads to the weakening of their unity, of their capacity to fight against the class enemy." [164]

It will be noted that his opposition to interference is limited to that which weakens communism. And since by definition any interference by the Soviet Union does not weaken, but strengthens communism in other countries, Ceausescu was expressing approval, not dissent.

Which is precisely the dialectical twist which Tito used when he discussed the Soviet intervention in Hungary which smashed the Budapest uprising. Communist Yugoslavia was emphatically against any intervention, asserted Tito. However, since the Soviet intervention saved communism in Hungary, it was justified.

As for Enrico Berlinger, assistant-secretary-general of the Italian Communist Party, his "dissent" had a distinct Brezhnevist flavor:

> "Our internationalism is based on the recognition of the complete independence of each country and each party. It leaves room . . . for points and motives of disagreement and divergence, but this does not weaken the solidarity in—and commitment to—the struggle for great common objectives." [165]

8. There is not the slightest indication that the attitude of world communism towards the U.S. had undergone any change. America remains the main target of communist total political warfare. On all problems, and especially on the issue of Viet Nam, no observer of any intelligence and powers of observation can fail to notice that world-wide propaganda, psychological and political war is being waged against the U.S.A. The reason is as clear and self-explanatory as can be: The U.S. is the leader of the world; if they destroy her, they have conquered the world.

9. Thus, there is no single point of importance in the characteristics of world communism where any substantial change has taken place. The communists have expanded from 200 million people they ruled in 1941 to the nearly one billion they rule today. That in itself is a momentous change and must necessarily entail deep and far-reaching changes in communist strategy and tactics.

But there have been no changes in communist basic aims, in the devotion of all world communists to the realization of that aim, and the total orientation of all their policies and use of all their resources for that basic aim.

So, the talk about the change of communism in the USSR and the communist satellite countries is devoid of any factual basis. All the changes inside all those countries and their mutual relations are strictly changes of strategy and tactics for keeping communism in power and consolidating it.

The talk about national independence of Soviet satellites is senseless and politically irresponsible, for the simple reason that all the satellite bosses know that their basis of power is not in their people but in Moscow. Therefore, the Western policy of helping the local communists make a going concern of their regimes, allegedly against Moscow, is based on baseless assumptions. The present policy is achieving precisely that which the philosophy on which it is built proclaims: that in the choice between the oppressed peoples who are for freedom and for the U.S., and the communist regimes imposed on them and mortal enemies of the U.S.—the policy-makers have constantly preferred to side with the regimes, against the people.

For the communist side, Titoism, i.e. the liberalization, democratization of communism, its struggle for national independence, is pretense, sham, to deceive and disarm politically their own people and the West. For the free world, or rather its liberals, it is an excuse not to face communism's implacable and unchanged hostility, and thus the obligation to fight it. It is much easier to pretend that communism is changing and thus justify a policy of appeasement and coexistence, which otherwise is absolutely indefensible.

In other words, the U.S. policy of helping communists, based on the theory of the change of communism, is not disrupting, but helping world communism. It is as elementary and incontrovertible as that.

The Fate of the Communist Dissenters

It is in this light that the problem of dissent, opposition and revolt under and against communism can only be properly assessed.

We have seen that among the dissatisfied there is the greatest variety of individuals, motives and purposes. The first distinction which must be made is between the sincere searchers for improvement and the communist "self-critics" who will subordinate every human, spiritual consideration to the supreme one: preserve communist power. This group then cannot be considered as rebels, but as communist agents infiltrated among the true fighters for freedom.

Those who are really concerned about human freedom, must realize the existence of the device of communist self-criticism and its satanic modes of operation, destined to take the wind out of their sails, to steal the thunder of their indignation and revolt and channel them into submission to communist power. Unless he is aware of the trap and strong enough to resist pressure, a sincere seeker of freedom may, unbeknownst to himself, become a consolidator of the spiritual jail which is strangling him.

That is apparently what has happened to Mihajlo Mihajlov, who started out by writing *Moscow, Summer 1964* and ended—in spite of all his dialectic juggling and contortions—as a typical "self-critic" of communism. In his essay "What we want and why we keep silent," [166] Mihajlov says that "the struggle for freedom in one's own society is at the same time a struggle for the freedom of all mankind." (Who can disagree with that?) However, intellectuals in communist countries must keep silence; they are "condemned to silence."

In the free West intellectuals ("from Sartre to Hochhuth") can criticize their society "without running the danger of being jailed or deprived of their means of subsistence." That fact, declares Mihajlov, creates respect in the socialist countries and thus cannot be used against the West!

Now, in socialist countries, free criticism of existing conditions is impossible. And that being so, an intellectual from the socialist world who would openly speak to Western public opinion, would somehow feel like a traitor! "That feeling of treason is a more decisive factor than reprisals, to which the intellectuals in socialist countries are usually subjected." Intellectuals under communism keep silent because they fear "that our struggle for freedom may jeopardize the struggle for freedom in capitalist countries" (!!)

For the struggle for freedom is not a struggle for capitalism. It is a struggle for Christian, non-communistic socialism. "I have no sympathies for communist ideas, but when communists are persecuted in the Western world, I become a communist" (p. 248).*

"We keep silent," concludes Mihajlov, "for fear of making the struggle for the liberation from the pressure of the economic powerholders of the West, more difficult. And we wish we had that

* This is an essentially Leninist-Stalinist attitude, succinctly expressed by Mao Tse-tung: "No matter whom you follow, so long as you are anti-communist, you are traitors."

The same philosophy was echoed by the secretary general of the leftist Community of European Writers, Vigorelli, at the Conference of European Writers held in Leningrad in August 1963: ". . . One does not have to be a communist, but one must not be an anti-communist. Who declares himself as an anti-communist, is already a fascist."

which free thinking people have in the West—in the first place the possibility of free thought and a free press. Then we would not have to keep silent any longer . . ." (p. 251)

In other words, in Mihajlov's perverted "self-critical" logic, free criticism is proper in "capitalist" countries, because it is permitted. But it is improper or rather tantamount to treason in communist countries, because they do not permit it. The only course left is to beg the communist tyrants to permit free criticism!

Mihajlov has apparently never asked himself: what kind of men fight against tyranny only with the license of the tyrants, and what results can they achieve?

The Crucial Question

Which brings us to the crux of the whole question: are communism and freedom compatible? Everything depends on this.

If they are, if it is possible, even in the future and gradually, if not today—immediately—to have at the same time communism and freedom, then the course of coexistence and the gradual change, evolution of communism towards freedom, may be viewed as justified.

But if there is no possible compromise between freedom and communism, then all the policies of coexistence and all the hopes of the gradual evolution of communism towards freedom are baseless and irresponsible.

The question is obviously of decisive importance, for the fate of all the intellectual ferment, dissatisfaction, opposition and revolt under communism depends on it.

The communist stand on the problem of freedom and communism has been established once and for all. It is simple, utterly cynical, shameless and unchangeable. Possibly the bluntest formulation had been put forward by Ernst Fischer, the well-known Austrian communist veteran in a recent interview in the German weekly magazine *Der Spiegel*: "Communism is Democracy." [167]

Therefore, anything that might endanger communist power— and freedom of thought, discussion of the printed and spoken word, endangers it—is by definition undemocratic. Conversely, anything that contributes to communist power, even if it is the most rigid control and restriction of freedom, is automatically proclaimed democratic.

Thus, freedom of discussion under communism is solely, strictly and exclusively the right to think and devise new ways and means of consolidating communist power under constantly changing conditions.

It is as simple and elementary as that.

No communist has ever taken a different position, nor can any communist ever take a different position as long as he remains a communist. Communism, in theory and in practice, is total dictatorship unrestricted by law. How can human reason then conceive of freedom under communism? Unfortunately, and to its lasting disgrace, it is only the West which toys with the idea of somehow reconciling communism and freedom. The communists do not.

In 1950, Tito, to lend some credibility to the fantastic stories about Yugoslavia's democratization, spread by his Western idolators, had announced the liberalization of the regime. But only after a few short weeks, the chief of the secret police, Alexandar Rankovic, reminded the public of Tito's warning of August 1949 that "only one thing . . . mattered today: who is for socialism and who is against socialism."

A few years after coming to power, Mao Tse-tung announced a new policy of spiritual freedom in Red China, inviting "a hundred schools of thought" to bloom. But the buds had hardly begun to sprout, when Mao chopped several times a hundred heads and the schools of thought never materialized.

In November 1962 the champion of anti-Stalinism, Nikita Khrushchev, announced a policy of liberalization in Soviet literature and arts. But after a few short weeks, he fulminated against those who would indulge in "free" literature and arts:

> "The press, radio, literature, music, the cinema, and the theater are a sharp ideological weapon of our Party. And it sees to it that this weapon is always in fighting trim and hits the enemy without fail. The Party will not allow anyone to blunt this weapon or weaken its effect." [168]

In 1966 Eastern Germany had a new minister of education, comrade Gysi, who announced that the authors in the German Democratic Republic had "full freedom of creative work and ex-

perimentation." However, he did not forget the fine print:
". . . of course, only in accordance with the wishes of the
Party." [169]

In December 1966, twenty-one Polish authors published an appeal for artistic freedom. According to *The New York Times* (December 8, 1966), "Zenon Klisko, Politburo member with special
responsibility for ideology and culture, at a Congress of Polish
culture last October . . . said, in effect that writers were free to
write any way they choose, but the subject matter must not run
counter to approved ideology."

Recently (December 1969) the Philosophical Society of Serbia,
facing the fact of ever increasing repression of cultural life: (1)
official condemnation of the ideological "extremism" of the critics;
(2) interdiction of published literary works and works of art; and
(3) preventive censorship (in the press, theater, film and television) organized a Conference to discuss the basic aspects of cultural life in communist Yugoslavia, under the overall theme of
Socialism and Culture. According to keynoter, Sveta Lukic, the
repression in culture had in the last few years surpassed all that
had been done in the previous twenty. About one hundred leading personalities and representatives of cultural institutions and
organizations had been invited. Over three hundred turned up at
the first session. At the second session, there were over one thousand! Understandably, the authorities were alarmed. The (communist) Rector (President) of the University of Belgrade, Dr.
Branko Pribicevic, found that not only concepts and views hostile
to the existing order in Yugoslavia, prevailed, but that their forces
were getting organized. Therefore, he drew the sharpest distinction between the "struggle of opinions" (which was fine) and political struggle, which was intolerable: "We cannot view political
struggle as if it were an academic debate." Political action must be
encased in the known and established Marxist-Leninist "vision of
the future world towards which we are striving." According to Dr.
Pribicevic, the Yugoslav "League of Communists" (C.P.Y.) is "the
main factor of freedom and democracy in this country." Therefore,
clearly, who is against the policy of the League, is automatically
against freedom and democracy, for what does not fit into communism, is not freedom and democracy! The dissenters, astutely
remarked this Yugoslav communist official, were interested not in

(communist) democratization, but in democracy. Instead of being content with communist liberalization, they demanded "freedom for everyone" and "true freedom." Those, of course, were "bourgeois" categories, which the communists could never accept.

Evidently there cannot be the slightest doubt about the stand which the communists take on the problem of freedom and communism, nor is any vacillation detectable. The confusion is on the side of the West, and it seems that no amount of factual evidence or official communist pronouncements or policies can affect the totally wishful belief of some Western circles in the improvement of communism, nor shake their determination to pursue a policy of coexistence, based on it.

An undoubtedly valuable documentary publication of the U.S. Senate Internal Security Subcommittee under the title "Aspects of Intellectual Ferment and Dissent in the Soviet Union," [170] is unfortunately deeply afflicted by the belief in the improvability of communism and the possibility of peaceful coexistence with it. In the foreword, the late Senator Thomas J. Dodd, generally considered a conservative and a staunch anti-communist, spoke of the

> ". . . hope for the peaceful evolution of totalitarian Communist society into a more open society which will . . . be more responsive to popular needs and the popular will, less conspiratorial and less prone to engage in subversion and aggression abroad. With such a society the free world would have no difficulty in achieving that degree of basic understanding essential for peaceful coexistence." (p. 8)

The author of the study also seems eager to put a strong disclaimer on any possible conclusion about the downfall of communism ("predictions on such points or on any points about Russia are games for fools"). He just points to "the existence now in the Soviet Union of a body of educated, public-spirited and informed people who . . . must be persuaded by real facts into a rational and honorable support of a state, one which can be depended upon to uphold freely and unreservedly its constitutional and legal commitments." (p. 81)

The insistence of the author of "Intellectual Ferment" that protest in the Soviet Union has absolutely no revolutionary character, is "not against the political system," but strives for the "redress of grievances within the framework of the Soviet Constitution and the existing institutional order, the validity of which they did not question" (p. 36)—is hardly in accordance with known facts.

First, among the critics and dissenters there are people of the most diverse ideas, temperaments, political awareness and maturity. Few have been as explicit as Valery Tarsis, an author who escaped from the USSR a few years ago and told Edgar Ansel Mowrer in June 1967 in Frankfurt:

> "Within the next few years we shall destroy tyranny in Mother Russia in spite of anything the United States administration can do to save it." [171]

More important is the relationship between spiritual revolt, literary protest and political action. As the Swiss newspaperman and author Lorenz Stucki astutely remarked in the weekly *Weltwoche* of January 4, 1963, the Soviet leaders "have hardly forgotten that in Budapest it was the "searching" communist authors and students who, without being properly aware of it, sparked an anticommunist revolution. The road from a spiritually rebellious poet to the author of a manifesto against the regime which suppresses his spiritual development, is short."

So, in taking seriously the literary protests and expressions of dissent, the communists are right, and those in the West who stubbornly wish to see in them strictly loyal communist opposition, are wrong.

The gist of the matter is: if we want freedom, we must do away with communism. If we want to preserve communism, we are practicing deceit and self-deceit when, in the same breath, we speak of freedom. That is the essence of the problem. For communism is not changing in any vital aspect and certainly not in its attitude towards freedom.

As far as the West is concerned, Karl Radek was apparently right when he said (to Charles Bohlen) that it would never understand bolshevism. And as far as the dissenters themselves, the critics of communism, are concerned, they must choose either freedom *or* communism, for they cannot have both.

The communists will always permit all "freedom" whose beneficiaries strictly and unconditionally observe the rules and postulates of communist power. Under such conditions, they can discuss socialism, culture, arts, human problems, even world events, anything, but only and exclusively from the positions of established communist power, of "socialist realism" or communist "self-criticism." Any discussion outside of that frame of reference, is tabu, for it is not considered discussion, but political action, insurrection.

The dissenters, critics and rebels must make up their minds. They can decide to spend their lives playing little games, producing essays, stories or novels, bold enough to suggest that under communism everything is not 100% perfect, but drawing no definite conclusions, condemning nobody, calling for no action; they can spin out analyses of super-refined irony, they can indulge in toothless criticism, in abstract protestations of democratic loyalty, unrelated to the existing reality of communist oppression. All this they can do, but it will not hurt communism one bit, nor will it advance freedom one step. It only may create and spread demoralization and hopelessness. And such critics, instead of gaining self-respect, will lose it completely and gradually sink in the gutter of communist-licensed liberalization and democratization, while the noose around their spiritual necks tightens.

Or, they can decide to fight for real freedom, without communist license, but against communism, in defiance of all its rules of "socialist realism" and the restrictions of its "self-criticism." They can struggle to be free to create what their conscience tells them and their talent enables them to write, thus gaining meaning and fulfillment to their lives and influencing events.

The choice obviously is not easy. But what vital problems was man ever able to solve easily? In the last resort, the decision depends on their values, and on the moral fortitude and solidarity of all freedom fighters on both sides of the Iron Curtain. The two basic questions are: what kind of life is worth living, and is man able to shape his destiny, or is he reconciled with being a powerless object of the winds of change and "historical" forces sweeping the world.

The dissenter and critic who decides that, after all, the main thing in life is to be physically alive, no matter how oppressed, how humiliated, how deprived of the most elementary attributes of human dignity he may be—should stop posing as a critic of communism and a fighter for freedom, either spiritual or political.

And if the individual makes the decision to live a life worth living, then he has no right to delude himself and others that it can be realized within communism, within communist legality, within the socialist system.

The Polish communist philosopher Lescek Kolakovski, brought forth the crux of the question when he stated (in an interview with the German magazine *Der Spiegel*)[172]

"If we had to admit that socialism can exist only where culture is trampled underfoot, that would be an admission, that socialism is impossible."

The communists will, of course, never word it that way, but that is precisely the truth of the matter, the inescapable consequence of the confrontation of freedom and communism. Communism is rigidity, restriction and suppression of all freedom and all cultural development, in the interest of communist power. Being in its core contrary to the values and all the noble impulses which make man, communism cannot survive under freedom. It needs the protection of force, of oppression, of terror. It can survive only by force, by utter violation of truth, by total distortion of the most elementary human decency.

Freedom today is a global problem, and its solution depends mainly on the United States. But the role of the dissenters and rebels under communism and the influence they can bring to bear on the course of events depend on their being made aware of the incompatibility between freedom and communism.

It is less dishonest to toe the line of communist official "socialist realism" than to pretend to fight for freedom while actually knowing that all communist-regulated, -licensed and -approved "struggle for freedom" is, is a service to communist oppression, tyranny and slavery.

And those who cannot reconcile with a life without freedom, must clearly realize that the communist prison* must be torn down.

---

* "The whole place is a prison" was the verdict of a young Russian interviewed for English television, about the USSR. (*New York Times*, Nov. 17, 1967)

PART FOUR

Liberalism

★

9 Vietnam

[This chapter was written early in 1968. Except for a few adaptations imposed by developments, the author found no reason to change anything pertaining to the essence of the problem of Vietnam.]

"Mr. Nixon said that any softening of policy toward Communist China or any hint of recognition of Peking would be the "straw that broke the camel's back" in Southeast Asia. Anything less than a get-tough policy, he said, will result in a complete Communist take-over."
The New York Times, April 17, 1964

"If America gives up on Vietnam, Asia will give up on America . . .
"The battle for Vietnam will determine whether the Pacific will become a Red sea."

RICHARD M. NIXON
(February 25, 1965, in Chicago)

In the controversy which has been raging for years about the war in Vietnam and the sub-questions which compose it, in all the acrimonious debates and irreconcilable positions taken of the issues, two facts stand out undisputed:

1. The problem of our intervention in Vietnam has affected all areas of our national life. It is today the nucleus in which all our problems are contained or mirrored.

2. It has shattered the basic unity of the nation and created deep rifts in its mind and soul.

With our present foreign policy, our military intervention in Vietnam will turn out to be a complete failure. Instead of guaranteeing the independence of South Vietnam, it will pave the way for the communist takeover of that country. And instead of creating conditions for peace, it will create conditions for and inducements to new aggressions.

The present analysis, written in April of 1968, at the moment of President Johnson's peace offer to North Vietnam (coupled with his announcement that he would not seek reelection), is not conditioned by the time element. It pertains to the essence of the war in Vietnam, and its validity does not depend on any particular developments within the war nor any of its particular aspects or phases.

Until recently, it seemed that in facing its new tasks in a revolutionary age, and in spite of all the errors and reverses of U.S. foreign policy as well as the rise of new domestic problems, the U.S. could still rely on a national consensus on some elementary values and principles which Americans shared today, as they did in 1776.

Vietnam Poses All Questions Anew

Vietnam, i.e. our intervention against communist aggression in Vietnam, has shattered whatever unity existed in the early sixties. Instead of uniting us, the war effort has produced unprecedented disunity. Instead of firming and expanding the national consensus, it has made every position and concept questionable and opened a debate on practically all national problems.

Our position, role and responsibility in the modern world; our place and mission in history; our foreign policy; our military policy; our basic stand on communism; our relationship with Asia; our relations with Allies in the various defense pacts which we have formed around the world (NATO, CENTO, SEATO, etc.); the related problem of fulfillment of our treaty obligations and the preservation of the world's trust in our pledged word; the relationship between our domestic policies and our foreign commitments; the problem of morality and war; the political, social, economic consequences of the war in Vietnam; the problem of the basic philosophy, educational standards and ideals for the youth of America—all these and many other questions are encompassed by or mirrored in the problem of our intervention in Vietnam.

The debate on Vietnam has created deep splits in public opinion, cutting through the lines of outlook and philosophy, liberal and conservative bent of mind, religious beliefs, national origin, color, etc.

While the complexity of the situation is staggering and the danger of oversimplification close at hand, there seem to have been two factors which were determinative in producing a situation unique in U.S. history.

Among those who in 1964 voted for President Johnson were elements who expected him to make an end to the war in Vietnam as soon as possible, at any price. Instead, President Johnson, under the pressure of the responsibilities of power, pursued a policy which in the public mind was identified with the name of the defeated Republican candidate, Barry Goldwater, labeled and vilified as "warmonger." Necessarily and increasingly, a part, the most aggressive, vociferous and ruthless part, of the support for President Johnson, turned against him with the same hatred and hostility they had previously evinced toward Barry Goldwater. Feeling "cheated" in their peace-at-any-price expectations, they provided the emotional fuel to inflame the passions, whip up rabid extremism and transform differences of opinion into irreconcilable, dogmatic positions on vital issues facing the nation.

The other factor is the very conduct of the war. To yield to communist aggression in Vietnam was one possible course, which, no matter how detrimental to U.S. interests, was nevertheless unambiguous. This course would have endeared President Johnson to the communists and their liberal followers, but it would have solidified the opposition to such policies.

Concomitantly, the opposite course, of resisting communist aggression would, for all communist-liberal opposition, have won the approval and the support of the overwhelming majority of the American people, thus preventing a nation-wide split. But President Johnson did neither. He decided to oppose communist aggression and impose tremendous sacrifices upon the American people, but he did it in a way which was encouraging communist aggression, since he never rose to waging war for victory. The decision to resist aggression cost him the support of the extreme Left. But the decision to wage an extremely costly war without the only conceivable justification of winning it, lost countless millions of patriots, or created deep misgivings in their ranks.

The inevitable consequence of such policy was that, in the words of (the then former Vice-President) Richard Nixon, "bitter dissension has torn the fabric of American intellectual life, and whatever the outcome of the war the tear may be a long time mending." [173] President Johnson himself blamed the "dissension and criticism" dividing the nation for the difficulties in the conduct of the war in Vietnam.[174]

With the passing of time and the rise in the emotional temperature of the participants, the debate about Vietnam degenerated into a battle of clichés, headlines and slogans, which achieve nothing except making the confusion worse, the search for a solution in Vietnam more difficult, and the forging of a new, sensible U.S. foreign policy much more complex.

The war in Vietnam is not a separate problem, which burst on the scene like a comet and will disappear as soon as the rifles, grenades and guns grow silent. It is an inseparable part of communist world strategy, and on the other hand it is inseparable from our foreign policy. The grave situation which we face today has been brought about not only by communist aggression, i.e. by the existence of communism, but also, and decisively, by our foreign policy and the accumulation of its effects. The paramount importance of foreign policy in the present world is too evident to elaborate on. It necessarily affects and determines, directly or indirectly, all areas and all concerns of our national life.

With the problem of Vietnam, the moment of truth has arrived for the U.S. policy-makers and for the American people, who have to suffer its consequences. For if it was possible until now to pursue a policy of self-deception, of make-believe, of incongruity, of moral contradiction—reality has finally caught up with us. Whether we like it or not, we have to face its consequences and its true, dead-end face: Vietnam.

The leaders of world communism can be calm and content. For the war in Vietnam has confirmed overwhelmingly the correctness of communist strategy of using local armed conflicts to bring us every few years to the conference table to negotiate and sign away parts of the world and parts of our will to live.

But what about us? What do we do and what are the lessons we must learn from the experience of Vietnam?

In our age of brainwashing, mind-conditioning, and "expertocracy," we can bridge the gap which exists between the hard facts of the world we live in today and the tragically inadequate ideas we entertain about it only by going to the elements of the Vietnam problem and analyzing them rationally.

The Elements of the Problem

Two questions have been kept on the stage by the communists and their unconscious dupes and willing associates: the question of war and peace (with special emphasis on the relationship between morality and war) and the question of our involvement in South Vietnam (do we "have business being in Asia" and waging war in it, or should we pull out our troops, "now"?)

The great majority of the American people do not share the views of the pacifists and "moralists" nor their motives and aims.

Do We Have Business in Vietnam?

It is well known that the communists and their allies of various shades are opposed to the U.S. involvement in Vietnam, simply because they resent and oppose any attempt to prevent the communist conquest of the world. Unfortunately, they are not the only ones to argue this point. There are a number of well-meaning Americans—ill-informed or not very deep thinkers—who in 1968 think in terms of 1787 and believe that all our troubles and problems as a nation of 200 million people and leading power in the world, stem from "meddling" in the affairs of other countries and continents. "Foreign entanglements" are our undoing! What we should have done, is stay at home, mind our business and tend our gardens. The isolationists, regardless of their motives, are thoroughly and very naively wrong.

The consideration of the hard facts of international life at this time, i.e. the fact that the war in Vietnam is not a local, strictly Vietnamese affair, but a confrontation between world communism and the United States, makes it obvious how necessary it is for the U.S. to be there and how irresponsible it would be to stand aside and away from it.

Morality and War

The war-haters and peace-lovers who oppose the war in Vietnam, i.e. the U.S. military action against communist aggression in

Vietnam, are not against every and any war, any violence done by man to man, or nation to nation, but they are specifically against U.S. military intervention in South Vietnam, which is opposing U.S. troops to communist troops. That is what arouses their ire, what offends their humanity, therein lies, in their estimation, the horrible offense against humanity and morality.

Many of the professional war-haters, draft-card burners and peace-lovers are certainly too young to remember or have any personal knowledge of World War II. Or they were too young to be able to take a position on war and peace at that time. But many of the key organizers of propaganda and agitation, the most vicious accusers of the U.S., were mature men in World War II and not only were they never heard to protest "man's inhumanity to man" in the U.S. war-making at that time, but they were enthusiastic bellicists and considered the slogan of "killing the Nazis" as the epitome of military wisdom and necessity, as well as a morally acceptable and commendable concept.

Why and wherefore the about-face in the case of Vietnam?

It suffices to pose the question.

As for those born after World War II, they may to an extent be excused for their lack of knowledge about that war, although every new generation knows and must know that the world is older than they are and that the basic problems of man and mankind did not start at their birth. But, there is certainly no excuse for their one-sidedness, and that in favor of the enemy.

No decent human being can rejoice in killing, especially not when the victims are non-belligerent, defenseless citizens. But no decent human being can passively tolerate the crimes committed by evil men, without being irresistibly impelled to oppose evil. Often there is no other way to stop evil but inflict it on the evil-doers. Therefore no decent human being can condemn the war actions of his own people while overlooking, passing in silence or condoning the deliberate, utterly inhuman crimes of the enemy. (God gave iron to man, says a famous Serbian poem, but he also gave him the responsibility to decide what purpose he will use it for. If evil men will forge chains to enslave their fellow-men, there must always be those who will use it to forge swords of justice to stop the enchainers.)

Nobody knows whether war as an instrument of settling disputes among different groups of men, can be abolished. But it is certain that it cannot be abolished by yielding to those who have utter contempt for human dignity and human lives and whose concept of power is "dictatorship unrestricted by law" (Lenin), and condemning those whose concept of power is to guarantee "liberty and justice for all."

War cannot be defended on strictly moral grounds and by absolute ethical standards. But since the beginning, force has had to be used to limit or impair the physical integrity or freedom of some (evil-doing) individuals, because there was no other way to protect other people and guarantee the blessings of civilized life. Effective resistance to evil includes the use of force. Nothing encourages evil as much as non-resistance to evil.

To ignore these basic truths and proclaim absolute morality in the face of communist total world-wide aggression, is not to promote morality, but to pave the way for the destruction of the U.S., for the extinction of all morality and freedom in the whole world and for the imposition of the rule of crime throughout the world.

A policeman using his gun to stop a crime being committed or a criminal trying to escape, is not the equal of a criminal from any viewpoint, including the moral one. And by the same token, a soldier doing his duty and using his rifle, stands at the opposite end of the spectrum from the criminal who shoots to inflict harm and gratify his low passions and instincts.

Only enemy agents, traitors or weak-minded individuals can equate U.S. soldiers in Vietnam with the criminals whom they are trying to stop and deter.

In other words, the problem is not whether war itself, i.e. the killing of people by other people is moral, for it is not. The problem is does the war action serve to defeat the forces of evil and prevent more evil than it inflicts and causes? And concretely, in the case of Vietnam, the question is which is the worse evil: U.S. military action or communism?

So today, to object on moral grounds to U.S. military action against the armed forces of communism, the most immoral, evil and murderous power system in history, is totally immoral or totally insane.

The Real Issues

But the questions of our role in South Vietnam and the morality of war are not the real problems. To dispose of them is just to clear away the heaps of communist propaganda and mutual confusion which have accumulated in the course of the whole anti-Vietnam agitation, so that we can approach the real questions with a meaningful discussion in view.

The real national picture is far more complex than the opposites of intervention vs. "hands off," war vs. peace-at-any-price, and the morality or immorality of our military involvement in Vietnam. It is not that the U.S. Government and all patriots are in favor of intervention and against it are only communists, traitors, pacifists and useful innocents. The real controversy and the real problem are mainly among Americans who realize that the intervention was proper and necessary and that our military action was not "immoral."

U.S. Official Position on the War in Vietnam

Insofar as it is possible to ascertain a definite official view of the conflict in Vietnam and discern a definite policy, the following could be considered as a fair and adequate presentation:

The conflict in Vietnam and the need for our intervention stem from the military aggression of the communist regime of North Vietnam against the republic of South Vietnam, with the apparent aim of imposing communism in that free half of the country.

This we cannot allow because it is contrary to our basic concept of the nature of international life and the ways international disputes should be settled. Besides, we have been invited by the government of free South Vietnam to support their struggle for the preservation of their independence and we must fulfill the obligations we have assumed.

Third, South Vietnam, like the whole of Asia, is a strategically important area that affects U.S. security, so that we could not possibly remain passive witnesses of the military conquest of that area by the communists.

Realizing that a communist military conquest of South Vietnam would have far-reaching consequences, we have evolved a plan of action which consists of several operational phases:

First is U.S. military action against the invader from the North and his communist allies in South Vietnam (the Vietcong). Since we have no quarrel with and do not intend to overthrow any regime or destroy any nation in the world, our military intervention does not aim at a victory over communism, i.e. at a full military victory which would unavoidably entail the downfall of the communist regime. No, our objective is limited: to stop communist aggression. Therefore our struggle, our war, also is limited. It serves not to win, to achieve victory, but just to stop aggression by teaching the communist aggressors the lesson that they cannot win and impose their will by force, because aggression is too costly. They must be induced to realize that aggression does not pay, and thus change their minds, mend their ways and make an end to their war to subvert and conquer South Vietnam.

Once that objective of our armed intervention is achieved by the display of our commanding military superiority, the road would be paved for negotiations, leading to a peace conference to settle the problem of Vietnam by the participation of all parties involved, South Vietnam, North Vietnam, the Vietcong, and of course the representatives of the interested big powers.

The main objective of the U.S. at that conference, would be to strike a compromise between the "aspirations" and "just claims" of North Vietnam, and the concern for establishing guarantees to preserve the national independence of South Vietnam and thus lay the foundations for a lasting peace and peaceful development of Southeast Asia.

One of the basic moves in that direction would be to form a "government of national unity" in South Vietnam, broadly representative of all segments of the nation and of all trends of opinion and forces in the country. The next would be to guarantee the neutrality of reorganized South Vietnam by international agreement, similar to the one regarding Laos (1962).

To give a proof of its good will and peaceful intentions, the U.S. would: (a) agree to withdraw its troops from Vietnam, and (b) finance a huge project for the economic development of the Mekong basin, to the extent of $1 billion (as President Johnson offered in his speech of April 7, 1965). Destined to serve the interest of all people of that area, it would bring about international cooperation, contribute decisively to blunt the edges of ideological conflict and create a sense of collaboration for common interests.

This way of solving the present conflict in Vietnam would by its very success serve as a warning and deterrent to the communists everywhere and an encouragement to all free nations in their struggle to preserve their freedom and independence. It would give to the whole world a shining example of the benefits of international cooperation, as opposed to the policies of national rivalries and ideological warfare.

Clearly, our Vietnam policy rests on a number of basic assumptions:

a) that the war in Vietnam is essentially a local military aggression which can and must be solved locally and mainly by military means. Insofar as political and ideological overtones are present, they obviously stem from poverty and economic underdevelopment. The Mekong project and other similar projects would, by eliminating poverty, also eliminate political trouble.

b) that the main problem and source of trouble in that area is military aggression and that the problem will be solved if by the use of superior military power we force or induce the communists at North Vietnam (as well as the Vietcong) to desist from aggression and revert to peaceful means;

c) that the aggressive traits of communism will be extirpated or at least tamed by our military superiority, so that the problem will change after military peace has been attained;

d) that our accent on aggression means that we are not concerned with communism, i.e. the communist regime in North Vietnam, or with whatever regime may develop or be created in South Vietnam after aggression has been stopped;

e) that we rely on communist good will and communist respect for their word to keep their promises and fulfill assumed treaty obligations;

f) that communism is undergoing deep and radical changes, evolving from the use of force and imperialistic ambitions and aspirations to peaceful methods and concern for domestic improvement. The deep conflict between the USSR, which is the carrier of the new approaches and policies, and Red China, which remains ferociously "stalinistic," aggressive and bellicose, serves to underline the depth and importance between acceptable (coexistential) and unacceptable (militant) communism and thus indicates our vital interest to cooperate with the first and resist the second.

Logically, we must discourage militant, forceful, violent, bellicose communism of the Mao Tse-tung variety and encourage the peaceful, reasonable, pro-Western, Titoist, Libermanist (pro-capitalistic), Kosyginist (technocratic, consumer-oriented) brand of communism, with which we can cooperate for the attainment of world peace.

In Southeast Asia, the positive program of action, especially in the Mekong area, would doubly contribute to peace in that area and in the world: by turning North Vietnam and South Vietnam from internecine struggle to collaboration, and by raising the standard of living of the people, thus eliminating the roots and sources of revolutionary nationalism and militant, bellicose communism.

Evidently, our policy in Vietnam stands or falls with the validity or invalidity of these premises. How true are they? Do the proclaimed goals of our foreign policy make sense and can they be attained by our present policies? How accurate are our appraisals, how realistic our goals, how adequate our means and methods?

As the following analysis will show, our premises are imaginary and wishful, our appraisals erroneous, our goals unrealistic, our means and methods inappropriate.

The Nature of the Conflict in Vietnam

The conflict in Vietnam is not a strictly military conflict for local territorial gains. It is part of the global and total warfare which the communists are waging against the free world, above all the United States, the leading world power, the only one which can prevent the realization of their aims. The military struggle in Vietnam is just a phase, an aspect of the basic conflict between communism and free men and nations.

So, it cannot be solved exclusively on the military plane. Military operations make sense only as tools of political warfare, but not as an aim in themselves. The military aspect of the war cannot be separated from the political aspect.

The war in Vietnam being part of a global political conflict, the actual opponents in the war are not South Vietnam and the United States vs. North Vietnam, but world communism (Moscow and Peking) vs. South Vietnam and the United States. For it is not Ho Chi Minh who decided to invade South Vietnam in the "national" interests of North Vietnam, but his actions were part of the strategic operations decided by the leaders of world communism. Thus the conflict cannot be solved in Vietnam by Vietnamese forces alone.

The aggression in Vietnam was premeditated and planned within a definite global strategic plan. The main aim of the action is not to conquer territorially South Vietnam, but to make another step forward in the fulfillment of the communist strategy of wearing out materially and disarming mentally and politically the United States, sapping its strength (in manpower, resources, arms, patience and perseverance, prestige, etc.) through countless local "wars of liberation," while the military strength of the leading communist power, the USSR, remains unengaged, unimpaired and free to develop and grow with the increase of its political strength and influence.

Wherein must that communist victory and U.S. defeat consist? Not in the defeat of U.S. arms. This is a most important, cardinal point. The communists are not irrational. They know that U.S. military might precludes any communist military victory. But they also know the invaluable lesson of World War II and Korea, that communist political victories over the United States can be attained and that political victories are more decisive than military ones, i.e. that political defeats can hurt more than military defeats.

For the plain facts of the matter are that the decisive contribution to victory over Nazi Germany and Japan in World War II was made by the USA, but that the political victor, which means the only real winner, was the USSR and world communism.

In the Korean war, where U.S. troops for the first time in history fought under a flag other than the U.S. flag (the international flag of the U.N.), they, for the first time in history, failed to achieve victory. The magnificent operation of General MacArthur at Inchon turned the tides of the war, but he was expressly forbidden to achieve victory and removed from the scene. The war in Korea, which was a vital part of the permanent political war which the USSR is waging against the USA, without engaging any Soviet troops and sacrificing any Soviet soldiers, ended in a military draw, but in a distinct political communist victory. For it gave the world the spectacle of a tie between capitalism and communism, thus destroying the belief in the West's military superiority and invincibility.

The same is the case in Vietnam. American military power cannot be beaten in the field. But if the war lasts long enough, if the U.S. is forced to send a considerable contingent of troops to fight in Vietnam against the aggression of a small, poor, underdeveloped, communist-dominated country of 16 million people, if the U.S. is induced to fight a limited war, suited to the conditions and interests of North Vietnam and aiming at no victory, then the will of the U.S., which since 1933 has never been very strong where world communism was concerned, will falter and its mood will change from a peace based on victory, to a peace at any price, amounting to U.S. political surrender and communist political victory, like Yalta in 1945 and Panmunjon in 1953, or worse.

The communists of North Vietnam and the Vietcong can afford to lose the military campaign now. After sustaining successfully a long war against the strongest military power in the world, they have built up their prestige, acquired enough face and created conditions for achieving political victory at the conference table, regardless, and in spite of how bad their military failure may be. Actually, they have already been successful politically, by holding out in the field for such a long time against overwhelming odds. All they have to do now is to transform partial success into complete political victory. And that consists in: (a) having the Vietcong recognized as a full-fledged partner at any peace talks; (b) consequently, having their "share in the responsibility of power" in any future government in South Vietnam, which would obviously be a mortal blow to the prestige and face of the present South Vietnamese government and all South Vietnamese freedom fighters, and (c) having the U.S. troops withdraw from "united," "pacified," "neutralized" and "guaranteed" Vietnam.

Now, whose concepts, plans and strategy (those of the U.S. or those of the Soviet Union) are more realistic, concrete and precise, and have better chances of winning out?

The preceding analysis should contribute toward explaining why:

Our Policy in Vietnam is Self-Defeating

Our Rusk-McNamara policy in Vietnam is characterized by so many fatal weaknesses and contradictions, that it is doing more to destroy the prestige and influence of the U.S. and make a U.S. success in Vietnam impossible, than communist action and communist propaganda ever could do.

There is first the glaring contradiction between our military effort to "stop communist aggression" in Vietnam, and our global policy of fraternization with communism.

We are fighting a military war against communist aggression in South Vietnam, which requires huge financial and other investment, efforts and sacrifices, and 500,000 troops in the field; our casualties have passed the 100,000 mark. But on the other hand, we pursue globally a combination of coexistence and pro-communist policy, our foreign policy-makers increasingly regard the communists as companions-in-arms in the war for peace, rather than as enemies in the war for freedom, and we actually and actively help communism in Yugoslavia, Poland and many other countries.

That is the first incomprehensible, paralyzing contradiction, which does not make sense and cannot inspire anybody's confidence in the U.S. and its policy-makers.

We find communist aggression intolerable in South Vietnam, i.e. one particular spot on the map, but we seem to have no objection to the policy of the USSR, the center of world communism and aggression. While they (a) openly and actively support North Vietnam 100%, and (b) wage a fierce political and propaganda war against the U.S. which they brand as the most ruthless aggressor and imperialist before world opinion—we abstain from any act of unfriendliness, speak with respect and consideration about them, seek their friendship and sign treaties of cooperation with them.

To make the paradox more glaring, we make a huge effort and sacrifice the pick of the nation in South Vietnam, because we find communist aggression intolerable twelve thousand miles from our shores, but we tolerate, stabilize, after helping it to be installed, a communist regime and center of subversion for all Latin America, in Cuba, 90 miles from our shores!

The contradiction is murderous, unexplainable and disastrous for us. Whom can we expect to believe that we do have a definite anti-communist policy?

To make matters even worse, there is the second paradox: our huge effort is explicitly and emphatically directed, *not* against communism, but only against communist aggression.

Which means that our concept of a limited war and the conduct of such a war is based on the strange notion, or rather the conspicuous fallacy that communism and aggression can be separated. They cannot. Communism and aggression are inseparable, because aggression is a constituent part of communism. The essence of communism is world conquest, attainable only through ruthless and relentless total aggression, i.e. aggression in all conceivable forms. Non-aggressive communism is a contradiction in terms. Communism exists for the purpose of committing aggression. That is the reason for which it was created. Thus aggression cannot be divorced from communism.

When we proclaim as our aim and intention to keep our word, help the people of Vietnam save their country and remain free and independent, but at the same time firmly refuse to use our efforts to bring about the downfall of communism in Vietnam, which is the vital requirement upon the fulfillment of which the realization of our objectives decisively depends—we are defeating our own aims.

That is why our conduct of a limited war, with a limited objective, is confusing for everybody concerned (except the enemy, of course, who welcomes it).

To pull punches, to restrict targets, to establish sanctuaries, to tie the hands of our pilots, to suspend bombardments and allow the enemy to rebuild and regroup and improve its positions, is inexplicable, because all those actions are clearly in favor of an enemy whom we are fighting.

The only way we can possibly justify sending the pick of the nation to kill and be killed, and their share in inflicting untold sacrifices and misery on the civilian population of Vietnam, is that it should be used for the purpose of victory, which alone could guarantee peace. But to make the immense effort and at the same time to preclude victory, goes counter to the most elementary laws of logic and common sense.

And the same laws are badly violated also by the fact that the Rusk-McNamara conduct of the war, which is supposed to limit the war by sticking close to peace, is actually escalating and prolonging it, needlessly and devastatingly. Limited struggle, limited engagement in a struggle, can only goad the enemy to make further efforts and thus escalate the conflict, not induce him to restrict his hostilities and turn toward peace. This is, of course, precisely what has happened in South Vietnam, and was 100% predictable, but inaccessible to Messrs. Rusk and McNamara and their experts. So, our limited warfare has prolonged and escalated the war, we had to increase our engagement from a thousand advisers in 1961 to over half a million fighting men, the determination of the enemy has been enormously strengthened by our display of weakness, the devastation of South Vietnam has, unnecessarily reached catastrophic proportions, and the problem of our intervention in Vietnam has grown into a national crisis of unprecedented scope and gravity.

It is a mystery how Messrs. Rusk and McNamara could fail to grasp the imperative of ending (by victory) the war at the earliest possible date. In the first days of 1965, when we had some 70,000 troops in South Vietnam and our casualties were well under two thousand, Secretary Rusk spoke against withdrawal from Vietnam, but also against the expansion of the war, because that would "multiply casualties by the thousands, subject Asian people to devastation and lead down a trail, the end of which no one in any country could possibly see with assurance." [175]

Since that time the war and U.S. involvement in it have increased immensely, and so have the casualties, devastation and uncertainty. But that has apparently left Secretary Rusk unimpressed. At a hearing before the U.S. Senate Foreign Relations Committee (on August 30, 1966), he answered a question by Senator Thurmond who was expressing his concern about the irresolute way the war effort was being pursued, that we could easily escalate the war, and have a much bigger war on our hands, but that our aim was the opposite, to keep it in the narrowest possible limits and "bring a little peace to the world!"

Senator Thurmond could not help being stunned by this reasoning. For Secretary Rusk was basing his policy on the assumption that war can be limited unilaterally (as if it did not depend on the enemy(!), and saying in so many words that our main concern in a war in which we were deeply committed was not to win the war but to save peace (as if peace did not depend on our achieving victory!).

Evidently, Mr. Rusk has failed to draw the lessons from our experiences in Vietnam, which conclusively indicate that the policy of avoiding escalation, i.e. a "bigger war," has produced precisely the results it was meant to avoid, heavier casualties and more devastation. It apparently never occurred to Mr. Rusk that had our war in Vietnam been used for a re-appraisal of our policy and its re-orientation from coexistence with communism to political war against communism, our conduct of the war in Vietnam may have changed from helplessly being drawn into escalation by the communists, to making a bigger effort for victory and shortening the war. Quite probably, the war by now would have been won, the casualties would have been much smaller and the conditions for peace much more favorable.

The contradiction contained in our concept of limited war and its function, is demonstrated in the horrible devastation of South Vietnam, which is directly related to the duration of the war.

We speak about the salvation of South Vietnam from communism, but our needlessly and senselessly protracted war of deliberate and planned futility is gradually destroying—physically, politically and morally—the very fabric of the nation, woven in the course of long centuries. Its economic life has been all but destroyed. Not only the villages, the homes, the temples and graveyards, the fields, gardens and forests which have shaped the character of the Vietnamese and which contain their very soul are being destroyed, but the toll in terms of human values and relations, moral standards, customs and traditions, philosophy and religious beliefs, is devastating.

This is an utterly disturbing consequence of our war which imposes huge sacrifices on U.S. resources and men, inflicts irreparable damage on the Vietnamese and their country, with the proclaimed aim of *not* removing the clear and obvious source and cause of all the trouble, but attempting to change communists into nice, well-behaved boys who will, if stopped by U.S. arms, renounce communism and become faithful adherents of democratic procedures of settling the conflict at the conference table.

That does not make sense at all because it flies in the face of the elementary facts and factors of the situation.

This conduct of the war is particularly objectionable because at a moment in history when the fate of freedom and civilization decisively depends on the strength of the United States, it makes her appear hopelessly powerless.

As early as 1957 the then Vice-President Nixon had stressed the crucial importance of Asia for the security of the United States and in that context the importance of preventing Southeast Asia from falling into communist hands.

The whole world, including the communists, is well aware of the fact that the military might of the United States can prevent any military conquest it would consider intolerable. Secretary McNamara himself had spoken of the fabulous military strength of the U.S. And in the words of President Johnson (on November 5, 1964), the armed might of the United States is today not only superior to that of any other country in the world, not only bigger than the armaments of the whole world today, but it exceeds the total sum of all armaments of all countries in history! Yet that country, with first-rate generals in command of operations, with troops not only superbly trained and equipped, but with great dedication, cannot win against what is, comparatively speaking, a handful of ill-clad and ill-fed communist troops, with low morale? The conclusion imposes itself that the war in Vietnam, i.e. our grand strategy there, is shaped as if an invisible hand from Moscow and Peking were directing our decisions and instructions, with the unmistakable *intent* of proving to everybody concerned that the U.S. *cannot* win.

The decisive element of war and victory is the will to win. The hugeness of our materiel (military, logistic, etc.) serves only to show and accentuate the debility of our will to fight and win, i.e. really to stop the communists and safeguard Vietnam, Southeast Asia, the United States and the world.

Thus the conduct of the war feeds the communist propaganda line that the U.S. is a weak giant, a paper tiger, even if it has atomic teeth.

Now, when the war in Vietnam has lasted longer than World War II and we have dropped in Vietnam, a small Asian country, more bombs than on Germany, the mightiest military power of 1941, and are unable to achieve decisive success—the wildest communist propaganda slogans begin to appear as probabilities at least. Especially if comparisons are made between the devastating efficacy of the U.S. military machine in World War II, against Nazi Germany and Japan, and its impotence in the war against communist North Vietnam.

This state of affairs, discounted or ignored by Secretary Mc-Namara and his advisers, is a factor weighing heavily against us in the war between the U.S. and world communism.

Communists everywhere—in Moscow and Peking, in Poland and Yugoslavia, regardless of all differences or conflicts, are not passing up the opportunity to make the most of the spectacle of U.S. military difficulties in overcoming Vietnamese communist troops, as the most telling illustration of U.S. ruthless imperialism, and at the same time of its powerlessness to achieve its aims and effectively protect its friends.

The American "Vietcong"

This impression of the absence of our determination to win is strengthened by the unaccountable tolerance of the openly and crassly treasonable activities of the "opponents of the war in Vietnam" in the U.S.

The attitude of some outstanding public figures (Senators), accusing in the midst of a war against the most cynically arrogant power in history, their own Government of "fatal arrogance of power that has sometimes destroyed great nations" (Senator Fulbright, Chairman of the Foreign Relations Committee of the U.S. Senate, on April 22, 1966) or offering their blood to the enemy in North Vietnam, has certainly made a very detrimental impression on the public. Senator Barry Goldwater on several occasions commented that "such remarks by highly placed individuals which

could be used by the enemy against the U.S., were close to treason." [176]

To accuse and condemn shamelessly our own government in
time of war, brazenly flout the war effort, burn draft-cards and
make propaganda for the enemy, openly display in time of war
the flag of the enemy in our national capital, organize riots which
are leading to civil war, stop trains transporting our soldiers, organize a massive demonstration against our participation in Vietnam, with the chief aim of forcibly blockading and paralyzing the
headquarters of our war effort, the Pentagon—is not to exercise
the right of dissent, but to give help to the enemy.

Unfortunately, even the spectacle of U.S. troops being called in
time of war to defend the headquarters of national defense from
its citizens, failed to clarify the muddled notions of some high
officials about free speech, honest dissent and democratic freedoms, and thus failed to open their eyes to the plain fact that the
leading fomenters of anti-war demonstrations and subversion
were nothing but organizers of enemy troops on U.S. soil with the
special assignment of disrupting the base of our war effort in Vietnam, the U.S. itself.

Our experts have made much of their idea of training special
counter-insurgency troops to deal with any emergency anywhere
in the world promptly and effectively. But they have somehow
overlooked the brazen insurgency on U.S. soil, which is worth to
the enemy more than entire divisions on the battlefields of Vietnam, and which, if allowed to continue and grow, could be as
deadly for the U.S. as was for Germany the Allied bombing which
broke the back of Hitler's war effort.

We are trying to win friends and influence people in Asia, and
induce them to trust us, help us, cooperate with us, join their fate
with ours, and yet we treat the Prime Minister of Laos and the
Prime Minister of Singapore, Lee Kwan Yew, to the spectacle of
U.S. citizens openly doing work for the enemy by assaulting the
Pentagon!

Premier Lee, who had bluntly stated that the purpose of his
official visit was to find out, for the benefit of his people and country, whether the U.S. had "staying power in Asia," i.e. the unshak-
able determination to influence the course of history in Asia in

favor of freedom, left the United States with his doubts unre-
solved.

Our Political War Against South Vietnam

To complete the picture, we must turn to a most important
aspect of the war in Vietnam which has hardly been mentioned in
all the reports and debates on Vietnam filling our newspapers,
magazines, books and television programs. That is the hostile attitude of our policy- and opinion-makers toward our ally, the government of South Vietnam, which amounts to a political war
against it.

South Vietnam was created (in 1954) in the process of the disruption of Indochina. The new country, "temporarily" divided between North Vietnam (under communist control) and free South
Vietnam, had to grope its way toward real independence, full
statehood and political development under the most adverse conditions. For the communists were continuing their "anti-colonial"
revolution, where the breakup of Indochina was only the first step
in the realization of the Leninist formula: first the anti-Western
revolution, then the "anti-bourgeois" revolution. In South Vietnam, Emperor Bao Dai, devoid of influence, popular support or
dynamic qualities of leadership, lasted only one year. His Prime
Minister, Ngo Diem, arose as the natural successor and won popular approval in a free referendum in 1955, thus becoming the first
president of the Republic of South Vietnam.

For several years Diem enjoyed the favor of U.S. liberals, perhaps on the mere ground that he was symbolizing the liquidation
of monarchy and "feudalism" and because as a young and ambitious politician, he was not supposed to be inclined to endanger
his political fortunes by any "reactionary" tendencies or nationalistic stubbornness, especially not after witnessing what had happened to Chiang Kai-shek in China and Syngman Rhee in Korea,
not to speak of European leaders (like Draza Mihailovich) who
would not bow before the leftist "winds of change."

The liberal expectations were soon let down. Diem was a politician, so that he did not hesitate to take the place of Bao Dai as
head of state. But he was also a patriot and statesman, so that he
refused to go along with or yield to communist plans and

schemes. He realized that the issue was national survival in the face of communist aggression and he devoted all his life and energies to defending his country. He was re-elected with a landslide majority in 1961.

But as Diem's anticommunist firmness grew, so grew the liberal hostility to him. He was exposed to malevolent criticism, harassment and charges of dictatorial methods, suppression of democratic freedoms, corruption. In November 1963, after a year of conspicuous success in fighting communist external and internal aggression, he was publicly reprimanded, rebuked and threatened by President Kennedy, following which, Ambassador Henry Cabot Lodge played a decisive part in encouraging a group of generals headed by Duong Van Minh to remove him forcibly from office. He was murdered on November 2, 1963. It was a signal communist triumph.*

The story of South Vietnamese resistance to communism under a number of governments rapidly succeeding one another until Marshal Ky and General Thieu took over, is outside the scope of this analysis. But the key fact that the South Vietnamese did not give up when their legal anti-communist government was overthrown owing to the connivance of the U.S. Government, its powerful ally in opposing communist aggression—is a signal testimony to the patriotism, strength of character, and tenacity of the South Vietnamese.

But from then on to this very day, the South Vietnamese government has been exposed to devastating criticism which has been used to the full by communist (North Vietnamese and Vietcong) propaganda to influence, morally disarm and break the will to freedom of the South Vietnamese and their confidence in their government.

Under absolute standards, no government, especially in time of war, can stand the test of full democratic freedoms and a morally clean-as-a-hound's-tooth administration. Most governments can-

---

* According to correspondent Keyes Beech, quoting communist Wilfred Burchett, the Vietnamese communists "could hardly believe their good fortune when they heard of Diem's death . . . They said the Americans had done something that we haven't been able to do for nine years and that was get rid of Diem." *Long Island Star Journal,* November 14, 1964, "Diem Overthrow Pleased Viet Cong".

not stand it in time of peace. But when a nation is engaged in a fight for its survival, the overriding concern is to defeat the enemy, and all the help received from allies (economic or military) must serve that purpose.

However, the value of military and economic help in the total balance of the struggle for survival is annulled if we fight a political war against the government we are helping militarily and economically. And that is what has been taking place in South Vietnam. When representatives of the U.S. Government intervene in favor of communist subversion cloaked in Buddhist garb, when outstanding and highly publicized U.S. public figures speak disparagingly of the South Vietnamese government and its chances of success in fighting communism, and praise the communist enemy, when indignation is turned on, not against any communist outrage, but against the Gulf of Tonkin resolution, which was a most important decision in our military strategy in Vietnam, when mass communications media are filled with adverse criticism of our ally and admiration for the enemy, when we insist that reforms should have priority over the conduct of the war* or even threaten to remove their top officials if they are not ready to negotiate with the enemy**—there is no other word for it but political warfare against an ally whom we are supposed to help win—not lose—the contest against communist aggression.

It apparently never occurred to our brilliant sociologists, political scientists and Asiologists advising our policy-makers, that representative democracy was not the easiest, but the most difficult political system on earth and that if it was ideally suited for the United States in 1776 and since, it might not be the best system for South Vietnam. It may not even be viable at all under the conditions of war-torn South Vietnam. Therefore, the insistence on implementing "democracy now" and putting it ahead even of

---

* "American officials have suggested reforms. But Diem doesn't want reforms. He wants the Vietcong destroyed." (Milburn Akers, Editor of the *Chicago Sun-Times,* in an article entitled "The Tottering Diem Regime," June 17, 1963).

** According to *The New York Times* of Jan. 23, 1967, Sen. William Fulbright, Chairman of the Senate Foreign Relations Committee, said that ". . . the U.S. should replace Premier Nguyen Cao Ky if he refused to negotiate with the Vietcong."

the task of waging war, may not be strengthening, but fatally debilitating the country and its war effort.*

A heavy tome could be filled with instances of psychological and political warfare waged against our ally, South Vietnam (and in favor of our enemy, North Vietnam—such as the disgraceful visit to, and reports from, Hanoi by Harrison Salisbury of *The New York Times*). But it will suffice here to quote Secretary of Defense McNamara who, in the midst of the war (speaking in Montreal before 500 U.S. and Canadian newspaper editors) stated that the U.S. "had no mandate to police the world," advocated a "realistic relationship" with the Soviet Union and Red China, and then declared that

> "We have no charter to rescue floundering regimes who have brought violence on themselves by deliberately refusing to meet the legitimate expectations of their citizenry." [177]

A few months later, McNamara stated in Saigon that "We do not intend to destroy the Communist regime of North Viet Nam."

Such were the concepts and intents of the man in charge of the U.S. war effort to defeat communist aggression, safeguard U.S. interests and help South Vietnam in its struggle for national independence!

The Problem of the Independence of South Vietnam

To achieve and guarantee the independence of South Vietnam is one of the key considerations which led the U.S. into armed intervention. "The United States, like the Republic of Vietnam," wrote President Kennedy to President Ngo Diem on December 14, 1961, "remains devoted to the cause of peace and our primary purpose is to help your people maintain their independence."

---

* In World War I, the exigencies of the war and struggle for survival had induced England, the home of a mighty world-wide empire, as well as of parliamentary democracy, to promulgate the Defense of the Realm Act, which practically abolished constitutional rights by giving dictatorial powers to the government. Such was the assessment of the need to subordinate every other consideration to the main one of defending the country and winning the war.

And independence is certainly a most fundamental principle of any decent international order.

But what *is* independence?

It avails naught to proclaim principles if the contents, sense and meaning of those principles are vitiated beyond recognition, i.e. into the contrary of what they always meant. That is what happened with the principle of national independence.

The measure of distortion which the concept of national independence has suffered is best illustrated by the fact that we have reconciled it with communism. A country can be either communistic *or* independent, so that the moment it becomes communistic it ceases to be independent. However, we have not only accepted, but proclaimed and made it a basic principle of our foreign policy, that national independence of a communist country is possible, that it is a good thing for everybody concerned, because it is allegedly weakening world communism, and thus is a fundamental concern of U.S. foreign policy. In other words, we replaced the traditional yardsticks of national independence on which the United States was established, and based our policy of lavish help to communist regimes (Yugoslavia, Poland, and others) on distorted concepts which discredit the very idea of national independence.

Can anybody assume that we would not apply those distorted concepts at the conference table when discussing the independence of South Vietnam?! There have been authoritative statements to the effect that we are not concerned with what regime would be created or evolve in South Vietnam after the war has ended, even if that regime were communistic, as long as the "independence" of the country is safeguarded!

Doesn't that mean that if Ho Chi Minh were to become president of a "united" Vietnam, we would have no objection, but would on the contrary do our best to help maintain his "independence" from Moscow and Peking? [178]

That occurrence should not be discarded as fantastic. It is a distinct possibility. If we continue to stress that we would accept (or even invite), besides representatives of North Vietnam, representatives of the Vietcong to the conference table, that would obviously deeply affect the mood of the people of Vietnam and the prestige of its present anti-communist rulers. The prestige of the Vietcong would rise sky-high and the fighters for the independence and freedom of Vietnam would suffer tremendous loss of face.

The takeover of the whole country by the communists under those circumstances, and regardless of all treaty provisions, would not be too difficult.

Would that be fulfilling our treaty obligations, saving a free country from communist aggression and guaranteeing the independence of South Vietnam?!

As for creating the conditions for peace by waging limited war, the first thing that must be remembered is that the communist concept of peace is different from, and irreconcilable with, our concept of peace.

Communism being permanent war, our concept of peace which rests on the assumption that peace reigns as soon as there are no military hostilities, does not make sense to them. Or rather our peace offers to them better chances to wage war by all other (non-military, diplomatic, subversive, economic, espionage, propaganda) means available.

Clearly, as long as our hostility against communism is confined to military action and theirs is total, permanent and unconditional, our military actions alone can never secure peace.

Our military actions can stop communist military aggression only if it is carried out within the framework of a wider, political war against communism, in the same way as the communists are carrying their military action within the political war they are permanently waging. Isolated military action which is conceived as the exclusive means of solving the problem of communist aggression, cannot succeed. To kill communist soldiers (mostly anti-communist civilians who have been forced into uniforms and into fighting "capitalism" and U.S. "imperialism" under control of communist commissars), and at the same time fraternize with the murderers who have enslaved those "communist soldiers" and are using them to realize their vile aims—is monstrous. Such a course, as World War II and Korea should have taught us, leads not to peace, but to more communism and more war.

If continued, it will induce the Asians to despair of the U.S. and turn to the communists as the only final winners. The more so since the U.S. is thousands of miles away, and Red China is just across the border.

The lust for war is the source of war. And as long as the communists agitate and wage war (civil wars, racial wars, wars of "national liberation")—there will be war. The cessation of armed hostilities in any local theatre of war will be nothing but a pause to prepare for further aggression, and all the pacifist prattle will only encourage war and the warmongers.

Today, no discussion about war and peace makes any sense if we do not consider the main source of the unrest, subversion, hatred, civil war and international war in the world—communism.

That is the source of the conflict in Vietnam; *that* is the problem we will face at the conference table; *that* is the main hurdle to peace.

The source of aggression is the mind of Kosygin, Brezhnev, Mao, Tito, Castro and the others, with whom we are fraternizing, and not in the minds of the Vietcong and North Vietnamese soldiers, whom we are killing. As long as we ignore this reality and try to reconcile ourselves with communism, we are steering toward disaster.*

Peace and Red China

And there is another element in the situation of Vietnam which cannot be omitted from any serious analysis of the conditions for achieving peace through limited war, and that is Red China.

Peace in Vietnam cannot be achieved and guaranteed solely by the active belligerents: North Vietnam, South Vietnam and the United States. As Secretary Rusk and Mr. George Kennan have

---

* Commenting on Secretary McNamara's testimony before the Senate preparedness subcommittee, that U.S. operations against North Vietnam could not bring them to the negotiating table, Senator Barry Goldwater wrote: "On that count McNamara has given more aid and comfort to the enemy than all of the ranting Vietnik marches and rallies, all the teach-ins and everything else. . . . On that point alone McNamara must be counted as more valuable to the enemy, and more damaging to our own men in the field, than a couple of new divisions of communist infantry." ("McNamara Should Be Fired," *Chicago American*, September 9, 1967.)

belatedly come to realize, we cannot make peace in Vietnam unless we make peace with the USSR and Red China.

After many years in office and many years of the war in Vietnam, Secretary Rusk apparently discovered the presence of Red
China behind Vietnam only in October 1967: "Within the next
decade or two there will be a billion Chinese on the mainland,
armed with nuclear weapons, with no certainty about what their
attitude toward the rest of Asia will be."

But Red China was there from the very beginning, or at least
from the time of the Yalu sanctuary, when we forbade General
MacArthur to bomb the concentration of Red Chinese troops
across the Yalu river!

Without Red China, and the encouragement of our non-victory
in Korea, there would have been no aggression in Vietnam. But
Mr. Rusk, even while he was announcing his momentous discovery of the Red China peril, was not sure of its intentions! Where
then is the peril? Why didn't our Secretary of State speak in public about Red China's crass communist imperialism and aggression? ! The natural duty of a war leader is not only to warn the
nation of dangers, but to point to the solution and mobilize, inspire and organize the forces to meet it. Mr. Rusk's warning was
completely devoid of this. But maybe by halting where he should
have picked up momentum in his denunciation of Red China, he
was trying to tell us something?

After all, his naive discovery of 1 billion Chinese in Asia within
a decade or two may not be so naive, but methodically presented,
to tell us that we have no chance of winning and that we should
draw the inevitable conclusions. He chose to forget that since he
was, with Mr. McNamara, the main architect of our policy of
"limited" war effort and "non-victory" in Vietnam, his warning
about Red China amounted to the most devastating indictment of
that policy.

For the logic is compelling: if the U.S.A. was unable to win
against a poor and poorly armed country of 16 million people in
1968 (i.e. from 1963 to 1968), how insane must be the idea of
opposing 1 billion nuclear Chinese! If we needed 500,000 of the
best U.S. troops against North Vietnam and the Vietcong (without being able to win), how many would we need against Red
China? Twenty, thirty, fifty million men?

The unavoidable conclusion, which is left unuttered, but to which we are led, is: to surrender. What else is there to do?

And should this seem arbitrary or far-fetched, let us turn to the main philosopher of our appeasement-containment policy, Mr. George Kennan. In emergency, our policy-makers are supported by their fellow-policy-makers out of office, and so Mr. Kennan came out with some views which seemed an attempt to clarify the views of Mr. Rusk for those who may have missed the point. He warned that the Soviet Union and Red China "cannot afford to let us end this (war) on our terms. They could increase their commitments there and they could raise very greatly the amount of difficulty we face in that area." Therefore, concludes Mr. Kennan, we should not "press this thing too hard." [179]

Which, apart from being an expression of complete defeatism, is an admission of the fact that the problem of peace in Vietnam cannot be separated from our relations with world communism, especially with Red China.

The inclusion of Red China in our debates about the attainment of peace in Asia is definitely a sensible innovation, even at this late hour. The most systematic views on the subject have been presented by Richard Nixon in his article: "Asia After Vietnam." [180] They deserve attention both on their own merit, and because of the author.

The Asian nations and the world are threatened by Red China, esteems Mr. Nixon, because it lives in "angry isolation." Isolated from the outside world, it is free to "nurture its fantasies and cherish its hates." What is to be done? "The world cannot be safe until China changes." And the way to influence events is to "'persuade China that it *must* change; that it cannot satisfy its imperial ambitions, and that its own national interest requires a turning away from foreign adventuring and a turning inward toward the solution of its own domestic problems."

We shall become persuasive when we help the nations of non-communist Asia "become so strong, economically, politically and militarily—that they no longer furnish tempting targets for Chinese aggression." Then the time will have arrived to begin "the dialogue with mainland China." By a "positive policy of pressure and persuasion" we would "help draw off the poison from the 'Thoughts of Mao.'"

And thus would be fulfilled the conditions for realizing our "long-range aim . . . to pull China back into the family of nations."

These views do not include some essential data of the problem. Mr. Nixon has shrewdly touched upon one of them when, speaking of Japan, he quoted an Asian Minister saying: "The Japanese are a great people, and no great people will accept as their destiny making better transistor radios and teaching the underdeveloped how to grow better rice."

But what about the Chinese? They certainly have as high an opinion of their nation and mission in the world, as the Japanese have of themselves. They are about seven times more numerous. And their present leadership on the mainland is communistic, which means exclusively power-oriented. If the Japanese reject a future of making better transistor radios, the Chinese communist regime views as the least desirable or acceptable thing to become a rational and knowledgeable, peace-loving, well-behaved member of the "family of nations," whatever the precise political meaning of that phrase may be.

If there is any chance of Red China renouncing its imperialistic aims, it is only if its ambitions and aggression are met by superior force, which will prevent the realization of its ambitions to rule Asia and the world.

Mr. Nixon rejects the solution of abject appeasement which would "concede to China a (big) sphere of influence" in Asia. We can agree with him that strengthening the non-communist nations of Asia must be a vital concern and task of U.S. foreign policy. But the absolutely decisive consideration in the whole picture is that the strengthening of those non-communist Asian nations must have a basis of support, or orientation, or reliance, on which and around which it can be built. Until they grow strong enough to defy and deter China, they must be able to rely on a force stronger than that of China to protect them, to give them the time to develop, grow stronger and organize their defenses.

Obviously, only one world power qualifies today for that role, the United States. However, in order to serve as a protective force and rallying factor, the U.S. must be strong not only militarily and economically, but above all politically. If the U.S. is unable to display convincing political force, strength of purpose, political will, the determination to be the rallying factor increasing a world system of security, freedom and justice—the nations of Asia, like the nations of Europe and Latin America and Africa, will turn not to peaceful pursuits and the solution of their domestic problems, but to Red China, despite U.S. military strength and economic aid.

In World War II our economic and military strength triumphed, but our politics failed us in the face of Stalin and world communism. In Korea, we fought a war of no-victory. The present no-victory policy in Vietnam is leading to a "peace" of surrender to communism, and the inclusion of communists in the government of anti-communist South Vietnam. With such policies and the ensuing rise in communist prestige—Red China can never be induced to change, especially if it reviews the history of communism in Russia in the course of the last fifty years, which owes its survival, consolidation and present strength to a great extent to the help of the West, which has facilitated the establishment and consolidation of communist power in Russia as well as in a number of other countries.

Is there any likelihood that the same would not happen in the case of Red China? Their will to power does not lag behind that of the Bolsheviks. Korea, in the case of the Yalu sanctuary, has shown that the West is inclined to refrain from opposing communist Chinese foreign adventures, for fear of "risking a war with Red China." And our present policy of non-victory in Vietnam, dictated (or rationalized) by the fear of war with Red China, encourages them not to turn to domestic problems and solutions, but to pay increasing attention to foreign adventures, which have served the Soviets so well, and which the West may condemn and fight with arms, only to yield and surrender to communist expansion at the "peace" conference table.

Tunku Abdul Rahman, Prime Minister of Malaysia, stated in December 1969 in Washington:

"What is happening in Vietnam today is not a war between North Vietnam and South Vietnam . . . It is a war in which China and communism aim to dominate the whole of Asia— first southeast Asia and then the rest of Asia . . . Their way of fighting is . . . by subversion . . .

They have been encouraged by the belief that America is soon going to withdraw." [181]

The Communist Concept of Peace

The communist concept of peace is entirely different from ours, as their concept of war is radically different from ours.

Their goal is to conquer the world. If they cannot do it by military force, they will be delighted to do it by peace conferences and treaties, as they have successfully (beyond dreams) done it at Teheran, Yalta, Potsdam and the two Geneva Conferences (1954 on Indochina, and 1962 on Laos).

President Johnson often and emphatically stated that we would not yield to force, i.e. allow North Vietnam to impose its system upon South Vietnam by force. But if strictly military means of conquest are unacceptable, what about political means? Through peace conferences, "coalition" governments, neutrality, etc.? Can they not lead to the same results and much more cheaply for the communists, so that "not a shot is fired," but power is seized?

That possibility has never been mentioned, considered or condemned in any of the many speeches and statements of our leaders. Why? Does it mean that the message of our official stand and the policy directed at the enemy is "limited": you will not achieve your political aims (which are the real aims, the aims of power), by the force of arms. Period! No mention of our determination to prevent them from achieving those same aims by "peaceful," political means, at the conference table and after. In any case, we have never explicitly ruled out that development.

In view of the communist idea of peace, peace negotiations and treaties, this position of ours seems to be made to order to accommodate them.

Chances For Peace

We are ready: (a) to stop all military action; (b) to invite the Vietcong to the conference table; (c) to accept, or rather work toward, a "coalition government" with the communists for South Vietnam; (d) to invest huge sums of money for the development of the Mekong basin; (e) to withdraw troops from South Vietnam.

They are willing: (a) to stop military aggression, and (b) to sign a peace treaty.

Let us analyze the meaning of the two peace positions.

(a) Our willingness to stop all military action is based on three assumptions: (1) that when the communists stop their military aggression, it will be because they no longer can carry it out, so that they have no choice but to negotiate; (2) that that point will be reached when they "have had enough," i.e. when we have convinced them that they cannot win by military aggression; (3) that their decision to refrain from aggression will be as final as our decision to stop military operations against them.

As for the first assumption, we have seen that when the communists come to the conference table, they do not come to make peace, but to continue war and conquest.

Second, that assumption rests on the very vague criterion of when the enemy has "had enough." But when is that point reached? Strictly militarily speaking, we may have convinced them that they cannot evict us from South Vietnam, although the disproportion between the size and might of the U.S. and that of North Vietnam on the one hand, and the long undecided war on the other hand, is a factor weighing heavily against us. So, if the communists agree to negotiate, that does not mean that they are willing to make concessions. It may simply be that their estimate of the elements of the situation, their prestige built in its wake, the TET offensive of January-February 1968,[182] the withdrawal of President Johnson from the presidential race of 1968, and the considerable, although ephemeral rise to prominence of Senator Eugene McCarthy, indicate that the U.S. is war-weary and thus more amenable to concessions than at any earlier stage of the war.

The present political situation and climate hold better promises for them at the conference table than their military aggression, and consequently they are ready to substitute for military aggression, political aggression at the conference table.

As for having had enough, the people of North Vietnam have had enough long ago, not only of the war, but of communism. However, if we are speaking of the communist leaders, of Ho Chi

Minh and Nguyen Giap, they will never have had enough, as long as cannon fodder is available.

As for the assumption that the end of communist military operations would mean the end of communist aggression in South Vietnam, i.e. the renunciation of their ambitions of conquest, the assumption is strictly wishful. The delegate general of the government of North Vietnam in France, Mai Van Bao, stated at a press conference in Paris in February 1967,[183] answering a question whether the cessation of U.S. bombing would be reciprocated by North Vietnam: "It would be impossible for the government in Hanoi to stop supporting and helping their brothers in the South in their struggle to liberate themselves from the American invasion and occupation."

As for inviting the Vietcong to participate in the peace negotiations, the invitation itself would be an admission of the failure of our intervention. It would inflict an irreparable loss of face, prestige and influence to the South Vietnamese, and it would correspondingly enhance the prestige of the Vietcong more than any battle and any communist propaganda could ever do. The point is so obvious that it can be missed only by people who have lost the sense of political realities and understanding of human nature.

Third, "coalition governments" with the communists have so far always served as a first step to communist takeover (Yugoslavia, Hungary, Rumania, Czechoslovakia). The monstrous neutralist-nationalist-communist coalition government imposed on Laos by the Geneva Conference of 1962, rendered the country powerless. It ideally suited the interests of the communists in North Vietnam, who used Laos as if it were their own territory, to station their troops and serve as a base of operations against South Vietnam.

And all this is not only a matter of practical experience, but it is in the logic of things. The very concept of a "coalition government" with the communists, never implies the infiltration of non-communists into a communist government, but always the infiltration of communists into a non-communist government. Thus, coalition governments with the communists, by the very fact that they are formed, are not a 50–50 compromise, but are a triumph for the communists and a defeat for us.

Thus we create conditions so favorable to their final and total conquest of power, that they do not need any more military aggression, since they are in the seats of power. And should they find it necessary to renew military aggression, the conditions for their success will be much more favorable and conditions for our resistance much more unfavorable.

Fourth, as for the development of the Mekong basin with enormous U.S. investment, it will not have the slightest influence on communism, except in the sense in which communists have, ever since 1919, welcomed capitalist financing as a means of strengthening communism. So, it does not deserve serious consideration as a move to affect the minds and basic aims of North Vietnam.

Finally, the withdrawal of our troops from Vietnam deserves attention, first of all because we cannot hold all strategically important positions and consolidate all existing non-communist regimes in the world with U.S. troops, and second, because in the concrete case of South Vietnam, it seems that both for reasons of foreign policy and in view of the mood developing in the U.S., they cannot stay much longer.

And this last aspect of the Vietnam problem is particularly important because of the stand adopted by many well-meaning patriots who say: "Let us win and then withdraw." Obviously none of them has properly studied the problem of victory, nor asked the question: what happens then? For, if the war in Vietnam were a local, military war, the question and answer would be simple, since our victory would mean that we are stronger, in a position to dictate the terms of peace and in a position to enforce them. But, as we have seen, the war in South Vietnam is an inseparable part of the total, global, never-ending political warfare of the communists against the free world.

So, a local military victory does not solve the problem of the global political aggression, of which the local communist military aggression is a part.

The less so in view of the fact that our aim is *not* military victory, not to speak of the political one.

For the slogan: "let us win and then withdraw our troops" to make sense, our military engagement should aim at victory and it should be fought within our global political war against communism. And since neither is the case, the withdrawal of our troops, under the policy pursued in Vietnam and under the terms of our peace platform, would make all our efforts and sacrifices in Vietnam pointless and would seal the fate of South Vietnam, Southeast Asia and then of all Asia.

Once we withdraw from South Vietnam, it would be well-nigh impossible to bring our troops back to meet the next communist aggression in Asia. And should we attempt to do so, the threat of World War III would certainly be brandished in our face, reinforced by the mass of "700 million Chinese." What would we do then, to "save peace and mankind?"

So, the only situation in which we could safely withdraw our troops from South Vietnam would be one of a political offensive against communism, that would turn the tides, put the communists on the defensive and bring about a radical change in the climate of public opinion—from fear of communist might, to confidence in U.S. might and right.

Our present peace policy is without any prospect of succeeding, for it is suited to communist aims, as is our policy of non-victory. In the same way that our limited war cannot win the war, our limited peace cannot attain peace. Our chances are proportionate to our policy of non-victory. Communist chances correspond to their ambitions of victory. The concessions which they are willing to make, are actually not concessions, since (a) being badly exhausted, it is in their interest to stop military operations as soon as possible, and (b) they can renew the aggression whenever they please, i.e. as soon as they have rested and reorganized.

The preceding considerations indicate how utterly unrealistic the concept of a limited war is, since it leads and can lead only to a limited peace, which is as empty and tenuous as its source. Just as limited war is no war, limited peace is no peace.

The peace which would ensue from a peace conference on Vietnam, held under the conditions of our present policy, would not deter the communists. On the contrary, communist North Vietnam would remain communist and its regime would be consolidated by its victory and by the discouragement and demoralization of its people. As for South Vietnam, it would be dealt a lethal blow by the inclusion of the communists (Vietcong) in the coalition government, and their people would become utterly discouraged after their untold sufferings.

So, not only would the road be paved for a total communist takeover of South Vietnam, but the communist victory in South Vietnam would mean, globally speaking, another step forward. It would improve communist positions everywhere and encourage them to grow bolder in preparing for new offensives toward the final aim, world conquest.

All communists in the world are agreed on Vietnam: that it must show conclusively than the U.S. cannot win. By our policy of limited war and military non-victory, we are doing precisely that: proving their point.

Conclusion

As long as we consider the communists the enemy (as they consider us) it is logical to defend Vietnam from communist aggression.

But to pursue the war in Vietnam while at the same time proclaiming that the cold war is over, that our business now is to build bridges between the communists and ourselves, to negotiate with them instead of confronting them, does not make sense. For we cannot at the same time go in two opposite directions. One of the two courses must be wrong. There is no middle course between them. If the communists are not the enemy of Vietnam and of the United States, then we should not be in Vietnam. But if they are the enemy, we must re-appraise our present policy, make a complete break with the policy of helping communism, coexisting with it, fraternization and collaboration, and inaugurate a policy of opposing communism and defeating it. As long as a policy of conciliation is pursued in Washington, no victory is possible in Vietnam, no satisfactory solution whatsoever. The problem of Vietnam cannot be solved in Vietnam, but chiefly in Washington.

The French lost the battle of Dien Bien Phu in Paris. A U.S. victory in Korea was made impossible in Washington, D.C. To win in Vietnam, we must first win in Washington, the seat of U.S.

power and policy-making. Only a change of heart, of outlook, of policy in Washington, can save at least part of all the military, moral and economic investments we have made so far in Vietnam. Otherwise, all our struggle in Vietnam will have been in vain.

Our soldiers in Vietnam are doing their duty admirably, the more so since for the first time in U.S. history they are exposed not only to the bullets of the enemy facing them, but to the treacherous war which the American "Vietcong" is waging against them back home. And it is only proper to give due credit for their valor, morale, strength, courage, and faith in their country.

However, *that* is not the issue. Everybody who wants to know does know that U.S. troops are fully doing their duty, in a manner worthy of their predecessors, from 1776 to the present day. But precisely because of that, Americans who care and who are proud of their sons, husbands and fathers in Vietnam, are puzzled, worried and disturbed by the contrast between the complete dedication of the troops in the field and the policy of non-victory of those whose decisions they are carrying out.

The true dilemma is not: to bomb or to scram; to bomb Hanoi to pieces or to withdraw from Vietnam. Not at all. When Messrs. Walter Lippmann and General Maxwell Taylor conduct a public debate within the frame of that dilemma (Lippmann: "Pull Out of Vietnam" vs. Taylor: "Keep Up the Bombing"),[184] they are misleading and confusing the public.

The real, vital dilemma, which offers the only true perspective for the solution in Vietnam, is: to surrender to communism or to destroy communism.

The fact that this fundamental dilemma has not yet made its way into the thinking of our politicians and statesmen, is at the root of our present predicament and crisis.

Vietnam may become the point of no return in a gradual process of U.S. surrender and communist advance. But it does not have to be. With our present policies we are going to lose the war in Vietnam, and we are not going to guarantee the national independence of South Vietnam or peace in that part of the world. But we must not lose the lesson of Vietnam. It is probably the last opportunity for a thorough examination of conscience, a reappraisal of our current standards, a radical reversal of our policies which, instead of safeguarding U.S. national interests and helping the nations of the world toward a life of freedom, have been facilitating the communist conquest of the globe.

The situation in which we are embroiled in Vietnam and the unique national crisis at home, which has to a great extent been engendered by the problems of our involvement in Vietnam, are due to the shocking, paralyzing unreason of a policy which fights communists in Vietnam, while fraternizing with them globally, and wages a costly and bloody war, with the aim of not achieving victory.

We wage a local military war against a global political enemy.

We pursue a policy of cooperation with the global enemy who is fully supporting our military enemy in Vietnam.

We fight a war with the explicit aim of not winning it.

We fight communists in Vietnam, but coexist with them in Cuba.

We strive for peace, while cooperating with the fomentors of war.

We seek to guarantee the independence of a country by forcing into its government the representatives of those who fight to destroy its independence.

We send our finest youth to the other end of the world to fight and die for the interests of America, but allow the worst elements in the U.S. to stab them in the back by waging a domestic war against the war effort and in favor of the enemy.

Such unreason cannot go unpunished, and we are paying the toll. A country whose national policy is not guided by reason, is doomed.

The lethal paradoxes of Vietnam must be resolved. They have inflicted on us untold harm, and the full consequences are yet to come. For if we do not resolve them, the countries of South Asia will not want the U.S. to "save" them. Our Vietnam policies will have reduced their options to outright surrender to communism or a heroic and suicidal resistance to concerted communist aggression.

Vietnam *is* our destiny.

10 The Reasons Why

> The U.S. is the most non-political country ever to emerge as the
> leader of the world, and that at a time when mankind is threatened
> by communism, the most political power in history.

The Historical Development of the United States
and its Position in the Modern World

Obviously, a crucial question imposes itself: how can the most
pragmatic nation fail to understand the reality of its historical position?

A policy detrimental to national interests can be pursued if the
international situation is wrongly estimated and the policies of the
enemy are not properly identified.

On the other hand, if the policy makers know the international
situation and are aware of the basic nature and policies of the
main antagonist, the only logical course is to formulate a foreign
policy accordingly.

What is inconceivable is to know the facts of the situation and
the objectives and nature of the enemy and yet pursue a policy
running counter to the incontrovertible facts, thus facilitating the
attainment of the adversary's aims.

The problem is utterly puzzling, the more so since there have
hardly been any serious attempts to solve it. To reduce everything
to treason is as wrong and sterile as to accept the situation as
historically inevitable.

To find an answer to the problem we must: (a) consider the
present stage of U.S. development (World War II and after) in
historical perspective, and (b) return to the central fact of communism: that it is a world-wide movement waging permanent
total war against the free world, with the U.S. as the main target.

That communist influences have definitely helped to bring
about this paradoxical situation is evident. It has been overwhelmingly and irrefutably demonstrated by a number of thorough and
scholarly studies, such as James Burnham's *The Web of Subver-*

sion, Lasky and Toledano's *Seeds of Treason,* Robert Morris' *No Wonder We Are Losing,* and many others.

All right! But then the question is: how were the communists able to penetrate so deeply, to infiltrate so thoroughly, to achieve such decisive influence? Were our officials just traitors or hopeless incompetents? Definitely not. Some people, like Harry Hopkins, obviously felt more obligated to the cause of U.S.-Soviet friendship than to the national interests of the United States. Some, like Edward Stettinius, were strangers and innocents in the field of problems dealing with communism.

But some, like James Byrnes, were people of great administrative ability and experience in public affairs and by nature and upbringing thoroughly disinclined to make any concession to anybody which would hurt their country. What incapacitated such people to understand communist aims, morality, strategy, and tactics?

In the valuable book, *The Grand Deceit,* which is a thorough documentary study of the work the Fabians have done over decades to change the United States out of recognition, there is one sentence in 337 pages about what loyal Americans were doing while the mind of the country was being assailed. They were ". . . too busy with their creative activities to counter effectively the massive and manifold mendacity of the well-managed propaganda of the left." [185] And even the bolshevik seizure of power in Russia did not affect the American belief in the supremacy of "creative activities," as opposed to "politics." "The business of America is business" asserted President Coolidge.

This non-political nature of the U.S. is the kernel of the explanation.

Communist and liberal forces were able to gain ascendance and exert the influence they have only under very propitious conditions for their operations. And these conditions relate to the specific historical development of the U.S., which has been different from that of any other nation.

Nobody can begin to understand the true position, burdens, dangers, responsibilities and chances of the U.S. in the modern world without bearing in mind the unique historical conditions of its development and the revolutionary changes of these conditions in the past half century.

A New Beginning. The first peculiarity of U.S. history is that it started in isolation from the world. This meant safety from aggression and invasion, it meant full freedom to live and develop. The fact, and the political implications of the fact, that no foreign soldier ever set foot on American soil have, amazingly, escaped the attention of historians and political scientists.

The new world was like a new planet, free from all the rules, regulations and restrictions of the old world, a planet where no kings or other established authorities could tell the people what to do—the people would take everything in their own hands and write entirely new rules.

The U.S. coming into being was felt and lived as an away-from-politics historical event, an entirely new beginning.

The Founding Fathers, true nation-builders in every respect, were endowed with amazing political maturity and a sense of full responsibility before their fellow citizens and before history. They had both feet on the ground and certainly struck the best possible balance between the striving for fullest individual liberty and the need for strong central authority.

But the conditions of U.S. life being so much different from those existing in Europe, the main accent and contents of the concept of politics underwent a radical alteration. In Europe the greater part of the nations' energies went into defense from foreign ambitions and aggressive ventures, as well as undertakings of foreign conquest. All internal political problems were subordinated to, as well as overshadowed and conditioned by foreign politics.

- In the U.S. it was the reverse. The primary object of politics was to make it possible for every individual to pursue happiness in his own way and develop his abilities under conditions of freedom. Most people conceived the U.S. only as a means to that end.

Immense Spaces and Rich Territory. What strongly contributed to the rise of such concepts is that the relationship between man and his "space for life" was the opposite from that in Europe, where one of the most potent reasons for war was the endeavor to secure enough breathing space for one's nation. In America that fundamental condition of European political life was totally absent. The spaces were so huge that nobody stood in anybody's way. There was more elbow room than anybody could possibly wish to have.

And once the Revolutionary War was over, there was no problem of national security at all. The struggles with the Indians required great individual courage and sacrifice, but the relationship of forces was such that the question of the outcome never arose, nor did they bear any similarity to the national rivalries in Europe.

Foreign policy was, for all practical purposes, a matter of secondary importance and interest. Bloody, passionate and bitter as it was, the War of 1861–1865 was an internal American affair, not an international problem.

Man vs. Nature. Being exempt from the need to devote its energies to safeguarding the security of the nation and having at its disposal unlimited territory with huge riches, the natural path of development for the young nation was, once the Union was consolidated, to devote its best energies toward conquering the forces of nature around her. This promised to make possible a life of opulence and general welfare such as the world had never seen.

And so, the mainstream of U.S. life consisted of problems bearing on the conquest of man's natural environment, not on the conquest of man. Political life in the U.S., always dynamic and animated by strong passions, consisted of struggles to create the best possible domestic order by realizing the goals and principles of the Declaration of Independence and the U.S. Constitution, not to make conquests.

Europe in America. The spectacular success of America has totally relegated to the background a fact of supreme importance not only in historical perspective, but also from the viewpoint of modern problems and the search for solutions. That fact is that those who had left Europe to come to America, had also taken with them all of Europe's civilization: its skills, knowledge, jurisprudence, literature, philosophy, customs and arts.

And while they would not reconcile with the political conditions of Europe which they considered too restrictive, they profited from all its achievements made between the time Christopher Columbus discovered America and 1776. That period in Europe's life was characterized by the tremendous development of human spirit and activity, by the Renaissance, by the most penetrating search for truth in philosophy and jurisprudence, by the Reformation, the creation of modern national states, as well as the birth of modern capitalism, which was considerably helped by the state. The citizen, often treated with brutal sternness by the authorities, was also encouraged to study and learn, he was goaded and financed to start new economic activity, he was taught the importance of discipline and self-discipline. Stern rule was not an end in itself; it was a rough means toward strengthening the newly arising national state.

The process was about the same in politics (enlightened absolutism) and in economic life (mercantilism): initially, the state had to push citizens to take part and unfold their energies, then the citizen gained confidence and viewed the state's guidance not as a support, but as an impediment. And finally, he wanted to get rid of any political paternalism and economic control. The result was liberalism and democracy in politics and laissez-faire in economic life.

The three centuries between 1492 and 1776 were a period of evolutionary changes, of struggle, self-discipline, effort and responsibility. They had developed the average citizen intellectually and politically. They had made him able both to take care of himself and to contribute to the strength of the community. Rivarol, at the end of the 18th century, stressed that centuries of stern discipline had taught the Frenchman the *culte du travail bien fait,* which is the indispensable ingredient of civilization and its unmistakable symptom. And there can hardly be any doubt that Alexander Hamilton had acquainted himself both with the problems of his country and with the essence of mercantilism, when he wrote his "Treatise on Manufactures" in 1781.

So, the U.S. was not only an escape from Europe. It was a product of Europe and a blooming of Europe under new conditions of the New World. Americans rejected the restrictions and old ways of Europe. But, while all other nations in history had to start from scratch, America started from Europe. Again a historical fact which it would be very foolish to neglect in considering present day problems and looking for sane solutions.

A *"Nation of Nations."* This term, incorrect in its strict sense, nevertheless indicates another distinctive trait of the U.S. It was made of individuals who belonged to some of the oldest nations of

Europe. So each individual came with a consciousness and mentality formed in the course of many centuries.

The American nation, to be formed, was not in a position to rely on time to evolve all distinctive traits of a new nation. The only solution was to establish principles and laws binding for everybody which would serve as the soil in which the new nation would strike roots and develop. That is why the law, i.e., general rules applicable to everybody, valid for everybody, regardless of his position in society or his national or religious background, were of greater importance than anywhere else. In his *History of the American Revolution,* Sir George Otto Trevelyan noted the extraordinary degree to which the study of law had developed in the population of early America. In this manner, the handicap of a heterogeneous population, was turned into an asset, for it allowed all energies to develop and cooperate for the good of the nation.

The other consequence of this unique origin of the U.S. is, however, that it fostered the conviction that compromise was possible between all peoples, no matter how different their national, historical or religious backgrounds. What is lost sight of is the fact that the problem of compromise in American society was between individuals who had come to America to become Americans, whereas the problem of compromise in the modern world is between states which intend to remain what they are and forces which strive to conquer the world.

These several basic factors combined to produce consequences which form the distinctive traits of America and its national character.

The natural sense of hostility, uncompromising rivalry, ruthless competition, life-and-death struggle, in other words, the instinct for survival, was badly stunted. Problems of economic development were solved by effort, capital, ingenuity, organization, mutual concessions and deals. Political problems, though solved by means both peaceful and violent, were also American problems solved by Americans, i.e. by people linked up together by national solidarity and by common concepts of political mores, fair play, and within the framework, in word and the spirit, of the U.S. Constitution.

The success of the U.S. in economic development, in securing political freedoms and uniquely high standards of living for the broadest masses of the population, created a deep faith in economic progress as the obviously rational path for all nations to take in trying to cope with their basic problems. The solution of those problems, common to all men and all nations, lay in satisfying their material needs, and fighting poverty and ignorance—not in politics, political struggles, ruthless competition and wars.

The U.S., having rejected class distinctions, autocratic authorities and old prejudices, and being the most successful country in history, was obviously the vanguard of mankind in its quest for a better life. Nobody could possibly be more progressive, more revolutionary, more democratic, for the ordinary people, for the common man, than America. The U.S. was the last word of progress, wellbeing, of opportunity for everyone. Wasn't the American Revolution the greatest revolution in history, concluding one era in the history of mankind and opening an entirely new one? How could anybody conceive of doing more? And should anyone try, let us engage in fair and friendly competition and may the better performer win!

In the American mind, this conviction that the U.S. had found the solution to age-old social problems and that practice had confirmed its validity beyond doubt, had acquired the strength of an evident truth. That is why the Depression was able to shake it so deeply. Once the wounds healed, the economy continued its progress, but faith in the U.S. economic and political system was never fully restored.

From World War II the U.S. had undoubtedly emerged as the world's leading military, industrial and technological power. That is what everybody noticed.

But from World War II it was the USSR which had emerged as its unquestionably leading political power. For it had used the material strength of the West (mainly the U.S.) to break its enemies and to advance, expanding its sway over hundreds of millions of people. And these achievements gave the most powerful encouragement to further communist imperialism and subversion.

Unfortunately, few people in the West took notice of this basic feature of the new world emerging from World War II.

Regardless, the new position of the U.S. in the world consisted of two new and revolutionary features:

(a) Because of her power, influence and decisive role in winning World War II, all the problems of a deeply shattered world in need of rebuilding, reorganizing and reordering, became its burden and responsibility. Everybody expected the U.S. to solve them by virtue of its economic, military and technological might.

(b) By reason of its rise to world leadership, the U.S. had become the main target of communist global warfare. The fact that the USSR was saved in World War II by the U.S. did not matter at all. Gratitude is an unknown concept in the communist scale of values.

The U.S. was not prepared for the first task. The burden of world responsibility had never so suddenly and so fully been thrust upon a great power in history. Nevertheless, the U.S. performed miracles of help to relieve world-wide misery resulting from the war. (Incidentally, in communist-occupied countries, the crates of goods sent by the U.S. were re-stamped "Gift from Uncle Joe," or simply, "made in USSR.")

It was much less prepared to meet the second challenge, especially since the wartime U.S.-Soviet collaboration, as interpreted by communist propaganda, had created an illusion of lasting friendship, based on alleged Soviet rejection of its imperialistic ambitions and the dedication of all its resources to the rebuilding of the USSR, and, jointly with the U.S., of the world.

In reality, the course and outcome of World War II were an added and irresistible stimulus for the communists *not* to renounce their basic aims, but on the contrary, to double their efforts to continue their march to world conquest.

World War II, which had resulted in a substantial decline of former world powers and the rise of the U.S. in their place, had simplified the task for the communist world movement. Now the U.S. took the place of the "bourgeois society" and the "imperialist powers." The destruction of the bourgeois imperialistic world was reduced to the destruction of the United States. If the U.S. went down, the whole world was practically conquered and the road to world power was open.

The U.S. owed its spectacular rise in the 19th century to the unique conditions of its birth and growth and to the habits of thought developed in full freedom. In the new situation, however, after World War II, those habits of thought were a heavy handicap. Faced with the immense advance of communism, which it had made possible, the U.S. was soon to find that its habits of thought, its basic approach to problems, its philosophy, its methods, were dangerously, almost tragically, out of tune with the requirements of the times. They had been formed under conditions of the past, which had changed in a revolutionary manner.

The historical problem of the U.S. was to overcome its political handicap, to make a truly superhuman effort to extricate itself from the anachronisms which had served so well in the past, and to take full cognizance of reality, to face the facts of international life in the middle of the twentieth century. The more so since the communists were busy turning against the U.S. its historical inadequacies to promote their revolutionary aims.

It was not too difficult to convince the U.S., proud of its revolutionary heritage, that the new revolutionary stirrings and movements in the world were just the same old U.S. revolution, going on under new conditions.

The ground for having the U.S. adopt a policy of peace at any price was also favorable, since the U.S. Government and people were inclined to think that the two world wars had finally broken the might of any would-be conquerors and that the terror of nuclear conflict was making war unthinkable.

The vital interest of the USSR in its drive for world conquest, to dismember the colonial empires of Western European powers, was easily presented to the U.S. leaders and public opinion as part of the great U.S. anti-colonialist tradition from 1776 on. In the euphoric atmosphere of wartime collaboration, it was not difficult to make anti-colonialism a fundamental principle of U.S. policy.

The communist vehicle of "social justice" and the stress on concern for the poor and underprivileged was also hitting a sensitive chord in the U.S. mind and soul. On the one hand, the struggle of man to conquer nature and improve his material condition had been one of the central occupations throughout history, and on the other hand the Depression had broken U.S. confidence that it had mastered the problem of poverty once and for all. Against that background, the rational course seemed to be to make a common effort with the communists to abolish poverty in the world, rather than to wage an elusive, wasteful and incomprehensible "cold war" against them.

And finally, the vital need of the USSR to have the U.S. adopt a basic stance of reconciliation, compromise and coexistence in the face of continued, aggressive, communist political warfare against the U.S., in the U.S. and in the whole world—was served by the U.S. tradition, based on its domestic experience, that in most ventures and situations in life, it was possible to strike some kind of deal even with the toughest competitor.

The tremendous success of the U.S. was also its predicament under the new conditions of its total involvement in world affairs.

For roughly three centuries (from the Mayflower Compact), the U.S. had escaped world international power struggle. Its life had run on a different level than that of the rest of the world, as if on a different, non-political, planet.

But gradually, as it grew, and as grew its international entanglements and interests, the U.S. came back to earth, to the real world from which it had escaped three centuries earlier. After World War II, the U.S. had to live not only under the same conditions of political rivalry, struggle and hostility as anybody else, but even more so.

For never had a country so suddenly become the leading power in the world, and in a situation more fraught with uncertainty, revolutionary unrest, dangers and immense hopes. Never did the world expect so much from a world leader as it did from the U.S. in 1945. And never had the rise of a nation to world leadership been accompanied by the simultaneous rise, expansion and threat of an implacable global enemy.

The change was too great, too sudden and too revolutionary even for a country like the U.S., born through a revolution and living in a permanent revolution of its ways and relations, due to its phenomenal growth and expansion.

Two years after the war (on June 5, 1947), while 100 million Europeans were already living under the imposed criminal regime of communism, and China on its way to the same fate, Secretary of State General George C. Marshall still could not notice communist imperialism and tyranny anywhere in the world: "Our policy is not directed against any country or doctrine, but against hunger, poverty, desperation and chaos."

The failure of U.S. leaders to grasp the fundamental facts of international life after World War II was bound to produce devastating consequences.

It has.

11 The Liberals

"America is in trouble today not because her people have failed, but because her *leaders* have failed."

(Presidential candidate) RICHARD M. NIXON,
in his acceptance address at the Republican
National Convention, on August 8, 1968.
(*Reader's Digest*, October 1968).

It is impossible to see things in proper perspective without considering the broad lines of the historical development of the United States and its radically changed position in the modern world.

However, that is not enough. The war in Vietnam, which is the culmination of our trouble, our unsolvable problem, proves that the key factor was the liberals, their concepts and policies. It is *owing to them* that the communists were able to wreak havoc with our psychological and moral defenses, as we saw in Chapter 6.

So, it is necessary to have a good look at the unbelievable type of leader who is on the way to bringing about the most paradoxical and most spectacular event in all history: the ruin of a country with tremendous achievements and with chances of even greater accomplishments, at the very moment that it has reached world leadership.

It is a sign of the times that until a few years ago the role of the liberal in shaping and conducting U.S. policy was badly neglected. Modern liberalism was accepted as: (a) expressing the natural, irresistible trends of modern times, and (b) as being the only answer to communism.

Lately, the gap of information on the subject has been substantially filled. The span built between William F. Buckley's *Up From Liberalism* and James Burnham's *The Suicide of the West*, contains some fundamental facts and considerations about liberalism which pertain to the gist of the problem.

In this connection, what the present study requires is a sharp and precise view of the relationship between liberalism and communism in the present world. And here the Sakharov Memorandum, with its unique invitation to U.S. "rulers" to cooperate with the USSR for U.S. surrender, offers some indications that cannot be ignored.

In his plan, Sakharov has not used the term "liberals." But he has used counterparts in the communist vocabulary: "the ruling group in the United States"; "progressives in the West"; "the reformist part of the bourgeoisie"; "the leftist reformist wing of the bourgeoisie"; "the leaders (of the two systems)"; and "leftist Westerners." And he has clearly indicated what role he expects them to play in the realization of his plan.

So, we can safely say that the term "liberal" covers or encompasses all the terms that Sakharov has used. U.S. liberals are "progressive," they can be classified as "bourgeois reformists," they are leftists (as opposed to rightists); they are the present leaders of our system, they have ruled the United States for a good many years (since 1933 anyway).

The term "liberal" has undergone a considerable mutation of political meaning and connotation in the past fifty years or so, and today covers a fairly wide range of the modern political spectrum. So, all liberals, i.e. people who call themselves liberals or who can be classified as such, are not people of the same philosophical bent and political attitude, nor can they be considered as "leftist Westerners." But those liberals who have been in power since 1933 obviously fit Sakharov's qualifications for a "leftist Westerner."

I am not talking only about individuals who have officially occupied the key posts in Government. Since we live in the era of expertocracy, we must include those personal advisers, experts in various fields and on various problems, chiefs of planning sections and offices, etc., who have—as for instance in the case of Defense Secretary McNamara's action against the military in 1961 and 1962—formulated and interpreted the concepts, laid down the rules, outlined the plans and carried out our national policies.

As indicated earlier, the tasks assigned to U.S. liberals by Sakharov are:

1. To help Leninist Communists in the Soviet Union win the world-wide struggle for social progress and peaceful coexistence.

2. Implement a program of rapprochement (convergence)

with socialism (effectuate a "peaceful transition to socialism").

3. Attack and defeat "the forces of racism and militarism" in the U.S.

4. Bring about substantial changes in the structure of ownership with a greater role played by government in the U.S.; check the growth of the U.S. population, see to it that the U.S. rate of economic growth seriously declines and with it necessarily the standard of living of its people—all this while in the USSR "the basic present features of ownership of the means of production" must be preserved.

5. Change the psychology of the American people, so that they reject their present nationalist, racist and militarist ideas and "adopt the point of view of the majority of mankind."

6. Teach and make the American people understand what their true goals are, i.e. that those goals "coincide with the universal tasks of bolstering peaceful coexistence."

7. Reduce differences in social structure between the United States and the Soviet Union and "lead to the creation of a world government."

Clearly, American rulers are invited to reject that which their country stands for and work for that which the avowed enemy represents! But if Sakharov has decided to make such a preposterous offer, extend such an impertinent invitation, he must have been sure of his allies. How justified is his trust?

First, there is a remarkable identity of approach and philosophy between the basic views of Sakharov and the basic theses of U.S. liberals. His whole plan is imbued with their ideas, their theories and their prejudices. It faithfully reflects their whole outlook on international affairs and the solution of international problems.

All the main liberal theses are there:

a) That the U.S. is threatened not by communist imperialism and subversion, but by the "division of mankind," especially the "'misunderstanding" between the U.S. and the Soviet Union;

b) that, consequently, any anti-communist policy is wrong and dangerous, since it increases international tensions and the danger of war;

c) that the radical change in international affairs from struggle to collaboration, is dictated by the danger of thermonuclear war, which nobody can win, and the problems of hunger and overpopulation in the world;

d) that the U.S. bears universal guilt at home (Negro problem, poverty, lack of freedom), and in the whole world, especially in Vietnam, where it wages an illegal and immoral war;

e) that white Americans are callous and inhuman, and thus must be re-educated;

f) that the U.S. economic system must change in the direction of "social change" and improvement and reforms of a socialist character;

g) that as far as the Soviet Union is concerned, it is already doing its share for the purpose of convergence, by its de-Stalinization and the developing trends of intellectual freedom;

h) that coexistence is the only alternative to co-annihilation (thermonuclear holocaust); and finally

i) that a one-world government is the only proper solution of international problems and lasting guarantee of world peace.

The identity of views and outlook between Sakharov and U.S. liberals is remarkable, but not at all surprising. For in reflecting and echoing liberal viewpoints, Sakharov has simply picked up echoes of communist propaganda, communist theses, programs and brainwashing. And this pertains to the essence of the communist-liberal relationship.

To avoid misunderstanding, let me repeat: the label "liberal" covers a great variety of people, with a great variety of individual motivations, outlooks on life and political philosophy.

At the farthest outskirts and fringes are those who simply and simplistically assume that who is for liberty must be a liberal; there are those who take it for granted that any educated person must be a liberal, i.e. inclined to question, to doubt, to ask for proofs before believing, to investigate, to give the benefit of the doubt to everybody, to listen to "the other fellow" and believe in the basic goodness of man and the inexorable progress of mankind. Then there are those who are sensitive to human suffering and injustice, are inclined to attribute them to the imperfections of society which has an obligation to give a fair opportunity to everybody, which in their minds is liberalism. Then there are the joiners, who believe that the trends of the times are liberal, and who would not want to be out of step with the times and be labelled conservatives, reactionaries, right-wingers, etc.

But all these and some other kinds of benign liberals, while going under the liberal name, are not aware of the essence of modern liberalism, its true beliefs and attitudes and its function in modern society. They especially are unaware of the relationship between liberalism and communism. Perhaps more than in any other group, the liberal "rank-and-file" are one thing, the leadership quite another. And whoever the liberal followers may be, the liberal leaders are definitely "leftist Westerners."

By naming names, Sakharov has removed any ambiguity regarding the kind of people he has in mind. Here is one of the most interesting parts of his plan:

> Typical representatives of the reformist bourgeoisie are Cyrus Eaton, President Franklin D. Roosevelt and, especially, President John F. Kennedy. Without wishing to cast a stone in the direction of Comrade N. S. Khrushchev (our high esteem of his services was expressed earlier), I cannot help recalling one of his statements, which may have been more typical of his entourage than of him personally.
>
> On July 10, 1961, in speaking at a reception of specialists about his meeting with Kennedy in Vienna, Comrade Khrushchev recalled Kennedy's request that the Soviet Union, in conducting policy and making demands, consider the actual possibilities and the difficulties of the new Kennedy Administration and refrain from demanding more than it could grant without courting the danger of being defeated in elections and being replaced by rightist forces. At that time, Khrushchev did not give Kennedy's unprecedented request the proper attention, to put it mildly, and began to rail. And now, after the shots in Dallas, who can say what auspicious opportunities in world history have been, if not destroyed, at any rate, set back because of lack of understanding.

It is questionable whether Sakharov is fully aware of what he has written here, especially about the late President Kennedy, and whether he has correctly estimated the impact of his statements.

But the choice of all three names is revealing, in spite of, or even more because of, the considerable differences between them.

The unbelievable detail about the Kennedy-Khrushchev meeting in Vienna cannot be verified. But, if anything, it cannot serve as a recommendation, but as a warning. (Sakharov has misjudged the American people.)

In any case, Sakharov's choice of those three names to symbolize U.S.-Soviet coexistence and collaboration for world peace tends fully to confirm what some people in the U.S. have been saying for years, only to be violently smeared and accused of prejudice, "McCarthyism," "right-wing extremism," obscurantism, etc., namely that the political global war which the communists are waging against the free world, is destined not primarily to win the masses, but to influence key personalities, to win them for communist views and solutions of world problems, and often in such manner that the victim would not know what role he was playing and by what device.

For reasons of self-protection, the communists have invented the cliché about the American people being inclined, under the influence of "McCarthyism," to see communists "under every bed." Americans do not look for communists under every bed, but an increasing number of them are beginning to recognize communist propaganda and influence when exposed to them, even when they come from some unexpected places such as prestigious desks, lecterns, microphones and pulpits.

Cyrus Sulzberger of *The New York Times*, a full-fledged leftist Westerner, stated several years ago that a favorite tactic of the communists was to hide and work behind well-known public figures and use them for their purposes.

And another well-known American liberal writer, Leon Uris, devoted the whole of his sensational novel, *Topaz*,[186] which has been presented as a fictional rendition of actual happenings, to the problem of communist infiltration in the highest levels of the present French hierarchy. In one scene, the high-ranking Soviet defector (N.K.V.D.) Boris Kuznetsov, is questioned by a panel of U.S. intelligence officials. The question is: "Are you charging that the President of France is being advised and briefed by a Soviet agent?" "Precisely," Boris Kuznetsov said, "precisely."

Anyway, by naming Cyrus Eaton, Franklin D. Roosevelt and John F. Kennedy, Sakharov has helped identify the causes of our unrealistic policy of collaborating with world communism.

The matter is far from simple, and oversimplification has not helped the interests of the U.S., but only those of the architects of such policies.

A communist is a traitor. A liberal is not. But without the liberals the communists would not have seized power in Russia (1917), nor would they have been able to increase their rule to one-third of the world at the end of World War II.

So, as it is fatuous to consider liberalism as an alternative to communism, it does not serve any useful purpose to speak of treason as the only possible motive for unexplainable liberal policies. Such explanations have helped the communists to hide more effectively behind the liberals, to conceal treason as dissent, and to play the role of innocent victims of "McCarthyism" when they were ignominiously betraying America.

To understand the reasons for the decline of U.S. foreign policy in the past 38 years or so, and to determine the conditions for a thorough change, it is of great importance to establish as precisely as possible the relationship between communists and liberals.

The Liberals and the Communists

The true liberal is inclined to reject the principle of nationhood (if not today, then in the future), national sovereignty and independence, as categories which the development of modern technological society and the present stage of international relations have rendered obsolete. Besides, sovereign national states have been the source of wars in all history, so that today the only way to eliminate war is to eliminate sovereign nation-states.

One of the most fervent advocates of this theory was Leo Szilard, an enthusiastic "Pugwashist." [187] More important, the main champion of the concept was one of the key advisors to two Presidents—Kennedy and Johnson—chief of the planning section of the State Department and personal adviser to the President on National Security Affairs, actual shaper of U.S. foreign policy, Professor Walt Rostow.

Once a thoroughly internationalist attitude is adopted, the acceptance of communism is greatly facilitated, in spite of formal and academic disagreements, exceptions and opposition. Typical is the statement of the British historian A. R. Burn: "As a British Socialist, I do not object to communism as such. I do object to some of the things Communists do." [188]

The acceptance of communism can also take the form of a surrender before presumed historical inevitability, such as voiced by the British Labor leader Aneurin Bevan in 1954 (quoted on page 43). Or it can take the form of the acceptance of unchangeable facts such as exemplified by the statement of the Rev. David Soper, of London, made at a lecture at Yale University in 1960, to the effect that "the West must reach for world government, and we must face the fact that Khrushchev will be the first president." Aside from the question of political foresight, this is a strange attitude to take for a man of the cloth and an Englishman. But it certainly speaks volumes on the modern crisis of religion.

Now, regardless of the strange and complex reasons for this submissive relationship which at the same time is a breach of trust and confidence of the public, and regardless of its genesis, which must be very interesting to follow, going back to Voltaire and the Encyclopedists and their next-of-kin "Gracchus" Babeuf, nearly two hundred years ago—the fact is that for a long time the liberals have lacked the courage or ability, or both, to dissociate themselves from the communists and draw a clear line of demarcation. Anti-communists in the United States have often been exposed to the criticism of well-meaning and poorly informed individuals: "I agree with you in your opposition to communism, but you fail to make the necessary distinction between communists and liberals." Which is wrong, totally wrong. For those who fail to make the necessary distinction between communists and liberals are the liberals themselves. It is they who talk "as if a Communist were merely one kind of liberal, though perhaps extreme." [189]

Herbert Aptheker, the chief theoretician of the Communist Party of America, maintains (quoting Professor Wright Mills) that: "Karl Marx remains the thinker who had articulated most clearly . . . the basic ideals which liberalism shares." The liberals who pose as champions of liberty, should have taken the strongest exception to this. Instead, they have for years, in the most crucial moments and situations, failed to raise their voice and take any action against the most flagrant communist assaults on liberty and their devastating results. "International Communism has been on the move for almost two decades," wrote *National Review* in 1962, but "American liberals . . . have been silent on the question of communism." They have "failed their own movement and the whole community by their failure to educate the American public about the true character of the Communist conspiracy." And that failure has been so complete that *National Review* concluded that: "The time is long overdue for the Liberal community to demonstrate conclusively that the term 'Liberal anti-communist' is not a contradiction in terms." [190]

The liberals seem to be inherently, by their very "residues" (innermost motives and yardsticks), predestined to serve the interests of communism. And the man who, a hundred years ago (1871) wrote the most penetrating analysis and the most devastating indictment of the liberals, was a famous Russian, Dostoyevsky. His book *The Possessed* [191] is as topical today as it was a century ago.

Talking to a young revolutionary who has accepted the slogan: "Close the churches, do away with God, break up the family, abolish the rights of inheritance, grab your knife . . . ," the governor of a state is doing his best to placate him: "I agree, I agree. I am in full agreement with you, but still it's too early for this country." To which the yippie retorts contemptuously: "What kind of government servant are you, agreeing that churches should be razed to the ground and saying that you are willing to march on Petersburg, making it only a question of timing?" (p. 298) Taken aback, the Governor tries to assure the yippie that "we are not your enemies" and to explain that they (communists and liberals in Russia) would be like Tories and Whigs in England. But the revolutionary nihilist remains disgusted and unconvinced: "Ah, whatever you say . . . you're preparing the way for us and working for our victory." (p. 300)

Incidentally, Dostoyevsky delves deeply in the mind and soul of his revolutionary "heroes" only to find that the "death of God" is a necessary prerequisite, that they believe in the creation of a "universal socialist democratic republic," in which human life would be organized on the all-pervading influence and importance of science; that the death of 100 million people for the cause is considered perfectly acceptable; and finally a concept of relationship between freedom and despotism which, although seemingly contrary to the Lenin and Dzerzhinsky concept, simply expresses its true nature: "I started out with the idea of unlimited freedom," says Stavrogin, the main revolutionary "hero" of the novel, "and I have arrived at unrestricted despotism." (p. 384)

Wouldn't modern statesmen, educators, sociologists and psychologists who are thinking, speaking and writing about the youth rebellion today, do well to re-read Dostoyevsky's *The Possessed?*

So, it is only natural that the early liberals reacted with indignation to the publication of *The Possessed,* that Maxim Gorky, forty years later called it a "slanderous and sadistic novel," and that under the Soviets the book "became the emblem of reactionary ideology" and was dubbed "socially obnoxious and detrimental to the cause of socialism." [192]

While the communists despise the liberals, they also realize that they desperately need them, because they would not be able to hide, maneuver, make their tactics effective, wield the crucial tool of the minimal program, without them. When Lenin proclaimed (in 1903) that the maximal program (communism) could not be realized without the minimal program (liberal reforms), he was actually saying that the communists cannot realize their goal without the decisive help of the liberals.

The lack of political sense and responsibility of the liberals prevents them from understanding the nature and meaning of Marxism-Leninism and dooms them to be, in the name of liberty, helpless promoters of communism.

The gist of the relationship between the communists and the liberals is in their different understanding of the *Communist Manifesto,* i.e. of its philosophy of history.

Reduced to its essence, that philosophy holds that the whole history of man is a record of injustice, oppression, inequality, exploitation of man by man and tyranny, which have been caused by the wrong organization of society. Man, the common man, is good, perfectible, means well and is inclined to live and let live. It is the "gentleman," the élite, the higher ups, the haves, who are greedy, ruthless, never satisfied, who crave to rule and impose their will on others, to force them to work for them and reap the fruits of their toil. The whole trouble in history has been those minorities of vile men (tribal chieftains, kings, feudal lords, priests, landowners, capitalists, generals) who have banded together to permanently control and exploit the huge majority of ordinary people. Those small groups have since the beginning of time made miserable the life of the common man, they have instigated wars, they have stemmed human progress, they are the source of all unhappiness and misery in the world. Without them, the masses would have prospered, progressed, lived in beauty, equality, abundance, brotherhood and happiness.

Obviously, to make an end to exploitation, injustice, unhappiness, inequality, oppression, misery and poverty, a new, radically different order must be created, based on equality and democracy, so that people will have the same amount of goods and wield the same amount of power. The rule of the wealthy, selfish and powerful individuals, must be substituted by the rule of society by all its members. And the product of the work of all must be shared by all. That would be the end of exploitation and the beginning of happiness.*

With smaller or bigger variations, this general theory of man's history and civilization as a record of injustice, oppression, wars and exploitation, has been built up into a sort of dogma, based on alleged truths so evident that no reasonable person could possibly question their validity.**

The Physiocrats, the Encyclopedists, the various Utopian socialists, J. J. Rousseau among others, have given their main contribution to this theory before the advent of the *Communist Manifesto* (1848), which was to give it definitive form and drown the vari-

---

* Nikolay Chernishevsky (1828–1889), author of the well-known novel *What is to be Done?* (1863), can be considered as the most typical and thorough proponent of this theory. "Lenin learned from and admired Chernyshevsky . . . and sometimes attributed to Chernyshevsky his own conversion to materialism, the dialectics, and socialism . . . Therefore, Chernyshevsky has had a great vogue in Communist Russia." (*McGraw-Hill Encyclopedia of Russia and the Soviet Union,* 1961, p. 93).

** ". . . the religious, social and economic systems of all times are soiled with blood; always the big oppressed the small, and the small oppressed the tiny," is the sweeping conclusion of Friedrich Dürrenmatt, one of the leading playwrights of our time, spoken at the meeting in Basel of September 8, 1968.

ous versions into the communist one. The essential novelty of the communist version was the insistence on the violent overthrow of the existing order, its "smashing to bits." And while many (among others most socialists) did not accept the idea of the violent overthrow of the existing order, the communist theory of history as a history of class struggle, has dominated the field and been, expressly or implicitly, accepted by all communists and by most liberals.

The practical consequences from the premises of the history-as-oppression-and-injustice theory are evident: if all history has been nothing but a record of aggression, oppression, wars and inhumanity, and injustice and exploitation of the huge majority, striving for peace and the brotherhood of all mankind, by a small minority of evil people and blood-suckers, it means that civilization was created at such a cost in human misery and degradation, that it was not worthwhile (a view held by John Ruskin). Consequently, the true builders of civilization are those who opposed the history-makers, the rulers, their laws, their ways and values. Rebellion, insurrection, destruction, revolution become synonyms of the only actions worthy of man and apt to change and improve his fate on this earth. In other words, there is only one solution, that of wiping out completely "all that" and starting from scratch on a totally different basis.

The liberals share the basic premises of the communists about the history of mankind as the history of the oppression of the great majority of honest toilers by small groups of ruthless and immoral exploiters; about the decisive role of the mode of production in determining social and political relations; about man's perfectibility and the interests of the "masses;" about the "common man" as the basis of all policy and the main factor of historical change; about the possibility of creating a final, ideal society.

The trouble is, however, that they do not understand the nature and purpose of the theory. To the communists, whose purpose is to change the world by achieving and wielding for an indefinite time unlimited power, all theory is nothing but a "guide to action," leading to the attainment of the desired objective. That is clear and logical. Therefore, the communists know that all "science" of Marxism-Leninism serves the only and avowed purpose of destroying the "bourgeois" society, i.e. making possible the communist seizure of power. It has nothing to do with any blueprint for any new society. Communism has become reality when its power has spread in the whole world.

This is the fundamental trait of communism which the Western world, with its liberal experts, has failed to realize clearly. Had the bourgeois victims-to-be done their homework a little more thoroughly, they would have found out that, except for a few meaningless generalities, such as "from everyone according to his work, to everyone according to his needs"—all the great minds of communism were unable to formulate the principles and mechanism of the better new world. All that Lenin was able to come up with was the asinine "withering of the state," after *ten thousand years* of the most ruthless oppression and exploitation by the "workers."

Thirty years later Milovan Djilas, who besides excelling in the murder of helpless victims in World War II, excels in intellectual confusion ("it is djilastically entangled," he admits himself in one of his articles), did his utmost to solve the big question. And all he was able to extract out of his grey matter was that communism aims at "creating normal relations between normal people."

In other words, neither before the seizure of power, nor after it, did the communists devote much energy to working out the principles of social life. They are too fully occupied with the concern of seizing power and consolidating it.

This perfectly logical attitude of the communists is beyond the intellectual and political capabilities of the liberals. They have never been able to understand Marxism-Leninism. They have always taken it to the letter as a blueprint, as the systematic presentation of the guiding principles for a new society, which would bring about a new dawn for mankind, free of all the evils which have plagued it since the beginning.

In this surrender to the positions and principles of Marxism-Leninism and their acceptance of communist "values" and the totally unwarranted assumption that it will serve liberty—while it can serve only permanent enslavement and oppression—lies the insoluble, lethal contradiction of modern liberalism, its historical and political tragedy. The "principles" of Marxism-Leninism make sense in the hands of the communists who have established them for the purpose of destroying the existing order. But they do not make any sense in the hands of the liberals, incorrigible utopians, who believe that Marxism-Leninism is a program for a new society, and want to use those same principles—created for the sole purpose of destroying the existing order—to build a better order, and run it nicely, humanly, democratically!

This does not mean at all that liberals are noble-hearted idealists. No. They believe in Marxism-Leninism because they crave to fill the void of their mind and soul. The liberals are Marxists who believe in the Utopia of Marxism. Communists are Marxists who do not, because they realize that Marxism-Leninism is not utopia at all, but a means to the paramount goal of total global power.

When H. G. Wells, a Fabian, i.e. most typical liberal, told Stalin, "I am more to the left than you . . . perhaps I believe more strongly in the economic interpretation of politics than you do," [193] he stated a fact, and he hit the nail on the head.

The Fabians have been much studied and discussed in the course of the past few years. The effort has not been wasted. Some excellent studies have resulted. But the Fabians have been overrated. Whatever they were once and might have become, today they are submerged by communist power and influence. They offer no new solutions, nor are their efforts leading to the creation of a society different from the one the communists envisage. The Fabians are, historically speaking, communist servants, assigned to the servant quarters of the communist structure. Should the communists win, they would owe a considerable debt to the Fabians, but political gratitude is a rare commodity in the world, and totally alien to the communists. Moreover, the kind of service which Sydney and Beatrice Webb rendered to the communists by publishing as their own "scientific" findings about the Soviet Union, texts prepared by the G.P.U. (Soviet secret police), can be immensely useful, but invites only deepest contempt.

The Fabians were able to become a factor in the modern world mainly as the "special forces" of communism, basing their operations on communist power and fitting in the communist overall strategy. Without communism, they would dwindle to a debating society.

To maintain themselves in power and run a government, the communists do *not* use their Marxist-Leninist "principles" and "values." They use them only to destroy us. But to consolidate communism they use time-proven, "bourgeois" values which build and strengthen society: love of country, personal responsibility, obligations of the individual toward the community, discipline, hierarchy, sacrifice. For a bad cause, but good principles. Is it then surprising that in the United States and other free countries, the liberal students want to destroy liberal society, whereas communist students want to keep and improve communist society?

And yet, all this has apparently left the liberals undisturbed and unaffected. They are unteachable. They are afflicted with a lack of political sensitivity and perception which forbids them to learn and change their outlook, views and ways.

To go back to Dostoyevsky, this is a trait which we find in 1871 as we find it today. When a group of "yippies" murders a man as a first revolutionary act and test of their elevation above the norms of bourgeois society, one of them, Virginsky, hauling the corpse, exclaims: "That is not it, no, no, absolutely not." As opposed to him the leader, a hard-core communist, undisturbed, explains that the "immediate aim must be to bring about the collapse both of the state and of the moral standards it represents. Then there will be no one left but us, and we will have been groomed in advance to take over power. We shall bring the smart ones to our side and ride on the back of the fools." (*The Possessed,* p. 625).

In 1917 Alexander Kerensky, the liberal, played precisely the role assigned to him by the communist minimal program: he was the bridge over which the bolsheviks rode to power. And the tragedy of the liberals is not that Kerensky did not then realize that he was being used for communist purposes, but that in the past 55 years the liberals apparently have not learned the lesson and have persevered in incurable political blindness.

Typically liberal was the conclusion drawn by a German Social-Democrat, who in 1933, berating a National-Socialist about the reasons for the failure of Social Democracy in Germany and the rise to power of national socialism, concluded: "We were idealists, but knew little about human nature" ("Wir waren Idealisten, aber schlechte Menschenkenner," in the periodical *Philosophie und Leben*).

Even a man of the intellectual and moral stature of José Ortega y Gasset apparently voiced not only indignation but surprise when he faced the reality of the Spanish Republican regime, riddled and increasingly controlled by the communists: "No es esto!" ("That is not it!")

Among the sharpest and most pathetic expressions of utter liberal helplessness before the elementary facts of political life is the reaction of Jawaharlal Nehru, the leader of a nation of 500 million people, who had blissfully signed and proclaimed to the world with Chou En-lai, the Red Chinese foreign minister, the lofty "five principles of peaceful coexistence" in 1955. When, seven years later, Red China attacked India, statesman Nehru was thunderstruck and completely lost: "This is not a border dispute. What we are facing is so nebulous, so immense, so vague, so deep, so complex, that it constitutes the most serious challenge that has ever been thrust at us." [194]

Of course, there was nothing nebulous or vague or bewilderingly complex about the Red Chinese aggression. For there is not the slightest contradiction, from the communist point of view, between the five principles of coexistence and the military aggression. Coexistence is, as the communists have told us countless times, not peace, not a truce, not a permanent condition; it is a specific form of struggle for the realization of communist aims of world dictatorship. Military aggression is just a more conventional form of the same struggle for the same objectives. So, without any malice, but rather in compassion, it can be said that nebulousness, vagueness and immense confusion were in Nehru's inability to understand the obvious.

And today, whatever else may be the ingredients of liberal philosophy, aims and policies, this lack of understanding of political reality and the substitution of Marxist patterns of thought and propaganda for real problems, is in the center of it.

It is the alienation of the liberals from reality and public responsibility, and the helpless submission to Marxist versions of reality and "correct" policies, which is at the basis of the Great Society, of the travesty of foreign aid, of the "war on poverty," of the assertedly insoluble "Negro problem" in the U.S., of the breakdown of law and order, of the elevation of the criminal element of society as the main benefactor of the rule and concern of the protection of the law, of the barbarization of American universities, and the rest.

The most eventful half-century in history, from Kerensky

(1917) to Richard M. Nixon, has not taught the liberals anything about history and politics. They still preach that we must either make liberal revolution, or else the communists will make violent revolution. Their sterile minds have not yet discovered that "liberal" revolution is not an alternative to communist revolution, not a way to avert it, but its preamble. (In Brazil, the people realized this before their liberal President João Goulart did, and they removed him from office in 1964).

It cannot be denied that the excesses of the rioters, New Left, Black Power advocates, etc., have produced a reaction among the liberals, that has expressed itself in articles by such liberal luminaries as Eric Sevareid, Stewart Alsop, and George Kennan, who has published a book on the New Left (*Democracy and the Student Left*), built around the main themes of his article "Rebels Without a Program," which contains some very sound, thoroughly non-communist and non-liberal ideas—such as effort and personal responsibility.

Besides, the arch-liberal of the Democratic Party, Hubert Humphrey, has voiced strong condemnation of and warning against anarchy and those who flout the rule of law and order. Even Senator Edward Kennedy, visibly shaken by the utterly irreverent and aggressive hecklers in his home town, Boston, in 1968, has expressed dismay and disapproval of their views of public debate and their practice of political action.

But while there is no reason to doubt the sincerity of their reaction, there is no indication that they have risen to the full understanding of the new phenomenon of fiendish hatred and absolute hostility of some American youth against their country. At the Convention of the Democratic Party (August 1968 in Chicago), which marks the high point of criminal subversion and brazen fomenting of civil war in America, there was nothing unexpected, sudden, inexplainable. On the contrary, the Democratic Party was reaping the whirlwind which its liberal policies, as well as those of the Republican liberals, had been sowing for many years. In vain was Vice-President Humphrey talking about the necessity of upholding law and order and stressing his determination to guarantee it to every American. The yippies, the rioters, the destroyers of law and order were formed, taught, schooled, trained and brainwashed by the many years of liberal, irresponsible leftist demagoguery, pacifist and defeatist thinking, by the promises and policies and brainwashing of the New Deal, New Frontier and Great Society.

For many years, too many, the liberals have been talking the language of demagoguery, irresponsibility, rights without duties, results without efforts, achievements without discipline, social order without self-restriction and freedom without law . . . paid lip service to liberty, but pursued policies of supporting communism. And the youth of America have listened, absorbed, learned, taken such talk seriously. The liberal policies and influences have heavily contributed toward confusing them intellectually and morally and turning some of them into hippies, yippies and the New Left. If the Johnsons and the Humphreys did not exactly mean what they preached, it is not the yippies who are to blame. They adopted and accepted what they heard from people who enjoyed a reputation for political wisdom and occupied high office.

And ideas have consequences. Yippie-like talk, no matter from whom it comes, and the higher the place the stronger the effect, will inevitably produce yippie state of mind and yippie action. Once that happens, it is futile to remind the yippies that "we did not quite mean it that way!"

In the same manner as the "anti-fascist" policy of President F. D. Roosevelt, and his determination to satisfy Joseph Stalin at any price by making sure that there would be nothing but pro-communist regimes in the countries bordering on the USSR, produced a communist bloc encompassing half of Europe and China —the policy of ignoring communist agitators, of tolerating open treason in Washington, D.C. (and throughout the land) in favor of the enemy with whom we are fighting militarily in Vietnam, of pursuing a communist-inspired and communist-directed policy of "gradualism" in the war in Vietnam—came to roost in Chicago on August 26–29, 1968.

That relationship of master and slave has characterized the relations between communists and liberals ever since 1917, when Kerensky, intending to make a small liberal revolution, opened the gates and prepared the success of the bolsheviks.

To the present day that relationship has remained unchanged. By definition the liberals should be the main champions of liberty.

They are anything but that. They pay lip service to liberty and advocate it only as long as they are not confronted by the communists. Then all love of, loyalty and dedication to freedom and humanity vanish in thin air. Their attitude adapts itself completely to the attitude of the communists. Indeed, the main concern and main moral yardstick of the liberals seems to be the interest of communist power. Talking about the attitude of the liberals in 1935, Arthur Koestler had this to say:

> "Liberals all over the world signed appeals demanding the liberation of Thaelmann, the Communist leader imprisoned by Hitler; not one in a hundred felt the same urge regarding the Communist leaders imprisoned and shot by Stalin. Yet this was the time when the Great Purge was ravaging Russia, a modern version of the Black Death—beginning with the execution of the leaders of the Revolution, ending with the execution of the executioners, and carrying off on its way more than ten per cent of the nation to slow death in the forced labour camps." [195]

That double standard is the main distinctive trait of the modern liberal. Today, in the United States, liberals are people who are deeply upset, morally indignant and up in arms whenever someone tries to defend America and combat communism, but are blissfully unconcerned whenever America is being destroyed, especially by the communists.

The liberals seem to be eager to render services to the communists, regardless of the consequences and with no gratitude or reciprocity expected. The credo of the French liberal parties has always been: *"Pas d'ennemis à gauche"* (No enemies on the Left). Having no program, no stand, no line of their own, they easily joined the communists (Léon Blum, Daladier) or turned to Hitler (Laval, Chautemps).

Services rendered and all help given to the communists do not cause any communist gratitude. They use the liberals for their ends, but always hold them in contempt and reject them as soon as their services are not needed. In World War II the U.S. Government did not get one simple "thank you" for all the $11 billion, not to speak of the military, political, propaganda and psychological support from the United States, which saved the USSR from certain disaster. According to Major Jordan (*Major Jordan's Diaries*), Harry Hopkins was deeply hurt by the affront he considered personal and unthinkable in view of his total and unconditional commitment to help the Soviets. When during a visit to Stalin, he brought up the subject, Stalin quietly replied: "And we were offended by the abrupt manner in which you ended your aid to the Soviet Union"!

The President of Czechoslovakia, Eduard Beneš, went to extremes at the end of World War II to accommodate and please Stalin. The result was that the key posts in the government were taken by the communists and the government was completely and openly taken over in 1948.

In Rumania, the leader of the Peasants' Party, Julius Maniu, intervened a number of times before World War II in favor of Anna Pauker. When the communists came to power, he was thrown in jail.

In Yugoslavia, before World War II, Dr. Dragoljub Jovanovich, professor of economics at the University of Belgrade, was a fiery and articulate orator and advocate of the revolt of the downtrodden, breathing defiance of established authority and preaching social revolution and a complete transformation of society. The only point where he disagreed with the communists was that his "proletariat" was the peasantry. But this theoretical difference did not prevent him from doing more subversive and disruptive work among the students than the communists themselves. After World War II, Jovanovich expected socialist democracy to be broad enough to accommodate his agrarian socialism. What happened is that he was "elected" member of parliament at a moment when Tito wanted to show a democratic face to the West, but as soon as the reins tightened, Jovanovich, who did not understand communist dialectics, was expelled from parliament, brutally beaten by a mob, exposed to persecution and finally disappeared from public life.

President Kennedy was assassinated not by a right-winger, but by a communist. Newspaper and magazine reports, articles and studies of 1963 indicated that the popularity of President Kennedy was seriously declining. Could there be a link between the two phenomena? Could Moscow allow the glorified John Kennedy to lose the next presidential election, as many were predicting? And wasn't the simplest way for Moscow to turn a political liability into a political asset to turn a living President into a dead martyr?

The similarity of the fate of his brother, Senator Robert Kennedy, is striking. Senator Robert Kennedy was an ultra-leftist Westerner in every respect. He offered to donate his blood to the Viet Cong in time of war. His views and actions were consistently on the radical left, sometimes indicating that his sense of U.S. national interests being distinct from those of other countries, especially hostile ones, was not very keen.

His speech in Toronto, in 1964 (quoted on pp. 42–43) would have been cheered at any of the Congresses of the Communist International.

And again, Senator Robert Kennedy was assassinated not by a right-winger, racist, nationalist, militarist, imperialist, but by a communist from an underdeveloped land, who was in the fullest possible revolt against the status quo Senator Kennedy was talking about in Toronto. Did Sirhan act alone? Or was it the interest of the communists to have another martyr to exploit, more important than having a politician symbolizing progressive ideas and politics, but declining in popularity and prestige?

I think that the answer to all these phenomena is above all the basic fact that the communists do not want to share power with anybody, and that includes leftist Westerners. They will use leftist Westerners to the full, but will discard them politically or by murder as soon as the situation changes. And if the leftist Westerners accept that relationship, why should the communists object?

In any case, there is absolutely no indication that today, because of some new world conditions and trends, either neo-Stalinists in the Kremlin or leftist Leninists, would be inclined to change the traditional relationship of master and slave with the liberals and enter into genuine partnership.

And there is no more telling proof to the contrary than the manner in which Lyndon Johnson's brilliant political career ended. His case certainly proves that he was a victim of historical circumstances beyond his control, and problems beyond his knowledge, experience and ability. His tragedy was that at a moment in history when the leading power in the world, the United States, had to take upon herself more suddenly than any other power before, the burden of all world problems, he had become its chief executive, with the main responsibility for the conduct of U.S. policies. The U.S. Presidency evidently needed a man of much greater stature, wider horizons, statesmanship, courage to make historical decisions, political consistency.

But there is more to the strange fate of a man who was elected with the greatest majority in the history of the United States and less than four years later was so thoroughly beaten that he had no choice but to withdraw.

The tragedy, the failure, the problems which President Johnson faced and the impossible solutions which he tried to enforce, are not exclusively his own. They are those of modern liberalism.

PART FIVE
The Alternative

12 Science and Technology

"We Scientists Have the Right to Play God."
DR. EDMUND R. LEACH

It cannot continue like this. But what can we do? Which way should we turn? Is there an alternative, and if so, what is it?

Among those who offer new solutions, one school of thought which must be considered, are those who claim that the very factors which have produced revolutionary changes in the life of mankind and its problems in the last few decades, also offer the solutions. This school deserves attention and scrutiny because it is powerful, because it has made the deepest inroads in the thinking of our policy-shapers, and because it is very alluring.

Ever since the end of World War II, we have been exposed to unrelenting propaganda through various media, that the development of science and technology, the devastating power of nuclear weapons, the gigantic progress in the speed of communications, as well as progress in the manufacture and distribution of goods and services—have revolutionized both domestic social relations and customs, and international relations and problems. The world has become so small, the power of man over nature so great, and the mutual dependence and interconnection of people and nations has grown to such an extent, that nuclear annihilation has become a distinct possibility and the main problems of mankind have become global.

Therefore, the world can no longer be considered in terms of nations and the policies of national states. The only sensible approach is the global approach and the only proper method is the scientific method. The more so since the problems of modern mankind, such as hunger, overpopulation, mass culture and pollution, are becoming much more problems of science and technology than political problems. And because of their non-political nature, they offer the possibility of real collaboration between states with sharply diverging political systems and philosophies.

In sum, owing to the unprecedented development of science and technology, man has now, for the first time in history, acquired the means of solving problems which have plagued him from the beginning.

Man's power to unearth the secrets and use the forces of nature has reached a revolutionary stage. Man can control the energy of matter, which enables him to travel in space and walk on the Moon (Mars next); he is able to harness the power of the seas and oceans and make full use of their abundance in vegetable and animal life to satisfy mankind's needs in energy and food; progress in the study of ecology brings us near the point where crops can be grown anywhere on the globe (in spite of the resounding failures of Matvey Lysenko and Nikita Khrushchev); man has reached not only the point where practically all diseases are under control, but where he knows all about his own behavior and possesses the biochemical knowledge and means of controlling and regulating it (pretty soon injections will take care of everybody's intelligence—nobody will be inferior, we will all be very intelligent); man's life span, which has been considerably lengthened in our lifetime, will soon be increased beyond all expectations (Western scientists foresee a life of 120 years as a perfectly normal perspective; some Soviet scientists speak of a life span of 300 years as quite possible). Moreover, on his long path of evolution, man has finally reached the stage where, for the first time in history, he can determine not only the sex of future babies, but by pre-natal biochemical or surgical intervention can decisively influence their aptitudes, talents and character. Man today, by using the latest achievements of medicine, biology and biochemistry, can produce exactly the kind of children he desires. So, new generations will produce hundreds and thousands of geniuses of arts, philosophy and science—Leonardos, Michelangelos, Descartes, Copernicuses, Newtons, Galileos, Shakespeares, Cervantes, Dostoyevskys, Bachs and Beethovens, Einsteins,[196] Edisons and Teslas. All are a distinct possibility. What glorious prospects!

As a result of the attainments of science and technology, the contemporary problems of mankind are becoming less political. (Several years ago, Daniel Bell proclaimed *The End of Ideology*). They are also becoming more international and less national.

Politics (of national states) have brought mankind to the brink of ruin. Science and technology will save it.

The war of all against all, which has allegedly characterized human history until now, has been greatly influenced by man's limited ability to produce, to wrest from nature the goods he needed. Instead of an equitable distribution of goods available, the greedy and mighty took the lion's share for themselves and left the crumbs for the masses. Social injustice and unhappiness in the world ensued.

But now, owing to the development of science and technology, man's capacity to control nature, to harness its forces for his own ends, has grown practically without limits. Man can today produce so much that there should be enough for every single human being on earth.

For the first time in history man has reached the point where he can satisfy the needs of all people, thereby eliminating the source of revolt, injustice, misery, unhappiness and wars, and ensuring universal peace. Thus man has reached the turning point in his entire existence on earth: the era of history and politics, with all its strife, unhappiness, misery and injustice is coming to an end, and a new era is being ushered in, the era of the satisfaction of human needs, the era of human happiness.

For the first time in his history, man now *can* do it. If he is able to walk on the Moon, it stands to reason that he can solve the problems of war, poverty, injustice, inhumanity and unhappiness on earth.

In one word, the task before modern mankind is very clear: to use its fantastic power over nature, its technology which is nothing short of miraculous, to create a life of abundance and happiness for everybody.*

---

* A typical example of this attitude was the commentary written by Archibald MacLeish after the flight of Apollo 8. This flight, according to him, divides the whole history of mankind into three parts. In the first, man considered himself the center of the Universe, and God's favorite. "From that high place they (men) ruled and killed and conquered as they pleased." In the second, when owing to the progress of science, the earth was no longer the center of the Universe, but "a small, spinning planet in the solar system of a minor star off at the edge of an inconsiderable galaxy in the immeasurable distance of space . . . men began to see themselves not as God-directed actors at the center of a noble drama, but as helpless victims also,

Briefly, science and technology can solve the problem of peace in international relations and of democracy in our social relations and institutions. For the global approach reduces international tensions resulting from the clash of opposed national and ideological interests, thus automatically reducing the danger of war and improving the chances for peace. And the practically unlimited possibilities of production of goods, combined with the new spirit of brotherhood and cooperation sweeping the world and human society, will eliminate the problem of need and poverty and thus the problem of inequality and social injustice.

How valid are these sweeping claims, which stem from a rather impressive lineage (St. Simon, Auguste Comte, Herbert Spencer, among others)?

Scientific and technological achievements do tend to convey the idea that man can do anything, solve all his problems, if he only wants to.

However, the plain truth is that there is no necessary causal, inevitable connection between scientific and technological progress and man's ability to assure human welfare and happiness. The reasoning that if man can go to the Moon, he must be able to solve all his problems by applying the same (?) methods, is based on a false and untenable analogy.

Science and technology have increased man's ability to produce and distribute material goods, they have increased his power over nature, they have increased his ability to conquer, subjugate and control other people and nations.

However, they have not increased but decreased man's ability to solve the problems of his existence and of a meaningful life for nations and mankind.

This is completely lost on a number of modern scientists whose

and millions would be killed in world-wide wars or in blasted cities or in concentration camps without a thought or reason but the reason of . . . force." The third era in the history of mankind begins with the flight of Apollo 8. Since Col. Borman and his two companions saw the earth "as it truly is, small and blue and beautiful in that eternal silence where it floats," we must, concludes Mr. MacLeish, "see ourselves as riders on the earth together, brothers on that bright loveliness in the eternal cold—brothers who know that they are truly brothers." [197]

propensity to climb into the clouds of fantasy is helped by their narrow human vision.*

Moreover, science and technology have, by giving man power over nature, deeply affected his sense of humility and vastly increased his craving for power. Man has proclaimed the death of God, and arrogated omnipotence to himself.

He has acquired so much knowledge and control over nature, that he can make anything. But this power has so debilitated and confused him morally, that he has become powerless to run his life properly, since he is unable to think properly about his human problems.

Therein lies the main danger today: in the gap between man's scientific-technological arrogance, and his human helplessness.

The champions of the almightiness of science and technology forget that for man to solve any of his human (political, social, cultural) problems, he needs first and above all a scale of values, to determine what he wants and the priority of things wanted, and second, that science and technology supply neither.**

Science and technology can help solve problems of production and distribution of material goods or services or travel. But no electronic brains, no machines and no computers and no science and technology at all can solve the absolutely decisive question of values, principles and standards upon which to base relations

---

* "Science does not think," is the verdict of Martin Heidegger, widely considered as the foremost living philosopher.[198]

** The danger resides not only in the inclination of modern man to place unreasoned faith in science to solve our problems of conscience, moral values and human relations, but in the loss of perspective, balance and humility of the scientists themselves. Dr. Edmund R. Leach, "one of England's most noted anthropologists," thinks that "We Scientists Have The Right to Play God." (*Saturday Evening Post,* Nov. 16, 1968).

And Harvard historian Donald Fleming, examining the new discoveries in biology and their sociological implications ("On Living In A Biological Revolution," *Atlantic Monthly,* February 1969) presents the program of the new biologists which includes "control of numbers by foolproof contraception; gene manipulation and substitution; surgical and biochemical intervention in the embryonic and neonatal phases." He speaks of "genetic tailoring," of "government license to have a child," of a "general sense of the inevitability to be manipulated by technicians—of becoming an object of manufacture," and forecasts that we will be "gradually adjusting our values to signify that we approve of what we will actually be getting."

between people and between nations, and upon which to organize power. Nor can they determine the goals to which the resources of a society should be devoted.

The same principles of mechanics and masonry are used to build all sorts of buildings, but none of them is more scientific than the next. Science and technology cannot tell a man which one of them he will or must build. He must choose.

Today—in the same way as in the 19th century (before airplanes, radio, movies, television, the atomic bomb, laser beams, space trips, nuclear weapons) and the same way as in the Middle Ages, or before Christ—man can solve his problems only by establishing and following some definite principles, truths and yardsticks.

Biochemical means can help sick and unfortunate people overcome their infirmities, improve their condition and lead normal lives. Or they can be put to Pavlovian use, to destroy the minds of free and healthy people and make them helpless slaves of monstrous political systems. No science and no technology can tell us what use we must make of biochemical means.

This should be evident if we consider the question: which human types are desirable and which should be stopped from reproducing. No computers can supply an answer. Man must choose.

Suppose that some society, i.e. its authorities, are facing the task of determining which type of man is preferable, George Washington or Joseph Stalin. And suppose that the decision comes out in favor of the Joseph Stalin type. The mere thought is enough.

Or suppose that the statesmen of the post-industrial society have to decide which kind of music will elevate mankind and what kind of musicians will make it happy. Theoretically, the decision could come out in favor of Bach, Beethoven, Mozart, Schubert, Handel, Cooper, Vivaldi, Debussy, Tchaikovsky and Verdi. But should the New Left ever come to power, anything outside of the Beatles, the Rolling Stones, Joan Baez, Bob Dylan, Janis Joplin, and the like, would be out! With science and technology in the service of that musicobiological project, who would save mankind?

The "Scientific" Solution of Political Problems

The inability of science and technology to solve human problems becomes perhaps most evident when we consider the question of their application to politics. What political system, what economic and social order is scientifically preferable, better, superior? It is enough to ask the question, to realize at once how preposterous the idea of scientifically determining the superiority of political, social and cultural values, is.

The very fact that the same attainments and products of science and technology are used by the most varied governments in the world, indicates their political neutrality. Science and technology can serve any regime, any goal, any political and social order, the best or the most ignoble.

At the very dawn of man's fabulous new era, the era of space travel, the first Soviet cosmonaut, Gagarin, stated after his space flight, that God was nonsense, since he, Gagarin, was up there in space, in heaven and did not see God! But U.S. astronaut Col. Borman, the leader of the first team (Apollo 8) which orbited around the Moon, was overwhelmed by his experience, which confirmed in a way he was never able to experience on earth, the presence, reality and infinite greatness of God.

Now, if on their first steps in space, the U.S. and the USSR have not been brought closer together, what chance is there that further exploration of space and building of space stations suited for military purposes, will produce that result?

Science and technology are giving more power to governments, to organized society, to destroy their enemies and achieve whatever objectives they set out to achieve. But they are patently and evidently not taking the place of political issues, ambitions, conflicts and struggles, nor reducing their importance in the modern world.

It is precisely the total moral neutrality and innocence of fantastically powerful means, their purposelessness, which is one of the most important ingredients of the moral crisis of our time. The development of science and technology has made possible huge increases in our production of material goods, but it has destroyed our scale of values and priorities and thus the sanity of our historical perspective. Prometheus, drunk with his power, has lost his balance. Man has lost the sense of his existence. The production of material goods and the wonders of science and technology have replaced the meaning of man's life, becoming ends in themselves.

The phenomenon is today world-wide. However, there is a vast difference between the stand of the communists and that of the West. For there is no depoliticalization of human affairs on a world-wide scale today. It is only we of the West who imagine that science and technology can somehow solve mankind's problems. Only the West is getting away from politics, only in the West do leaders believe that science is able to solve every problem, conquer any political differences, and bring about an "end of politics."

And this belief, or rather obsession, is so strong that Western man assumes that as long as the West leads in science and technology, it can control events and hostile political powers (communism) in a world which is increasingly becoming dominated by science and technology.

If this were really so, if the world were getting less and less political, and if science and technology were taking over, this big plan of Western man to control by science and technology what he cannot or is unwilling to control by political will and strength —would be great. But neither is the case.

The communists, being politically-minded, believe less in science and technology than Western man. They are interested in conquering and ruling the world and they know that it is not science and technology which will give them that power, but political warfare against the free nations.

It was 124 years ago that they proclaimed their aim to change the world, and used from the beginning the vehicle of science as a political tool to confuse the West's thinking. Today, at the height of Western de-politicization, they are not evincing the slightest inclination of becoming less political.

It is only *we* who are dedicated to the proposition that politics should be rejected, while *they* remain as political as ever; only we believe in the supremacy of science and technology, while they consider them as political weapons; only we are promoting nonpolitical internationalism, while they view internationalism exclusively in the light of their own world rule.

Thus the non-political endeavors of Western internationalists are doomed to failure both because there is no communist cooperation to implement them, and because they run counter to the political nature of man. If the U.S. rejects political struggle and political warfare, and would rather confine its statesmanship to coexistence, collaboration and internationalism, this orientation remains totally futile as long as the communists do not share similar inclinations.

In other words, if the whole West wants to stop being political, but the communists do not, the law of international life will still be politics and struggle, and not the rejection of politics in favor of internationalism, science and technology.*

The struggle for power, the political struggle for the world, never changes nor stops. What changes are the nations which rise to pre-eminence. Today the communist powers are not engaged in an effort to abrogate politics, but in a struggle to conquer the world and determine its fate.

What the world would be like if the USSR or Red China were to win, is not difficult to figure out: a global Vorkuta. Then the questions of society and mankind would not be solved by science and technology, but by the knout and machine guns. If communist Mao Tse-tung would think nothing of sacrificing the lives of 300 million Chinese to conquer the world and establish communist rule, would he have any compunction to deter him from liquidating, in the interest of "progress," some, let us say, one billion and 300 million non-Chinese?

The present "de-politicization" of the West is a continuation of the U.S. "non-politics" which in World War II resulted in the ces-

* In his famous novel *The Fall of A Titan* (W. W. Norton & Co., New York, 1954), Igor Gouzenko impressively tells (pp. 96–98) the story of a physicist, Professor Pyotr Glushak, who "was interested in nothing except science. Questions of politics interested him little." He "considered the revolution an occupation for madmen," and advised his students: "Forget politics . . . Politics will destroy you; only knowledge will save you."

However, after being arrested and hearing the horrible screams of his brother, "pure" scientist too, tortured in the neighboring cell by the Cheka (secret police), Pyotr Glushak breaks. "In the cell there was no longer the proud scientist Pyotr Glushak. There was a pitiful, hurt dog, suffering pain, pain, pain." "These blows behind the wall had beat out of his soul all faith in himself, in people, in everything breathing." Glushak becomes informer for the Cheka.

sion of half of Europe and China to the communists. That non-political approach to problems which are essentially political, is a policy of disappearing from the world stage and surrendering to the communists.

As for the correlative development of the de-politicization of the world, or rather its end result—internationalism—it is, regardless of the motives and concepts of its champions, a movement not toward liberty, but toward a curtailment of freedom and increasing oppression. Since human society cannot live without authority, without organized power, the substitute for national states would not be a world without politics, but an international super-state with more authority, more terror and more oppression than have ever existed under the system of empires and national states.

Internationalism is the concentration of power for the whole world in one place, thus requiring the maximal use of force, producing the worst possible injustice and breeding the most complete suppression of freedom. The ignoble record of the United Nations military action in the Congo and Katanga—and that in the name of humanity—gives us a clear premonition of what the unrestricted power of a ruthless group of internationalists ruling the world without responsibility would amount to.

When communists speak about the withering of the state, they are laughing in our faces, for they realize that we do not perceive the fraud, that their "science" is sheer propaganda serving the purpose of destroying existing society and making room for communist dictatorship and terror.

But when Western internationalists rave about the inevitable advent of a non-political international world, which they would rule, they indulge in dreams. Should such a world really come about, it is not Western internationalists who would run it, as John K. Jessup of *Life* magazine has astutely observed.* Politics being stronger than non-politics, the internationalist order to ac-

* "The World Federalists are up against the same old frustrating fact of Soviet global aspirations. For their brand of internationalism, indeed, Kremlin diamaticians have a special vocabulary of abuse: World Federalist leaders are called "agents of Wall Street," "debauched American maniacs," and "fascist degenerates" by the Soviet press. The communists have their own plan for world government, and no rival plan need apply." (*Communism, The Nature of the Enemy*), by John K. Jessup and the editors of *Life, Time*, 1962, p. 68.)

cede on the ruins of national states, would not be non-political, but thoroughly political, communistic.

The development of technology and the emergence of modern mass society and mass culture have undeniably produced revolutionary changes in the conditions and problems of mankind. The problems are too serious to be ignored or trifled with. The danger of war exists and the problems of overpopulation, pollution of our environment, hunger and many others, are real. But everything depends on the basis on which we seek to solve them, on the yardsticks we apply and the purposes they are to serve.

And science and technology by themselves cannot supply the answers to those questions.

Conclusion

Modern science and technology afford truly immense possibilities for influencing the life and future of mankind. But everything depends on the choice of aims, on the scale of values, on the standards of human behavior, on the political, moral and cultural principles we espouse and promote. There simply is no scientific objectivity or "scientific method" in politics. To claim that there is an objective scientific answer to human problems, independent from human will and choice, from our values and yardsticks—is hoax, deceit and charlatanry of the lowest kind.

It is on our first principles and basic values that everything depends, the solution to every problem and to all problems. And if we cannot agree on basic human values, we shall not be reconciled by any science and technology.

That is the problem today. Sakharov's assertion that we must get rid of the evil things of mass culture if humanity is to survive, of the "tide of filth and depravity," unrestricted by reason and human dignity, which is submerging man and society, is correct as far as it goes. But we must also get rid of power unrestricted by law, by reason and truth, which is dooming human decency and turning civilization into the jungle. It is a bold deception to assert that the problems of mankind can be solved by ignoring the unbridgeable chasm between the Declaration of Independence upon which the United States was founded, and the Marxist-Leninist concepts upon which the Soviet Union was organized, and by having them join efforts in international affairs under the guidance of modern science and technology—which is the essence of Andrei Sakharov's "ski-race" approach to the problem of U.S.-USSR relations.

The crucial issue facing mankind is not the comparative technological efficiency of the socialist and capitalist systems. It is much more fundamental: shall we allow human dignity to be mercilessly crushed, shall we (all men, all nations, all humanity) be reduced to the level of Pavlov's dogs, to be managed, maneuvered, brainwashed and controlled by Big Brother's police, using biochemical means and electronic devices—or shall men and nations be free to live and expand, using science and technology to develop their creative talents and potentialities. That is the issue.

Agreement on the use of science and technology depends ultimately on the agreement on the values upon which to base human life and organized political power. The communist concept of truth is the interest of the communist party; their concept of human dignity is dictatorship unrestricted by law; their concept of art and literature is unconditional service to their regime; their concept of peace is permanent war; their concept of the interests of mankind is the promotion of communist power. How then, and on what, can we agree to work together and apply science and technology, which can be used for freedom, as they can be used for communism?

The communists have achieved all their successes so far, and been able, through their unilateral total political war waged against the free world, to poison our mind, paralyze us, and even enroll our active support for their schemes—by invoking the interests of mankind, the danger of war, the common struggle against hunger, ignorance and poverty—and now science and technology!

Thus the main issue facing mankind today is not war, but communism, for the great majority of men on earth absolutely and unconditionally believe that men are not dogs and that two and two make four, and can never make anything else.*

* In 1984, one of the most important novels of the twentieth century, George Orwell has written the memorable sentence that "freedom is the free-

So, if mankind is to have peace, there is no other course but to stop the insane, criminal agitation of total hatred in the world, promoted by the communist forces of regression, inhumanity and total obscurantism, with the aim of realizing the barbaric dream of total world power.

---

dom to say that two and two make four. If that is granted, all else follows." At the end of the novel, however, the hero, Winston, is so inhumanly beaten and tortured, that he accepts and signs that "two and two make five."

But before gloating, the communists should consider not the truth of the novel, but the truth of real life. In the autobiography of Anatoli Granovsky, *I Was An N.K.V.D. Agent* (Devin-Adair, New York, 1962), the author relates the story of a young Soviet official, Gorodietsky, who during Stalin's purges was jailed, beaten and ordered to sign a "confession." Time after time he refused, in spite of merciless beating, castration, torture (including the hammering of phonograph needles under his fingernails), in spite of watching the horrible beating of his pregnant wife until she gave birth to a stillborn baby on the floor of the interrogation room. And he died of torture, beating, tuberculosis, complete exhaustion. But he did *not* sign! He made two and two remain four! That is the rock of human strength on which the fraudulent ship of communism will run aground.

13 United States Foreign Policy for the 1970s: A New Strategy for Peace

A Blueprint for U.S. Global Withdrawal

1963   "If the danger of war has been decreased, the danger of defeat without war has been substantially increased.

"A great new Communist offensive is being launched against the free world, an offensive without resort to war, an offensive all the more dangerous because it is so difficult to recognize it and meet it effectively.

"We cannot meet and defeat such an offensive by a static policy of defense . . . Our goal must not be simply to keep freedom from shrinking but to make it grow too. Our goal must be a free Cuba, a free Eastern Europe, a free Russia, a free China."

RICHARD M. NIXON
(*Saturday Evening Post,* October 10, 1963)

1970   "Today any nuclear attack—no matter how small, whether accidental, unauthorized or by design; by a superpower or by a country with only primitive nuclear delivery capability— would be a catastrophe for the U.S., no matter how devastating our ability to retaliate."

"By the example we set, we hope to lead the way toward the day when other nations adopt the same principles . . .

"We hope that other great powers will act in a similar spirit and not seek hegemony . . .

"We hope that the coming year will bring evidence that the Soviets have decided to seek a durable peace rather than continue along the roads of the past."

RICHARD M. NIXON
A New Strategy For Peace (1970)

In our search for the alternative to our foreign policy of surrender, we cannot by-pass President Nixon's message to Congress entitled "United States Foreign Policy for the 1970's: A New Strategy for Peace," which appeared on the political scene with the avowed aim of making an end to old formulas and habits of thought, outdated views, uncertainty and confusion, and tracing bold new lines, new concepts and new methods for our foreign policy at this time and in the decade of the '70s.

When the Nixon Administration took over in January 1969, it was expected that some rather fundamental changes would take place. Not only because of the ideas presented by President Nixon during the campaign, but because of the war in Vietnam, which had deeply affected the life of the nation, creating deep divisions, inflicting graver wounds and producing greater threats than any other event since the Civil War.

What could be more natural than to assume that in determining the basic course of its policy in regard to world communism, which has caused the Vietnam conflict, the new Administration would thoroughly study and courageously draw all the necessary conclusions from the traumatic experience of Vietnam.

President Nixon's Inaugural Address, with its overall emphasis on peace as the main concern of U.S. foreign policy, at the height of communist political warfare against the U.S. everywhere, was deeply disturbing. This particularly applies to the slogan "negotiation instead of confrontation," which sounded like a bugle of retreat.

However, these unmistakable signs of the basic foreign policy orientation of the new Administration were hardly noticed by those who elected it. First, it seems that inaugural addresses in modern times, with the U.S. being the leading world power, are expected to be more diplomatic and concerned more with world problems from a global viewpoint. And second, a number of speeches which President Nixon delivered on various occasions on various subjects, such as the speech at the State College in Madison (South Dakota) on June 6, 1969 and at the Air Force Academy in Colorado Springs, Colorado, on June 7, 1969, on his way to the meeting with President Thieu of South Vietnam, made a very favorable impression on those who trusted and elected him hoping that he would turn a new leaf in U.S. foreign policy.

So, when, on February 19, 1970, he addressed his foreign policy message to the U.S. Congress: "United States Foreign Policy for the 1970s: A New Strategy for Peace," it was obvious that the American people were presented with a very important document. Except for the Rostow Plan (discussed earlier), there had never been such a systematic and ambitious attempt to formulate the principles, machinery, objectives and methods of U.S. foreign policy, and that for a whole decade. And then the Rostow Plan remained confidential, while this document received full publicity. It obviously deserves careful analysis.

The age of expertocracy is certainly one of the names which fits the age in which we live. The growth of science and the spread of knowledge have produced an unprecedented division of labor and specialization of professions in modern society. Simultaneously, the role and influence of experts in formulating and conducting our national policies have grown to unprecedented levels.

Considering the responsibilities of the office of the President of the United States, it is clear that not even the ablest individual can know all the problems about which a U.S. President must make decisions. Therefore, he has to consult individuals with specialized knowledge. And, logically, the more complex the problems, the more he must rely on their knowledge, wisdom and advice. Incidentally, it was Walt Rostow who while working in the 1960 campaign on Kennedy's foreign and military policies . . . gave JFK the phrase 'get the country moving again' and Kennedy credited him with originating the 'New Frontier' slogan.[199] And it was Richard Goodwin, Deputy Assistant Secretary for Inter-American Affairs during President Kennedy's administration, who coined the well-known title 'Alliance for Progress' and later coined another famous phrase, 'The Great Society' for President Johnson.[200]

The "New Strategy for Peace" was, according to all sources, practically the work of one man, President Nixon's Assistant for National Security Affairs, Professor Dr. Henry A. Kissinger. It goes without saying that by approving and endorsing the text, President Nixon took before the nation the responsibility upon himself. However, our foreign policy and its genesis are too important a matter to permit us to confine ourselves to considerations of their formal aspects. On the contrary, it is more important than ever to clearly identify the author of a blueprint of foreign policy for a whole decade and to treat the message not as a Presidential message of anonymous or broadly composite origin, but as a document expressing the personal views and philosophy on matters of foreign policy and communism, of one outstanding expert, Dr. Kissinger.

The Kissinger Blueprint was obviously supposed to clarify the crucial issues of our time and the U.S. stand on them. Based on new ideas and new approaches, it was to indicate new solutions, leading to the liquidation of the present perilous impasse and eventually to the attainment of a durable peace.

The Structure of the Kissinger Blueprint

The world, according to Dr. Kissinger, has "dramatically changed" since World War II. "The postwar period in international relations has ended."

A quarter of a century ago, the key features of the situation were: (a) the overwhelming military superiority of the U.S., especially in atomic weapons; (b) the comparative weakness of its allies, who were ravaged and exhausted by the war, and thus dependent on U.S. help; (c) the monolithism of the communist world.

In the meantime, profound changes have taken place. First, the U.S. military preponderance has been drastically reduced. For some time the U.S. strove to maintain its nuclear superiority. However, in the crucial period after 1965, "the Johnson Administration decided not to step up (nuclear) deployments."

"As a result of these developments, an inescapable reality of the 1970's is the Soviet Union's possession of powerful and sophisticated strategic forces approaching, and in some categories, exceeding ours in numbers and capability."

Moreover,

"the Soviet missile deployments are continuing, whereas ours have leveled off. In the 1970's we must also expect to see Communist China deploy international ballistic missiles, seriously complicating strategic planning and diplomacy."

Second, our allies have recovered from the war and the relationship of dependence on the United States has ended.

Third, the nature of the communist world has also changed deeply:

". . . the power of individual Communist nations has grown, but international Communist unity has been shattered. Once a unified bloc, its solidarity has been broken by the powerful forces of nationalism."

The "powerful tides of change" which have transformed the world, include "unprecedented scientific and technological advances as well as explosions in population, communications and knowledge," which produce "a new element of insecurity" and "require new forms of international cooperation."

So, "the time has passed in which powerful nations can or should dictate the future to less powerful nations." Until now, the U.S. foreign policy has tried to dominate, to tell the countries of the free world what to do, to decide for them. Now, the U.S. must decidedly turn from leadership ("domination") to partnership in its relations with its allies.

Since both the United States and the Soviet Union "have acquired the ability to inflict unacceptable damage on the other no matter who strikes first," since "no one's interests are furthered by conflict" and obviously "peace is in everyone's interest," war can no longer be considered as a rational solution to any problem. "There can be no gain and certainly no victory for the power that provokes a thermonuclear exchange." "Thus both sides have recognized a mutual vital interest in halting the dangerous momentum of the nuclear arms race."

In view of all these developments a new situation has arisen which requires a new American policy.

Professor Kissinger first warns against the policy of weakness, which could encourage aggression ("military adventures"). But he does not seem to favor the opposite course—of increasing U.S. nuclear strength—either, for ". . . Soviet political positions would harden, tensions would increase and the prospect for reaching agreements to limit strategic arms might be irreparably damaged."

This conclusion is the more surprising since the author recognizes and stresses the grave threats of Soviet offensive arms. "There is a serious threat to our retaliatory capability in the form of the growing Soviet forces of ICBMs and ballistic-missile submarines, their multiple-warhead program for the SS-9 missile, their apparent interest in improving the accuracy of the ICBM warheads and their development of a semi-orbital nuclear-weapon system." Besides, there is also the potential danger of the nuclear development of Communist China threatening the U.S. population.

After stressing all these dangers, the author, instead of reaching the conclusion that U.S. nuclear strength should be increased, follows with a warning that any nuclear war would be a catastrophe for the United States:

> "Today any nuclear attack—no matter how small, whether accidental, unauthorized or by design; by a superpower or by a country with only primitive nuclear delivery capability—would be a catastrophe for the U.S., no matter how devastating our ability to retaliate . . ."

This uniquely defeatist consideration, which makes the United States nuclearly the most hopeless and doomed country in the world, necessarily leads to only one possible conclusion: adapt to the world, such as it is. And Professor Kissinger draws it: the U.S. must "harmonize doctrine and capability."

The U.S. must continue to protect its security and the lives of its citizens. But the "mutual hostility that flowed from deep-seated differences of ideology" belongs to the past. "For us as well as our adversaries, in the nuclear age the perils of using force are simply not in reasonable proportion to most of the objectives sought in many cases. The balance of nuclear power has placed a premium on negotiation rather than confrontation."

Therefore, both powers must concentrate on "issues that transcend national differences and ideology and should respond to effective multilateral action. In an era when man possesses the power both to explore the heavens and desolate the earth, science and technology must be marshalled and shared in the cause of progress, whatever the political differences among nations."

In spite of the Soviet Union building up its military, especially nuclear, strength, endangering the security of the United States, seeking a position of hegemony in the Middle East, Professor Kissinger's estimate of the chances for the progress of peace is optimistic:

"By the examples we set, we hope to lead the way toward the day when other nations adopt the same principles";

"We hope that other great powers will act in a similar spirit and not seek hegemony."

"We hope that as Vietnamization proceeds the Government of North Vietnam will realize that it has more to gain in negotiations than in continued fighting."

"We hope that the coming year will bring evidence that the Soviets have decided to seek a durable peace rather than continue along the roads of the past."

That is the structure of the Kissinger Blueprint, its main theses and lines of argument.

"This vision of peace built on partnership, strength and willingness to negotiate is the unifying theme of this report," says Dr. Kissinger.

Let us now see whether these three principles as conceived and presented by Dr. Kissinger, can lead to world peace.

Partnership

The first thing which speaks against the Kissinger concept of partnership, is that national policies are far more than a matter of momentary moods or individual whims. They are constantly shaped by a complex interplay of a thousand various factors and can be changed only by a complicated and rather lengthy process involving thorough study, and the cooperation of many official and unofficial individuals and institutions.

So, if the U.S. foreign policy until now has been selfish and overbearing, if we have failed to consult with our allies and substituted "lofty phrases" for "candid and constructive dialogue," if we have told everybody what to do, instead of listening to other nations' needs and opinions, if the various agencies planning our national security have been "using different assumptions about our policy objectives . . . and even the basic facts about our policy choices"—who can and on what grounds believe that all that will abruptly stop and change for the better just because we have announced it?

It is enough to ask the question.

Besides, what seriously undermines the credibility and sincerity of the criticism of our old policies and recommendation for the new, is the profuse rhetoric, sweeping generalities and slogan-reasoning ("we are not involved in the world because we have commitments, we have commitments, because we are involved"; our foreign policy for the 1970s demands "above all, imaginative thought"; . . . "bringing 20th century man and his environment to terms with one another"; "all voices are heard and none is predominant," etc.)—which take the place of sober analysis, matter-of-fact approach and realistic evaluations.

"Good words are not a substitute for hard deeds, and noble rhetoric is no guarantee of noble results," says the Kissinger Blueprint. The rhetoric and word games, generalities and flippant tone of the New Strategy for Peace undoubtedly speak and work against it and make any favorable results from this document for peace unlikely.

The "New" Is Too Similar to the "Old"

The next factor working against the credibility of our "new" policy is the fact that it bears too close a resemblance to the old, Rusk-Rostow policy. Except for the repeated assertion that the "new" policy is new, they are in essence identical. We find the same concepts, the same slogans, the same conclusions, the same misconceptions, the same fallacies. So, the trouble with the "new" view of the world is the same as with the old one: it is in conflict with the facts of the situation.

And the first and basic conflict with reality is that it assumes that we have peace today simply because there is no global nuclear war. It ignores the reality of communist political global warfare aimed at the destruction of states and nations, law and public order, religion and education, the whole fabric of civilization.

The towering fact of the international scene today is the total aggression of world communism. And so our chief problem is not poverty, not ignorance, not disease, not overpopulation, important as they are, but *communism*.

This is the aspect of the present trouble and strife in the U.S. which the communists and liberals do not want or are unable to face. Their standard retort is that all the modern problems of mankind would exist even if there were no communism in the world. They even say that to accuse the communists as the main fomentors of trouble is paranoiac and makes them appear all-powerful and increases their prestige.

In his article within the debate on the National Purpose in 1960, David Sarnoff had a very apt rebuttal to this liberal inanity. Obviously there were many problems besetting the world, not only the problem of communism. However, he added, ". . . if the Sino-Soviet bloc wins world domination, the other problems will cease to matter; they will have been solved for the free world in about the way death solves all bodily ills." [201]

In other words, without communism many present problems would *not* exist, and others would be essentially different and they would not be used as weapons to destroy America.

So, the political nature of the communist challenge and threat is overwhelmingly evident, and the theory about communism presenting a strictly military danger, where we have no choice outside of surrendering or engaging in a totally hopeless nuclear war, openly defies evidence and reason.

Ever since World War II, it is the United States that has been bleeding, in Korea (1950–1953) and in Vietnam (1964–1972), while the USSR and Red China have waged war by proxy, keeping their military machines intact and saving their immense manpower.

It is the political war waged by world communism against the U.S. throughout the world and in the U.S. itself, which has heavily impaired the prestige of the U.S. in the world, and at home has wrought havoc with the ingredients which make the nation.

And yet we find in the Kissinger Blueprint not only the general framework of the old estimate of the international situation, but also its main theses.

As early as 1947, General G. C. Marshall had proclaimed that "Our policy is not directed against any country or doctrine, but against hunger, poverty, desperation and chaos." President Johnson considered "a bigger bowl of rice" as the solution for Asia's woes and problems.

The "new" policy is also based on "economism," the belief in the supreme importance of economic factors in the life of nations: ". . . if peace and freedom are to endure in the world, there is no task more urgent than lifting the hungry and the helpless, and putting flesh on the dreams of those who yearn for a better life." (Nixon speech of October 31, 1969).

The non-political approach to eminently political problems is not new either. Modern science and technology, while creating new problems, are also, allegedly, creating a new world where "the importance of power is reduced"(!)

The position that "it will be the policy of the United States . . . not to employ negotiations as a forum for cold-war invective or ideological debate," is anything but new. It not only forms the essence of the foreign policy views of such influential politicians as Averell Harriman or Adlai Stevenson, but it has been a guideline of the State Department's policy.

The concept of normalization of relations with communist countries is not new. It is typical of Senator William Fulbright's philosophy that "the Soviet Union is a normal state with normal interests."

The explicit stand that we will not try to take advantage of Soviet-Chinese rivalry:

"Our desire for improved relations is not a tactical means of exploiting the clash between China and the Soviet Union. We see no benefit to us in the intensification of that conflict, and we have no intention of taking sides. Nor is the United States interested in joining any condominium or hostile action of great powers against either of the large communist countries . . ."

does not reflect a new attitude either. This most strange position is typical of the Walter Lippmann philosophy that "all wise statesmen give their adversaries the chance of saving face," which is demonstrably inaccurate. For, as everybody knows, wise statesmen have, since the beginning of time, done their utmost to embarrass their opponents, especially their sworn enemies, not to give them a chance to save face. As far as the United States is concerned, its wise statesmen have tried to embarrass their opponents from the days when George Washington embarrassed King

George III, up to the days when Franklin D. Roosevelt went out of his way *not* to embarrass Joseph Stalin.

This Kissinger attitude on Soviet-Chinese rivalry is also identical with the position and policy of his predecessor, Professor Walt Rostow, who, speaking on the growing alienation between the USSR and Red China, stated that "it would be a mistake if the U.S. were to try to take advantage of this rift to promote its own interests." The United States "should pursue its own policy and defend its most important interests in the world." [202] Professor Rostow did not care to explain the alleged contradiction between promoting U.S. national interests and taking advantage of the Soviet-Chinese rift.

Partnership and South Vietnam

The validity of the new principle of partnership in our relation to U.S. allies is seriously threatened in the very document where it is announced, by the attitude taken toward South Vietnam.

Dr. Kissinger trusts our adversaries and respects their interests as they see them. But when South Vietnam is concerned, he is not sure, after nine years, where the people of South Vietnam stand: "Are they truly being disaffected from the Vietcong or are they indifferent to both sides?" And then: ". . . are the Vietnamese developing the leadership, logistics, capabilities, tactical knowhow and sensitivity to the needs of their own people which are indispensable to continued success?"

The only possibility which apparently never crossed the mind of Dr. Kissinger is that the Vietnamese people may be for their Government, in favor of which they voted not only in the one-candidate elections of October 3, 1971, but twice before in perfectly free and internationally supervised elections.

The claim that the Saigon government was insensitive to the needs of the people, has been a standard thesis of communist propaganda. Where is the sense, the logic, the justification, to question publicly our ally in a most decisive area and in a manner which is intensely injurious to their prestige, as it is to ours?

And then why stress the absolute decisiveness of free elections in South Vietnam and its outcome, "regardless of the changes they may bring," and not consider the state of human rights and political freedoms in North Vietnam, and insist on the need for holding free elections there and seeing to it that the results be enforced, no matter which way they may turn?!

This discriminatory treatment of North Vietnam (our adversary) and South Vietnam (our ally) in favor of the former, casts an ominous light on the meaning of Vietnamization, which is our answer to the problem of communist aggression against South Vietnam.

The communist relentless drive for world conquest through "wars of national liberation" is not about to subside, nor is the pressure on all Asian lands by Red China. So, how can South Vietnam do alone, without us, what they were unable to do with the help and active participation of over 500,000 American troops? It clearly appears that we do not mean to strengthen an ally so that he be able to take care of his own problems, but that, under the cover of partnership, we are withdrawing U.S. power and influence and leaving it to the South Vietnamese to face alone the permanent and joint communist (North Vietnam, USSR, Red China, etc.) aggression in Southeast Asia.

Is that, in Dr. Kissinger's estimate, really the road to peace?

Who Wants Partnership?

In announcing the transition from U.S. "dominance" to "partnership," the Kissinger Blueprint has completely overlooked the question of how it will affect its supposed beneficiaries, our allies. It has simply been assumed that since people resent being ordered about, spoken to with condescension and having decisions made for them, and much prefer to be consulted and to participate in the making of decisions,—every nation will welcome the end of U.S. dominance and the advent of U.S. partnership.

But that logic is too simplistic to be valid.

There has been more talk of change as a factor of international life than of any other factor. But strangely enough, hardly anybody—and especially not those whose favorite "sociologico-political" explanation for all modern problems is change, and whose unique solution is adaptation to change—ever speaks of the most important change of all as a result of World War II, and that is the spread of communism, of communist terrorist rule from

200 million to nearly one billion human beings. They thereby naturally overlook also the fact that communist rule has killed an unprecedentedly large number of people, much more than all the casualties of both World Wars.

That is the change which is posing the biggest problems and which the U.S. has to face more than any other change or problem. What will the U.S. do? Resist, shape events? It has not so far. And now the Kissinger Blueprint tells us that the position of the Nixon Administration is "to reflect the forces of change in our approach and in our actions."

And that, most assuredly, is not what the world, above all our allies, want or expect from the United States.

The United States has become the leader of the world, the strongest country of the globe, not because it would have sought that position or dreamed of ruling our planet, but as a result of its unique growth, of world developments and its participation in them. That is how it emerged at the end of World War II as the leading country of the modern world. And while it is not a position it sought, it is also a position and responsibility it cannot lightly discard. Even if there were no communist movement and power in the world, the leading nation must lead, in the same way as leading individuals must play a bigger part and assume more responsibility in society. It is a law of nature.

Today, when the communist world movement is displaying increased aggressiveness and building its strength for new assaults and conquests, the free world needs a leader, not a partner! Our allies, all free countries of the world, as well as the enslaved in all communist-ruled countries, naturally expect the U.S. to lead, not to resign or betray its natural obligation of leadership.

So, partnership, as presented by Dr. Kissinger, cannot be justified, politically or historically. At his press conference (March 4, 1969) following his visit to Western Europe, President Nixon had stated: "We will be dominant . . . because of our immense nuclear power and also because of our economic wealth." Why then and wherefore would the U.S. all of a sudden renounce leadership ("dominance") and become "one of the boys"?

Our allies cannot be convinced by the explanation given and will search for the true meaning of the change. And in this search they cannot miss the connection between our new policy of seeking better relations with the communist world (negotiation instead of confrontation) and partnership. The former explains the latter. The transition from confrontation to negotiation explains the transition from leadership to partnership. It is a withdrawal from the world, from political reality, under the pressure of communist imperialism and aggression.

If U.S. leadership—it is characteristic that the word has been avoided in the Kissinger Blueprint, and substituted by the word "dominance"—has failed so far, it can only be a reason for making new efforts, finding new ways and implementing it with more serious intent and firmer determination. If we are unable to provide world leadership, we have condemned ourselves to death. And in that case partnership will not improve the chances of the free world, but accelerate its demise.

2. Strength

The second of the three principles proclaimed essential for the attainment of world peace by Dr. Kissinger, is U.S. strength. However, it does not take extraordinary efforts or unusual powers of perception to realize that Dr. Kissinger actually is not talking of U.S. strength but U.S. renunciation of strength. This is evident in the very strange logic applied in considering the unfavorable change in the relationship of U.S. and Soviet nuclear capability.

In the face of the deterioration of our military (nuclear) position, of the growing strength of the USSR, and of Soviet overwhelming temptation to continue communist imperialist aggression and subversion—what should be more natural for us than to examine and establish who and what policies were responsible for our decline, and then proceed with the greatest resolve to improve the situation.

Instead of that, Dr. Kissinger completely ignores the first question (apparently nobody is responsible or it does not matter who is). And then he chooses to put our policies down on the level of our weakness because our strength might antagonize the Soviets and make the attainment of peace more difficult. And yet it is a matter of record that the concept of U.S. position of strength was one of the key points of President Nixon's attitude on negotiations with the communists (North Vietnam and the USSR) during the whole presidential campaign of 1968, as well as after.

And it is more than obvious that if the U.S. strength, while it was overpowering, was unable to secure peace, U.S. weakness will much less be able to attain that end.

It stands to reason that if our position has so seriously deteriorated in the course of 27 years (1945–1972) and we are not trying to correct the situation, and if the Soviets are doing their utmost to increase their military, and especially nuclear strength,—there is no guarantee that our position will not continue deteriorating in the next 27 years, to the point of no-option, which then spells unconditional surrender!

The Kissinger Blueprint is based on the false assumption that the survival of the U.S. depends on peace. It lacks the awareness that peace cannot have any chance at all without U.S. strength. To base peace on U.S. strength is the only approach which makes political sense.

To rely on peace based on compromise with our enemies (and thus dependence on their will) to safeguard U.S. vital interests, is unrealistic, and the procedure is indefensible: We disregard all hard facts of increased communist strength and hostility; we proclaim that we have important values, concerns and interests in common with the enemy. And then we reduce all realistic options to the utterly perilous reliance on communist good will, to a "we hope"!

How can that be a policy? And a policy for the leading country in the world at a time of its greatest peril!

3. *Negotiation* (The Willingness to Negotiate)

The third Kissinger principle of the "new" U.S. foreign policy of peace, is negotiation.

One of the most conspicuous features of our "old" foreign policy was to ignore the real nature of communism and to assume or pretend that the communists were just the way we are, sharing our basic concepts about the world, politics, international life, agreements and obligations. Dr. Kissinger has operated with the same assumptions:

1. That the communists share our abhorrence of war and are as concerned about peace as we are;

2. That they believe, as we do, that there would be no winners in a nuclear conflict, but only losers;

3. That they, therefore, are trying as hard as we are, to avoid war and are endeavoring to arrive by negotiation at some sort of agreement with us, to settle the basic issues which divide us, so as to build, by common efforts with us, a better society and world of peace, well-being and prosperity. In other words, that they believe and practice peaceful coexistence and that they believe in and observe international agreements.

The trouble with all these assumptions is that they are demonstrably inaccurate.

1. *Peace and War.*—As stated before, the communist concept of peace and war is totally different from ours. We believe that peace, i.e. the absence of armed hostilities, based on the disposition of the potential belligerents to settle disputes peacefully, by negotiation, is in itself an important goal for everybody. But that is alien to the communist mind. Our concepts of peace and war do not make sense to the communists. For communism is permanent war. Only the means vary. War and peace are exclusively instruments of communist strategy. And since communism, by definition, is peace, as it is democracy, justice, progress, etc., it logically follows that anybody opposing communism is against peace, as he is against democracy, justice, progress, etc. Which leaves the communists complete freedom to do whatever they please, including waging war, while at the same time remaining deeply devoted to "peace" (communism).

It is only in this sense that it can be said that the communists are concerned with peace.

2. *No Winners in a Nuclear War.*—That is notoriously not the case. As we have seen (pp. 43–44), this is the thesis of the West. But the communist thesis is exactly the opposite: the casualties would, admittedly, be enormous, but communism would emerge victorious from a global nuclear conflict.

3. *Peace Through Negotiation and Agreement.*—They do not try to avoid war per se. They are not worried about a global war because: (a) they know that the U.S. will not start a nuclear war;

(b) because they are doing too well without it (they have conquered one-third of the world).

At the XXth Congress of the C.P.S.U. held in Moscow in 1956, Nikita Khrushchev stated that the world situation had changed so radically in favor of communism and was continuing to develop favorably, that war would only interfere with the process of the instant victory of communism. The only proper policy to ensure the "world-transforming . . . and complete triumph of communism," was that of peaceful coexistence.

And peaceful coexistence certainly includes negotiations. But before considering them as a means of solving "East-West" problems, we must first put them in proper perspective.

The communists want the world enslaved, powerless, at their mercy, subjected to a rule "unrestricted by law." And that is not negotiable. In that field, as Nikita Khrushchev, Mikhail Suslov, Ilyitchev and many other Soviet leaders have made clear a thousand times, they will never make peace, for it would mean suicide. They understand what our leaders do not, that our conflict with the communists is not about hijacking, or air and water pollution, or the exploitation of deep seabed resources, etc.—but about absolutes and absolute power. They want to conquer the world and enslave man, his body and his mind. Nothing else and nothing less. Coexistence is not a resolve to make peace with the free world, but the most effective form of struggle in the present world situation. And negotiation is part of it.[203]

The communist attitude towards agreements and treaties is a matter of record. From Lenin's "principle" that international treaties were like pie crusts, made to be broken, to Stalin's statement that he never broke agreements, just changed his mind about the issues they covered, to the "five principles of coexistence" of Chou En-lai (Nehru) in 1955, to the Geneva agreement on Laos in 1962, to the Brezhnev doctrine in 1968, etc.,—treaties and agreements were and today are for the communists strictly matters of strategy. This stands to reason: a movement created for the purpose of revolutionizing and subjugating the world may talk to gain time or make unavoidable temporary retreats, but it "does not discuss with its foes, its smashes them," and therefore it will not tie its hands with written and signed pieces of paper.

The communists go to the negotiating table, as they have done ever since Brest-Litovsk in 1917. However, to them, the negotiating table is not a place of peace, but just another battlefield. So, they never go to it with the intention or willingness to make any lasting concessions or compromises on substantial questions, but to exact political concessions, consolidate their power and establish the bases for future offensive thrusts. This has been their consistent line from 1917 (Brest-Litovsk) to 1972 (negotiations on Vietnam in Paris), and they have had no reason yet to change it.

What separates us from the communists are not specific, concrete, non-political issues. Our conflicting interests are rooted in irreconcilable philosophies, world outlooks, aims and policies. Dr. Kissinger forgets what he has aptly stated himself in his study on Bismarck: not all international conflicts are a matter of misunderstanding; some are rooted in irreconcilable, non-negotiable values and objectives.[204]

And if people are willing to settle amiably non-controversial problems, they are definitely not willing to settle amiably issues of religion, faith, values, ideology, lust for world power!

Therein lies the crux of the world crisis today. As odd as it may seem to Dr. Kissinger and other experts, the source of the danger of war and of our troubles with the communists, is communism. Its aggressiveness, its intolerance, its subversion, its hatred, its total and permanent political war against the free world. Can that be negotiated out of existence?

The issues which can be solved by negotiation, those which "transcend national differences and ideology," are irrelevant. The issues which make our conflict with communism, cannot be negotiated.

Moreover, the technique of breaking up the problem of communism, a problem essentially political, of will, of confrontation, into an intellectual debate about non-political, innocuous problems, where no wills are confronted, but logical arguments, reason and fair play prevail,—is in itself an admission of political helplessness.

Political War

This brings us to the second point of the Kissinger principle of negotiation, the importance of political will. Dr. Kissinger has neglected a vital aspect of communist imperialism and conquest: political war. That, not military warfare, has been from the very beginning, the main vehicle of communist imperialism and has brought them their conquests. The Soviets won half of Europe at the end of World War II, not through military victory over Adolf Hitler, but through political victory over Franklin D. Roosevelt. That is the kind of war which they have been waging with great effect ever since. They did not fight a military war in Korea. They fought a political war. The result was that the Korean war was the first war in her history which the United States did not win.

They are not fighting today militarily in Vietnam. American casualties run into hundreds of thousands, while the Soviet Union is at military peace and not one Soviet soldier has been killed. But there would be no North Vietnamese military aggression without Soviet political aggression. And it is this Soviet political warfare, not military action, which has created the greatest foreign and domestic problem in the history of the United States—Vietnam. On top of it, we are not fighting back, but are insisting on friendship and negotiation! So, how can anybody imagine that the Soviets would now cease and desist? Why would they now make peace, political peace? Concretely: why would they now renounce their political goals, their aims of world conquest, be content with what they have and turn their energies and resources towards producing more consumer goods for their people and preserving peace?

If all we want is to avert a global military war by negotiation, we are putting them in a position of commanding political superiority. For the USSR enjoys today military global peace, and their best guarantee for it is their certitude that the U.S. will not start a nuclear war against them. Moreover, this situation of global military peace is vital to them because it enables them to wage the politically very effective local wars (wars of "national liberation") throughout the globe, without fear of provoking us nuclearly. For, evidently the U.S. is not holding that against them. They are free to wage and instigate "wars of national liberation" and support them (Vietnam, Laos, Middle East, Cambodia, Thailand) without even being accused of warmongering, aggression or disturbing the peace of the world.

The obvious sum of it all is that the Soviets have no reason to engage in any new kind of negotiation and enter any new kind of agreement except those which have helped them put one-third of the globe under communist rule. And unless we base our willingness to negotiate on the strength of the nation and an unconditional will to safeguard our national interests, no negotiation can save the United States or world peace.

Disregarding all these considerations, Dr. Kissinger has gone out of his way to induce the Soviet Union to negotiate. He has pointed to Moscow's growing troubles. He has also praised them, acknowledged the legitimacy of their interests in Eastern Europe, interpreted their interests for them.

All this deserves attention.

Breakup of Communist Monolithism

Dr. Kissinger has uncritically made his own, the old clichés about the condition of world communism, summed up in the proposition that communist monolithism has been broken. Instead of a critical analysis, he simply proclaims that communist unity and solidarity belong to the past.

In pleading the case for the breakup of communist monolithism as an alleged reason for the communists to lean toward negotiation rather than toward confrontation, Dr. Kissinger has made the most unforgivable single error of his whole Blueprint. He says:

"The only times the Soviet Union has used the Red Army since World War II have been against its own allies—in East Germany in 1953, in Hungary in 1956, and in Czechoslovakia in 1968. The Marxist dream of international unity has disintegrated."

Here the contrast between the incontrovertible facts and the interpretation given by Dr. Kissinger is most flagrant and inexcusable. For the Soviet Army, in all mentioned cases, intervened *not against* communist power in those countries, to overthrow it, but on the contrary, *in its favor,* to save communism.

Writing for himself, and carrying full personal responsibility for the views expressed, Dr. Kissinger might have been entitled to whatever defiance of evidence he might have chosen. But writing for the President, as author of a Presidential message, he had no excuse.

His theory casts a completely deceiving light on a crucial problem. It distorts historical truth in a way which makes other important assertions questionable. And it certainly thoroughly demolishes the whole theory of the disintegration of world communism. Rather than being a proof of the breakup of communist monolithism, and an inducement to negotiation, it is exactly the contrary: the proof of the existence and efficacy of communist solidarity actively preserving communist power (monolithism). And it once more confirms that the communists, unquestionably and unchangeably, view the preservation of communist power, not negotiation with the "capitalists," as the best way to safeguard their interests.

The End of Communism?

The supposed disintegration of communist monolithism is not Dr. Kissinger's only "argument" to induce the USSR to negotiation. He is telling the Soviet leaders what disappointments the past twenty years must have brought them and what lessons they certainly must have learned from them: "Perceptions framed in the 19th century are hardly relevant to the era we are now entering." "The Communist world has had to learn that the spread of Communism may magnify international tensions rather than usher in a period of reconciliation as Marx taught." The leadership in the Kremlin must have recognized "that Marxist ideology is not the surest guide to the problems of a changing industrial society." "Today all 'isms' have lost their vitality."

Which all should make it obvious to the Soviet Union that it cannot "continue and . . . base its policies at home and abroad on old and familiar concepts," in spite of the "overwhelming temptation" to do so.

These assertions are so superficial and untenable, that it is almost embarrassing to refute Dr. Kissinger.

The relevancy of communist perceptions framed in the nineteenth century (1848) is indicated by the fact that today they rule one billion people. This fact also takes care of the insufficiency of "Marxist ideology." And where such growth occurs in the period of 32 years (1917–1949), international tensions are bound to increase.

As for the "loss of vitality" of communism, Dr. Kissinger must be reminded of the intensive re-stalinization in all areas of Soviet life, including its unopposed invasion of Czechoslovakia; of its aggression in Vietnam and politico-military offensive in the Middle East and the Mediterranean, as well as of the fact that all communist self-critical "heretics" swear by socialism and communism as do their dogmatic and bureaucratic colleagues.

Equally out of place and ineffective are Dr. Kissinger's blandishments about communist love of peace (world peace above "national" interests), humanity (humanity before politics) and reasonableness. For the communists have a mind of their own, especially in political matters. They do not need anybody to interpret their thoughts for them, to tell them what their views and positions are and what their policies ought to be. They decide all that for themselves.

This brings us to another important and intriguing feature of the Kissinger Blueprint, the defense of our "adversary's" interests.

Defending the Adversary and Confirming the Communist Status-Quo

"We are aware that the Soviet Union sees its own security as directly affected by developments in this region. Several times, over the centuries, Russia has been invaded through Central Europe; so this sensitivity is not novel or purely the product of Communist dogma.

"It is not the intention of the United States to undermine the legitimate security interests of the Soviet Union. The time is certainly past, with the development of modern technology, when any power would seek to exploit Eastern Europe to obtain strategic advantage against the Soviet Union. It is clearly no part of our policy. Our pursuit of negotiation and détente is meant to reduce existing tensions, not to stir up new ones."

These paragraphs are most unusual. What do they mean? The insistence on the "insecurity of nations" and the invasion of Russia in the past centuries are an old argument and favorite excuse for Soviet imperialism. Why is Professor Kissinger endorsing them? Does he not realize that the very adoption of that logic for settling international disputes, of going back in history and trying to redress wrongs of past centuries—is the most potent incitement to hatred, intolerance and war? As if we did not have enough inflammatory material in the world of today.

Why justify Soviet imperialism and aggression with the Mongolian invasion of Russia several centuries ago, or Napoleon's invasion, or Hitler's? First of all, there is no "Russia" today, but the Union of Soviet Socialist Republics. How can a highly learned man and trained historian possibly overlook that difference? Would we apply the same logic if there had been no revolution of 1917, and we had before us today a tsarist or democratic Russia, definitely less aggressive and less threatening to world peace than the USSR? Why induce the sufferings of Russia, i.e. the Russian people, to demand understanding for the aggressive policies and warmongering intolerance of the USSR? The United States neither launched Hitler against the Soviet Union nor helped him. On the contrary, it broke his back and saved Stalin from his ally (Hitler).

Second, the argument that the time is past "when any power would seek to exploit Eastern Europe to obtain strategic advantage against the Soviet Union," sounds unbelievable. For—unfortunately—no Western power has ever tried to "exploit" Eastern Europe against the USSR. It is the Soviet Union which invaded Czechoslovakia in August 1968. And yet *we*, i.e. Professor Kissinger for us, deem it proper and necessary to announce that we have no intention of using Czechoslovakia (Eastern Europe) against the USSR!

This indefensible move suggests that after all the Soviet propaganda line about Western agents stirring trouble in Czechoslovakia and thus provoking and justifying the Soviet invasion, may have some solid foundation in fact! The opposite logic seems alien to Dr. Kissinger: if Eastern Europe should not be used against the Soviet Union, it is *a fortiori* entitled not to be oppressed, invaded and occupied by anybody, including the USSR. But that angle is not even considered by Dr. Kissinger. We have here one more example of the old foreign policy philosophy: the communists conquer and impose slavery, but we (President Eisenhower) beg the world to believe that *we* should be trusted!

The assertion that:

"By the same token, the United States views the countries of Eastern Europe as sovereign, not as parts of a monolith. And we can accept no doctrine that abridges their right to seek reciprocal improvement of relations with us or others."

would at first tend to convey the impression that if we intend to respect Soviet security interests, we also intend to see to it that the rights of Eastern European nations are respected. But that, despite appearances, is unfortunately not so. The Kissinger Blueprint says:

"We will regard our Communist adversaries first and foremost as nations pursuing their own interests as they perceive their interests, just as we follow our interests as we see them. We will judge them by their actions as we expect them to be judged by our own. Specific agreements and the structure of peace they help build will come from a realistic accommodation of conflicting interests."

First, this statement of "new" policy which equates communist regimes with independent nations follows the pattern of the old, which was based on the Rooseveltian thesis that communism was just a different brand of democracy.

Second, this is a grave disregard of historical and factual accuracy, and that not in favor of the United States, but in favor of our communist enemy.

The elementary facts of the Eastern European situation are that the nations of that area were at the end of World War II brutally, ruthlessly, in defiance of elementary justice and most solemn promises (Atlantic Charter), deprived of their sacred right of self-determination. They were never allowed to exercise their natural right to "determine their own future," to decide about their form of government. And their status has never changed since. They are not nations "pursuing their own interests," but communist regimes imposed on nations, regimes which never pursued any *national* interests, but only interests of the consolidation of communist power.

By solemnly proclaiming that we will not "undermine the legitimate security interests of the Soviet Union" in Eastern Europe, we have announced a policy of letting communist power in that area be consolidated. However, by rejecting the Brezhnev doctrine (the abridgment of "their right to seek reciprocal improvement of relations with us or others"), we have not taken a stand in favor of freedom and self-determination, as it may at first appear. On the contrary, by failing to take any action against the Soviet invasion of Czechoslovakia (in August 1968), and recommending to the USSR to normalize its relations with communist East European states, we have actually put a second lock on the communist jail into which those nations were thrown at the end of World War II.

President Roosevelt's policy of appeasement made it possible for the Soviets to enslave half of Europe. The sense of our "new" policy, which considers the communist regimes as sovereign "nations," seems to be to consolidate those regimes under the guise of challenging and defying Moscow's monolithic policies.

The Kissinger Blueprint endorses another old liberal slogan which has unalterably been at the roots of our old policies: the claim about Soviet mistrust of our intentions. The argument is untenable and injurious to the U.S. The communists (Moscow, Hanoi, etc.) do not mistrust our intentions. They are engaged in a total permanent war for the conquest of the globe. This has nothing to do with mistrust. Mistrust is a propaganda and diplomatic weapon, an excuse, not a reason. The very fact that we speak of their mistrust, i.e. acknowledge that the motive (or one of them) is mistrust, obscures the fact that their lust for power is the driving force of their actions and policies, and lends moral justification to their aggression.

Dr. Kissinger, after stressing the need for the USSR to "recover from its anachronistic fear of Germany," in the same breath stresses the need for the USSR to "normalize" its relations with Eastern Europe! In view of the U.S. stand that we consider the communist occupation of Eastern Europe as an untouchable status quo, the Soviet Union can only accept the recommendation with delight.

Solemn proclamations are judged by the practical policies which implement them. So, if our "new" policy proclaims that the rights of each nation must be respected: "the right of national independence, of self-determination, the right to be secure within its own borders and to be free from intimidation"—but accepts as a historical *fait accompli* a situation created by the most cynical violation of all those lofty principles—that will inevitably give a powerful boost to the Soviet policies based on the "Brezhnev Doctrine," paving the way for new adventures of invasion and to policies of permanent enslavement, in the name of the very principles which are being violated.

Anybody with the slightest inclination to doubt this, should be reminded of the unspeakably abject statement of Gustav Husak, the quisling stooge of the re-occupation of Czechoslovakia, to the effect that under Soviet occupation Czechoslovakia was "a fully sovereign, independent state, politically, economically, and militarily."

Conclusion

In composng his Blueprint, Dr. Kissinger has made a most serious error of scope and perspective. He has promised us "a coherent vision of the world and a rational conception of America's interests." He has given us neither. Instead of viewing the world as it is, and communism as it is, utterly ruthless, imperialistic and subversive, sharing none of our values and principles, he has viewed the world situation from a strictly diplomatic viewpoint, where all states are "normal states with normal interests," to speak with Senator Fulbright.

However, that is not the real world of today. It is an impermissibly oversimplified version of reality, in which Dr. Kissinger assumes that we have basically to play the game of international diplomacy like chess,[205] with well-known, given quantities and factors, where every piece has well-defined rules and limits of action and where the decisive factor is the skill of the participants. Dr. Kissinger leaves out of consideration the fact that today the rules of the times of Richelieu or Metternich or Bismarck or even World War I, cover only a small part of the field. In the meantime, all categories have been revolutionized.

And the chief factor which has made the world less "normal" than ever, is communism, which today holds nearly 1 billion people under its sway and wages permanent political war, with new concepts of human and international affairs.

So, when Dr. Kissinger talks about the contemporary world in terms of the willingness to negotiate, of the fundamental interest of all states in building the structure of peace, the concern of every nation for the interest of others, the Soviet and Red Chinese renouncing their hegemonistic policies and aspirations, of U.S.-communist common purposes, of restraint, of "mutual respect" and "mutual forbearance"—he is talking of some imaginary world, totally different from the world we know.

The question is then, why has an intelligent man, trained in international affairs, who cannot be so alienated from the world to be unaware of all this, composed a plan based on propositions and conclusions which cannot be accepted and defended? What are the reasons, what is his logic?

Let us proceed from the known to the concealed.

If the United States has declined and does not want to inquire into who and what wrong policies and concepts were responsible for our decline, nor do we want to make an effort to move forward;

—if we recognize the serious defects of our U.S. foreign policy until now, and expect our allies to believe that we will change all that drastically with the emergence of the Kissinger Blueprint;

—if the enemy is growing in strength and is as ever inclined to use his old methods, which have propelled him from Point Zero in 1917 to one-third of the globe in 1949;

—if we are not looking for weak spots of the enemy, but are, on the contrary, making it a policy not to take advantage of his weaknesses, and are moreover extolling his strength and virtues and finding justification and excuses for his aggression;

—if we proclaim that "there is no 'status quo'—the only constant is the inevitability of change," but recognize the communist-imposed status quo in Eastern Europe;

—if we disregard the unprecedented communist record of crimes, as well as their present imperialistic policies, and invite them to "transcend the past" and consider everything as normal;

—if we have no alternative whatsoever for the prospect of failure of this whole elaborate peace plan, but just a series of "we hopes,"—

then there is no other conclusion possible except that the plan rests on a vision of hopelessness, an estimate of unavoidable defeat and an attitude of despair and surrender.

For what Dr. Kissinger is unmistakably telling us is that, in view of the radical change of the international situation and our decline, we are no longer in a position to influence events decisively. We must adapt ourselves to the world. We are caught in the vicious circle of Vietnam. At home the mood of anti-war, anti-intervention, anti-commitment, is growing, thus making impossible a strong stand in foreign policy. And then the failure of our effort in South Vietnam strengthens the defeatist and isolationist mood at home. If we cannot win against North Vietnam, how can we win against the Soviet Union or Red China?

Dr. Kissinger totally ignores the fact that U.S. decline and Soviet growth have arisen from our strategy and philosophy of non-victory. His conclusion is, in essence, that the relationship of forces is turning in favor of communism. So, we have no other way but to Vietnamize Vietnam, and to "Vietnamize" our whole foreign policy, which means to ask and exhort our allies and potential victims of communist aggression, to do alone what they cannot do together with us.

There are, to be sure, statements of encouragement. We allegedly have a chance of achieving peace, because: (1) our allies are getting stronger; (2) the communists are no longer monolithic; (3) the satellites are getting nationalistic and resenting Soviet hegemony; (4) we have a nuclear deterrent; (5) the communists have an interest in peace as we have; (6) all mankind craves for peace and will support our efforts, etc. But all those grounds for hope are, as we have seen, non-existent.

And the reassurances that we intend to keep our commitments, that we will take strong and effective steps in Vietnam if necessary (!); that we are opposed to the Brezhnev doctrine, etc., sound hollow for they are at odds with reality, with our present policies and with the main lines of our "new" policy.

As we have seen in the chapter on Surrender, the idea of deducing the inevitability of surrender from the relative deterioration of our nuclear capability, in relation to the Soviet Union, is not new.

In 1962 it was, strangely enough, a conservative columnist, George Sokolsky, who wrote that in view of the changed relationship of power between the U.S. and the Soviet Union, which had made "enormous progress and strides," there was no other road for the U.S. but to "negotiate for survival." [206] Exactly the same idea, in a more covert form, was expressed in the President Kennedy-Stewart Alsop interview of March 1962. And it has been carefully concealed but powerfully operative in the J. F. Kennedy-Dean Rusk concept and policies of the "winds of change."

And now comes Dr. Kissinger with a blueprint for world peace which is supposed to be a new beginning, a watershed, an opening of bright new horizons, an inspiring message, but actually contains a hopeless outlook for the future of the United States. For the Kissinger Blueprint is built on the acceptance of historical defeat.

Dr. Kissinger speaks repeatedly and emphatically of change, of the powerful tides of change which are transforming the world, as a crucial factor in determining world events and relationships: "Most important, a durable peace will give full opportunity to the powerful forces driving toward economic change and social justice."

It is strange that Dr. Kissinger has not elaborated on that which he considers the most important factor of a durable peace, but has confined it to one sentence. What does he mean? How do these concepts relate to the three principles of his new foreign policy?

The slogan of "social justice" is a favorite communist war horse. So, without any explanation to the contrary and precise definition of meaning, it does not cut both ways, but works only against the U.S. What about social justice in the Soviet Union?

Economic change is in itself a fact of life. But again, it has been used by communist and liberal propagandists to demand basic changes in the U.S. economic system in the direction of socialist concepts. Is that too part of peace? And if Dr. Kissinger does not accept the communist meaning of economic change and social justice, wherein does he see the most important feature of a durable peace? Could it be that he has answered that question by stating that

> "the best means of dealing with insurgencies is to pre-empt them through economic development and social reform and to control them with police, paramilitary and military action by the threatened government," and that "peace . . . is . . . a renunciation and a constructive alternative to revolution"?

These are strange statements coming from the President's Assistant for National Security Affairs. For they reflect the theory of economic determinism and the imminence of revolution, according to which economic and social backwardness and injustice are the source of revolution. The communists use this theory to assert that they never "export revolution," never foment trouble anywhere, but that it comes from poverty, exploitation and injustice. This runs counter to historical experience, which demonstrates that the root of revolution is political. If a country cannot produce adequate political leadership, no economic development, no social reform, and no police and military can save it—nor can they save peace. There is no necessary relationship between peace and revolution. To maintain that we must have peace at any cost for fear that we cannot stop revolution, is to confirm communist propaganda.

Has Dr. Kissinger never heard of the communist cliché-theory that World War I gave birth to the first communist state, World War II made communism a world power, and World War III would mean its global victory?

If we must avoid war at any price, since *any* kind of nuclear war would be a catastrophe for the United States, and if peace is also the "alternative to revolution,"—it means that we have no option left at all. The powerful tides of change, the concern for economic change and social justice, the forces of revolution, are working irresistibly in favor of communism. Communism, then, *is* the "wave of the future"!

If so, the communists, who are politically literate, may interpret the Kissinger Blueprint not as a plan for peace which would safeguard both communist interests and those of the free countries, but as a plan for doing in a "civilized" and businesslike manner, without war, revolution and nuclear conflict, that which will come to pass anyway.

So, the "new" Kissinger policy is a throwback to the tragic days of Yalta and F. D. Roosevelt's surrender of half of Europe to Stalin, an endorsement and resuscitation of the policies of appeasement, containment and coexistence. Such policies have produced tragic consequences since World War II. Today, 25 years later, they would be final. If the main ideas of the Kissinger Blueprint, for the 1970's, were to be applied for a decade, there would probably be no 1980's for America.

It is possible that "no nation need be our permanent enemy." But our enemy today is no *nation*. It is communism, in the USSR, in China, in half of Europe, wherever it exists. It is impossible to avoid that confrontation, not only because success and leadership necessarily invite envy, resentment, hostility, and impose responsibility, but because communism has taken since 1848 a position of "either-or" and on that basis has pursued its policy to the present day. So, if we equate communism with nations, and proclaim that "no nation need be our permanent enemy," then there is only one possible sense in which that position can be interpreted: surrender.

That is why the Kissinger Blueprint must be rejected. For no expert has the right to reduce the policies of the greatest country in the world to the non-choice between surrender and "we hope," and give the advice of despair to the President of the United States.

In 1962, Senator Barry Goldwater suggested to President Kennedy that the first need of U.S. foreign policy was for him to fire some of his chief foreign policy advisers. Eight years later, Vice President Agnew took the same dim view of certain foreign policy experts when he stated:

"As one looks back over the diplomatic disasters that have befallen the West and the friends of the West over three decades, at Teheran, Yalta, Cairo—in every great diplomatic con-

ference that turned out to be a loss for the West and freedom
—one can find the unmistakable footprints of W. Averell Harriman." [207]

Should Professor Henry Kissinger remain the chief shaper of our
foreign policy, the '70s will bear his "unmistakable footprints,"
and that would be a major American tragedy.

No nation, and especially not the leading country in the world,
can go in two opposite directions at the same time. It cannot "reflect the forces of change" in the world, and at the same time
"shape the future." It must choose.

To shape events, the President needs not the advice of despair,
but the advice of courage, of faith in the values which made the
nation and make its present strength, advice based on the resolve
to make the U.S. and freedom stronger in the world.

For all its shortcomings, the Kissinger Blueprint for world
peace has one incontrovertible merit: it proves beyond the
shadow of a doubt that the United States vitally needs a really
new foreign policy.

14 The Liberation of the U.S. Mind

"If we cringe from the necessity of meeting issues boldly—with principle, resolution and strength—then we shall simply hurdle along from crisis to crisis, improvising with expedients, seeking inoffensive solutions, drugging the nation with an illusion of security which does not really exist.

"The United States has matured to world leadership; we must steer by the stars, not by the lights of each passing ship. If we are to scamper from crisis to crisis fixing principles and policies to the whims of each day, we shall place ourselves supinely and helplessly at the mercy of any aggressor who might play on the public opinion and decimate our resolution at will . . ."

GENERAL OF THE ARMY OMAR N. BRADLEY
"That We May Learn To Live as Bravely as They Died"
Parade magazine, June 1, 1969

If science and technology do not offer the alternative we are seeking, but pose more problems than they solve, and if our new policy, announced in the Kissinger Blueprint, is identical with the old—does that mean that there is no alternative?

That is what the experts are saying when they claim that facts are not facts, that evidence is not evidence, that communism is not communism, and—even if they were—we must hope that nevertheless everything will somehow turn out all right.

Concomitantly, they assert that what is not, *is* (communism is falling apart, communists are willing to coexist and cooperate, the nations of the world crave for peace, our supreme interest is peace at any price, etc.). Explicitly or implicitly, deliberately or unwittingly, they would like the U.S. to reconcile with a situation of no alternative to surrender.

The crucial point where liberal thinking is confused is nothing less than the question of U.S. survival, of its existence. Instead of this being a matter beyond any dispute, it is precisely there, at the core, that the controversy has been infiltrated: isn't maybe the U.S., such as we know it, obsolete as a national sovereign state, behind the times, out of step with the realities of the modern nuclear world? And isn't it thus advisable to strive for a merger with other nations into a world-wide community, a global family of nations?

This question amounts to asking: has the U.S. a right to live, to assert itself, continue, develop, progress, *or* must it now that it has reached the peak, spend all its remaining days apologizing to everybody and atoning for all the sins it has committed since 1776, and possibly for its pre-natal sins dating from 1620; or, why not even from 1492?

This means that what the communist offensive has done, by confusing our thinking, making questionable our values and subverting our yardsticks, is to induce us to violate some elementary laws of international life, (which they have scrupulously observed), and on the observance of which the survival of nations depends:

1. The law of struggle.

International life is made not only of struggle, but of cooperation and mutual help. But as long as communism is on the world scene, the struggle for the elimination of others, the Western world, will remain the absolutely dominant feature of world politics. We, however, are suicidally pretending that the cold war belongs to the past and daily proclaim to the Soviets that our salvation depends on their willingness to cooperate for world peace.

2. The law of national identity.

To live, a nation must defend what it is, as distinct from what other nations, especially the enemy, are. We must be faithful to ourselves, to our traditions, customs, principles, ways, values, yardsticks, interests. The assertion of a nation's identity is the cornerstone of its life. Politics is the art of self-protection and self-assertion, not of adaptation to others and submission to other nations' interests and ambitions.

3. The law of political strength.

In international life the survival of the nation depends not on its merits, achievements, excellence and performance in various areas of life and culture, remarkable as they may be, not on its economic, or military might, of science and technology—but on the will it can produce to assert itself. It is only if that will exists, that its moral and natural resources count. Otherwise, if they do not inspire and do not impel to action and struggle, they are irrelevant.

This lesson has forcefully and tragically been brought to our attention by the experiences of World War II, Korea and Vietnam. In all three instances, U.S. military, economic, technological power was vastly superior. But in all three instances we lacked the will to victory. In World War II the military victory, in which the U.S. armed forces played the decisive role, was lost in favor of the total political victory of the communists (Stalin) in half of Europe, to be followed by the communist conquest of China a few years later.

In Korea, certain military victory was transformed into an inglorious stalemate, which has solved no problem, but has severely shaken the prestige of the U.S. which until then never waged a war without achieving military victory.

In Vietnam, the lesson is even more forceful. Therefore, without political strength, without strength of will to defend ourselves and defeat the enemy, all strength is in vain.

4. The law of selection

is actually the perennial problem to which such men as Plato and Confucius, as long as 2500 years ago, devoted their best intellectual efforts: the secret of good government and national security. And if their work has laid the foundations for the thinking of other outstanding men and if all the efforts of all of them, no matter how diverse, have pointed to one certain thing, it is that a nation, to prosper and go forward, must always select the best among its citizens, the best qualified, ablest individuals, most completely dedicated to the preservation of the nation (group) and the safeguarding of its interests, to positions of leadership, especially in the Government.

As we have seen in Chapter 6, the present unprecedented crisis of the U.S. is rooted in the policy of reconciliation of its liberal governments since 1933 with America's mortal enemy, the Soviet Union, leader of world communism.

It is thus most important to stress that if there must be selection, or "excellence" (to speak with John Gardner) in intellectual life, in economy, business, labor, education, etc., there must above all be excellence in politics, in the area of safeguarding the interests of the nation as a whole, defending its political foundations and strength, on which everything also depends.

It is by disregarding and violating these laws that we have become vulnerable to the enemy's political offensive. And it is because the thinking of our experts is strangled by a maze of liberal slogans which serve communist ends, that they cannot possibly see an alternative to a policy of surrender.

It so becomes obvious that it is in the *liberation of the U.S. mind* from communist and liberal control and influence, that we must seek the alternative. That process of liberation must enable us to return to the observance of the inexorable laws of international life.

The more so since the enemy is observing them scrupulously, by 1. espousing and practicing a philosophy of constant and merciless struggle aiming at unconditional victory; 2. by waging a permanent total political war, where the will to conquer dominates and coordinates all their activities; 3. by unconditionally defending communism in every respect, treating it as a religion, rejecting any criticism (except communist self-criticism) or blame for any ill or shortcoming, and considering its preservation and growth as the most important thing on earth; and 4. by always selecting for the top posts individuals who have above and beyond any other consideration, given proof of their total and ruthless dedication to the furtherance of communist power at home and abroad.

In other words, while we have been practicing a policy of surrender, they have, by implementing the four basic laws, practiced self-assertion, for that is what the four laws amount to.

And that fact, that the basic four points of the communist minimal program, peace, the U.N., anti-colonialism and co-existence,

are the basic four points of U.S. foreign policy, proves, if anything, the vital need for the liberation of the U.S. mind. So, let us
take a critical look at peace, the U.N., anti-colonialism and coexistence.

1. *Peace*

Only criminals and imbeciles can take the danger of a nuclear
war and devastation lightly. But precisely because the problem is
very real, everything must be done not only to prevent war, but
also to prevent the use of that issue and of the horrors of nuclear
war for the attainment of reprehensible political ends which may
very probably include nuclear (one-sided) massacre.

The pacifist propaganda to which we have been exposed for so
long has so befogged the issue of war and peace that rational
discussion about nuclear war has yielded to conditioned reflexes
and reactions of Western surrender as soon as the very nuclear
name is mentioned. It would appear that since both powers capable of waging a nuclear war at this time (the U.S. and the
USSR) are deeply concerned about it and doing everything in
their power to prevent it, the danger of nuclear war is everywhere and nowhere in particular—save in science and technology
—ready to strike out of the blue. In his inaugural address, President Kennedy urged "both sides" to engage in a quest for peace
"before the dark powers of destruction unleashed by science engulf
all humanity . . ."

There may be politico-diplomatic situations to which vague formulas and an abstract formulation of responsibilities may be
suited. But that approach is unsuited for the issue of nuclear war.
It can only aggravate the danger.

The slogan that "in an atomic war there would be no winners;
mankind would perish," is, to say the least, hypothetical. Besides,
it is entertained and propagandized by *our* rulers, not by the
rulers and agitprop experts of communism. Former Secretary of
Defense McNamara, with the computer brain, has told us that
he simply knows that in case of a nuclear conflict there would be
100 million dead Americans, adding that the death of 100 million
Russians (again a computerized figure) would be no consolation.

The quest for peace has become a slogan dinned into the minds of the American people by all communications media, Government officials and politicians, as well as by communist agents. Any attempt to consider the problem rationally is immediately drowned and smothered by vile smears and accusations of war-mongering, inhumanity, "fascistoid" tendencies, etc. But this over-whelming love for peace and sharp alertness against any active or potential warmongers, somehow bypasses the communists. Our peace-lovers are totally blind not only to the unlimited, total political subversive war which the communists are waging against the free world everywhere, but they are equally impervious to all communist blatant military aggression throughout the globe. (They are blindest in regard to Vietnam.)

If there is to be war, someone must wage it. Weapons alone do not shoot, do not go off, do not kill by themselves. There must be soldiers to operate them, there must be an army within which they act, a government which decides about the military action, an organized political force of some kind, national or international. Now, since, thank God, there is not yet any international force capable of starting and waging a war of world scope—the question is who, what army, what government, what country in the modern world, is likely and able to start a nuclear war?

"Accidental war."

There is, of course, the theory, so dear to Western nuclear leftists, their last refuge before facts and reality, about the danger of an accidental war, which would supposedly start if a "G.I. Joe" on this side or an "Ivan" on the communist side, would, to kill boredom, take a few swigs more than advisable of some good bourbon or vodka, and press a button releasing an I.C.B.M. or the like, just "for kicks." Then, even without the slightest intent of any government, the war could not be prevented from developing in full scope and horror.

But regardless of the puerility of the hypothesis, we are told that our noble-hearted liberals who have advanced the devastating possibility, have also advocated an effective antidote and put the achievements of modern science and technology to good use: the red telephone line between Washington and Moscow, linking directly the President of the United States and the head of the

Soviet government. Characteristically, the genius who recommended that such a line be installed, was a liberal U.S. newspaper editor who illustrated the hypothetical situation by assuming that the devastating missile had been fired from the Soviet Union. In such a situation, Nikita Khrushchev (or Kosygin or Brezhnev or . . .) would get on the hot line and with all the seriousness and deep feeling suited to his statemanship, responsibility and love of mankind, and appropriate for the occasion, announce approximately the following: "Dear John (or Lyndon, or Dick) a terrible thing has just happened. . . . An I.C.B.M. will hit New York (or Chicago, etc.) in a few moments and we have no way of stopping It. The city will be reduced to ruins. But it was all a bad accident, I am terribly sorry and we now have the crushing responsibility to see to it that there is no war, which would, as we both know, destroy both our countries." The U.S. President, knowing the sincerity of the Soviet head of state, would readily agree and make sure that no American warmonger came near any U.S. nuclear button. So, peace would be saved. . . . As we all know, a hot line between the White House and the Kremlin has been established since. So, that takes care of that.

Now, returning to the basic consideration: who today is going to start a nuclear war? Under present conditions, the very question eliminates those who do not have the atomic bomb. So, for the present time at least, the number of potential nuclear war starters is reduced to two powers, the United States and the Soviet Union. Which of the two is likely to start a nuclear war?

To answer that question, we must start from one clear and incontrovertible fact: that peace begins in the mind and war begins in the mind. People wage war when they entertain ambitions, which cannot be satisfied by peaceful pursuits, when they decide not to talk, discuss and make mutual concessions, so as to arrive at peaceful change, but to impose change by overpowering, beating, destroying the enemy. This is the crux of the question of peace and war.

If the U.S. and USSR took basically the same view of the problem of war and peace, if those two words had the same meaning for them, and if they shared the view that a war would be devastating for both sides and for mankind—then the preconditions for peace endeavors and cooperation would be fulfilled.

But that is notoriously not the case. The U.S. and the USSR do not have the same idea of peace or the same idea of war. The U.S. concept of war is confined to military hostilities and the concept of peace is just the absence of military hostilities. The Soviet concept of war is total and permanent, in all fields, by all means and all the time. And their concept of peace is strictly unilateral: peace exists when the "capitalist" powers do not oppose communist aggression, subversion, imperialism, when they wage no military or political war against communism. Any Western resistance against communist aggression is aggression, and any resistance to communist war is war. By communist standards, mankind is progressing toward peace exclusively through Western surrender, and it will have peace only when communism wins and conquers the world.

The total and permanent war which communism is waging for the destruction of the West, is directed not only against "powers and thrones," principles and institutions, but against the peace of mind of the world's masses, against the acceptance not only of all things as they are, but of peace as a basic precondition for changing things for the better. Communists are all the time stirring dissatisfaction in the free world, sowing the seeds of trouble, revolt, revolution and violence in the minds of people, poor or affluent.*

The reality with which we are confronted all over the globe is that of unchanged communism, in its three main and essential aspects: power, war and hatred. That is the fundamental fact of the world situation. The forms of that unrelenting global and total war for the conquest of the world are manifold. But whether it is the military aggression in Vietnam, the heavy arming of Egypt for war in the Middle East, the invasion of Czechoslovakia, or "peace" negotiations in Paris, or Soviet naval penetration in the Mediterranean, or nuclear negotiations in Geneva, or the "hot summers" in the U.S. cities, or the disruption of the Convention of the Democratic Party in Chicago (August 1968), or the sacking of

* In 1848 (Communist Manifesto) and until recently, the main source of personal unhappiness and social trouble was poverty. Now that the U.S., a "capitalist" country, has performed the miracle of a high standard of living for the broadest masses, it is affluence. Paradoxically, poverty too! The affluent are stirred to dissatisfaction and rebellion for having only a good material life, but spiritually empty, and the poor are stirred to dissatisfaction and rebellion because they are poor in the midst of opulence!

U.S. universities, etc.—it is *war*, waged with total hatred, which leaves no room for peace at all, be it in social relations, or racial relations, or international relations.

So, this is the acid test of communist sincerity in talking about peace. As long as they proclaim peace, but stir all the passions of war, there will be no peace, there *can* be no peace, because they do not want it, because their program has remained permanent war.

If world peace is threatened, permanently, it is not by the U.S., which does not want war or a revolutionary change of world conditions and order—but by the communists, whose aim is to destroy the present world order and bring about an entirely different one, by wars of all kinds, military aggression, wars of "national liberation," civil war, espionage, agitation, propaganda.

So, while the danger of a shooting war cannot be dismissed, it is still only a possibility. But the communists are waging every day, in every area of human endeavor, in every country, all the time, offensively and relentlessly, a war which can destroy the U.S. and civilization, and that total political war is the dominant fact of our time. And yet U.S. foreign policy is based on the potential threat of nuclear war, while it ignores the reality of communist political warfare, which is most likely to lead to communist nuclear aggression.

It is only within this framework of facts that the problem of the threat of nuclear war can be considered soberly and realistically.

Asked after World War I why France was not disarming when Germany was without an army, the French Foreign Minister, Aristide Briand, is quoted as answering: "We cannot disarm militarily as long as the Germans are armed mentally." Authentic or not, the anecdote points to the moral of the case: regardless of their military strength and preparedness, the communists are permanently, unconditionally war-oriented. To take an attitude of unconditional peace toward them is to commit suicide.

At the close of World War II we possessed an atomic monopoly, and thus enjoyed a commanding position in the modern world. However, we not only did not use it politically, but during that U.S. atomic monopoly era, we surrendered to the communists half of Europe and China.

Moreover, we not only helped the USSR to develop its own

atomic bomb, but no traitor encountered any serious difficulties in passing or selling U.S. atomic secrets to the enemy.

From 1949 to 1965 we enjoyed considerable nuclear superiority over the USSR, but instead of taking full advantage of that superiority politically, we pursued a policy of U.S. weakness, unaccountable by reason and by U.S. national interests.

From 1965 on, we neglected the building of our nuclear power, as attested by our top expert in matters of nuclear policy, Professor Kissinger himself, in his foreign policy program for the 1970s.

And now he recommends that we refrain from strengthening ourselves nuclearly, for fear that Soviet political positions would harden and the attainment of world peace (through U.S.-Soviet collaboration) would be made more difficult.

From this, several aspects of the nuclear problem should emerge clear as daylight:

1. that there was no danger of any nuclear holocaust in the period of U.S. atomic monopoly, and that the danger arose only from the moment when the USSR started producing atomic bombs;

2. that the danger increases in proportion with the nuclear strengthening of the communist powers, i.e. with the relationship of nuclear capability changing in favor of the communists;

3. that the decisive factor in this deterioration of nuclear relationship against the United States, is the U.S. foreign policy of coexistence, appeasement and fear of provoking (!) the hostility of the communists;

4. that therefore the danger of nuclear war has grown not only owing to communist nuclear efforts, but was encouraged by our policy of political weakness, which accepts communist nuclear strength and strengthening as unalterable facts of life, but sees peace endangered by U.S. nuclear strength, and thus rejects a policy of the increase of U.S. nuclear power as a dangerous "nuclear arms race";

5. that, should we persist in our philosophy of the unthinkability of nuclear war and in our policy of peace at any price, the present trends of the increase of communist nuclear might and the (comparative) decline in U.S. nuclear might would be enhanced, thus turning the theoretical danger of nuclear war into the likeli-

hood of unilateral nuclear warfare, into a nuclear massacre of the free world by the communists.

Our striving for peace at any price is against nature. For the law of international life is struggle, not peace. Young nations, eager to change things and make history, love old rules. Peace is possible only if men give up making history. But no such thing is on the horizon, for the end of history is the end of man.

Lenin made a bad "Freudian slip" in 1919 when he spoke of the communist state as one where the rule over people would be substituted by the administration of things. After 10,000 years of communist rule, people would be reduced to vegetables, and administration of things would be a fitting term for such a political system.

Only those who have nothing to stand for, to live for, to express, to create, who have no answers to the problems of mankind, who have no will, no yardsticks, no absolutes, nothing to oppose to other contenders for world power and their will, their yardsticks, their solutions—only such nations can reconcile with or strive for absolute peace.

That is what the communists know and that is why they have set the greatest store by achieving control of our thinking and invalidating our values. For they know that a nation which has no absolutes, no longer has any identity; it has nothing to fight for. And that is the case with nations whose foreign policy consists of sheer adaptation to the enemy.

So, it is utterly unreasonable and damaging to busy ourselves exclusively with communist military aggression and strive for military peace while ignoring the basic, political aggression. The danger of a potential nuclear war, considered apart from the political situation, is in essence spurious, because it depends decisively on the outcome of the political war. As long as we see only the specter of the nuclear war (which the communists do not need to conquer the globe), but are blind to the reality of the political war, which they are waging to conquer the world, we are working against our proclaimed desire to prevent a nuclear conflict.

If the U.S. is to live, our chief concern must be not to work for general disarmament, but to arm ourselves with moral and political power, with the will to defeat our global political enemy. The

failure to grasp this elementary trait of the situation is at the root
of our policy of non-victory in Vietnam, as it is at the root of our
adulation of the United Nations Organization.

2. *The U.N.*

The most important fact regarding the U.N. and the one which
has received the least attention is that the very concept of this
organization is deranged. For it consists of an insoluble contradiction: the nations of the world, especially the U.S., want peace and
a world free of oppression. The USSR wages permanent war
against the free world, it has subjugated half of Europe and is re-
affirming in word and deed its unchanged determination to conquer the globe and impose everywhere the ruthless dictatorship of
the communist party. And thus the U.S. and the Soviet Union
agree to work together for peace in the world and guarantee to all
nations the exercise of the right of self-determination and freedom! A worse surrender of the U.S. to the USSR and world communism can hardly be imagined. The very fact that we accept the
USSR as a member of the U.N., washes from it all its (Stalinist
and other) crimes, it absolves all communists from their unsur-
passed inhumanity, and it accepts the realization of communist
aims as compatible with the ends of the U.S. and other free nations.

The U.N. Organization is the child of capitalist-communist collaboration and fraternization in World War II. It is the realization
of the very bold communist plan to continue, and institutionalize,
the concept of anti-fascism which so brilliantly served their interests in the conditions of wartime collaboration of 1941–1945, that
it would further impose restrictions on U.S. policies in the new era
of U.S.-Soviet relations, characterized by unchecked Soviet imperialism and open hostility against the United States.

This basic concern, to make the U.N. into an instrument of Soviet policies, is visible in the very setup of the United Nations,
since in the name of common (U.S.-Soviet) concern and responsibility for peace, we, i.e. our top peace expert at that time, Alger
Hiss, gave the Soviet Union three seats in the General Assembly,
while every other country obtained only one. For every other

country the principle was: one nation, one vote. Only for the USSR the principle was one nation, *three votes*. By the logic adopted for the Soviet Union, the United States should have obtained forty-eight votes.

The argument about the U.N.'s peace-keeping function is patently spurious, since the period between 1945 and 1972, has been anything but a time of peace.

After obtaining from the very outset a favored position of 3:1 over everybody else, the USSR instituted the veto in the Security Council and used it to bend to its will the decisions of the U.N. The Undersecretary for Political and Security Council Affairs, head of the most important department in the U.N., has always been a communist. The first three were Soviet delegates, then one Yugoslav, then an uninterrupted string of Soviet officials.

But in spite of all this, the communist attitude has been never to concede that the U.N. should be above the Soviet Union. On the contrary, the USSR was "a law unto itself," and Nikita Khrushchev made it unmistakably clear when he stated:

> "Even if all countries of the world adopted a decision that did not accord with the interests of the Soviet Union and threatened its security, the Soviet Union would not recognize such a decision but would uphold its right, relying on force. And we have the wherewithal to do this." [208]

In Korea, where U.S. troops for the first time did not fight under their own flag, there was no victory, in spite of the excellent prospects for it. Perhaps that had something to do with the fact that Lt. General A. Vasilev, who from 1947 to 1950 was the Soviet representative on the Military Staff Committee of the United Nations, closely connected with the Undersecretariat for Political and Security Council Affairs,—was in June 1950 a Soviet "adviser" to the North Korean Army! According to some witnesses, he even personally gave the order to attack on June 25, 1950. [209] The communists accept only and exclusively one kind of internationalism, international law and international order: world-wide communist dictatorship. And therefore they recognize the U.N. only insofar as it contributes to the realization of that objective. Otherwise, they do not consider themselves to be under any obligation. In that sense, Robert Strausz-Hupé is right: "Outside of the Free World, the U.N. does not really exist." [210]

Consequently, all the talk about the rule of the majority, the interests of mankind, as opposed to the interests of sovereign states, become empty verbiage before the reality of communist unchangeable aims, yardsticks and policies.

As for the United Nations being a nucleus for a future world government, it is probable that such was the intent of many of its founders, but it is hardly a cause for rejoicing for Americans.

3. Anti-Colonialism

Here again we totally disregard the realities of the world situation and the notorious communist position on the colonial question, epitomized in the words of the Program of the Communist International (Sixth World Congress, September 1, 1928):

"Colonial rebellions . . . although not in themselves revolutionary proletarian socialist movements, are nevertheless objectively, insofar as they undermine the domination of imperialism, constituent parts of the world proletarian revolution."

This basic position has not changed one iota since Stalin formulated the official communist views on the problem, which were accepted 100% and faithfully adhered to as a guide to action in the colonial question, by the Congresses of the Communist International.

President Roosevelt, at the same time that he was ruthlessly sacrificing the freedom and independence of half of Europe, among whom were some of the staunchest allies of the United States (the Serbs and the Poles), and giving it to Stalin, considered it a sacred duty to liquidate the colonial empires of U.S. allies from both world wars, the free countries of Europe (Britain, France, the Netherlands and Belgium), all of this, of course, in the name of the good of millions of oppressed people concerned, and of the principle of self-determination.

While de-colonization has been most effectively pursued as far as Western European powers are concerned, the principle of self-determination has been brutally bent to the political exigencies of the situation and denied to some colonial people (Katanga, Biafra), inflicting more misery, brutality, bloodshed and starvation than any colonial rule did in several centuries.

The liberal theory of unavoidable change ("winds of change"), inexorable trends and irresistible revolutions, on which anticolonialism rests, is at least as spurious as the liberal thesis about war and peace. For it presupposes man's total inability to determine the course of human events, which is in itself a preposterous assumption. And it becomes utterly preposterous when applied unilaterally against the U.S., which is called upon to assume a stance of impotence before political developments in the world, while at the same time the most voluntarist movement in history, the communist world movement, is inventing, creating, setting afoot and promoting all sorts of explosions, expectations, revolutions and winds of change, to influence the course of events and impose its will on the world.

While there is unrest among the masses of Asia, Africa, and Latin America, they have not come out of the blue, unexpectedly, all of a sudden, but they have been the result of internal developments, technical progress, foreign influences, the growth of international commercial and communications links, domestic policies and, more than anything else—of communist policies, subversion, agitation and planning. So, the winds of change are not an abstract category. They are blown from Moscow and Peking.

The principle of national self-determination which is an irreplaceable cornerstone of a just international order, must certainly apply to all peoples of the world, which definitely includes all those peoples who until World War II had a colonial status.

But to proclaim the principle of national self-determination as sacrosanct only as regards colonial peoples and reconcile with communist imperialism which at the same time violates with utter cynicism the right to self-determination of centuries-old European and Asian peoples with great political and cultural tradition and achievements, makes a mockery of the principle of self-determination and brands such a concept from a general principle of international order, to a tool of Soviet policy.

Thus, "anti-colonialism," as practiced today, makes sense as a principle of policy, only from the communist viewpoint. From the viewpoint of the United States and freedom, it is utterly indefensible. It will start making sense only when the Moscow- (and Peking) blown "winds of change" are substituted, for a change, by American winds of liberty.

4. Peaceful Coexistence

The premises of Western (U.S.) coexistence policy are false for the simple reason that they are based on the assumption that the communist concept of coexistence is identical or at least compatible with ours. And that is patently untrue.

The gist of the communist concept of coexistence has been succinctly expressed by Dmitr Shepilov at the Twentieth Congress of the CPSU in February 1956:

> "The fact that the prerequisites for the transition to Socialism mature at different times in different countries, the fact that individual countries break away from the capitalist system at different times, means that the simultaneous existence of both capitalist and socialist states is inevitable on our planet."

In other words, coexistence is a temporary factual situation, which does not affect the essence of the problem, i.e. the unchanged striving of communism to conquer the world. Communist coexistence is neither a substitute for (shooting, nuclear) war, nor is it a substitute for the political war which is the essence of communism. It is simply a new means of conquering the world, a new form of struggle in a new world situation which the communists consider vastly improved. As Molotov stated on the same occasion: "We now have an international situation of which we could have only dreamed ten or fifteen years ago."

So for the communists there is no question of coexistence as a lasting condition, since "the capitalist and socialist outlooks cannot be reconciled." Coexistence means that in the total perpetual war against the West, the only field where the warfare is suspended, is a shooting international war between the great powers. Period. As for the rest, subversion, espionage, psychological warfare, wars of liberation, civil wars—go on unabated.[211]

In April 1958, eighteen months after the Budapest anti-communist uprising, Khrushchev visited Hungary and made one of the most unmistakable statements on coexistence. Under the headline "Khrushchev Says Russia Will Help Crush Revolt," the *Washington Post*[212] reported that Khrushchev had stated that Soviet troops would be "at any time at the disposal of Socialist countries if needed." "The capitalists may live quietly as long as the workers in their own countries let them do so . . . But we advise the capitalists not to poke their noses—or, as we say, their pig-snouts—into our Socialist gardens. That's how we interpret peaceful co-existence." (Evidently, the "Brezhnev doctrine" was formulated and applied many years before the Soviet occupation of Czechoslovakia, August 1968).

Eighteen months later, Khrushchev used more "cultured" language, but the essence was the same: "Co-existence means the continuation of the struggle between two social systems . . . We consider it to be an economic, political and ideological struggle, but not military" (October 10, 1959).

Western liberals have hailed "cultural exchange" as a vital ingredient of peaceful coexistence. However, the most competent Soviet source, Georgi Alexandrovitch Zhukov, chairman of the Soviet Committee for Foreign Cultural Relations, seems to disagree substantially:

"We have declared and we will declare again, honestly and openly, that the peaceful coexistence of ideas is as nonsensical as fried snowballs." [213]

Pyotr Demichev, secretary of the Central Committee of the CPSU, castigated the thesis of "bourgeois propaganda" about the "rapprochement between socialism and capitalism" and "categorically rejected all peaceful coexistence in the realm of ideology." [214]

Passing from cultural experts to military experts, it is worth presenting the views of a leading Soviet military authority, Colonel I. A. Zheleznev, contained in his book *The War and the Ideological Struggle*, published in 1965.

After stressing that the relationship between war and politics has "today become closer than ever," and that "the use of weapons of mass destruction does not take war out of the framework of politics," but, on the contrary, increases "the dependence of the military leadership on political leadership," he concludes that "a modern war cannot be imagined without an ideological war." These considerations determined the meaning of peaceful coexistence:

> "If under peaceful coexistence we mean the solution of all international controversial questions by negotiation, an agreement can be reached only on the basis of reasonable compromises and mutual concessions. Such concessions and compromises pertain only to questions of detail, but not to the essence of the social-political order. Peaceful coexistence excludes any compromises and concessions in the area of ideology." [215]

Far from being the personal views of one man, these considerations contain the essence of Soviet contemporary thinking on the problems under discussion, which Professor Milorad M. Drachkovitch, of the Hoover Institution, has presented in his noteworthy article "The Selling of the Soviet Pentagon," published in *National Review*.[216]

From the choice thoughts and positions of four leading Soviet military personalities, Major General S. Ilin; General A. Epishev, head of the political directorate of the Soviet Army; Marshal Ivan Yakubovsky, First Deputy Defense Minister of the USSR and commander of the forces of the Warsaw Pact, and Marshal A. A. Grechko, Minister of Defense of the Soviet Union—the following casts revealing light on the Soviet concept of peaceful coexistence:

> "If a third world war should become a fact, it will differ greatly from previous wars. It will take the form of a decisive class struggle between socialism and imperialism on a global scale."

> ". . . educating men in the spirit of proletarian internationalism and the unity of the fraternal socialist countries and their armies . . . assumes particular importance in connection with the expansion of the USSR armed forces' international tasks."

Statements and definitions of peaceful coexistence from communist sources could be quoted endlessly, without any deviation of meaning. What we have presented here should suffice to demonstrate that, as opposed to the Western concept of coexistence, the communist concept is that of a new form of struggle to disarm and destroy the West and ensure "the world-transforming . . . complete triumph of communism." [217]

The gist of the matter is that the communists do not believe in peace, the U.N., anti-colonialism and coexistence. They believe in (1) war; (2) the subordination of the U.N. to their power and interests; (3) the subjugation of nations; and (4) no coexistence with the free world.

Clearly, to win, they had to induce the West to adopt and follow the path of (1) peace above all; (2) the U.N. above all nations, especially the U.S.; (3) anti-colonialism (strictly anti-Western, never anti-communist), and (4) coexistence, i.e. accommodation and compromise with communism. That is why they have made these four points the pillars of their strategy, i.e. their minimal program at this stage of their relations with the free world.

By the same token, the U.S. has every reason to thoroughly reappraise those same principles as bases for its policies, for they are serving the interests of the enemy.

So, the path of liberation is to recognize that the challenge of communism is essentially not economic, not social, not cultural, not military, but political.

The struggle going on in the world today is not about the best social system that man can devise, it is not a "competition for human happiness," as the French socialist leader Guy Mollet said in a toast offered in the Kremlin, where he talked with Nikita Khrushchev,[218] nor is it a gentleman's contest of performance, nor a test of coexistential adaptation and mutuality. Least of all is it a struggle to eradicate "hunger, poverty, desperation and chaos," as G. C. Marshall formulated it.

The contest is above all a contest for power, and thus a contest of wills. Which in plain English means that the world, and especially the United States, is threatened not economically, not culturally, not militarily, although warfare is waged on all these fields —but politically, in its very existence. The will of the communist enemy is directed not toward outproducing the U.S. industrially, or outperforming us (in culture, arts, science, technology), not toward excogitating some fascinating ideas about human society and happiness—but toward destroying it.

And the political war, waged by the communists, by tearing ruthlessly the moral fabric of the nation, sowing dissension and creating disunity, can destroy us without military war. That is the gist of our present situation. The issue, in other words, is not whether we are at war or not, but whether we are strong enough to recognize the plain fact and whether we shall surrender or fight back and strive for victory.

The communists have understood from the first moment (the Communist Manifesto, 1848) that the history of mankind is decisively its political history. It is made of human actions pertaining to the order of things, human relations, the question of who is going to rule society and nations, and how, who will decide the fate, the life-and-death issues of people, of nations, of all mankind.

The problem is as old as the world. It is the problem of the eternal struggle of the existing order to affirm, defend and assert itself, its identity, against enemies, and the forces of change trying to destroy existing conditions, institutions and order.

There have always been in history satisfied nations and those who were not. And it is always the dissatisfied, the lean nations who have made history. The moment a nation reaches the point where it is satisfied and does not want to go further, it is doomed, because it tends to please its enemies, appease them, withdraw before them, surrender to them. When General MacArthur proclaimed in 1951 that there was no substitute for victory, he was not innovating or inventing, he was just forcefully expressing an old and basic truth. In revolutionary times, this truth is more important than ever.

Today, however, the old powers seem to have lost their historical virility and would like now to change the rules of history-making by eliminating struggle and violence. But that cannot be, because the rules are unchangeable, and because there are always nations which are not terrified of them. On the contrary, they like them.

The West today, with its radical pacifism and moralism, appears to the world as the old roué who, upon hearing about a torrid love story, tiredly exclaimed: "Do people still do those things"?

They do, and the communists more than anybody else.

Nevertheless, the West would apparently like to live unpolitically, to live without making history, to reduce all the life of society and nations to issues which do not involve any "either-or" choices.

Western man's message to mankind, to the other continents and races seems to be:

"So far, there have been tyranny, oppression, injustice, inequality, national states and national conquests, colonialisms and imperialisms. But not from now on. All that has to stop; all that must change. We have had enough. We are going to be nice to everybody, and everybody is going to be nice to everybody else. (Of course, should anybody refuse to be as nice as we want him to be, we can always send U.N. mercenaries to silence him as was done in the Congo and Katanga.) In any case, with the new approach of universal kindness, all ills which have plagued mankind since the beginning, will gradually disappear."

But why? This attitude of behaving non-politically at a time of maximal political aggression, is utterly unrealistic and contrary to the laws of international life.

It has been induced by communist brainwashing, i.e. political warfare. By accepting deliberate, preposterous and strategically operated communist falsehoods as the truth about politics and history, we have paralyzed ourselves and become unable to develop and build any political strength.

This attitude is the less excusable since the communists never tire of updating and re-asserting their basic views as events unfold and new power situations arise.

The latest, most convincing and forceful instance is the study, "Topical Problems in the Theory of the World Revolutionary Process," by Boris Ponomarev, one of the most important men in the Soviet hierarchy, published in the periodical, *Komunist,* of October 1971.* Ponomarev was promoted to secretary general of the Central Committee of the CPSU—after writing the article.

Ponomarev's presentation is strictly in keeping with the basic principles of Marxism-Leninism, theoretically and tactically. He

* *Détente and the World Revolutionary Process,* An Analysis of Current Soviet Revolutionary Aims. Prepared for the use of the Committee on the Judiciary of the U.S. Senate, U.S. Government Printing Office, Washington, 1972.

is evidently trying to keep up the pretense of "scientific" analysis, but at the same time his whole essay is a typical act of communist political warfare, utterly aggressive and vicious.

He first makes very clear the fundamental Marxist-Leninist concept that communist theory, today as always, serves the needs of communist policy. Speaking of the 1969 International Conference held in Moscow and the 24th Congress of the CPSU of 1971, he states that they both "guide the communists toward the comprehensive utilization of the new opportunities offered by the current historical stage." (p. 11)

The present situation, according to Ponomarev, is anything but a situation of ebbing conflict or rapprochement between the two world systems, of convergence, accommodation and cooperation. No, it is a situation of strife, of inevitable conflict: "As we know, the main direction of the world revolutionary process is determined by the struggle between the two opposite social systems. There is no realm of social life or area on earth where the growing impact of the antagonisms between the two systems is not manifested." (p. 12) "It is also important to emphasize that . . . since it is a question of two essentially irreconcilable lines of world development, all countries, classes, social strata and political currents become involved in their struggle, directly or indirectly, more or less actively, yet, in the final account, inevitably." (p. 13)

Evidently there is no neutrality in the modern world for anybody. In true communist fashion, Ponomarev cynically makes clear that diplomatic niceties and negotiations do not affect in the least communist basic objectives of world subversion and revolution: "It is also noteworthy that the current sharpening of the class struggle is taking place not under conditions marked by overall international tension, as has been the case in the past, but under conditions marked by a clearly growing trend toward international détente." (p. 20)

In other words, President Nixon's spectacular politico-diplomatic offensive of coexistence and collaboration in Peking and Moscow not only does not affect communist basic policies, but it makes the communists less tractable: "The ever greater intensification of the ideological struggle is a noteworthy feature of our times. The more restricted the capitalist possibilities to fight socialism militarily become, the greater the tension of the ideological battles in the world rises." (p. 20) It is impossible not to be reminded of Lenin's famous thesis that a lasting coexistence between capitalism and communism is impossible, and that eventually "a funeral dirge will be sung over the Soviet Republic or over world capitalism."

Ponomarev entertains no doubts whatever about who will bury whom, since he maintains that communism is getting stronger all the time: "The socialist comity is proving its capability to impose upon the imperialists a solution of the problems in the interest of peace and peaceful coexistence." (p. 19)

Concomitantly, capitalism is growing weaker in every respect. One of the most important facts of the situation is "the growing instability of capitalism as a social system; the historical limitations of its attempts to adapt to the new circumstances." (p. 12) "The imperialist possibilities to maneuver are becoming ever more restricted." (p. 19) And the U.S., "the bulwark of imperialism" is in greatest trouble: "Unparalleled political upheavals are taking place in this principal capitalist country . . . Huge anti-war demonstrations in the course of which war veterans are throwing away their orders and medals, unparalleled actions by youth and the fighters for Negro equality, marches of the poor to Washington . . . *America has never had this before.*" (p. 19) (Emphasis added).

"Serious failures" in foreign policy and "mass discontent" at home have forced U.S. leaders to reappraise "their political direction," promote "a new policy" and acknowledge that "their former claims to so-called world rule cannot be pursued." (p. 19)

The new attitude of U.S. leaders reflects "a serious erosion of the international prestige of the United States and of its growing moral isolation." (p. 19) "From a kind of ideal of a capitalist society, the 'American way of life' is becoming a standard of vices which even the bourgeois leaders of other countries are now doing everything possible to reject." (p. 19)

Ponomarev feels no need to assuage the West with tales of communist change. On the contrary, he stresses the unchanged character of communism. One of the basic characteristics of the communist party is its "ability systematically to follow a course toward the revolutionary liquidation of the capitalist system." (p. 26) "The communists always remain the party of the socialist revolution, a party which never tolerates the capitalist order, and is always ready to head the struggle for the total political power of the working class and for the establishment of the dictatorship of the proletariat in one or another form." (p. 26)

The communists have always waged war against the free world and they are today fighting as intensely as ever for the conquest of the globe: "Our party does not implement random international measures. It would be entirely justified to consider them as the expanded foreign political offensive for the sake of peace and the security of peoples." (p. 18) "Our foreign political measures are restricting further and further the aggressive imperialist circles. They are paralyzing their actions aimed against other peoples and countries. They contribute to the creation of ever better international circumstances for the expansion of the struggle of the revolutionary forces the world over." (p. 18)

While Western top experts and advisers drug themselves daily with political LSD about communist change and mellowing, Ponomarev states openly that "not the bourgeois, but our own socialist ideology is in a state of historical offensive," (p. 20), and that communist policies of the past 25 years have promoted the *"increased revolutionariness"* of "the masses." (p. 24) (Emphasis added).

Communist leaders have repeatedly denied that they were promoting revolution abroad, and claimed that revolution grows everywhere from the social and economic conditions of injustice and exploitation under capitalism. Ponomarev openly admits communist international subversion: "We must strongly emphasize that the successes of the national-liberation movements would have been impossible without the existence of the Soviet Union and the tremendous and irreplaceable political, moral and material support which it gives the peoples fighting imperialism." (p. 40) And this help to world revolution will continue: "The CPSU, as always, is giving practical support to the revolutionary struggle of the Chilean people." (p. 35)

These are the main ideas of what may be called the "Ponomarev Blueprint for World Conquest" within this book, and at this point it does not require much comment. But it should not be too difficult to notice the fundamental identity of views and world outlook between a top Soviet official, like Ponomarev, planning conquest—and a "heretic," like Andrei Sakharov, planning U.S.-Soviet reconciliation and collaboration for peace.

More important, the Ponomarev Blueprint irresistibly invites comparison with his American counterpart, Dr. Henry Kissinger and *his* Blueprint. Ponomarev speaks in terms of realities; his evaluations and plans are those of hard facts and firm purposes; his yardsticks in the world of international affairs are political; his clear aim is victory. Dr. Henry Kissinger speaks in terms of diplomatic chess and games; his evaluations are unrelated to the real world of the 1970s; his yardsticks in dealing with the communist super-powers are abstruse and "humanistic"; his aim is a thorough depoliticization of politics, and his strategy is global withdrawal.

This puts in proper focus the chances of Dr. Kissinger coping with and outwitting the Brezhnevs, Ponomarevs and Chou En-lais of the communist world.

To face and confront the challenge of communism, we must above all liberate ourselves from the lethal fallacies upon which our foreign policy has been based since 1933, and rediscover the basic truths about history and civilization, which are the only possible basis for a policy of U.S. survival and victory.

Truths about Civilization and History

Civilization has been a very costly process representing the victory of man over hostile outside forces and over his own boundless ignorance, blind passions, uncontrolled lusts and paralyzing fears. It is not "exploitation," but on the contrary, it is an unending struggle to overcome man's limitations and make him master of his own destiny through the development of his moral sense and the exercise of his free will. It is anything but easy. It requires a tremendous amount of insight, of wisdom, self-control, self-discipline and self-respect.

Civilization begins with rational organization. And the capacity for organization, for seeing things in wider perspective, perceiving relationships and truths not visible or easily accessible, and for bringing law and order out of confusion and disorder, is rather uncommon. Progress from savagery to civilization has been a process of differentiation, of hierarchical distinction and organization, because civilization, i.e. any sort of civilized society requires "uncommon" people, men with a keener intelligence, endowed with more wisdom and perception than the rest, more skill, organizational talent, courage and will, than the "average man." It requires individuals able to run the affairs of the community, to perceive and formulate the general interest and find the proper relationship between individual freedom and the rule of law which limits it. It is only when society reaches that stage of development that conditions are created for every individual to develop his capabilities to the full. Without organization, hierarchy and coercion based on law, man would have remained in the jungle, and the common man would have been much worse off.

In other words, it is not that man was free in his first stage of savagery and that civilization enslaved him, (the Jean Jacques Rousseau thesis). It is exactly the other way around: man was initially helpless, enslaved by nature, by ignorance, by lack of vision, by total disregard for others and for the future. Civilization made him free.

Civilization did not develop spontaneously and effortlessly, from the noble qualities abounding in the masses, in spite of the evil doings of the handful of greedy and power-hungry individuals—but on the contrary, it has been a gigantic effort and achievement of overcoming man's shortcomings, his foibles, his narrow horizons, his selfishness, his stupidity, his cruelty, his concern with the material and the immediate, his passions and his lusts.

Common sense, generosity, idealism, wisdom, capacity for hard work and sacrifice, are not the privilege of a minority. Most people strive to go beyond the search for food, shelter and the gratification of the senses. And we may also readily agree with Descartes and Eric Hoffer that reason, the chief lever of progress, is widely distributed among the masses of the people.

And yet, the fact is that what makes all the difference in the world, between barbarism and civilization, between progress and the stagnation of society at levels of poverty, injustice, anarchy and chaos, are exceptional individuals, leaders, who are the architects, the sculptors, the shapers, the creators, the mobilizers, the catalyzers of the people's energies, talents, aptitudes, noble urges and potentials for good.

Whether a mass of people is a nation, an efficient army, a scientific team, a factory, a university, a community, a church—or a shapeless agglomeration of people, a disorganized mob; whether they create things of beauty and lasting value or exist from day to day—depends on the small number of leaders.

The raw material of the masses is there, but it takes the artist of history to give it shape, to breathe life into it, to elevate it, to kill the weeds and to encourage all the noble instincts. And this is not done nor can it be done once for all. There are no *final* solutions to the great problems of mankind. The only solution is constant effort and resulting progress. The making of history and the building of civilization is a permanent, never-ending job, as necessary and vital and as never-ending as the job of the tiller of the ground which produces the food we eat, the materials we use and the beauty we enjoy and without which we cannot live.

That is the role of the leaders, the builders of civilization, wherever they may be or emerge from. Ortega y Gasset's mass man is not a category of social status, nor is his uncommon man. Much before Gasset, Vilfredo Pareto had formulated his well-known theory of the "circulation of the élites," which calls our attention to the elementary fact that among those who rise to the social and political tops, degeneration, i.e. deterioration of leadership quality, may set in soon, after one or a few generations, and also that the qualities of leadership are all the time reborn out of the depths of the nation. In any case, the true leaders always give infinitely more to their fellow-men in human dignity, in meaning, in self-fulfillment, in happiness—and yes, in material goods, too—than they take for themselves and than they exact from the common people in terms of toil, suffering, self-discipline, self-restraint and privation.

So the truth is that civilization is not easy, that it requires toil and sacrifice, and that it requires the leadership of the best.

The liberals, mesmerized by the masters of their minds and souls, the communists, fundamentally reject the most vital principle of sacrifice, without which there is no creation, no achievement. Actually, that is the main weapon which the communists use to justify the foulest of their crimes and inhuman policies. But in the war against our minds they have imposed on us the "double-standard" idea that we, having committed so much injustice in the past, have no right to demand any sacrifice from anybody for whatever purpose. Naturally, the communists know what our liberal leaders do not, that if you eliminate the principle of sacrifice, you also inevitably eliminate civilization, which can be achieved only by sacrifice, by constant personal effort, and which necessarily involves suffering, pain and unhappiness.

Only if we recognize the creative and noble efforts, the superhuman toil, which was necessary in the past to keep people from sinking to the level of animals and, especially today, what superhuman effort it takes (bigger than ever, as anybody watching the protesters and destroyers can easily recognize), only then can we establish the truth about history and the U.S. in it, and can we defend the U.S. as it deserves to be defended.

Then we will realize who the real men were, who toiled and sacrificed and built and helped mankind uphold human values and human dignity—and who are the real villains, the destroyers, parasites and demagogues of Utopia, the "ideal society," and the "final solution."

If the history of mankind is nothing but a record of villainy, then the communists are right in their philosophy that man is unquestionably evil and incapable of achieving anything worthwhile in freedom, but must be subjected to ruthless tyranny and doglike conditioning.

If however the history of mankind is not merely a record of human villainy, but also of overcoming human villainy, of great endeavors, moral greatness and accomplishments, then obviously man is free, able to change things and improve them. He is not a dog, to have his reflexes conditioned, but a man to perfect his moral sense, exercise his free will, to develop and create.

Freedom implies the determination that no man shall be permitted to extinguish the inherent dignity and creative spark with which God has endowed man. These are absolutes, more important than life itself.

There have undeniably been injustices and suffering and wars and devastation and selfishness and exploitation and poverty and inhumanity throughout history. But first and basic, they were and are rooted in man, in his nature, his character, his weakness, his inability to control his low and evil instincts. The history of man is the reflection of man. If it is not better than it is, this is because man is not better than he is. And if there have been wars and

privation and suffering unnecessarily inflicted upon man by evil individuals and groups, there also have been wars and privation and
suffering absolutely necessary, unavoidable to preserve man's
freedom, welfare and dignity. They are the price of achievement.
Iron has been used to enslave but also to liberate. And swords
have smitten not only the just but also the tyrants.

So, the picture of civilization propagated by the rebels and accepted by the Liberal Establishment, is untrue in its very core. All
art, philosophy, literature, music, architecture, buildings, gardens
and monuments which enrich everybody's life—the masses as well
as the "élite"—are aspects of civilization. And it is not true that the
masses would prefer to reduce life to food, clothing, shelter and
gratification of the senses, rather than bear suffering, privation and
sacrifice in order to live spiritually as well as physically.

It is the few materialistic do-gooders who reduce all problems
to material needs, and the masses of the common man to an animal to be fed, tamed, controlled and ordered about. Man, regardless of his station in life, aspires to go higher, to rise, to elevate
himself.

In international life struggle never ceases and history never
stops, nor can it be stopped. It is impossible to freeze historical
situations. Nations which stop going forward, decline. But there is
no stopping history. What few Western politicians, experts and
social scientists have realized, although it is unmistakably expressed in the Communist Manifesto, and Lenin explained it very
clearly in *State and Revolution,* is that the realization of communist society spells the end of politics altogether, the end of the
political life of man, of history.

Communist logic is clear: all trouble in history and society is
social, i.e. due to the wrong organization of society. If we organize
human society right, all problems will be solved once for all. If so,
we will ask, won't then human history end? But precisely. That is
what the communists have in mind for us. Communist power forever. That is the gist of the "withering of the state." [219]

So, whether Western leaders realize it or not, we are, by accepting communism, i.e. coexistence with it, renouncing our right and
duty to make history. And that is utter folly and disgrace. For it is
impossible to stop history, as it is impossible to step out of history.
"Stop the world, I want to get off," may be an amusing title for

a New York musical, but it is a very poor precept for Western policy, especially for the U.S., when it is the leader of the world.

Man cannot live without making history. He cannot live without changing, improving, creating, tearing down and building, without influencing the conditions of his life. His life is more than biology. And if he wants to reduce it to biology, he dies. To end history, is to kill mankind.

That is why the communists want to have man stop struggling and submit to evil. Since history cannot stop as long as man exists, the communist theory of the end of history amounts to the perpetuation of communist power.

However, it is not terrible that the communists want to make an end to history by claiming the exclusive right to make it. Terrible is that we accept it. We no longer have the ambition to make history. All our present policy consists of adapting ourselves to communist-made history.

The speech of General George C. Marshall of June 5, 1947 is the fundamental document of the "end-of-history" school of thought. ("Our policy is directed not against any country or doctrine, but against hunger, poverty, desperation and chaos.") Should this concept continue to guide our foreign policy, the U.S. will be destroyed, and hunger, poverty, desperation and chaos will be unleashed on the globe.

For nobody, no nation and no country, can solve any non-political problem unless it solves the political problem: to be strong enough to oppose its enemies and safeguard its vital national interests.

If the U.S. surrenders the right and duty to decide about the problems of power in the world, to indicate the road, to make history, the USSR and Red China will not be so hesitant. On the contrary, they will do everything to expand their power. And it will be curtains for the U.S.

So, for the United States to reject adaptation to communism, and shape events, make history, assert itself, is a matter not of choice but of survival. Man being by nature a history-maker, there can be no end to history. What may end, if we yield and submit, is *our* history, our role in the history of mankind.

History-making is based on the full awareness that nothing of value can be created without effort and sacrifice. This is a basic truth of which Theodore Roosevelt reminded his fellow-countrymen at the beginning of this century:

"Nothing in this world is worth having or worth doing unless it means effort, pain, difficulty . . . Let us therefore boldly face the life of strife."

Mankind cannot be confined to the private lives of the individuals that compose it, nor can evil history-makers be stopped by appeasement, or appeals to humanity, or lofty oratory, or better performance, or by withdrawing into our private ivory towers, far from the battlefields of history.

They can be stopped only by superior history-making capacity, i.e. by people who possess greater strength of will and character, determination, ability to arouse the resources and energies of the nation and weld them into a superior history-making force.

This is a vital point today in the relationship between the West and communism.[220]

Gentle history-making is a contradiction in terms. For history-making is inevitably, inherently, very rough business.

So, today, as always a fundamental law applies: those who possess the courage to make history, will win, no matter how vile their cause may be. Those who lack the courage to fight and win, will lose, in spite of the loftiness of the cause they represent.[*]

Nobody was more keenly aware of the importance of politics than the Founding Fathers. They knew that the political organi-

[*] Arthur Koestler is certainly one of the most deserving, articulate and convincing exposers of communist villainy, dishonesty and inhumanity. And yet, in his portrait (*Darkness at Noon*) of the old "idealist" revolutionary Rubashev, who, jailed, is facing the new generation of bolsheviks, in the person of the robot-like bureaucrat-interrogator, Gletkin, he has done a disservice to the free world. For since Rubashev has spent all his life making history (the bolshevik revolution), which knew no sentimentality or humanity, he is now at a disadvantage. Not for being the jailed facing the jailer, but because he appears as a sentimental dreamer and idealist, facing an implacable revolutionary and history-maker. His change of heart, from revolution to humanism is unconvincing. Therefore he has no message for the freedom-fighters, but can appeal only to the quitters, to Western tired intellectuals, who lack the fortitude to oppose communism and are just strong enough to deplore their ruthlessness. Which, of course, is a green light for communism.

zation of a nation was the foundation for its life and progress, both as the natural framework for the unfolding of all its activities and as the expression of its beliefs and values. That is why their first concern in 1776 was not economic, nor military, but moral and political. They put first things first. The U.S. was not conceived on an economic basis, as a capitalist country. The Founding Fathers of the United States thought not of capital and wealth, but of human freedom, of the dignity of man, of life, liberty and human happiness based on the right of developing one's life in liberty. They were anything but Utopians. They were aware of the necessity of Government, of the rule of law, of sacrifices and the limitation of individual freedom in the interest of the country.

George Washington stressed at the same time the importance of the Union as the basis of the life of the new nation, and every one of its citizens, and the importance of "religion and morality as the indispensable support of political prosperity" and "necessary support of popular government."

The same trait of putting first things first, distinguishes Alexander Hamilton. And that concern for the Union as the guarantor of individual rights and freedoms is not confined to these two giants. It was a general trait of all the Founding Fathers, regardless of the differences which separated them. In a letter of 1780, written to his wife Abigail from Paris, John Adams says:

> "The science of government is my duty to study . . . I must study politics and war, so that my sons may have liberty to study mathematics and philosophy, geography, natural history, and naval architecture, navigation, commerce, and agriculture. In order to give their children a right to study painting, poetry, music, architecture, statuary, tapestry and porcelain . . ."

The chronological order in which Adams puts various pursuits unmistakably indicates that the importance of the "science of government" was perfectly known to him.

These are the things which the Founding Fathers knew to the marrow of their bones. They risked everything because the ideals they cherished, the values from which they drew their strength and the goals which guided them, told them that it was worthwhile risking everything, for they had a world to win. And they succeeded.

(A nation of three million people produced true nation-founders and empire-builders. Too many of our liberal leaders today, in a nation of over 200 million people, are nation-destroyers and wasters of the nation's heritage.)

Had George Washington's advisers at Valley Forge been experts of the caliber of Harry Hopkins or George C. Marshall or Robert S. McNamara or McGeorge Bundy, and had he been inclined to take their advice, he would immediately have "sent the boys home." And the "boys" would have gone home and spared themselves much suffering, frostbite, hunger, and, of course, many would have lived longer . . . And there would have been no United States of America.

But George Washington, the father of the nation, was just that. He did not recognize anybody's accomplished facts or unchangeable situation. He knew the nation to which he belonged and he sensed without fail that the nation wanted to make history and that no earthly power could stop it. The U.S. grew, became wealthy, strong and surpassed all expectations because its principles were right, because its founders were true nation-builders, because they knew the distinction between eternal things and things ephemeral, because first things were put first, because their aims were based on absolute values and beliefs and because they pledged their lives, their fortunes and their sacred honor to fulfill their dream.

Man and his Values

And here we come to the crucial problem of civilization, which no country, least of all the leading nation of the world, can ignore or bypass, a problem on which basically the alternative to our policy of surrender depends. It is the problem of values. Has man, Western man, any values worth living, fighting, and dying for? Or not? If he has not, if mere physical existence has become his supreme value, then nothing can save him. No disarmament, no pacts, no treaties and no peace. For there is peace which is death, as there is war which is life. Those who have no values, surrender, for they have nothing to fight for, nothing to defend. And then they are wiped out, in dishonor.

History and civilization and culture are made of activities based on the self-evident truth that there are things more valuable than mere physical existence, things so important that life is dedicated to their attainment or sacrificed to them.

This is how great things have been created and this is how the United States came into being. When Patrick Henry stated that he valued liberty so highly, that he preferred death to "chains and slavery," he was not orating. He was pointing to an essential trait of man, which is the root of life, as it is of human dignity.

There is obviously no compromise between this position and the liberal position of "rather red than dead." One must be right and the other must be wrong. Even if we assume that nuclear war is an impending threat and that it would devastate the world as no other war ever has—does it mean that anything is preferable to nuclear war? Anything? Is communism, on a global scale, unrestricted by law, by "capitalism," by the armed might of the United States?—is a global Vorkuta preferable to a nuclear war?

To come back to the question and put it in a more inescapable form: is Nazism preferable to a nuclear war? It certainly was not in 1945. Would it be in case of a Nazi resurgence? Can anybody claim that the inmates of Nazi concentration camps in Dachau, Mauthausen, etc., would have preferred "life" under Nazism to a nuclear war making an end to it?

Some 100 years ago John Stuart Mill, who certainly cannot be accused of callousness and disregard for the condition and welfare of his fellow men, thought that there were things worse than war:

"War is an ugly thing, but not the ugliest of things: the decayed and degraded state of moral and patriotic feeling which thinks nothing worth a war is worse." *

But why go so far back? The champions of peace at any price and acceptance of anything rather than nuclear war,—are deceitful. Their ultra-pacifism emerged only after the defeat of Nazi

---

* One of the latest books (1968) of the well-known author Miodrag Bulatovic, who does not enjoy the favor of the authorities of communist Yugoslavia, bears the characteristic title: *The War Was Better*.

Germany in World War II, and as the basic antagonism between the Soviet Union and the Western democracies, papered over during the wartime alliance, was re-appearing. So, the main concern for unconditional peace transpires as a concern for the unconditional preservation of communism. And as for their concern for the "small people," the "common man," maybe the voice of those people is more decisive than that of their liberal self-appointed protectors. And those people have spoken an unmistakable language in the revolts of East Berlin, Poznan and Budapest. And wasn't Jan Palach, the Czech student who set himself afire on January 19, 1969 in Prague, proving the Patrick Henry point?

Millions of people behind the Iron Curtain are still willing to have war rather than communism, because they know from personal experience that there is a certain life which is not worth living.* Several years ago, an elderly man, a Serb, from Belgrade who had toiled very hard all his life to provide for his family and for a good education for his children and who in his old days owned a very modest house, which represented all his earthly belongings, told me: "I am not a very literate man to analyse all the aspects of communism, nor give you statistics nor present impressive descriptions of what it means to live under communism. But I think that it will suffice if I tell you that if war is the only path of deliverance from communism, then I am for war, even if the first bomb should hit my own house!"

But most important and interesting is the feeling and stand of U.S. fighting men who have recently experienced the reality of communism. In the words of one of the members of *Pueblo's* crew, Lawrence E. Strickland: "We used to hope that Americans would drop a nuclear bomb on the place. We felt we were at ground zero. We just wanted to see the flash." This was not an old, fat, cynical member of the "military-industrial complex" talking about other people's lives in the safety of his plush office! No, it was the voice of a 21 year-old Engineman 3 C facing the communists.

---

* In a film of 1943, presented on television (NBC) on July 15, 1971, a French schoolteacher in occupied France, played by Charles Laughton, exhorts—on the eve of his execution by a Nazi firing squad—his fellow countrymen to unconditional resistance, including every sacrifice, with the exalted philosophy that "though it increases our misery, it shortens our slavery."

So, one thing is sure: the advocates of peace at any price are not moved by any humanitarian motives, nor do they speak for mankind. They are either doing their utmost to protect communism, or they have departed so far from the concept of man as a being endowed with dignity and free will, that the preservation of life, regardless of any moral value involved, i.e. destroyed in the process, has become an exclusive, supreme concern.

Modern Western man seems to have forgotten that since the beginning of time, men have, in the presence of great danger, been afraid and have trembled. But since the beginning of time, there have also been men who have not trembled, but have overcome fear and done their duty.

Some people think that because man has only one life, it must be lived to the hilt, leaving considerations of conscience and moral imperatives aside. Others, however, as Alexandr Solzhenitsyn stresses in *The First Circle,* think that since man has not only one life, but only one conscience, he must try to live it as a man.

The desperate fanatic believers in physical existence as the supreme value, who have proclaimed the death of God and follow Jean-Paul Sartre, pave the way to the Chardinist man of the future, who will have divested himself of all manhood and humanity and returned to the hypothetical primitive amoebic condition of life on earth.

No society can live without absolutes, i.e. if everything is considered relative and if truth depends strictly on circumstances, exclusively as a compromise between divergent viewpoints, as some neutral middle ground. An atmosphere permeated with moral relativism, devoid of standards, contemptuous of truth, indifferent to wrongdoing, favors and breeds evil-doers, traitors and destroyers. The fantastic career of spy Kim Philby, whose ambition, in his own words, was "determining the course of events in the world," [221] which he greatly did, was made possible by the lack of moral yardsticks and fortitude in the society in which he was living and against which he was working. He was, by all immutable standards, a most despicable traitor. But when a famous writer, Graham Greene, agrees to write the Introduction to Philby's autobiographical book, *My Silent War* and therein says:

"He betrayed his country—yes, perhaps he did, but who among us had not committed treason to something or someone more important than a country? In Philby's own eyes he was working for a shape of things to come from which his country would benefit, . . ."

then we clearly understand that Philby's success as a traitor was not due to his exceptional mind or whatever ability he may possess, but to a state of affairs which favors treason and traitors.

The most important thing we must realize today in the search for an alternative, is that we are at war, and that this is an unchangeable category of our existence.

Therefore, our chief concern must not be to avoid violence and war at any price, but to prevent at any price the destruction of all that makes man and America, its values and achievements. If America is not good, then the enemies are right. But if America is good, it must be defended.

It is indispensable to bear in mind that struggle and violence can be used for freedom, for law and order, as they can be used for destruction, for chaos, for anarchy, for killing.

That is where we have to beat the communists. As long as we stay on the position of no struggle at all, and no violence at all, we are lost, because it is against nature. It is only when we come on the right battlefield, *what for,* that we stand a chance of beating them, because the ground favors us. We must not reconcile Americanism with communism but oppose it to communism.

Our trouble is that we have come to conceive politics in terms of sheer adaptation to situations created by others and to the will of the enemy. Our policies have been reduced to tactics: adaptation, negotiation, surrender.

The communist concept is entirely different: impose their will by any means. They subvert our mind and our institutions all the time. We consolidate their status quo and peace of mind all the time.

We recognize them as a "fact of life" ("You cannot ignore 700 million Chinese"). They do not recognize us. We must be swept away from the stage of the world. We respect their facts and try to adapt ourselves to them. They use facts or deny them, or make them, as the interest of communist power dictates. (As Igor Gouzenko, through the hero of the novel, Feodor Novikov, brilliantly explained in *The Fall of a Titan*).[222]

Our reconciliation with historical defeat is so thorough that we refuse to see the enemy's actions and perceive his intentions: ". . . so deep is the euphoria into which many Americans have tranquilized themselves that Soviet threats are actually accepted as promises of peace." [223]

The main trouble in the world today is that the basic values of Western civilization are being betrayed and rejected and the basic communist concepts and ideas are being accepted and implemented. They will commit any crime to stop the dissenters of communism. We destroy our foundations to placate the enemy.

The foreign and domestic enemies of the U.S. have the courage, boldness, gall and effrontery, of lies, nonsense and treason. Our liberal leaders lack the courage of plain patriotism, of defending the truth and U.S. basic interests.

The present U.S. policy, torn by the contradiction between the principles and philosophy of freedom and the policies of coexistence with communism, is destructive of any belief, any principles, any certainty.

We have been saddled with a guilt complex which consists of the proposition that the enemy is right and the U.S. is wrong, thus precluding any rational discussion of the most important problems pertaining to the very survival of the U.S.

The main asset and strength of the communists is that they know that the West will not try to subvert them. On the contrary, it is helping them to become going concerns.

Why is this so? How is it possible that we, who are always concerned with objective truth, never seem to attain it and never know what to do, except yield? And how does it come that they, whose views are utterly biased, always know what to do?

There is no mystery, no enigma and no puzzle about that at all. They know that international life is not a search for truth, but a search for political strength, not a debate, but a struggle.

They know what they want: to destroy us, and so they at all times know what to do. And we not only lack the wish and will to destroy them, but we do not want even to defend ourselves. Therefore, we are all the time puzzled and confronted with the "enigma" of communism, whereas they never encounter any "enigma" in capitalism.

So, if one of the two sides does not know the true state of affairs, does not know life and its plain facts, its dangers and the sources it springs from, it is we—not they. To want to destroy an enemy may be inhuman and morally reprehensible; but it is not irrational. What is irrational is to ignore the nature of communism and base our policy on totally arbitrary concepts about the enemy.

It is thus we who need enlightenment about the real world, not the communists, in Moscow or Peking or anywhere else.

So the liberation of our mind must necessarily bring us to the realization that our violation of the basic laws of international life must stop. We must stop surrendering and start fighting for what we have and what we are.

Instead of waiting for the communists to change and turn to peaceful pursuits, it is we who must change from a posture of surrender to one of confronting and defeating communism.

If our objective is really freedom, we cannot expect it from the "withering" of the communist state. It can be attained only by the solution of the problem of power in the last thirty years of the twentieth century.

For the problem of freedom is contained in the problem of power. Unless and until the problem of power is solved, the problem of freedom will not be solved. To ignore or deny the problem of power is to indulge in moral escapism and irresponsibility.

And it is a complex problem. Why, otherwise, would the Founding Fathers have taken such pains to work out a difficult, complicated system of checks and balances? Why otherwise, would Benjamin Franklin have warned the inquiring lady: ". . . if you can keep it, Madam"? (meaning the Republic).

The communists recognize only power, for they consider the problem of human liberty non-existent. The West would like to counter that with liberty without authority. And that certainly is no answer to the problem. If the West, i.e. the United States, is to win, it must determine the yardsticks by which to combine power and authority, i.e. to organize power so that human liberty can still be preserved under the most adverse conditions of modern technological and mass society.

To live, a nation must have an aim, a dream, an ideal to lead it, to serve as a guide and moving force. For a nation is a spiritual creation, a spiritual reality. Whatever the other bonds which connect the people who make up a nation, they are held together above all by the same spirit, different from the spirit of other nations. To survive and go forward, a nation must constantly renew itself by fighting for its interests, defending its identity and finding answers to the new problems and challenges it is being confronted with.

Obviously, the communist drive for power cannot be opposed with a spirit of permanent defensive and pacifist commonplaces. An utterly aggressive, bold, fanatical movement of world changers and history-makers, cannot be stopped by withdrawal, preaching of universal friendship and with the philosophy of the enjoyment of everyday life. You cannot stop revolution by looking away from political reality and opposing moralistic whimper to the ruthlessness of those who want to change the world and impose their will.

The communists, because their supreme interest is power, and because they realize the utter complexity of power, have not neglected any aspect of man and of human existence. And they have appealed not to man's economic interests, but to his sense of justice, his urge for big and lasting achievements, his religious bents, his lust for power, his idealism, his capacity to love and hate, his craving for sacrifice, thus yearning to play a part, to contribute to the total transformation of the world, to make it different from what it has been since the beginning of history. They have harnessed the eternal and immensely powerful longing of man to create a good world to their vile, satanic aim of totally enslaving him. But, reprehensible as the means are, the yearnings to which the communists appeal and the force which they capture and exploit for their ends, are real, a million times more real than the "ideal" of a full stomach.

That is why materialism which today is strangling the West, cannot compete with communism. It is we, not they, who apply the philosophy of "a bigger bowl of rice" to all world problems.

Our "ideal" is to have everybody have his filet mignon and enjoy his private life. Their approach to man is to have him participate in the transformation of our planet.

Who then is materialistic and who is more apt to inspire people, win the battle for their minds and create political force to conquer, control and change the world?

It is not surprising that Alexandr Solzhenitsyn, the greatest living Russian writer, who is in bad trouble with the Soviet regime, has raised in his book, *The First Circle*, the basic question that life is impossible without meaning, and that to live, man must have some values more important than life itself.

It is a very sad commentary on the disorientation of our leadership when, after accepting the premises of Marxist-Leninist "materialistic" philosophy, which in reality was never anything but thoroughly political, we are the champions of the economic approach to the problems of mankind, while the communists pose as the champions of the spiritual approach.

Several years ago, a novel was published in the Soviet Union with great world-wide publicity, under the title *Not By Bread Alone*, by Vladimir Dudintsev. It was strictly a novel of communist self-criticism, but the point is that it was the Soviet Union which was reminding us of truths as old as the world which went into the foundations of Western civilization, and which we had rejected.

And Yevgeny Yevtushenko, the court poet of the Soviet Union, wrote in his book, *A Precocious Autobiography*, this incredible apotheosis of the supreme importance of ideals in the life of man, more important than bread itself:

"However prosperous, a man will always be dissatisfied if he has no high ideals . . . But if even the rich feel burdened by the lack of an ideal, to those who suffer real deprivation, an ideal is a first necessity of life. When there is plenty of bread and a shortage of ideals, bread is no substitute for an ideal. But where bread is short, ideals are bread." [224]

While making the necessary allowances for demagoguery and for the limitations of socialist economy which would impel to make virtues out of necessities, Yevtushenko's statement expresses an irrefutable truth of the human condition, which no nation can disregard with impunity.

It is by the spirit that they have confused us and weakened us, and it is by the spirit that we must liberate ourselves[225] and rise to positions of which our Founding Fathers had a clear vision in 1776, and to which our sights and our responsibilities in the modern world call us in the 1970s.

The most pressing, the crucial need for the U.S., is to *face reality*. And that means to realize the two main changes in its position in the world which have taken place in the course of the past fifty years and which have revolutionized the world:

1. There is no isolation for the U.S., which is in the midst of all dangers, and moreover the main target of the most aggressive and most political force in history, communism; and

2. the U.S. is no longer "one of the boys," but the leader. Political childhood is behind us. World responsibility and leadership are the new imperatives for the U.S., for the present moment and for the future.

It is impossible to survive in the world of the late twentieth century, with ideas, concepts and habits of thought based on the realities of the 19th century. Much less is it possible to ignore reality and operate with irrelevant commonplaces which destroy our vision, confuse our mind and sap our morale, while they win no friend and ally, deter no enemy and solve no problem.

That is why it is so important to liberate ourselves from the stranglehold of that theory and face the truth about history and history-making, about man, and about the importance of politics in the infinite variety and complexity of man's pursuits.

Communism is a fact, and the war which the communists are waging to destroy us is a fact. Our liberal leaders are too intelligent not to realize it, and the communist leaders are too intelligent not to know that we realize it. So, when we try to dodge the confrontation by our pitiful theories of communist change, of the breakup of communist monolithism, the emergence of national communism, the liberalization of communism, etc., we are not fooling the communists, but only provoking their contemptuous amusement and confirming them in their claim that the liberal West is too cowardly to fight, as Nikita Khrushchev explicitly stated. Our expectations that communist troubles, communist blunders and internal difficulties, communist "liberals" and "democratic socialists" will save us from communism, only indicates that we shy away from undertaking the job ourselves.

Especially ludicrous is the theory that the whole conflict between communism and the free world is really a big misunderstanding, due to the lack of information about each other. This is patently false. The communists themselves have been busy for 124 years telling us the contrary. They have an aim, based not on ignorance, or confusion or misinformation, but on purposeful selection and relentless pursuit. They want to rule the world and we stand in their path. Therefore they wage total political war to remove us from their path. There is no misunderstanding whatsoever on their part. We misunderstand them. But they do not misunderstand us. It is we who need information about the real world, about the reality of communism, not they about us. They know us.

Power conflicts are seldom, if at all, the result of misunderstanding. Most of the time, they reflect opposite political goals and interests, and quite often profound disagreement on issues where there is no reconciliation. And no international problem and conflict has ever been rooted in deeper disagreement on more important issues and values than the present struggle for the world, opposing the U.S. and the U.S.S.R.

So, the real alternative is not surrender or nuclear war, but surrender or political war.

15   Self-Assertion

"Freedom is the claim for vigorous self-assertion"
ALFRED NORTH WHITEHEAD
(*Adventure of Ideas*, Mentor, 1955, p. 280)

There is no magic formula to solve our problems. Least of all can they be solved by reforms based on fallacies which have produced the problems. But magic formulas we do not need, for there is an answer so elementary and natural that it is magical and miraculous beyond anything the liberals are capable of conceiving. It is self-assertion. That is the road to the liberation we are seeking. For if, as Alfred Whitehead so aptly defined it: "Freedom is the claim for vigorous self-assertion," [226] then there is no freedom without self-assertion.

Self-assertion is no magic wand which produces ready-made solutions for every and any problem (peace, civil rights, youth rebellion, etc.). But it is the answer of reason, of common sense, of decency, of responsibility, of affirmation of life. It is the only sane, logical basis on which the solution must be sought and can be found.

Self-assertion is the recognition of the fact that to survive and go forward, a country must all the time re-affirm the bases of its existence: its values and principles, its institutions, its traditions, its vital interests. It is the realization that the evidence and assertion of the U.S. is the prerequisite for the solution of any problem.

How can the U.S. be free if it does not strive to assert itself? How can it otherwise help make other nations free? How can it secure individual freedom and civil rights to anybody if the country is not strong and safe? This does not mean that ends justify means and that political expediency precludes moral considerations as a factor in our national policies. It means that to build, we must preserve and strengthen the foundations. To improve, we must defend against all enemies what we have and what we are.

Instead of adopting the course of the liquidation of the United States for the sake of "higher" interests and values, allegedly those of mankind, we must re-assert America, for only so can mankind be served.

The U.S. is not only its military might, or its economy, its industry, science and technology, its unique standard of living, but it is the eternal moral values and age-long wisdom of man which went into the Declaration of Independence and the U.S. Constitution, and it is what the U.S. has come to mean today, after nearly 200 years of its life, in history and in the world, its distinct identity, its national character, its message to the world. Self-assertion is a declaration of faith in values upon which the U.S. was founded, a categorical "yes" to the achievements of the nation, an unqualified commitment to defend what the U.S. stands for, because it is worth defending and because the future of the nation depends on it.

Self-assertion is anything but a rejection of change and progress. On the contrary, it is a basic principle which puts priorities in order and establishes the necessary conditions for creative change and progress.

To neglect and ignore historical changes of 200 years and present conditions would be foolish.

Worse would be to reject the leading principles upon which America was built, on the theory that they are invalid because they are 200 years old!

The political wisdom of a nation is to be able to distinguish between the *ephemeral,* pertaining to changing social conditions and relations, and the *eternal,* pertaining to the nature and basic categories of man's existence.[227]

No nation can live only by changing, nor can any nation live only by preserving. The genius of a nation, as expressed in the policies of its statesmen, is to combine tradition and change, by distinguishing between the fundamental principles which have lasting validity, and the temporary forms of their application, which must change with the times.

There are no recipes, no short-cuts, no panaceas for the solution of any of the great problems of the contemporary world. But the first and basic requirement for finding the best possible solutions, is to have clear and firm principles.

That is why self-assertion must be at the basis of all our re-evaluation and liberation of the U.S. mind. If those values and those substances which make America have come to be questioned and doubted, it is because we have failed to stand for them. A value is not a nice spun-out abstraction. It is an abstraction which has come to life by being defended and fought for. The finest values become empty when they are not defended. By re-asserting our values, we shall make them alive and powerful.

Our predicament is the predicament of unreason.

The West is like a man trying to walk in all conceivable ways: jumping on one leg, walking on his knees, upside-down on his hands, rolling over on the ground in wheel-like motion, all except walking *upside up*. And then he is puzzled, amazed, that he cannot move forward, that he has so many headaches, that his vision and perspective of things, people, powers and thrones, and especially communism, is blurred, faulty, confused, upside-down!

So, it is a matter of utter urgency to restore true perspective and start viewing things as they are. And to do that we have nothing else but the gift of human reason with which our Creator has endowed us. We must not reject it, but use it. We have no other solution, no other answer to the communist war of annihilation in all its forms and on all its fronts. Self-assertion is the path of reason.

It is the only principle that can put back sense and meaning in public affairs and in our perspective of our basic problems. It is the only answer to the two foremost needs of the U.S. today: a.) to combat communism, and b.) to lead the world to freedom.

Self-assertion has eternal validity and it is ultra-modern. In an age saturated with cowardice and surrender, it is utterly revolutionary because it proclaims an unyielding struggle for freedom and for one's identity. It springs from the foundations of America, i.e. the values expressed in the writings and deeds of the Founding Fathers, and imposes itself from the confrontation of the needs of our survival as a free and sovereign nation, with the conditions and challenges of the 1970's.

It opposes communist political warfare, imperialism and subversion, not by military action, but head on, with the U.S. will to exist, to stop communist imperialism and subversion, to break the backbone of their power; in short, to destroy communism.

Self-assertion stands for the self-evident truth that the survival of the U.S. is the basic precondition for solving all and any of our problems. If we continue tearing down the foundations of America, no problem will be solved, neither the problem of civil rights, nor the problems of youth, and certainly not the problems of "hunger, poverty, desperation and chaos." On the contrary, should the U.S. be destroyed, hunger, poverty, desperation and chaos would be unleashed on the globe, there would be no peace, but a "hundred Vietnams." And those who are protesting against the evils and shortcomings of modern America would curse the day they started their protests.

By proclaiming that we must defend our national heritage, values and interests, self-assertion appears as the only principle which can unite Americans, who have been disunited by our liberal policies of tearing down America and basing U.S. foreign policy on considerations superior (!) to U.S. national interests.

As for those who are most worried that U.S. policy might follow any path save that of absolute morality towards its enemies, they are the ones who have displayed the least moral concern about U.S. national interests in the last 40 years. The most immoral thing in America today is the liberal pro-communist policy which denies and undermines all our values, far more effectively than all communist propaganda and subversion. So, instead of being disturbed by what liberals may think about the danger of potential U.S. immorality, our concern must be to stop liberal immorality against America.

No matter how much liberals may protest and wail about the "wrong priorities," one thing is sure: the top priority for anyone who really cares about this country and about finding real answers to its problems, is the preservation of the United States. To improve, the United States must exist, live, fight back, defend itself, assert itself.

To sum up, self-assertion amounts to recognizing that—

1. It is high time to stop joining the communists and to start beating them.

2. It is high time to stop bowing to the communist-made "winds of change" and change winds. What is needed are gales of American winds of freedom and anti-communist change throughout the globe.

3. It is high time to put an end to our sickly posture of chronic defense and impotence. A nation cannot solve any problems kneeling before its enemies, or sitting on the bench of the accused before them. It can survive only by standing up and defending its identity.

4. It is high time to stop apologizing to every scoundrel anywhere on earth who happens to dislike the United States.

5. It is high time to stop deprecating the accomplishments of the U.S. and admiring those of communism.

6. It is high time to stop recognizing, communist-made *faits accomplis* as the will of history, to start demolishing the communist world penitentiary for a billion human beings, and to muster the will to make history against the communists and without them.

Which all amounts to saying that once we adopt the principle of self-assertion as the basis of our policy, our answer to the communist political war becomes political war against communism. This is the only way to save America, to solve our problems, to make history. Self-assertion will clear the U.S. mind, eliminate the poison of surrender and become the great mobilizer of the nation's energies.

The vital importance of propaganda in our utterly political age is evident. And yet we have no propaganda of our own. For propaganda makes sense only insofar as it serves the political aims of a country. It is the art of convincing the world that we are right and the enemy is wrong. So, how can there be any true U.S. propaganda if our basic stand is coexistence with the enemy? With no goal and policy of U.S. victory, no U.S. propaganda is possible.

Our most distressing problems (youth rebellion, civil rights and Vietnam) have been caused or turned into nightmares largely as the result of our rejecting self-assertion as a basic tenet of all national policy. They have resulted from spiritual emptiness, despair, the lack of sense and hope, lack of yardsticks and values, the rejection of reason.

Amazing as it is, it seems that Americans have not yet fully grasped that the main thing which the world expects of America, is not foreign aid, not military support or loans, not technical know-how and gifts, but leadership. The U.S. is expected to know the road to follow, to be able to determine the choices best for mankind in this historical era, and possess the strength to pursue a corresponding policy.

The need for global order is evident. But the problem is how to achieve a stable and meaningful order: by self-liquidation of the U.S. or by U.S. leadership?

By adopting the principle of U.S. self-assertion we can answer that question.

There is no need to elaborate on the strategy of this political war, nor its means and fields of operation. It would naturally consist of two distinct operations:

1. Discontinuing all help to world communism of any kind, economic, financial, military, psychological or political.

2. Immediately mounting a mighty offensive in all those fields, where the clear aim would be to weaken communist positions, shatter the lies of their propaganda, expose the fundamental deceit of the most impudent hoax in history, unremittingly hit at the foul foundations of Marxist-Leninist theory, expose in detail and with untiring insistence the appalling inefficiency of communist economy, the corruption of their administration, the disorder and endless confusion of their production and distribution of goods and services, the fantastic waste of time and efforts in obtaining the most elementary foods, the murderous drabness of their everyday life, the constant fear from the secret police, the basic and incurable inherent backwardness of communism, as well as its intrinsic dishonesty in dealing with people, their corruption rooted in their system of unlimited privileges for members of the abjectly conformist power élite.

And for the standard liberal excuses that "we don't know how to do those things," "we are inept at subversion," "we simply cannot cope with the totalitarians" (incidentally, a thesis of Thomas Mann), "democracies cannot use totalitarian methods," etc., they are plainly and ridiculously untrue. For, as Senator Barry Goldwater has pointed out, the same individuals and groups who assert with a straight face that we absolutely do not know and do not have the makings of political warriors because the U.S. is unpolitical and inexperienced in subversion and revolution—knew

how to fight Hitler and were very efficient at it. Why wouldn't
they know how to fight the communists? The question answers
itself.

To visualize and assess the impact and consequences of this
change of our policy, we must bear in mind the immensity of the
change. It would bring about a revolution in the basic relationship
which has existed so far. Until now, U.S. policy has subordinated
U.S. national interests to those of mankind—which includes the
Soviet Union and all communists—always trying to avoid increasing tensions and "provoking" their irritation, or anger. Most of the
press and communications media adopted the same attitude of
being highly critical of the U.S. and most indulgent regarding the
Soviet Union. All this in the face of Soviet (and generally, communist) policies and propaganda which unremittingly tear down,
vilify, discredit, accuse of corruption, hopeless rottenness, injustice, U.S. and Western society, while never yielding an inch in
their defense and glorification of communist society.

The fundamental truth, which has been kept hidden from the
public of the West, is that the world situation of 1972 is not the
result of a stalemate between communist political warfare against
the West and the West's political warfare against communism.
Not at all. It has ensued from a communist political war against
the West and a Western policy which has offered little resistance
to communism, most of the time facilitating its operations and
conquests, never fighting to destroy it, and at best acting only to
slow down its expansion.

In other words, if the present situation—no matter how serious
and pregnant with grave consequences and possible deterioration
—is all that the communists have been able to achieve by strain-
ing all their forces and resources and with all the help they have
obtained from the West—then they hardly stand a chance once
we stop helping them and start fighting them.

In 1958 George Allen, head of the U.S. Information Agency,
and thus Commander-in-Chief of our psychological warfare, declared that the U.S. was "willing to have its international broadcasts monitored by the United Nations." He thought that this
"would be a very good way toward bringing some kind of decency
out of the international air waves." (Since there was no mention
of any monitoring of Soviet propaganda, this clearly amounted to

the sensational indication that the offender against international radio decency was the U.S.!). He then emphatically assured the press that "we are making no inflammatory broadcasts" (!) [228]

Is it difficult to imagine the results if we started making them?

The effects of a basic change in our attitude and policies toward world communism would be those of a psychological and political atomic bomb. The main battlefields of the war would move from the free world to the communist world. The main topics of propaganda over the air and in the printed word would not be the evils of the West, but those of communism. The main devastation would be done in their bailiwick, not in ours, the positions crumbling would be theirs, not ours, the attention of the world would be drawn to their shortcomings and incurable defects, not ours. And the main resentment, indignation and emotional explosiveness of the world, the dissatisfaction with whatever trouble may befall it, would turn against the communists, not against the West.

In the shortest time, the communist offensive against the West would be in hopeless disarray and they would be forced into fighting a desperate defensive political war, instead of the offensive one they have been fighting all the time.

So, political warfare based on U.S. self-assertion, offers the best solutions to our domestic problems, as well as international.

Nuclear War?

The idea may appear shocking, of course. For we have so long been conditioned to look for all kinds of explanations save the true, logical, natural and sane ones for modern problems, we have become so resigned to accepting our upside-down relationship with the USSR—that they must live, and we must disappear—as the only one possible, and that political war, a solution based on the fundamental elements and considerations of our situation, must, for some time at least, be met with alarm, resistance and denunciation.

And if the political war which the communists are waging against us all the time with maximal intensity is not leading to nuclear war, why would a political war waged by us against the communists, lead to nuclear war?

If today the communists are not waging against the U.S. a nu-

clear war, it is not out of the goodness of their hearts, love for the
U.S. or mankind, or the people they keep enslaved, but: a.) because they are (still) militarily weaker, and b.) because they are
doing exceedingly well by political war, marching toward the
realization of their objectives.

So, why would our decision to start waging political war lead to
nuclear war?

If what is holding the communists back is their military inferiority, that element would not be improved, but would deteriorate,
since our political offensive would deeply affect the morale of all
the communist-enslaved peoples, making them very unreliable
soldiers.

Considering the real situation, and particularly the vulnerability
of the communists and their regimes in various countries, from the
Soviet Union to Albania and from China to Cuba, it is evident that
political warfare against communism would not lead to a hot war,
but is the best, nay the only thoroughly effective way to prevent a
shooting world war. For it would knock out all the props upon
which communist military strength and potential military aggression rest, and to which the Polish communist "heretic" writers,
Kuron and Modzelewski are referring. (see pp. 168–169).

As things stand now, the strength of the communists consists
above all of our disposition to counter their war with peace, their
hostility with friendship and co-existence, their aggression with
surrender.

Which means that politically, even more than in any other field,
they are at our mercy, because it needs only us to change the
present situation of Soviet strength into a situation of weakness.
Their present strength is based on our policy of sparing them and
building them up, thus creating in the U.S., behind the Iron Curtain and in the whole world, the myth of communist overpowering strength and invincibility. By withdrawing our props under
their phony might, by carrying the torch of unrest, riots, rebellion
and civil war to their house, we would reverse the situation radically, take the reins in our hands and show the world that the U.S.
is not only right, but strong enough to control the course of
events.

People behind the Iron Curtain hate communism with all the
emotional intensity they are capable of, but they will remain pas-

sive as long as they consider that there is no hope of overthrowing it. Despair and the feeling of being forsaken, lead them to the conclusion that all efforts to destroy tyranny would be in vain.

The hold of communism over the enslaved peoples was immensely strengthened by the fact that the West, instead of giving a helping hand to the enslaved in 1953 and 1956, when they demonstrated their staunch determination to fight for freedom, gave support to their communist enslavers by taking no action against them. All that the embattled freedom fighters obtained were sentimental platitudes about liberty, humanity, self-determination and democracy. The lesson was not lost on any other enslaved people, including those in the Soviet Union: "If we were to start a revolution here, would the Americans come and help? I suppose it would be the same as Hungary." [229] These words of a young Russian just about sum up the prevalent feeling.

A change of U.S. foreign policy from surrender to self-assertion and struggle for freedom, would produce incalculable consequences: despair would turn into hope, obedience to the communist regimes into defiance, submission into revolt, passivity into activism, anti-Westernism into anti-communism. And the communists know that—should despair drive them to start a war—the command of "fire!" in the direction of Paris, London or Washington, would be followed by the soldiers turning around their rifles, machine guns, guns and missiles in the direction of Moscow and Peking and all other communist-enslaved capitals of the world, against the communist powerholders.

A sure indication of the panic that grips communist leaders whenever the idea of the liberation of the enslaved peoples of Eastern Europe is mentioned, is Nikita Khrushchev's hysterical reaction against the totally emasculated and innocuous Captive Nations Week, proclaimed in 1959 by President Eisenhower. The move was made in the later days of Eisenhower's second Administration and clearly bore all the marks of a policy whose reality was coexistence with the communists and where anti-communism was relegated to the realm of political vacuity and day-dreaming. But, regardless, communists know their Achilles heel and cannot control their reaction of panic.

So, communists dare not start a military war, even if they had a mind to do it, for communist war chances are mainly the despair of the people and the pro-communist foreign policy of the West. Once these two basic conditions are reversed, and the oppressed people progress from despair to hope as a consequence of the change of Western policy from surrender to struggle for freedom —the communists do not stand a ghost of a chance of successfully waging a war against the West.

And if it could be objected that it takes two to keep peace, i.e. to avert war, this is entirely true and this is the second real reason why there would, there could be no shooting war: because the West's positions are so overwhelmingly favorable, that neither the U.S. nor the oppressed *need* military war to overthrow their imposed communist regimes and become free.

The Kremlin powerholders, in spite of all their bluster, have not forgotten the lesson of 1941, when Adolf Hitler, the representative of "the most extreme elements of finance capital," the arch-enemy of the workers, the mortal enemy of Russia and communism, the most reactionary political figure in history, was supposed to be smashed by the armies of the Soviet Union, if he were not liquidated before that by the oppressed proletariat of Nazi Germany. Instead, the Soviet forces disintegrated before his onrush. Not because the Soviet soldiers did not love their country or were cowards, but because, no matter how much they hated the foreign fascist Hitler, they hated still more the domestic communist Stalin.

The example of Budapest has not been forgotten either. In October of 1956, when the people revolted against their communist rulers, the domestic (Hungarian) troops turned to the rebels, and moreover a considerable number of Soviet troops of occupation did the same. It is the West which obliged Khrushchev by assuring him that it would not move a finger to help the Budapest anticommunist revolution, but would let the Soviet might deal with them without any foreign interference. This made it possible for Khrushchev to come back with 5000 tanks and fresh Mongolian troops to save communism, which had been beaten by the people, with the help of the Hungarian communist troops and Soviet troops switching over to their side.

So contrary to all the propaganda and brainwashing about nuclear war inevitably resulting from the slightest stiffening of the

West's spine, there is not the slightest reason to assume that a change of U.S. policy would or could possibly mean war. And there is every reason to assume that it would make impossible a shooting, nuclear war.

The Czechs and Slovaks possess a very keen sense of discipline and organization. It is a matter of common knowledge how much they harassed, embarrassed and confused the Soviet occupation troops in 1968 just by opposing a marvelously coordinated passive resistance, without violence, i.e. military means, and that in spite of their awareness of being let down by the West. Is it difficult to imagine how paralyzing for the Soviet occupiers that ability to organize, that national solidarity would be in case of a real war situation or revolutionary action where the West would not side with the communist powerholders, but would offer at least its political and material help (which would be enough) to the people struggling to be free?

This does not mean that bloodshed could be avoided. The communist planned coup in Indonesia was averted (September 1, 1965) and there was no war, although Red China had actually made all preparations to lend the necessary assistance to the new powerholders, had the coup been successful.

There has been serious bloodshed, the number of victims has been estimated at over half a million. But it is a generally accepted truth that the tree of liberty must be fed by the blood not only of the freedom fighters but also of the oppressors. And, in any case, the death of half a million people who had accepted the idea of liquidating without the slightest pang of conscience, many millions of Indonesians ("reactionaries"), is a modest price to pay for preserving freedom for the 105 million Indonesians.

Far from leading to nuclear war, the change of U.S. policy from surrender to struggle for freedom would establish the only possible basis for the solution of our problems.

Self-Assertion and Domestic Problems

". . . Kill your parents . . . And I mean that quite seriously, because until you're prepared to kill your parents, you're not really prepared to change the country . . .

". . . Quit being students. Become criminals. We have to disrupt every institution and break every law."

> Jerry Rubin (quoted in W. Trohan's article
> *Chicago Tribune* May 29, 1970)

"Stand up, older generation . . . Don't give us what we demand. We're testing you and you're failing . . . It's your society . . . It's your country; you fought for it . . . bled for it, dreamed of it . . . It's time to reclaim it."

> Jennie Fisher (same source)

"Stop capitulating to the stupid demands of Negro students."

> Bayard Rustin (*Time* magazine, May 9, 1967)

The adoption of a revolutionary new course in U.S. policies, from surrender to self-assertion would produce effects so thorough and far-reaching, that under present conditions of upside-down, surrender and unreason, it may be difficult for many people to visualize the immense transformation that would take place.

Our elected leaders, our educators, university professors, philosophers, sociologists and psychologists, newspapermen, radio and television commentators, and movie-makers have too long exercised ruthless criticism of all our values, institutions and achievements, while at the same time adopting an attitude of respect and inferiority before the enemy. Consciously or unwittingly, they have played into the hands of the communists, who have systematically distorted the facts, selected the evidence, whipped up passions and drowned every problem in sociological and psychological "newspeak." As a result, every sane perspective of every problem has been distorted and rational discussion made impossible, thus inducing a feeling of powerlessness and hopelessness.

The change of U.S. policy from surrender to self-assertion would completely change this situation.

The Youth Rebellion

An exhaustive analysis of the rebellion of our youth is outside the scope of this book. The irrationality and destructiveness of the rebels, turned against themselves as much as against society, brand them as pathological, as "crowd madness," but also as a symptom of deep trouble in the society which spawned them. The phenomenon of Woodstock, with half a million young people reducing themselves morally to animals and mentally to vegetables, is as grave as the demonstration of several hundred thousands of young Americans demonstrating with obscenities, and under the Vietcong flag, in the nation's capital with the avowed aim of "stopping the Government," and exhibiting before the whole world the unspeakably sordid spectacle of the desecration of U.S. war decorations. And the presence of thousands upon thousands of young Americans throughout the world, as draft dodgers, hippies and drug users, who automatically bear testimony about their country, even when they disown it, is a disgrace for the United States and does nothing for its prestige at a time when it is exposed to the most comprehensive and merciless war in history. Therefore, the nature and origin of the phenomenon must be properly identified.

There are always, in any society, at any time, compulsive protestors who, for whatever reasons, turn against the society to which they belong and try to bring about a "better" society by destroying the existing one. And then no explanation of the present protest movement can be attempted without considering the role of the communists in fomenting dissatisfaction, and creating all the conditions for organized action against the U.S.

Nevertheless, the phenomenon calls for additional explanation. Without denying the complexity of the problem, it can be reduced to the following three traits:

1. Destructive and violent as the actions of the youth in rebellion are, the movement has no comprehensive outlook, no philosophy of history, society and politics, no coherent program. It is a movement of deepest despair, emptiness and hatred, not a movement to attain a rational political end.

The rules they go by (including the one of denying the existence and validity of any laws) are rules of suicide, for no society, no social order can be built on them (barbaric ignorance of the human condition, of history, of the problems of the modern world; the adoption of feelings and impulses, momentary whims and moods, as the supreme yardstick of happiness and culture;

the unrestricted use of drugs, the rejection of reason and decency, unlimited sexual promiscuity, refusal to work, rejection of personal responsibility.)

2. The rebels are not interested in the redress of any grievances, in the correction of any social or moral ills, but in destroying America. As Jerry Rubin has said, the moment their demands are met, they come with new demands, bolder and more difficult to meet, until a spirit and mood of surrender is induced in the leaders of "the system." They are waging war against America.

3. The rebels are not an antithesis to the Establishment, but its children. The rebellion of the youth within the present crisis of the U.S. is usually viewed in an entirely wrong perspective, as if the two, the rebels and the Establishment, were opposed to each other, the one attacking law and order and traditional American values and principles, the other upholding them; the one destroying the United States, the other safeguarding it unconditionally.

Nothing could be farther from the truth. The rebels are an inevitable product of the Liberal Establishment. There is little difference in the attitude towards communism and the war in Vietnam between the representatives of the Establishment and the leaders of the protest movement: the victory of the U.S. must not be achieved; communism must not be destroyed, the only way to end the war is to strive for a compromise, the U.S. must urgently solve its social problems or face destruction.

The Liberal Establishment could not help produce the New Left.

As we have seen in Chapter 2, a nation is never inalterably completed, never secure, but dying every day and being reborn every day. It cannot exist if it is not constantly protected and strengthened by the devotion of its citizens, who must have the right to criticize, but have the duty to watch its ramparts. And the process of decay or renewal, disintegration or bloom, depends decisively on its leaders, on how they fulfill their natural responsibility of preserving the values of the nation, upholding its rights, safeguarding its interests.

The vital need of youth is to have principles, values, truths, absolutes to believe in and be guided by. Sound, creative individuals and responsible citizens do not grow like weeds. They are reared and educated by their elders.

Youth needs someone to tell them the truth about man, about the essence of his being, about his duties, his dignity, his responsibility, about the United States which must be preserved if there are to be any free Americans and free people in the world. Every new generation needs the guiding hand, the care, above all the good example of parents, at home, in church, in school, in government. Without that there is no continuity and no civilized society.

If, however, the young, in their search for values, meaning and ideals, encounter only uncertainty, wavering, inconsistency and opportunism, they will turn against their parents and the society which deprived them of the spiritual food by which man lives. And they will be easy prey for those who, however vile their aims, know how to appeal to youth's need for commitment, direction and meaning.

A French adage says that to educate is to encourage (*éduquer, c'est encourager*). The essence of education is to enlighten the mind of the young and give them courage to face, explore and change the world. And since evil, the seamy side of life, the hardships, difficulties, sufferings are easier to notice, the task of the educators is to go beyond the evil, ugliness, corruption and depravity in life and society, and indicate to young minds and souls the glory of life, its beauty, the greatness of man's achievements, his enormous chances as opposed to his limitations. It is easy to be cynical and drag everything in the mud. For that, no education is necessary. Education is enlightenment, discovering things and truths, sparking faith, bringing to life, developing mental and moral energies.

That is the function, the sacred trust of parents, teachers, churchmen, statesmen.

But the fact is that the young generation has never heard their liberal elders, at home, in church, in school, in Government, say: "This is true and this is false; this is right and this is wrong; and in vital issues we will not yield and compromise." No, everything has been relative, debatable, negotiable. Faith and affirmation pertaining to the U.S. or to the human condition and its basic categories, have been replaced with universal doubt. Nothing was left to believe in, no principles, no values, no achievement, no task. "The American Dream is over," [230] proclaimed Dr. Grayson Kirk, president of Columbia University, a few years ago. The tragedy is that when several years later he watched the ignoble destruction wrought on his University by his students and exclaimed, "My God, can human beings do this?", he did not realize that he was witnessing fruits which could not have matured without his educational seeds being sown.

On the communist side, there has all the time been total, absolute and unconditional assertiveness and self-confidence, with always the same unmistakable message: "We communists are right; we know the score; we will not yield, we will defend our power and system at all costs; we will win."

This contrast was bound to produce disastrous consequences and alienate American youth from America. Reconciliation with communism breeds self-contempt, because it *is* self-contempt. If the leaders do not believe in the country they rule, where can youth turn for encouragement and faith? How can they possibly be inspired with belief in America and enthusiasm to live and battle and sacrifice for it? Those whose ideals have been sullied by the official recognition of communist "values" have nothing to fight for.

Today, the scene is dominated by youth who carry the Vietcong or North Vietnamese flag and look up to "Chairman Mao" and Ché Guevara as idols and the leaders of mankind, and give their enthusiasm and toil to Fidel Castro, cutting sugar cane in communist Cuba.

But disgraceful as this adulation of American youth for Mao and Guevara is, the truth is that they have been pushed in that direction by the U.S. policy of self-betrayal which deprived them of the chance and yearning to identify with Patrick Henry and Nathan Hale.

This aspect of the problem is absolutely vital. What our youth have rebelled against and are increasingly rebelling against, is not Government and authority, "U.S. imperialism and militarism," "repression" and "incipient fascism," but on the contrary, the lack of authority, the renunciation on the part of Government to do its duty, the moral, military and political surrender of America. They are rebelling against the emptiness of their lives, resulting from the policy of U.S. surrender.

It is here that we meet with the problem of

Law and Order

One of the fundamental truths which young people must be taught is the validity and importance of laws, moral and formal. Aristotle stressed some 2300 years ago the absolute need for man to respect laws,* and Goethe renewed the emphasis 21 centuries later: "Only the law can give us freedom."

Man, nations and mankind cannot live without laws, for the simple reason that the moral law in man is his strongest reality. Formal, written and enacted laws are based on unwritten laws, on spiritual truths and moral values. But to have validity, the laws must be enforced. And they can be enforced only if their spiritual foundations are upheld. *If we reject the truths, we violate the laws.* The talk about law becomes pointless and order cannot be kept.

Modern youth's contempt for law and order is deplorable. However, lawlessness begins not when the mob begins to riot and loot, but when the rulers stop ruling, when they fail to apply the law and to uphold the basic values of the nation.

Today, we do reject these values by a policy of *reconciliation with communism* and non-resistance to the enemy who is undermining the foundations of the United States. Under such conditions, the rule of law and order is impossible.

The unreason of the New Left has inevitably resulted from the unreason of the Establishment. For if it is outrageous to destroy, to riot, to smash windows and set fire to buildings, to destroy scientific papers and documents which are the result of decades of work and research, to defy law and order, to behave like the demonstrators of August 1968 in Chicago, to substitute obscenities for language, it is even more outrageous to defy the basic laws and standards of logic and ethics, of decency and civilization, by pursuing a policy of coexistence, collaboration and reconciliation with communism, as well as by proclaiming that the war of the destroyers against America was legitimate dissent and that the

* For everyone to live "as he pleases . . . is all wrong; men should not think it slavery to live according to the rule of the constitution; for it is their salvation." (*Aristotle's Politics,* Translated by Benjamin Jowett, Carlton House, New York, p. 237)

Establishment, while disagreeing on methods, shared their goals.

The protesters and destroyers have adopted a typically communistic attitude of blackmail towards the Establishment, amounting to the following proposition: "We, being angry, have the right to smash everything to pieces, and you, being wrong and guilty, have no right to oppose us. If you resist our aggression, you are guilty of aggression."

The acceptance of this Bevanist logic (see page 43) obviously means blatant surrender.

If the foundations of the U.S. are wrong, if Vietnam is nothing but a huge enterprise in killing, if the Negroes have been exploited for 300 years and are being exploited today by white Americans, if poverty and social injustice are the main traits of the United States, then there is no case for law and order, because then the destroyers are right and the rule of liberty and justice for all in the U.S. is a sham.

But if the foundations of the United States are right and the leaders of the U.S. believe them to be right, then they are expected to say so, to stand behind them, and to stop the destroyers.

The trouble is precisely that the destroyers have never met real resistance on the part of the advocates of law and order, nor have they ever heard them say:

"So, you want to change and improve the world? Fine! But then: learn to know the world, the nature of communism, and your own country. Get acquainted with its history, with the efforts of those who created it and those who made it the leading and most prosperous country in the world. Compare what others have done with what the U.S. has done. Decide what your goal is, and then work for it.

"But, for heaven's sake, don't be stupid puppets, tools used by the communists, masters of deceit and political warfare, for their own ends!

"At this juncture, you are wrong, you are ignorant and you are vile. You are not concerned with the redress of any grievance, nor do you care about the black man, or the working man, or the peasants of Vietnam, or the youth of America. Least of all do you care about freedom and justice. You feel empty, you feel sorry for yourselves, you are full of self-contempt. Too cowardly to confront the enemy, you are turning your despair and bitterness against your own country, to which you owe all you have.

"You follow leaders without conscience, without courage and without decency, who despise you and use you for their ends.

"You want to destroy America, not to make a better one, but to escape your own hopeless inner chaos, to vent your pathological urges and compulsions.

"Well, kids, you won't have it!

"The U.S. does stand improving. But it also, and much more, deserves defending. Because it was created by men infinitely better than the New Left with all its hippies and yippies and weathermen and black panthers will ever be. And today, in spite of all its shortcomings, it is kept together by people with whom you can never hope to compare.

"So, you have no right to destroy America and you will not have it your way. Not for the fun of playing your sick games, and not for world communism."

That is the only kind of talk which could have brought the destroyers to their senses and turned the tides. And that is the kind of talk they have never heard.

There has been much talk about the "generation gap." The expression is a misnomer. The gap between children and parents started with Adam and Eve and their children and has existed ever since. Today the generation gap is deeper than ever before not because of the conditions of our technological society, but because for the first time in the history of the U.S., a good part of U.S. youth has been deprived of moral education and guidance by their parents.

The parents of the rebellious youth have seen to their physical, material needs, and have been "pals" to them. But they have failed to tell them about right and wrong (because questions beyond the satisfaction of material needs, urges or passions, never entered the field of their vision or discussion). They failed to tell them that there is no human dignity without personal responsibility, that there are values which are not advertised in the press or shown on television, among which are self-respect and respect for others, and the unique pleasure which comes from the fulfillment of duty. They have failed to give them an example of behavior, to set standards which must be upheld if man and mankind are to live in dignity and not sink into the jungle. Modern parents have given their kids everything—except love and care about their souls and characters.

That is the main sin of the fathers of today's rebels, protesters and rioters: that whenever U.S. principles, values and interests were challenged, they did not stand their ground to defend them, but looked for compromise and yielded to the enemy.*

Deprived by their parents of that moral and educational essence, how could the children possibly have been encouraged to trust and respect other people, to believe that human society, imperfect as it is, had nevertheless been built by untold toil, dedication, sacrifice and selflessness and cannot be preserved without them. How could they have developed self-respect, self-reliance and a sense of preserving the bases of civilized society, the noble ambition of improving the world and leaving it to their children as a better place than the world they were born in?

How could they possibly have learned to take a responsible attitude toward society, to love their country, to develop anything but contempt for their parents, with the inseparable consequence of self-contempt, disrespect for society, a cynical attitude toward the United States, and a destructive attitude toward the world?

As things now stand, we have mortally imperiled them by depriving them of everything, denuding them not only physically to mini-skirts which until a few years ago no prostitute would wear, —but destroying every and any moral concept and reducing them to bundles of instincts and impulses, the only thing left to them to guide them in their lives. The parents do not dare speak of that which is essential to life, moral principles, because they either do not believe in them, or are unaware of their existence and vital importance, or know about them, but have lost the fortitude to stand for what they know to be right.

The problem of sex education is a case in point. What our youth need is not *sex* education, but moral education and moral example. For the best sexual education is moral education, based

---

* The notable movie of nearly twenty years ago, "Rebel Without A Cause" (James Dean), clearly identified the tragic cause of the incipient rebellion of the youth: the inability of the fathers to take a position of principle and recommend a definite stand on any issue.

on the reverence of the human person and for the relationship of sex, which cannot be divorced from the relationship of love.

A teenage girl will be saved from bad company, moral debasement, pregnancy, venereal disease and other trouble which can ruin her life, not by charts of male and female reproductive organs, or by learning all there is to know about sexual intercourse, not by anti-pregnancy pills, but by the development of her moral sense. She must be taught that the life of every one of us is made not only of physiology, but of human dignity and free will, without which we cannot build a decent life. And the substance out of which happiness is made consists of accomplishments of toil, effort, hard work, self-discipline, which alone can produce the supreme joy of beauty, of self-fulfillment, of overcoming the difficulties, adversities and ugliness which constantly come our way, as well as the foibles and limitations of human nature. Only so can the fullness and true joy of life be attained and the human condition improved.

When recently the case of pregnancy of a girl of eleven was reported, many of the sexual education experts immediately pounced upon it to prove their case: she was pregnant because she had received no sexual education! But this is totally and demonstrably wrong. She got into trouble because she received no human education. She was not taught how to be a decent human being, respecting herself and upholding her human and female dignity. There is all the difference in the world between a female who knows the techniques and owns the pills to avoid getting pregnant by the many males with whom she is "free" to engage in sexual intercourse, and a decent girl who first respects herself and in that self-respect finds the best defense against all trouble, including getting pregnant out of wedlock.

There has never been more kissing and less love in the world; more denudation and less honesty, more "baring of our insides," to use Paul Newman's expression, and less sincerity.

This vacuum could not have come about without the failure of those in authority to exercise authority, the failure of parents to be parents, the failure of the men of God to preach the word of God instead of, as cowards, turning their efforts to transforming the Church into an agency for "social change"; the failure of the teachers to develop the mind and character of youth, the failure of Government to govern. And that vacuum is intolerable. It drives people to rebellion.

This is not putting the blame on "society," instead of the individual. Personal responsibility is inherent in man and transcends social conditions and the influence of others. But the decisive responsibility of the leaders must be fully faced, for there can be no solution of any problem unless improvement is effectuated at the top.

There cannot be law and order in the streets and in the behavior of youth unless and before there is law and order in the minds and souls of the leaders. And the natural allegiance of Americans to the American flag and all it represents will be undermined as long as GIs are called upon to die carrying it, but are forbidden to achieve victory under it.

As long as we recognize the enemy's values and goals and disagree only on methods, there is no solution. On the contrary, the problems will be escalated and lead to final disaster.

The problem will not be solved before we tackle the question of values, of the reason for fighting in Vietnam and the reason for observing law and order in the United States. In the name of what? That is what must be clearly answered. As long as we agree with the destroyers on principle, on the premises, there is no reason to observe law and order, there is no reason not to withdraw U.S. troops from Vietnam unconditionally and let South Vietnam be overrun by the forces of victorious communist aggression; and there is no reason not to let the destroyers destroy America. Only when we say "no"! to the destroyers, shall we have on the side of America not only the physical force of the police, and the National Guard, but the incomparably greater force of moral right.

The solution is self-assertion, a "yes" to America and all that makes it, all that men, good and strong men, Americans, dreamed of, toiled, suffered and accomplished. Nobody has the right to despise that. Everybody has the duty to respect it.[231] Everybody, but above all those who are at the helm.

Youth craves not for glib and clever politicians who mean whatever anybody pleases to read in their statements, and will reverse themselves on any issue in any direction as the situation changes and take the opposite position.

It needs statesmen who will stand and fall for their beliefs, for beliefs on which a nation can be founded and on which this one *was* founded.

When we give that to our youth, and that, let us make no mistake, we *do* owe to our youth, we will not have to worry about obscenity, about morals, about pot, about self-contempt and self-destruction, about the exodus of draftees, about the vandalization of our colleges and universities.

For then our youth will have the most important thing in life: an example to follow, to lean on, a faith to be sure of, a meaning to fill their lives.

That is why self-assertion is the answer to our problems, the true alternative to the policy of surrender which we have practiced too long.

We repeat: self-assertion is no magic wand, no cure-all, no panacea. But it is the precondition for law and order, for the solution of our problems. It is the natural basis of our life. For it says yes to the fundamental values of the U.S., it straightens out the misguided, it gives support to the believers in America. And it says no to the destroyers, to their violence, and to the inane, preposterous, shameless, pathological, barbaric premises from which they derive their violence and nihilistic fury.

Self-assertion is the answer to life for America; it eliminates surrender which spells its death.

Is it difficult to imagine what a formidable change it would be if the youth of America were to discover that the Establishment, those who are supposed to represent us all and whose foremost duty is to defend the country and fight its enemies, were really and unwaveringly doing just that? All of a sudden their yearning for belief, for sense, for pride in America, for guiding ideals would be fulfilled. And concomitantly, is it difficult to figure out how shatteringly discouraging it would be for all the dropouts from Americanism to discover that the overriding concern of U.S. policy makers is no longer coexistence with communism and readiness to negotiate for survival, but unconditional defense and assertion of America, both against the foreign enemy and the domestic traitors who are helping the foreign enemy.

It is of the essence for Americans to keep as strong as possible their links with the principles of the Founding Fathers and with American traditions hallowed by effort, suffering and achievement. Today, in the age of science and technology, whose spectacular feats and moral relativism tend to upset our intellectual, moral and political balance, it is a matter of survival.[232]

Self-Assertion and International Relations

"China does not traffic in principles, nor do we sell out *our* comrades-in-arms, never."

Chou En-lai

The international repercussions which the fundamental change of U.S. foreign policy from surrender to self-assertion and freedom would produce in our international relations, are palpable.

Our foreign policy experts have never tired of stressing the importance of

a. world public opinion, the respect we owe it and the restraints it imposes on our policy; and of

b. the struggle for the minds of men, which is the main battle going on in the world between powers with different political ideologies and systems.

Now, it cannot be denied that both points have validity: 1. the success of U.S. foreign policy, as of any other country's policy, depends not only on economic potential and military strength, but to a great extent on psychological factors, on how our policy affects other countries and what reactions it elicits; 2. in the present world, caught in revolutionary turmoil involving basic, age-old beliefs, ideas, traditions and institutions, there is no static situation nor are there positions conquered and assured once and for all. As a result, people are less sure of anything than ever before.

So far, so good. The question is, however, how do we earn the respect of the world and how do we win the battle for people's minds? Are the record of our foreign policy of the past few decades and its present practice likely to impress favorably the opinion of the world and win the minds of people around the globe?

There is a distinct and widespread tendency to speak of our foreign policy in terms of confusion, ambiguity, vacillation, lack of consistency and continuity. The plain truth of the matter, however, is that in spite of all diversity (real and apparent), our foreign policy since 1933 (the recognition of the USSR by the U.S. under President F. D. Roosevelt) up to the present day has not been one of fighting communism, trying to stop its advance, break its aggressiveness, defeat its drive for world conquest—but one of seeking compromise, accommodation, as well as of active help to communism in various countries, under diverse pretenses, explanations and excuses.

There is an equally widespread tendency to accuse our allies of dragging their feet when it comes to fighting communism, which allegedly makes the burden of the U.S. heavier. But this story is in collision with the plain and known facts that U.S. allies everywhere on the globe have taken a firmer stand against communism than the U.S., wondering why the U.S. was pursuing a course opposed to the evidence of communist policies and contrary to its own interests.

To start with World War II, Colonel (later General) Draza Mihailovich defied Hitler when he was at the peak of his power and considered by many as the sure winner, and when the Yugoslav communists, and all world communists, headed by Joseph Stalin, were his allies. Pictures of the three "greatest generals of World War II," Douglas MacArthur, Semyon Timoshenko and Draza Mihailovich were printed and distributed in millions of copies throughout the United States. However, Draza being nobody's mercenary, but his people's faithful servant, also fought the communists who were vying with the Nazi invader and his henchmen as to who would kill more Serbs and more thoroughly devastate the country. That struggle against the communists was Draza Mihailovich's unforgivable sin. He was harassed, left without supplies, slandered and betrayed. The rest of the story is known. It is the worst disgrace and injustice of World War II. When Tito caught Mihailovich (1946) and staged a "trial," there was an upsurge of public opinion and conscience in America, but nothing officially was done. The U.S. Government let its most loyal and gallant ally of World War II be murdered by Stalin's agent, Tito. In 1949, under President Truman, Draza Mihailovich was awarded the Legion of Merit medal, the highest U.S. decoration for aliens. But, probably for fear of incurring Tito's displeasure, this fact was kept secret until June 19, 1967, when it was dug out owing to the efforts of Congressman Edward Derwinski (R.-Illinois).

The story of the Poles is well known too. They did not drag their feet, but fought with their customary valor all over Europe, in Norway, in Italy, in England, in the Warsaw uprising (1944), ignominiously betrayed by their Soviet allies, who let the German troops massacre the rebels. But the Polish freedom fighters were sacrificed to the communist traitors of the Lublin Committee.

In 1966, prompted by a suggestion of Senator Robert Kennedy that a coalition government was needed in Saigon to end the war in Vietnam, Ferenc Nagy, former Prime Minister of Hungary (1946–47) came out with a significant statement:

". . . In my government the Communist Party had only 17 per cent of popular support while my party alone was supported by more than 60 per cent of the voters and the parliament. Still the communist party could get in power in two years because they were supported by the Soviet Union and I was overthrown because no outside power gave me any help.

"Similar was the fate of all coalition governments in central and eastern Europe." [233]

Equally well known is the story of China. There was never any reluctance on the part of the Chinese (nationalists) to fight the enemy, and today it is not Chiang Kai-shek and his soldiers who are shirking the battle of any kind against communism. A most interesting view on the problem was expressed by President Eisenhower, who stated that "in effect the United States Navy (under the Truman Administration) was required to serve as a defensive arm of Communist China." [234]

Of more than passing interest, especially in view of the fact that the Middle East has become in the meantime a potential source of global trouble, is the article which Nuri es Said, pro-Western Premier of Iraq, wrote in July 1958 for *Life* magazine. He was murdered before the article was published (July 28, 1958).

"The sense that the West has abandoned us is as strong as it was in 1955 before Nasser electrified the Arab world by his arms deals with Russia, or even stronger . . . Speaking as an Arab and friend of the West, I'm fed up. Most responsible Arabs feel the same."

When President Eisenhower on his world tour in December 1959 stopped in Ankara, Turkish students met him with a "banner stretched across an arch through which President Eisenhower rode into Ankara." "Honor and Freedom at all costs, not peace at all costs." [235] Writing about Turkey a year later, Frank H. Bartholomew, President of the United Press International, stressed that the Turks were an ally "that does not need to have its spine stiffened against communism. Instead it needs assurance that the spine of the West has not softened." [236]

Edgar Ansel Mowrer equally contrasted the firmness which our allies expected from the U.S. and the "flexible firmness" which President Eisenhower gave them:

". . . President de Gaulle, Chancellor Adenauer, the governments of Italy, Portugal, Turkey, Spain, Iran, Pakistan, Thailand, Korea, the Philippines, National China on Formosa, Peru and others, want greater firmness if the world is to be saved.

"President Eisenhower's answer was, 'firmness with flexibility —resistance with relaxation of tension.' (He early forgot the 'liberation policy' with which he won the 1952 elections.)" [237]

The story of Syngman Rhee of South Korea, is also the story of a staunch U.S. ally, who, at a crucial moment, was not supported by the U.S. Government, but ousted through support given to his enemies.

To get closer to home, trouble in Canada did not start with Pierre Trudeau. Back in 1961, the voices predominant in the Liberal Party (of Lester Pearson) were neutralist and socialist to the point of taking the stand "that any defense is suicidal and the only hope for survival is to come to terms with communism." [238] Without entertaining the slightest doubts regarding Lester Pearson's personal inclinations, the strengthening of leftist influences in Canada can hardly be divorced from the trends expressed in U.S. policies of that time.

The mood south of U.S. borders, in Latin America, which was

made unmistakably clear during a recent visit (July 1969) of Governor Nelson Rockefeller, President Nixon's special envoy for the task, also has long roots. One of them is certainly the very timid and yielding policy toward Castro, i.e. communism in Cuba. After the dismal failure of the Cuban invasion of April 16, 1961, promoted and scuttled by U.S. policy-makers, a well informed correspondent and authority on Latin America, Jules Dubois, of *The Chicago Tribune*, visited a number of Latin American capitals and made a survey of the local moods and opinions. In his findings, Dubois wrote:

> "Latin Americans like a winner and they were disillusioned that the United States proved to be the loser."

> "We wouldn't have admired your government for what it would have done," they would say, "but we would have respected you. We have never been partisans of halfway measures." [239]

Dr. Carlos Urruttia Aparicio, Guatemalan ambassador to the Organization of American States, expressed identical feelings. The U.S. Government should "show less timidity" in dealing with hemispheric problems. "We would admire you more if you showed more initiative, firmness and leadership. The Communist Doctrine is wrong, but at least it has vitality and an implacable plan of action. You are too timid."

In January 1962, the main political event was the Conference of the Foreign Ministers of the American Republics held in Punta del Este (Uruguay), for the purpose of deciding "how to meet the mounting Communist offensive in our hemisphere . . . spearheaded by the present regime in Cuba." *The New York Times* (January 21) wrote that "a clear condemnation of Cuban communism . . . would be a victory for the United States."

But it is precisely on that key resolution that the conference attained the least unity. The majority of two-thirds (of the states) was just barely achieved. But the thirteen countries voting for the exclusion of Cuba from the Inter-American System, had a population of 55 million. The six countries abstaining (Brazil, Argentina, Mexico, Ecuador, Chile, Bolivia) a total of 140 million.

What happened? According to several sources, one of them the

U.S. News & World Report (February 5, 1962): "Anti-Castro diplomats complained to Secretary Rusk that (his advisers) Rostow, Schlesinger and Goodwin weakened the U.S. position with many Latin countries by giving the impression that they favored a 'go easy on Castro' line of policy."

Latin Americans were disturbed not only by U.S. policy in the Western Hemisphere. They were following U.S. policy around the globe, unable to understand it. At the time when Angola was blown into a big problem of anti-colonialism before the U.N., some Latin American delegates were "surprised by the willingness of the United States to split with its allies on a colonial issue." [240]

The Korean war, the Geneva Conference of 1954, the solution of the Laotian problem and then the nightmare of Vietnam should have shed enough light on the problems in Asia to show again that it is not our allies who are lagging behind our State Department in their anti-communism, but exactly the opposite.

The Australian Ambassador to Washington, Howard Beale, issued a warning regarding the consequences of the "loss of heart" in Asia:

"The fate of mankind ultimately rests with 1,500,000,000 Asians . . . If we lose the East to communism, we will lose the world; surviving no doubt for a while in isolated countries, but gradually being worn down by erosion and loss of heart until in our countries, too, the lights will flicker and go out and another Dark Age will descend upon the human spirit everywhere." [241]

In the Philippines, the statement of President Carlos P. Garcia (1957–1961) that "We will never recognize Communist China, even if the United States does," [242] was much more than one man's opinion.

When the then Attorney General of the United States, Robert Kennedy, visited Thailand during his Asian tour of 1962, he found a vast difference between his stand on Laos and that of Asian statesmen. While the U.S. policy was favoring a neutral coalition (including the communists), Thai Premier Sarit Thanarat told him that "the Thai would prefer an all-out fight against the communist rebels." [243]

As for Europe, here again, in the same way as anywhere else, the repercussions of U.S. policy moves and trends were quick to announce themselves. Nikita Khrushchev's triumphant visit to the United States inevitably dampened the anti-communist spirit of U.S. allies. There were reports of Sweden cutting down its military expenditures, which caused shocked surprise in U.S. official circles. But the explanation given by a Scandinavian diplomat was plain logic:

> "We can only make our policy on what we see happening . . . And what we see is Khrushchev visiting the United States, Eisenhower preparing to go to the Soviet Union and a summit meeting in the future. On that basis, can we go to our people and say we must have more money for more soldiers, more planes and more tanks?" [244]

At a press conference in Bonn in November 1963, Secretary of State Dean Rusk was assailed with questions about the possible withdrawal of some U.S. troops from Germany. Visibly annoyed, Mr. Rusk told German newspapermen: "You seem always willing to ascribe the lowest motives to us. We cannot live this way." [245]

But Mr. Rusk's anger was misplaced. Distrust of U.S. foreign policy in Germany, in Europe and in the world, was not the result of anybody's inclination (save the communists, of course), to "ascribe the lowest motives" to U.S. policy-makers, but simply of the unequivocal record of U.S. foreign policy, of its unmistakable trends and spirit. We reaped what we sowed.

In July 1966, President Johnson was prevailed upon to take a peaceful coexistence initiative in the direction of Red China. First, Secretary Rusk visited Taiwan and warned the Nationalist Chinese Government that "it must face a possible unfavorable vote on representation in the United Nations." [246] A few days later, President Johnson himself asserted "the United States is not trying to wipe out North Vietnam, *nor is this country hostile toward Red China*" (Emphasis added).[247] *The Chicago Tribune* could not help comment:

> "If admission of Peking is indeed the administration's new policy . . . the switch comes at a curious time. Its own leaders admit that Red China's international influence is now at its low-

est ebb since the Korean War. Peking has just lost out in Indonesia and is beset by purges and internal strife. At this juncture, with Peking on the ropes and suffering from internal miseries, the Johnson administration arrives in time to boost it back into the ring. Most curious timing." [248]

However, considering the timing of Franklin D. Roosevelt's recognition of the Soviet Union 33 years before (1933) under similar conditions, the timing does not appear curious at all. It is even less curious in the light of President Nixon's initiative of July 15, 1971, which indicates the existence of some powerful forces assuring the continuity of the U.S. foreign policy of appeasing communism.

At the Geneva fourteen-nation Conference on Laos of June 1961, Thailand's Foreign Minister Thanat Khoman expressed dismay at the U.S. ignoring Thai proposals and supporting communist proposals. He concluded that "the country which claimed to be our great friend likes its foe better than its friends." [249]

Edgar Ansel Mowrer, an experienced observer of international affairs, agrees: "The U.S. has what it calls a victory policy only against its allies." [250]

Can that inspire anybody, win anybody's mind, impress world opinion in our favor? The world knows that the Soviet conquest of Eastern Europe was actually made possible by F. D. Roosevelt's policy of not antagonizing Stalin. Now, if we have not changed that philosophy and if we are determined to preserve the status quo in Eastern Europe and China—how can anybody fail to conclude that by proclaiming communism to be good for half of Europe, for the largest country in the world, Russia, and for the most populous country on earth, China—we are also saying that it is acceptable for the United States too?

Today, there is confusion in the ranks of the free everywhere, in France, England, Germany, in Asia, in Latin America, because one thing is becoming increasingly and painfully clear: that U.S. foreign policy is not to defeat communism, but to find a compromise with communism.

De Gaulle realistically assessed the course of U.S. foreign policy: appeasement, anti-colonialism, one sided nuclear morality (in favor of the enemy). That regrettably consistent course was made unmistakably clear on all issues of importance and everywhere in the world (Summit conferences;[251] Cuba, the Congo and Katanga; Laos; Korea; Vietnam; the test-ban treaty, etc. with the reconciliation with Red China being assiduously worked on by Adlai Stevenson, Roger Hilsman, John Galbraith, and a host of other influential liberals.)

So, De Gaulle logically concluded: if the U.S. does not do what only the U.S. can successfully do—fight to defeat communism—but does that which anybody can do—yield to communism, cooperate and coexist with it—then obviously I don't need the U.S.

And that attitude is by no means limited to De Gaulle. It is a widespread phenomenon. If Europe is going left, it is because that is where the U.S. is leading it, incredible as it may be.

What people in various European countries usually say is: U.S. foreign policy is against our basic interests. In England they tell you that it is anti-British, in France that it is anti-French, and so down the line in Italy, Spain, Germany, etc. Which is all true to an extent, and only to an extent. For what is not true is the implication (or sometimes, open accusation) that the U.S. is pursuing some diabolically clever selfish imperialistic policy, good for the U.S. but bad for its allies.

The fact is, of course, that in World War II it was not the U.S. Government, acting in defense of some U.S. selfish imperialistic interests, which neglected and sacrificed the interests of its allies, but that some people in Washington, D.C. who were supposed to defend U.S. interests, failed to do so, and favored Soviet interests instead. And, naturally, if Americans are willing to accept any political interests as superior to those of their country, then why not sell down the river the Serbs, the Poles, or anybody else, if it pleases Moscow, and helps create an atmosphere of mutual trust and peace?!

The same monstrous idea that U.S. foreign policy must be adapted to communist interests, and the interests of U.S. allies must be subordinated to that concern, is in operation today.

So the truth is that the anti-British, anti-French, anti-Italian, etc. (anti-European) U.S. foreign policy is first of all *bad for the U.S.* If it is imperialistic it is also a new phenomenon in the history of world politics, for it is imperialistic in favor of the enemy, as Vietnam glaringly demonstrates.

This is so patently true and yet so incredible and paradoxical, that reason rebels against accepting it. And nevertheless the plain gist of the matter is that:

they, the communists, want to destroy us, are destroying us, our political and economic positions, our beliefs, our values, our morale, our institutions, our legal system, our economic system, our historical presence, our right to live, whereas

we, faced with this aggressive and lethal challenge, pursue a policy which does not consist in safeguarding U.S. national interests, concepts and influences. On the contrary, U.S. foreign policy is *not* to fight communism. That is the incredible essence of the situation. For while they are doing everything in their power to destroy us, *they are in no danger from us* at all, at any time. At no moment do we jeopardize their existence.

In the communist world, no anti-communist rebellion has any chance, not because the communist regimes are against the people, but because the West is against them (Berlin 1953, Budapest 1956, Czechoslovakia 1968). The oppressed get the West's "humanitarian" sighs and tears, but its policy favors the communist regimes in their struggle against their peoples, either openly or implicitly, by ignoring the fact they are communists by treating them as "normal" regimes. For example, whenever Red China is discussed, we hear the argument that "we cannot ignore 700 million Chinese." But the same experts who sound the supposedly matter-of-fact, realistic warning, totally ignore the fact that those 700 million Chinese are ruled by communists!

It is that total and deliberate disregard of reality, that surrender in the face of open and aggressive hostility, which deeply harms U.S. interests, defies reason and puzzles, as well as demoralizes, the world.

The Struggle for the Minds of Men

The elementary truth which escapes the political perspicacity of our experts is that the decisive human battles are, in the last resort, fought and won or lost, *not* in the realm of material forces and social conditions, but in the realm of the minds and souls of people.

In the present world situation, the success of the U.S. struggle for the minds of men depends not on the products of its industry or the generosity of its State Department, nor can it be won by the patently abstruse, confused and inappropriate products of various official or semi-official "idea-factories"—but it depends on the quality of our working ideas and on the policies which we actually pursue. The struggle for the minds of Europeans, Latin Americans, Asians, Africans, etc., is being fought in the minds of Americans. That is the essence of the problem. All those people judge us by our policy, and our policy is shaped by our concepts, by our minds.

Being the world leader, we are necessarily looked up to, watched closely, imitated in good or evil, followed along sound paths and along roads of disaster. What the world thinks of us and the attitude it takes toward us, is to a great extent an echo of the message we send into the world, a mirror of our attitudes, our influences, our policies.

The men in Government (Administration and Congress), their basic attitudes, convictions and capabilities, reflect the real state of mind, concern, interest, awareness and dedication of the country, of its 200 million citizens. And if the outlook of America is one of impotence and hopelessness, and our policies are policies of weakness and despair, if our leaders, following some tortuous reasoning, direct us to reject our friends, who share our ideals and beliefs and stand for what we stand, and to yield to our sworn enemies, to try to win those who hate what we cherish and despise what we venerate,*—how can we possibly expect to win any

---

* An A.B.C. comment (Channel 7, on January 4, 1970, 10 P.M.) on some of Vice-President Agnew's remarks made at the time of his trip to Asia goes to the heart of the matter:

"Vice-President Agnew made today a statement which sounded rather enigmatic:

'Some people in Washington are so anxious to make friends of our enemies, that they are apparently making enemies of our friends.'

"The Thais, who liked the statement, apparently understood what he meant."

This brief TV comment contains the essence of what is wrong with our for-friends and favorably influence the minds of any people? How can we win them if by our deeds we show that it is unsafe to be on our side? How can the political leadership of any country turn to the U.S., the most powerful country on earth, when it is committing suicide and thus appearing as the sure loser?

By our present policy of surrender we are creating in the whole world a pro-communist climate of opinion, instead of a pro-American climate. Under those conditions, it obviously does not make any sense talking about winning anybody's mind for America, for freedom, for democracy. Not only can we attract nobody, but we are forcibly alienating the minds of men throughout the globe.

Various experts on communism and anti-communism never tire repeating that the only solution for the West is unity. We are failing, and the communists are succeeding, allegedly because they are united and we are disunited. Therefore: let us unite!

The argument is patently wrong. It is another liberal cobweb which must be cleared from our mind. As Salvador de Madariaga stressed in his booklet, *The Blasting of the Parthenon* (1961), unity, united action, presupposes common aim, common objective. Unity for what, to achieve what end? So far, Western unity has been promoted as an end in itself without discerning either the common goal or the ways and methods by which to attain them. That explains the failure.

Besides, the communists have never practiced unity at any price, and consequently that can in no case be the source of their strength and success. The history of communism is not a record of brotherly love, agreement and unity, tolerance and forbearance, but a record of constant conflict, ruthless strife, treacherous intrigue and merciless liquidation. The bolshevik party was born in a rift. And from the original conflict between the bolsheviks and the mensheviks to the liquidation of Trotsky by Stalin and the countless liquidations of most of the leaders of the revolution of 1917 to the present day everywhere, there is no movement where

---

eign policy, points to the self-evident fact that it alienates our allies, and evinces the formidable inability (or refusal) of some TV commentators to face reality and their equally strong inclination to consider the obvious, enigmatic.

there have been more struggles, more conflicts, more acrimonious confrontations, more dissensions, more liquidations, than the communist world movement.

Their strength is not in formal unity, but in the unity achieved on clear premises of thought and action, which can be attained by the existence of a concrete political aim and a thorough examination and precise determination of the most efficient ways to realize it.

So, before the slogan of the unity of the free world can begin to make sense and acquire validity, the free world must determine what is the common concrete political aim (not high-sounding generalities), which all free countries share and what is the best strategy to attain it, on which they agree.

And it is only natural that the basis for Western unity should be provided by the leader of the West, the United States.

However, our present ideas and policies are so inadequate, that —as two of our Presidents have stressed—there is today worse disunity among Americans than in all our history. And if our present ideas and policies cannot unite Americans, how can they unite the nations of the world?

The slogan of unity is a favorite of assorted experts on Europe. The United States is strong because it is united. Europe is weak, because it is disunited. So, again let us unite. Apart from all the historical and other differences which thoroughly disqualify the analogy and its authors, the fact they lose sight of is that European unity is impossible as long as Europe is half free, half communist-enslaved. And when U.S. leaders, like President Kennedy (in his interview with Nikita Krushchev's son-in-law, Alexei Adzubei) [252] talk about securing peace in Central Europe, they talk about recognizing and consolidating the communist status-quo in Europe, i.e. surrendering, thus making peace and European unity impossible, except on Soviet terms, (precisely like the Kissinger Blueprint nine years later).

Anybody who knows Europe and has talked to Europeans unofficially, is fully aware of the widespread feeling that U.S. foreign policy, in spite of the North Atlantic Treaty Organization (N.A.T.O.), or perhaps because the N.A.T.O. has been such a signal failure, is not based on U.S.-European solidarity, but bent on achieving a *modus vivendi* with the Soviet Union, at the expense of Europe.

And this is a source of dissatisfaction and despair, even when totally hidden behind wordly wisdom or optimistic commonplaces. To quote some personal experiences of a few years ago:

A. In Germany, the late Wenzel Jaksch, Socialist member of the Bundestag (Parliament) told me in the course of a long conversation:

"When you go back to the U.S. please tell your friends in the State Department, not to push us to Moscow." After I interrupted him to tell him that I hardly had friends in the present composition and structure of the State Department, he continued: "Have a look at the map. The distance from Bonn to Moscow is much shorter than from Bonn to Washington to Moscow. If we *have* to go to Moscow, we do not need you. . . . This is tragic, but we have no choice. If we were some 200 million people, we would not wait for you. But we are not. We are under 60 million. So we cannot view and solve our main problems regardless of what you do." He added that while he personally was fully aware of Soviet true policy and intentions, the idea that by turning directly to Moscow, Germany would be able to attain a much more favorable settlement than through the U.S., was definitely gaining ground.

There was compelling political logic in Jaksch's argument. According to C. L. Sulzberger of *The New York Times*, "last month Khrushchev confided to a foreign diplomat: 'If the West Germans lose faith in the West they will turn to us. They have no place else to go.' "

B. In a smaller country, the assistant secretary of state (or its European equivalent) listened carefully to what I had to say, but answered: "I agree with you entirely. However, I am very sure that Mr. Harriman whom we are expecting here in a few days, will talk an entirely different language. The U.S. is a nation of 200 million people. Nobody in Europe can change its policy. That must be done by Americans. I prefer to hear you, but meanwhile I must listen to Mr. Harriman."

C. In France, a retired Army colonel, with great experience in the Far East, concluded our series of conversations by saying: "It is wrong to view U.S.-French relations in the light of (alleged)

French ingratitude for what the U.S. has done for us in World War II and after. We appreciate your help and are aware of its importance. But that is not the point. We are worried not about what the U.S. will do for France, but about what the U.S. will do for the U.S."

With our present foreign policy, we are coming into conflict with everybody, free and enslaved, except the leaders of the communist world. The oppressed are bitter for being betrayed and forced into communist slavery at the end of World War II. The anti-communist freedom fighters are bitter for being let down in favor of their communist slave-masters. The free nations are resentful for being pushed and led toward the unnatural and impossible reconciliation with the communist enemy whose only concept of reconciliation is our surrender. And the communists despise us for our weakness in the midst of wealth and might.

The experience of the Budapest uprising of October 1956 was a terrible blow not only to the Hungarians who rose against communism, but to all freedom fighters in the whole world. The revolt had shown the organic, inherent weakness of communism and the deep hostility of the popular masses. The slightest help of the West (probably even without any military intervention at all, but just through moral and political support and pressure), would have ended communism in Hungary in a matter of weeks, if not days. And the revolt would have spread and swept like wild fire, bringing down the whole communist empire in Europe.

But the West chose the path of unconditional cowardice and self-betrayal. The revolt was crushed and so were the hopes of the enslaved.

One million people fled North Vietnam to go to South Vietnam. And three million people fled Eastern Germany to go over to free Western Germany. The meaning of this is obvious. But it is *we* who by our policies of coexistence with communism are forcing the enslaved Eastern Germans and North Vietnamese to reconcile with communism and adapt to it.

That is the reason why the communist-enslaved peoples are not revolting against communism. Not because they would like to be reconciled with it, but because at the moment they have no alternative. And they are deprived of the alternative by the West's policy which betrayed them in 1944 and 1945 and ever since.

The most important thing is to realize the nature and background of the contention that there is no alternative to communism, that we have no choice but to surrender or blow up the world and be blown to pieces. It is a cover and an excuse for those who do not *want* an alternative to communism. Apart from all moral considerations, the truth is that what is going now, i.e. what we are doing now is against all common sense and logic, against reality, the real relationship of forces between the U.S. (and the forces of freedom in the world) and the communists. The situation is bad because we, our policy of surrender, make it bad. The communists alone could never bring it about.

The Question

The most important fact which emerges from these considerations is that it is not the communists who are ruining us by their actions, varied, multiple, systematic, well studied and murderous as they are.* No. We are suffering from self-inflicted wounds, by pursuing a policy contrary to our basic interests, to logic, to self-respect and self-preservation.**

The fundamental, revolutionary and seemingly paradoxical conclusion from that fact is that the fate of the U.S., the fate of communism and the fate of the world are not in the hands of Moscow or Peking, but in our hands, in Washington.

This is something which the whole world sees, but fails to find an answer to the question why are we helping the enemy, instead of fighting back and winning? Why are we forfeiting our vital chance? That is the question which we must answer or the com-

---

* "Our communist adversaries are neither very strong nor very wise. Their seeming strength and wisdom thus far are actually no more than the reflection of our weakness, shortsightedness and cowardice." (David Dallin: "An Indictment Written in Blood," *The New Leader*, February 4, 1952).

This opinion is shared by Henry J. Taylor: "The Russians . . . are not inherently as strong as we make them strong by the weakness of the policies we employ against them." (Article "Unvarying Soft Policy Stymies U.S. in Parleys With Reds," *New York Journal American*, June 23, 1961).

** Robert Morris could not have chosen a more apt title to his book about the "dismantling (of) our ramparts" than *No Wonder We Are Losing*, The Bookmailer, New York, 1958.

munists will answer it by annihilating us, with or without nuclear weapons.

The big question is, why has the U.S. Government made possible the enslavement by the communists of 100 million people in Eastern Europe and 500 million Chinese, and why has it made it a policy to coexist with the communists everywhere, instead of fighting back?

As long as the question remains unanswered, there is another fundamental question which imposes itself, not only in the minds of the enslaved, but in everybody's mind, particularly in the minds of the leaders of the new nations, and that is: How can we trust you? In World War II you betrayed your most faithful and gallant allies. Why would you give us a better deal?

So, today what the peoples of the world want to know is *not* whether the U.S. is good, compassionate, rich, efficient, but is it strong of will. They know that the U.S. is nice, they know that it is militarily strong, that it is achieving miracles in science and technology. What they want to know, is whether the U.S. believes in itself, whether it has a will to assert itself to win. That is the question. For, evidently, if the peoples of the globe have the choice only between two forces, one which strives to live, win, conquer and rule the world—and the other which in spite of its overwhelming strength, strives to please everybody, especially its mortal enemy—then everyone will join the victorious murderer, rather than the kindly giant who is committing suicide.[253]

The Teheran and Yalta policy has shattered the faith of countless millions throughout the world in the validity of Western (American) values and in the word and reliability of the West. Because, otherwise, why were those Western values not defended and why were the countries behind the Iron Curtain sold to communism?

Should the present course continue to the end, the final result will not be resignation, inaction and apathy, but an explosive accumulation of resentment, hatred and lust for revenge. For their fondest hopes and ideals are constantly betrayed by the only power in the world that is their natural ally, supporter and defender, to whom they can turn. Thus their loyalty makes no sense. The supposedly sacred community of ideals, values, civilization is cynically betrayed in the name of those ideals and values in the name of which it is proclaimed and preached!

Is there nobody among our foreign policy experts to notice that by betraying Draza Mihailovich and rejecting (and slandering) the Chetniks who fought under his command, we did not win Tito and the Yugoslav communists; that by rejecting the Poles who fought alongside the U.S. in World War II, we did not win the Lublin Committee Poles (communists); that by letting down the river Nuri es Said, we did not win any leftist Iraqi; that by showing disapproval of Syngman Rhee and facilitating his overthrow, we won nobody among the communists of North Korea; that by liquidating Ngo Diem, we did not win Ho Chi Minh nor one single North Vietnamese communist or Vietcong?

So the policy based on the assumption that by betraying our friends we shall win over our enemies, not only is immoral, not only runs against vital U.S. interests, but it is senseless. We cannot keep our allies guessing all the time whether we are freedom-fighters or communist collaborators. We must make up our minds. For otherwise, should that policy continue long enough, it would bring about what no communist power and propaganda could ever do: turn those peoples against the United States and the free world. For people will, in despair, turn rather to those who oppress them, than to those who betray them.

Therefore, the change of U.S. foreign policy from surrender to freedom is a matter of life and death, because it is impossible to continue "as usual." Only by a radical change of policy can we remove the paralyzing contradiction in the minds of people throughout the world, which all can be summed up in one question: why isn't the U.S. fighting for itself?

We have everything to gain and nothing to lose by an either-or approach. Respect in the world (world opinion) begins with self-respect. How can others respect and trust us if we do not respect ourselves?

Our assets are still tremendous. Never in the history of mankind has there been a country to catch the imagination of people throughout the world as is the case with the United States of America. Never such a world-wide legend about a country as is the *legend America*, which is a part of real America.

To use that legend as a mighty weapon against communism and its subversion and propaganda of lies directed against the U.S. or any other country, is the obvious duty of U.S. responsible leaders. The more so since practically every nation on earth has a double stake in the success of America in the world: a. practically every nation on earth has invested in America its people, its know-how, its culture, its ideals, its spiritual and material forces. Almost every nation on the globe has contributed to and participated on the early or later achievements of the U.S. by giving it men of wisdom, or statesmanship, or of the pen, or of the sword, or of science, or of untiring toil, or adventure and imagination. So, the success of America is at the same time a matter of pride and satisfaction for most of the nations of the globe; b. if the U.S. does not win, if the U.S. loses and communism wins, there will be no freedom, no independence, no national sovereignty and no self-determination for anybody.

So, all the problems of reversing the present trend of the victory of communism in the world, can be summed up in one absolute requirement, one upon which everything depends: *U.S. foreign policy must serve U.S. interests.* Instead of using all our (experts') ingenuity and all our resources to attain accommodation with the USSR at any price, we must use them to promote U.S. interests and destroy the internal peace and the political positions of communism throughout the world.

In 1960, the then Secretary of State, Christian Herter, following the current accepted line of proving U.S. limitations and impotence, stressed the fact that it was difficult to fight communist subversion, because the USSR had some 350,000 agents throughout the world, with their efforts especially concentrated against the U.S. The figure is probably accurate and it has certainly increased in the past ten years. But what Mr. Herter was apparently unable to conceive, much less to clearly grasp, is that, as opposed to that considerable subversive force in our midst, undermining our foundations, we have an incomparably bigger force in the communist world, in the midst of their realm, and that is the nearly one billion people enslaved by communism.[254] With a little moral solidarity and encouragement from the West, they could become in shortest order, such an elemental force, that no army, no police and no secret police in the world would be able to offer any serious resistance. But if those billion people who were enslaved against their will, are constantly sacrificed in the interests of coexistence and peace with communism with whom there is no coexistence and no peace, then that huge force is dissipated and gradually turned into a force against the free world.

It is futile to try to console or deceive ourselves about the real situation in the world by invoking the "breakup of communist monolithism," and hoping that communist internal conflicts, and difficulties might save us from communism. Whatever internal communist conflicts may exist, there is, in their confrontation with the West—basic, inherent communist unity among all communists.

There is no corresponding cohesion and solidarity among Western powers. The fundamental unity of civilization and values they all share, has not been spelled out in clear terms of concrete aims and political militancy. And, in the absence of that common goal, everybody is talking Western unity, but trying for separate coexistence with communism. Without common denominator to hang together, the countries of the free world are embarking on the course which leads to their hanging separately.

That situation can be changed only through a common goal, cogent, politically sound and inspiring. And the only natural common goal to unite the West, which is threatened by communism both in its political existence and in its spiritual values, is to fight down the common enemy, communism.

A radical change of U.S. policy toward world communism, from surrender to political war based on self-assertion, would automatically create unity among the nations of the West on a common platform made of all the essential values of Western civilization. By our present policies we are solving all the crucial problems of the communists, as we are creating or aggravating our own problems. A policy of U.S. self-assertion would make an end to that unnatural situation, because we would stop helping the enemy, as we would stop poisoning and debilitating ourselves. The U.S. would regain its freedom of action, win the public opinion of the world and start winning the struggle for the minds of men. U.S. self-assertion would expand into the self-assertion of the free world, of all the people and all nations who believe in liberty and insist on their non-negotiable identity.

U.S. Fate Is Inseparable From That Of The Oppressed

The gist of the situation can be summed up in three points:

1. Communism is being kept alive not by Brezhnev and Mao, but by the West's policy of giving encouragement and help to communist regimes and denying help and encouragement to any anti-communist movement and action;

2. That Western policy is suicidal;

3. It can be reversed very effectively by stopping aid to communists and giving support to the enslaved. If the U.S. has the will to do this, there is nothing that the communists can do to prevent it and render it ineffectual. It is later than we think. But if we pull ourselves together, it will be later than the communists think.

The very fact that the U.S. has a position of world leadership means that the fate of the world decisively depends on U.S. policies. But, equally important for the U.S. is never to lose sight of the fact that it cannot separate its fate from that of the free world nor of the peoples enslaved by communism.

The U.S. cannot save the world if it does not save itself. But it cannot save itself if it does not save the world. Which means that without liberation of the enslaved there is no freedom for the free. The free cannot remain free if the enslaved remain enslaved. Should the darkness of communist slavery remain in Warsaw, Belgrade, Bucharest, Budapest, Sofia, etc., it will some day engulf Washington, D.C. And if the torch of freedom is to remain lit in Washington, it must be re-lit in the capitals of the peoples enslaved by communism.

We cannot divorce our fate from that of the oppressed and enslaved. We cannot buy our freedom and life at the price of their slavery and death. Either soon people in countries which today are under communism, will be able to live like human beings, or they will not be able to live in human dignity in these United States.

We may betray the whole world and all our allies, but that would not save us. We have no choice but to beat the communists. On the course of surrender, everybody will desert us and turn against us. On the course of the assertion of U.S. values and interests, the whole world will join us as the irresistible victor in the struggle against communism.

The liberal slogan about the need of recognizing "reality" is spurious. For the only reality the liberals recognize, is the reality of communist power. But the potentially much stronger reality which they ignore, is that the communists are oppressing one billion people, that they are bending all efforts to destroy the United States, and that the accumulated hatred of the oppressed against their communist oppressors is a political and moral hydrogen bomb which can blast communist power to pieces.

Once we reject the chains of communist brainwashing and mind-conditioning and realize that the world is craving for U.S. leadership, the balance of power in the world would be totally upset in our favor. All the energies which are being dissipated, all the hopes which are now being frustrated, all the pro-American affection which has so far been reciprocated with liberal abuse, cynicism and pro-communist betrayal, all the pro-American forces in the world which are now being wasted—would be mobilized and swell to the proportions of an elemental might to seep communism from power.

With the present U.S. foreign policy, there is no hope for the U.S. Anybody (e.g., North Vietnam) can beat us, the mightiest power ever.

If, however, we decide to fight, rejecting surrender and waging our political war for freedom, nobody can beat us. Not one of them and not all of them together. For all our energies will be brought to life and mobilized, and the whole world will be with us.

With belief in Divine Providence, with a clear mind, with faith and courage, with proper leadership, nothing is impossible for Americans. If America fulfills its assignment of 1776, it will open undreamed of avenues into the future for man to reach higher than ever before.

But should America betray itself, thus also betraying mankind, it will go down. And Americans will have nobody to blame but themselves, that a venture of freedom, promising to lead mankind to unique heights of self-fulfillment, ended in the most abject abdication of human dignity and betrayal of the divine spark in man.

Footnotes by Chapters

CHAPTER 1

1 Frank Meyer: *The Moulding of Communists* (The Training of the Communist Cadre), A Harvest Book, N.Y., 1961

2 Ibid., p. 126

3 A point insisted upon by Karl Jaspers in his memorable study *Die Geistige Situation der Zeit* (1931), Sammlung Göschen, Band 1000, Walter de Gruyter, Berlin 1960

4 *Life,* June 13, 1960

5 Much intellectual spade-work towards the liberation of the U.S. mind has undoubtedly been done. Frank Meyer, (*The Conservative Mainstream,* Arlington House, New Rochelle, N.Y. 1969), is right on this point. But if the intellect is not to be doomed to sterility and reduced to academic exercises, it must be complemented by the will.

CHAPTER 2

6 Edwin Canham, editor of the *Christian Science Monitor,* by no means a war-mongering "right-winger," was quoted as saying: "Our failing was to allow the erecting of the wall which now divides the city. The moment they started laying barbed wire, our forces should have been there rolling the wire up again . . ." (*Chicago American,* September 27, 1961)

7 According to *The New York Times,* (Nov. 13, 1962, "Rostow Says Soviet Faces Vital Choice"), Walt W. Rostow, at a news conference in Detroit, "warned that the United States must be prepared for total peace or total war."

8 Quoted by Senator Stuart Symington, in his Senate speech of May 26, 1961 (*New York Times,* May 27, 1961)

9 *Chicago Sun-Times,* March 27, 1962

10 *Winds of Freedom,* Boston, The Beacon Press, 1962, p. 16

11 *New York Times,* September 12, 1962

12 Speech at the Mary Sawyer Auditorium, Rhinelander, Wisconsin, on February 21, 1968 (*Chippewa Herald-Telegram,* Feb. 22, 1968)

13 The article was written for the Encyclopedia Britannica and published
    in condensed form in the *Reader's Digest* for February 1969

14 Article, "England, Whose England?" In *Suicide of A Nation*, edited by
    Arthur Koestler (The Macmillan Company, New York, 1964, p. 31)

15 "Cloak-and-Dagger Behind the Scenes." (After twenty years of silence,
    a former government scientist describes the diabolical workings of our
    World War II espionage), by Stanley P. Lovell, *Saturday Evening Post*,
    March 3, 1962

16 "The Hidden Problems in Negotiating with Asia's Reds." (*Look*, March
    5, 1967)

17 Title of Arnold J. Toynbee's article in the *New York Times Magazine*
    of April 5, 1964

18 "Laos and Tibet Open our Eyes," *Chicago Sun-Times*, September 1,
    1959

19 Arnold Beichmann, in the *Christian Science Monitor*, July 6, 1953

20 *New York Times*, July 16, 1959

21 *Chicago Tribune*, November 6, 1967 ("Warns Reds Won't Accept Viet
    Defeat") and *Chicago Sun-Times*, November 6, 1967 ("Soviets Can't
    Afford U.S. Viet Victory: Kennan")

22 *Newsweek*, March 14, 1960

23 *The Private Papers of Senator Vandenberg*, Houghton Mifflin, Boston
    1952, pp. 525 and 539

24 *New York Times*, January 19, 1960

25 Editorial, "What Mr. Khrushchev Won't See," *New York Times*,
    September 10, 1959

26 Quoted in a *Philadelphia Daily News* editorial, December 2, 1953,
    (italics added), and in excerpts from Ickes' *Memoirs*, published in *Look*,
    December 15, 1953, p. 127

27 *The Forrestal Diaries*, New York, The Viking Press, 1951, p. 72

28 Quoted in Stewart Alsop's column of November 26, 1952, in the *New
    York Herald Tribune*

29 *Washington Star*, August 15, 1958

30 "The Galbraith Plan To End The War," *New York Times Magazine*,
    Nov. 12, 1967

31 *Congressional Record,* November 20, 1963, Page 22536

32 Allen-Scott Report, "Attorney General Makes First Political Commitment," *St. Albans Messenger,* Vermont, May 19, 1964. Also: "R.F.K. Seeks to Lead 'Youth Revolution,' " by Robert S. Allen and Paul Scott, *Long Island Star-Journal,* May 19, 1964

33 *Time,* July 26, 1954, p. 18

34 "Bang or a Whimper" (*Long Island Press,* November 13, 1968)

35 "Too Convenient" (*Long Island Press,* January 27, 1969)

36 W. W. Rostow, *The United States in the World Arena,* Harper Brothers New York, 1960, p. 549. (Quoted in Alice Widener's review of the book in the publication *U.S.A.* of June 29–July 13, 1962)

37 *Chicago Sun-Times,* September 26, 1961

38 *Chicago Tribune,* May 23, 1962, (Editorial, "Victory Is A Nasty Word")

39 *Chicago Tribune,* June 5, 1962. ("Ball Defends Kennedy Cold War Policies; Tells U.S. Hope for Changes in Red Bloc," by Willard Edwards)

40 *Chicago Tribune,* May 6, 1962 ("Censors' Code: Speak Softly of Communism," by Willard Edwards)

41 *The Wanderer,* January 4, 1962

42 *Chicago Tribune,* May 6, 1962 ("Censors' Code: Speak Softly of Communism," by Willard Edwards)

43 *Chicago Tribune,* June 18, 1962 ("Rostow Backs 'Education' on Soft Red Line; Policy Draft Eyes Conciliation of Russia," by Williard Edwards)

44 *Chicago Sun-Times,* Marquis Childs, "McNamara Speech A Strategy Outline," July 17, 1962

45 This was the fifth "fundamental dimension" of Rostow's "top-secret, master strategy plan." (*U.S. News & World Report,* May 7, 1962, Interview with Walt W. Rostow, "Where U.S. Is Headed in Today's World," pp. 62–68)

46 *Chicago Tribune:* June 18, 1962 ("Rostow Backs 'Education' on Soft Red Line; Policy Draft Eyes Conciliation of Russia," by Willard Edwards)

47 *Chicago Sun-Times,* June 22, 1962 ("Senators to Quiz Rostow On Soviet Policy," by Frederick Kuh)

48 *Chicago Tribune,* June 19, 1962, (Editorial "Washington's Flight from Reality")

49 *Chicago Sun-Times,* June 22, ("Goldwater To Quiz Rostow on Soviet Goals," by Frederick Kuh)

50 *New York Times,* June 20, 1962 ("The McNamara Doctrine of Limited Nuclear War," by James Reston)

51 *Chicago Sun-Times,* July 17, 1962 (Marquis Childs, "McNamara Speech A Strategy Outline")

52 *Chicago Sun-Times,* August 14, 1962, "Rusk Says U.S. Will Defeat Communism," by Marguerite Higgins

53 *Chicago Tribune,* August 14, 1962

54 *New York Times,* August 14, 1962 ("Rusk Declares U.S. Has a 'Win' Policy," by Austin C. Wehrwein)

55 "Son," the father replied, "if a law is bad, you do not have to obey it." *Masters of Deceit,* Cardinal edition, 1959, p. 107

56 *Chicago Tribune,* February 25, 1966, "Charge Violations in King Flat"

57 *Chicago Tribune,* April 5, 1967

58 *Chicago Tribune,* August 28, 1967, "Mob in Detroit Roars as Brown Calls for Rioting"

59 In Philadelphia, on September 6, 1970

60 *Chicago Tribune,* April 6, 1967, Editorial, "Inflammatory Talk"

61 *Chicago Tribune,* August 5, 1967, Editorial, "If It Isn't Sedition, What Is It?"

62 *New York Times,* August 2, 1967

63 *The New York Times,* March 14, 1967 ("In The Nation: The Malaise Beyond Dissent," by Tom Wicker)

64 T.V. Channel 13, Eau Claire, Wis., October 11, 1969, 10 p.m. news program. Also *Chicago Tribune,* October 12, 1969

65 *Esquire,* February 1961, article "The Angriest Negroes," by William Worth

66 *Chicago Tribune,* July 28, 1967

67 *Chicago American,* April 2, 1967, "Raps King Shift to Viet Protest"

68 In an address at Yale University, April 20, 1967; "Wilkins Raps King Viet View," *Chicago Tribune*, April 20, 1967
   Vice President Agnew had the same reaction: ". . . the criminal misfits of society are glamorized while our best men die in Asian rice paddies." (*Chicago Tribune*, June 4, 1970)

69 *Chicago Tribune*, March 29, 1967 ("LBJ Urges Major War Against Crime," by William Kling)

70 *New York Times*, May 26, 1971

71 *New York Times*, January 24, 1967

72 *New York Times*, November 23, 1970, "G.I.s in Germany: Black is Bitter, and Morale, Discipline and Efficiency Decline," by Thomas A. Johnson

73 *Chicago Sun-Times*, January 18, 1961

74 *New York Times*, May 2, 1961, "Eisenhower Asks Banning of a 'Witch Hunt' on Cuba," by Russell Baker

75 *Chicago Tribune*, September 18, 1961

76 *Reader's Digest*, October 1968

77 At present U.S. naval bases are in Naples and Gaeta (in Italy), Piraeus (Greece), Suda Bay (Crete), Izmir and Iskenderun (Turkey). Soviet bases are in Mers-el-Kebir (Algeria), Alexandria, Mersa Matruh and Port Said (Egypt), and Latakia and Tartus (Syria)

78 *Time*, July 27, 1970

79 *New York Times*, January 6, 1969

80 *Minneapolis Tribune*, October 31, 1969

81 *Chicago Tribune*, February 28, 1970, "U.S. Admiral Warns of Red Navy Threat"

82 *Daily Telegraph*, London, March 4, 1971

83 *Chicago Tribune*, November 23, 1969, "Russian Arms Peril is Bared"

84 *Chicago Tribune*, May 10, 1971, "Laird Warns of Russian Gains"

85 *Milwaukee Journal*, July 3, 1970, "New Military Chief Raps Defense Critics"

CHAPTER 3

86 Incidentally, Sakharov has not done his homework on Lenin properly.
For Lenin never "used to say that every cook should learn how to govern." What he wrote is that, after many centuries of communist rule,
all enemies of communism would be wiped out, democracy would become reality, people would have learned to observe "the elementary
rules of social life" without force and compulsion. And that would so
greatly simplify the problems of society, turning them from problems of
ruling people into problems of administering things,—that "a kitchen
maid would be able to run the affairs of state."

87 Quoted in the German weekly magazine *Der Spiegel,* September 30,
1968

88 "African Students at Iron Curtain schools flee a hateful epithet *'cherni
maimuni'* " (Special Report), *Life,* March 15, 1963

CHAPTER 4

89 Frank Meyer, *The Moulding of Communists,* p. 54

90 *"On People's Democratic Dictatorship,"* Foreign Language Press, 1957

91 *New York Times,* April 7, 1963

92 Vyacheslav Molotov, *Time,* February 20, 1955

93 Marshal Vasili I. Chuikov, *New York Times,* January 16, 1960

94 Nikita Khrushchev, *New York Times,* January 18, 1964

95 *Chicago Tribune,* July 13, 1960

96 Article in *Sovietskaya Rossia,* quoted in *The Chicago Tribune,* August
31, 1969 ("Russ Boss Rattles Rockets at America," by Frank Starr,
Chief of Moscow Bureau)

97 Quoted in *Time,* May 2, 1960

98 Quoted in the article of Keyes Beech, "Has U.S. Already Suffered Its
Dien Bien Phu?" (*Long Island Star Journal,* March 12, 1968)

99 "The free world is invited to weaken itself to make communism strong—
that is Khrushchev's definition of peace." (Testimony of Professor Stefan
T. Possony before the Senate Internal Security Subcommittee, June 10,
1961)

100 Dell Books, New York, 1968, pp. 510–511

101 Nathan Hare, director of the Negro studies program at San Francisco State College, may never have heard of Hervegh, but he certainly breathes the same spirit, with the addition of the Bible(!) as his inspirational source: "The Bible says there is a time for everything. I think this is a time for hate." (*U.S. News & World Report*, January 27, 1969, p. 9)

102 "Not all the wealth of this affluent society could provide an adequate compensation for the exploitation and humiliation of the Negro in America down through the centuries." (Martin Luther King, "Why We Can't Wait," *Life*, May 15, 1964)

CHAPTER 5

103 Stalin expressly stated to Harry Hopkins that "without American production, the war would have been lost." (Cited by Robert Sherwood, *Roosevelt and Hopkins*, Harper Brothers, New York, 1948, p. 793)

CHAPTER 6

104 The most authoritative source of information on the Soviet concept of coexistence is the 20th Congress of the C.P.S.U., held in Moscow in February 1956, whose main thoughts were presented in my book, *Tito, Moscow's Trojan Horse*, Henry Regnery, Chicago, 1957, pp. 255–261

105 Supreme Court Justice (1916–1939) Louis Brandeis, quoted by Henry J. Taylor, *St. Louis Globe-Democrat*, August 18, 1970

106 Stalin, *Marxism and the National and Colonial Question*, p. 61

107 Personal communication to this author at a meeting in New York in 1954. Benjamin Gitlow's, *The Whole of Their Lives* (Scribner, 1948, Western Islands, 1965) is a most valuable testimony, based on personal experience and observation, on the war waged by the communists against the United States.

108 *La Maladie Infantile du Communisme*, Paris, 1945, p. 62

109 *Europe-Magazine* (Brussels), October 25–31, 1966, p. 14

110 N.C. (initials of Norman Cousins, editor), in his article "The Higher Patriotism," *Saturday Review*, July 4, 1970

111 "The Hidden Costs of Opportunity," *Atlantic Monthly*, February 1969, p. 90

112 "Infidelity Held Not Always Sign of a Sick Marriage," by Martin Tolchin, *New York Times*, April 12, 1962

113 *Chicago Tribune,* May 21, 1970 (Article, "Liberal Stand Urged for Church")

114 *Chicago Tribune,* December 30, 1970, "Psychologist Says Love Is 'Lousy Basis for Marriage,'" by Bernie Moss

115 "Motherhood—Who Needs It?" *Look,* September 22, 1970

116 Quoted in Harriet Van Horne's column, "Liberation? More Like Frustration," *Chicago Today,* June 10, 1970

117 In 1963, when Brazil's finance minister San Tiago Dantas visited Washington to ask for a loan, he had formulated the view that, "The lack of development of our nation is not the result of history or incapacity, but was determined in great part by the exploitative process. Foreign aid should be considered as a means of indemnity for damages caused." ("Dantas: U.S. Owes Brazil Aid," by Gerry Robichaud, *Chicago Daily News,* March 19, 1963)

118 Edward Gottlieb, former chairman of the W.R.L. (War Resisters League) stated after the riots of August 1968 in Chicago: "The politicians only reflect the climate in the country . . . it's my job to change the climate . . . being pacifist . . . means being more militant than anyone else." (*Rocky Mountain News,* Denver, September 3, 1968)

119 "Reds . . . continue to use every available technique, ruse, and artifice to capture the minds and control the behavior of loyal Americans . . . We must all realize that the Red conspirators in our midst . . . continue to wage a relentless campaign to pervert our thinking and undermine our freedoms." (J. Edgar Hoover, "The Communists Are After Our Minds," *American Magazine,* October 1954)

120 "The Soviet press . . . is a powerful ideological weapon of the communist party." Its task is "to wage an untiring struggle against the bourgeois ideology, to unmask . . . the aggressive plans of imperialism, to expose the inhuman character of the capitalist world." Ideological struggle is "one of the most important domains of the class struggle between socialism and capitalism." ("The High Function of the Press Consists in Waging a Tireless Struggle Against Bourgeois Ideology," Dispatch from Moscow by Robert Lacoutre, *Figaro,* Paris, May 6, 1969)

121 The Movies, *Life,* December 20, 1963

122 "In Red China . . . there is no sex in films. Movies behind the bamboo curtain are devoted to preaching revolution and the thoughts of communist party chairman Mao Tse-tung." ("Film Nudity Losing Favor Abroad," by Sherry Conohan, *Chicago Tribune,* September 6, 1970)

123 *Life,* March 13, 1964 ("The Strange Case of Strangelove," by Laudon Wainwright)

124 Theodore H. White's study, "The Action Intellectuals," published in three parts (June 9, 16 and 23, 1967) in *Life* magazine is highly informative and enlightening.

125 Stewart Alsop, although trying to minimize the importance of the press in influencing events, nevertheless admits that, "although the news is what matters most, reporters and editors decide what is news and what is not, and what commentators say about the news influences this decision." (*The Center*, Popular Library, New York, 1969, p. 156)

126 "Newsman Criticizes Biased T.V. Coverage" (*Chicago Tribune*, February 24, 1970)

127 A typical example is *The Liberal Papers*, Edited and with an Introduction by James Roosevelt, A Doubleday Anchor Original, 1962

128 *Communism* (The Nature of the Enemy), by John K. Jessup and the editors of *Life*, 1962, p. 68

129 In a comic strip published in one of the leading newspapers of the Middle West, the story glorifies Grisha, a Soviet intelligence major, who reveals himself not only as a war hero of the Soviet Union, but, after the war, as a non-conformist, anti-Stalinist, who serves "his country" while despising its leaders. On a secret mission to Yugoslavia, he is saving the life of an American actress, wife of a newspaper correspondent, and in an encounter with some brigands on Yugoslav soil, he beats their leader to a pulp, whose name is given as "Drazha." Accident? In WW II communist propaganda glorified Stalin's agent Tito, and conducted an intense smear campaign against the champion of anti-Hitler resistance in Europe, General Draza Mihailovich.
    In a crossword puzzle of *The New York Times* (Feb. 1, 1964), the 8-letter word with which to fill the space is given as "Tito's people," and the word is: Serbians. Which is like calling the Jews "Hitler's people."

130 The peace ballot in San Francisco, on November 7, 1967, asked the voters to vote yes or no on the proposal, ". . . that there be an immediate cease-fire and withdrawal of U.S. troops from Vietnam, so that the Vietnamese people can settle their own problems." The same kind of proposal in Madison, Wisconsin, on April 2, 1968, had a slightly different ending: ". . . so that the Vietnamese people can determine their own destiny."
    The dishonesty of the wording of the question is glaring, for it implies: (a) that the problem of Vietnam is a strictly Vietnamese affair, and (b) that it is the presence of U.S. troops which is preventing the Vietnamese people from settling their own problems and determining their own destiny.
    Although the proposal was defeated (in San Francisco 64%–36%; in Madison 57%–43%, the defeat of the peaceniks would have been disastrous had the text been honest and factual: ". . . so that the aggression of communist North Vietnam, supported by Red China and the Soviet Union, against free South Vietnam, can succeed unhindered."

131 "The Congress-Left? Right? Or Neither?," *New York Times Magazine*, April 22, 1962

132 *New York Times*, July 29, 1964

133 Salvador de Madariaga, quoted by Charles Poore, in his review of E. A. Mowrer's book, *An End To Make Believe, New York Times*, September 23, 1961

134 *U.S. News & World Report* of October 1, 1954, "Reds Try Puritanism," published a story from *Trud* (Labor), official newspaper of communist workers, about the downfall of a young woman who, in search of an "exciting life," ended as a prostitute. After recognizing that the parents and society are to blame to an extent, *Trud* concluded: "But who is to blame first of all? Olga, herself . . . She ran after the 'beautiful life,' meaning by this not work, not a family, but cafes, dances and fashions."

CHAPTER 7

135 "Henry Pollitt it was, I think, who said, '. . . Every Communist in capitalist society is a capitalist at heart.' This wasn't a matter of benevolent tolerance, it was a warning to all comrades to beware of the non-Communist fifth column within themselves. When a Communist is disturbed by the voice of his conscience he remembers the words of Harry Pollitt and drowns it." (Frank Meyer, *The Moulding of Communists*, p. 187)

136 Frederick A. Praeger, New York, 1957, p. 197

137 Article "Césars Fous" (Mad Caesars) *Figaro*, Paris, May 5, 1971

138 Andrei Sinyavsky, in *On Trial*, The Soviet State versus "Abram Tertz" and "Nikolai Arzhak," Translated, Edited, and with an Introduction by Max Hayward, Harper & Row, Publishers, New York, Evanston and London, 1966, p. 130

139 Ibid., p. 113

140 Arthur Koestler: *The Invisible Writing*, The Beacon Press, Boston, 1954, p. 15

141 Jacek Kuron and Karl Modzelewski: "Monopolsozialismus" (Open Letter to the Polish United Workers' Party, Hoffman und Campe, Hamburg, 1969)

142 Speaking about "liberals" in the U.S.S.R., Andrei Amalrik, the author of *Will the Soviet Union Survive Until 1984?*, branded them, without using the word, as typical "self-critics" of communism: "Poets (Yevgeny) Yevtushenko and (Andrei) Voznesensky engage in polite opposition to the system . . . but they are very much a part of it." (*Newsweek*, June 1, 1970, p. 43

143 Andrei Amalrik, quoted in *Newsweek*, June 1, 1970, p. 43

144 Published in the German weekly newspaper *Die Zeit*, April 2, 1968

145 *New York Times*, January 23, 1966

CHAPTER 8

146 Anatoli Granovsky, *I Was an NKVD Agent*, Devin-Adair, New York, 1962

147 *Briefe über die Grenze*, Hamburg, 1968

148 German weekly, *Die Zeit*, September 3, 1968

149 Ladislav Mnačko: *La Septième Nuit* (Les Russes Occupent la Tchécoslovaquie), Flammarion, Paris, 1968

150 Bertram D. Wolfe, "The Durability of Despotism in the Soviet Union," *Russian Review*, July 1958

151 *On Trial*, p. 118

152 Quoted in Philip Moseley's article "Soviet Foreign Policy," *Foreign Affairs*, July, 1956, p. 546

153 The phenomenon of Titoism, both as a communist strategy and as a Western policy, has been thoroughly analyzed in my book, *Tito, Moscow's Trojan Horse*, Henry Regnery, Chicago, 1957

154 *The Reporter*, April 4, 1957, p. 34

155 Interview published in the French magazine *Paris-Match* ("Guerre ou Paix," Le Maréchal Tito Dialogue avec Raymond Tournoux), November 16, 1968

156 This, according to the *Wall Street Journal* (June 4, 1971, "Tito's Troubles, A Slumping Economy and Ethnic Divisions Threaten Yugoslavia," by Felix Kessler) is the latest astronomic total of the West's support to the Yugoslav communist regime: "In 1965 the country was . . . at the edge of financial disaster despite Western aid of $5 billion over the previous 20 years. After committing itself to major economic reforms . . . Yugoslavia over the next five years got another $2 billion in loans and aid, mostly from the West."

157 *New York Times*, November 5, 1956

158 Published in the German liberal-socialist weekly, *Die Zeit*, September 3, 1968

159 *Chicago Tribune*, August 26, 1969, editorial "Two Views of the Czech Tragedy."

160 *New York Times,* August 10, 1960

161 Concluding words of Garaudy's speech at the 19th Congress of the French communist party, where he was divested of all official functions. (*Time,* February 23, 1970, p. 24)

162 "Investigators in Washington, New York and Los Angeles said that plans for the purges began shortly after Gus Hall, general secretary of the party in this country, and Henry Winston, executive secretary, returned in late June from a meeting of the Communist International in Moscow," (*Chicago Tribune,* October 2, 1969, "Top Leaders of U.S. Reds Are Purged," by Ronald Koziol)

163 "Romanian, Italian Red Leaders Hit Russ Intervention Doctrine," (*Chicago Tribune,* April 2, 1971, dispatch from James Yuenger, Chief of Moscow Bureau)

164 Ibid.

165 Ibid.

166 Mihajlo Mihajlov: *Russische Themen,* Edition Swiss Eastern Institute, Berne, 1969, pp. 244–251

167 *Der Spiegel* (Hamburg), August 26, 1969
     A prime example of this thoroughly Orwellian communist effrontery are the comments made by Walter Ulbricht, the most obsequious of all Soviet puppets, to some Czechoslovak newspapermen in Karlsbad, one week before the Soviet invasion of Czechoslovakia:
     "As we learned from the press that you had abolished press censorship, we were astounded, because we have never known something like that. We have never had press censorship, and, as you can see, we have prospered quite well without press censorship"
     ("The Press As Propaganda Drum," by Joachim Navrocki, *Die Zeit,* Hamburg, May 26, 1970)

168 Speech of March 8, 1963, cited in *Aspects of Intellectual Ferment and Dissent in the Soviet Union,* Government Printing Office, 1968, p. 23

169 *Neue Zürcher Zeitung,* August 17, 1966

170 Government Printing Office, 1968

171 *Gary Post-Tribune,* October 21, 1967

172 *Der Spiegel* (Hamburg), May 26, 1969, p. 174

CHAPTER 9

173 Article, "Asia after Vietnam," *U.S. News & World Report,* October 23, 1967, p. 87

174 *Chicago Tribune,* November 2, 1967

175 Quoted in the *Dan Smoot Report* of January 18, 1965

176 November 8, 1965; January 16, 1967; April 10, 1967

177 *Chicago Tribune,* May 19, 1966 ("McNamara Defines U.S. Role—Denies America Wants to Police the World," by Eugene Griffin)

178 This is the thesis of General James M. Gavin, soldier and diplomat, former U.S. Ambassador to France, presented in his article: "We *Can* Get out of Vietnam," in the *Saturday Evening Post,* February 24, 1968

179 *Chicago Tribune,* November 6, 1967

180 *Foreign Affairs,* for October 1967, and *U.S. News & World Report,* October 23, 1967

181 Quoted in the *Chicago Tribune* editorial, "Red China Moving Against Free Asia," December 28, 1969

182 The psychological and political impact of the TET offensive should not be underestimated. From the military viewpoint, it certainly cannot be appraised as an American Dien Bien Phu (Keyes Beech, "Has U.S. Already Suffered Its Dien Bien Phu?," in *Long Island Star Journal,* March 12, 1968.) And yet it may turn out to be a turning point in the war in Vietnam.

183 *Corriere della Serra,* February 25, 1967

184 *Chicago Sun-Times,* October 23, 1967

CHAPTER 10

185 *The Grand Deceit,* Social Pseudo-Sciences, A Veritas Foundation Staff Study, Introduction and Epilogue by Archibald Roosevelt; Research Director Zygmund Dobbs, Published by Veritas Foundation, West Sayville, New York, 1964, p. 104

CHAPTER 11

186 McGraw Hill, New York, Toronto, London, 1967

187 On this important, and little discussed subject, Duane Thorin's, *The Pugwash Movement and the U.S. Arms Policy,* New York, 1965, is a study which deserves attention.

188 *New York Times,* June 23, 1962

189 *National Review Bulletin,* May 15, 1962

190 Ibid.

191 Fyodor Dostoyevsky, *The Possessed*, a Signet Classic, The New American Library, 1962

192 Mark Slonim in his Afterword to *The Possessed*

193 *Joseph Stalin—H. G. Wells, Marxism vs. Liberalism*, An Interview, 1935, pp. 9 and 12

194 Interview with the correspondent of the French Liberal Periodical, l'*Express*, November 29, 1962

195 Arthur Koestler, *The Invisible Writing*, 1954, pp. 364–365

CHAPTER 12

196 In his article, "The Brave World of the Unborn," *Look*, November 4, 1969, David Rorvik says: "Human Breeding Farms could control the sex, brains and physique of babies, even produce 100,000 exact copies of Einstein."

197 "Will New Vision Help Man Know Himself?," MacLeish Asks Question in Apollo Tribute, *International Herald Tribune*, Paris, December 26, 1968

198 Quoted by Claus Grossner in his article about "The End of Science and Technology," in the weekly, *Die Zeit*, Hamburg, May 19, 1970

CHAPTER 13

199 *Look*, December 12, 1967, "The Dangerous World of Walt Rostow," by J. Robert Moskin

200 *Life*, April 14, 1966, "Speechwriter for Two Presidents," by managing editor George P. Hunt

201 "National Purpose: Sarnoff Program—Renewed Dedication of Traditions Urged in Fighting Communism," *New York Times*, June 2, 1960

202 Quoted in *Süddeutsche Zeitung*, Munich, December 4, 1962

203 Senator Henry M. Jackson (D., Wash.) evinced a clear understanding of the nature of communist negotiations when he wrote: "Some Americans see international negotiation only as a way of *ending* conflict. They are blind to the fact that negotiation as practiced by Moscow is equally adapted to *continuing* and *waging* conflict." ("Russia Has Not Changed Her Ways," *Reader's Digest*, June 1969, p. 95)

204 "Bismarck understood that disagreement reflected not 'misunderstanding,' but incompatible values." (Article, "Reflections on Bismarck," *Daedalus*, Summer 1968, p. 917

205 "The Pleasures of Global Chess" was the title of the article, by Hugh Sidey, in *Life*, February 27, 1970, commenting on the Kissinger Blueprint.

206 *Chicago American*, February 1, 1962. Sokolsky admitted that he had received letters from readers telling him that, in their estimate, he had "sold out."

207 *New York Times*, June 21, 1970 ("Agnew Asserts 8 Prescribe Defeat; Lists 7 Leading Democrats and Lindsay as Advocates of Surrender in Indochina," by James M. Naughton)

CHAPTER 14

208 These words were part of a speech welcoming President Nkrumah of Ghana on a visit to Moscow. ("Nikita Defies The World," editorial of *The New York Times*, July 13, 1961)

209 *Washington-Exclusive*, Editorial Commentary on National Affairs, by Robert Morris, issue of January 8, 1964

210 "A Policy for the West," *The Yale Review*, December 1956

211 This is perfectly clear to every communist. On the eve of Nikita Khrushchev's visit to the United States, Peter Lisagor of the *Chicago Daily News* wrote that "the most the Yugoslavs hope for in the Eisenhower-Khrushchev talks is a mutual acceptance of the status quo . . . in *communist thinking the status quo includes tomorrow's revolution* if it happens to be anti-West and pro-Soviet." (Emphasis added.) (*Chicago Daily News*, August 26, 1959, "Khrush Won't Give Up Much, Yugoslavs Say Status Quo Means Victory")

212 *Washington Post*, April 9, 1958

213 *New York Herald-Tribune*, March 3, 1961

214 Yugoslav daily *Politika* (Belgrade), January 21, 1968

215 Excerpts published in the Swiss magazine, *Der Klare Blick* (Bern), of Sept. 1, 1965

216 *National Review*, June 29, 1971

217 *Time*, February 27, 1956

218 *U.S. News & World Report*, June 1, 1956, p. 30

219 "The dictatorship of the proletariat, or rather the withering of the state that follows it, is literally the end of history." (Christopher Dawson: *The Dynamics of World History*, A Mentor Omega Book, 1956, p. 353)

220 The Pasternak case offers a most convincing example of surrender of the flower-smellers before the history-makers. Western liberals loved his "humanism," especially because it, allegedly, triumphed over bolshevism, the revolution. But the communists (Nikita Khrushchev and comrades), loved his humanism too, because it was withdrawal before the revolution, letting the history-makers make history, while we live our private lives. That is the ideal division of labor from the viewpoint of communist interests. By forbidding Pasternak to accept the Nobel Prize, they made him a martyr for humanism, champion of Western values and symbol of the West's obvious choice between making history or withdrawing into the realm of non-political, private living.

221 Kim Philby, *My Silent War*, Grove Press, New York, 1968, p. 109

222 "Historical facts . . . are no more than stones and bricks; only a well-trained Marxist can create of this material a graceful edifice." (*The Fall of a Titan*, pp. 190–191)

223 Editorial in the *Saturday Evening Post*, March 5, 1960

224 *New York Times*, August 20, 1963

225 In *Suicide of A Nation* (The Macmillan Company, New York, 1964) Arthur Koestler, who edited the book, quotes Ian Naim's diagnosis of Britain's ills: "We are at the moment dying by the mind . . . it is the mind which must will the change." (p. 13)

CHAPTER 15

226 Alfred North Whitehead, *Adventure of Ideas*, Mentor, 1955, p. 280

227 "The enemies of permanent things progress from personal anarchy to public tyranny," says Russell Kirk in *Enemies of the Permanent Things* (Arlington House, New Rochelle, N.Y., 1969, p. 300), an important book which deserves attention and study.

228 *New York Times*, August 18, 1958

229 Sally Belfrage, *A Room in Moscow*, Reynald Company, New York, 1958, p. 43

230 Quoted in a circular of the Young Americans for Freedom, of February 1969

231 In his "Report from Israel" (*Chicago Tribune*, August 18, 1968), Judge Abraham Lincoln Marovitz brought out very clearly the vital link be-

tween the obligation of every Israeli "kid" to defend his country, and the absence of destructive dissent in Israel:

"The unifying factor among almost all the students, male and female alike, is that nearly all of them have served in the Israeli armed forces, and like all other Israelis do an annual stint in reserves. The implications of this are enormous. One of the results of this particular military and political situation in Israel is that there is little if any genuine dissent.

"Policies and methods may be questioned—but the right to physical survival is a basic unquestioned concern for all of them. Thus, the equivalent of draft card burning is nonexistent."

232 In a New Year's message to Conservative Jews, Rabbi Henry N. Rapaport, president of the United Synagogue of America, made a point of universal validity: "Only by adopting the code of our prophets, can we hope to match the technological strides with equal progress in human relationship leading to universal peace." ("Jews Prepare Special Rites for New Year," by Richard Philbrick, *Chicago Tribune*, August 20, 1969)

233 "Urges Caution in Coalition Plan for Viet—Hungary's Ex-Leader Offers Pointers" (*Chicago Tribune*, February 21, 1966)

234 Quoted in Merlo J. Pusey's, *Eisenhower The President*, New York, The Macmillan Company, 1956, p. 162

235 *Chicago Daily News*, May 3, 1960

236 Article, "Turks, Anti-Red as Ever, Worry about West Going Soft," *New York World-Telegram*, Nov. 24, 1959

237 "This Flexible Firmness," by Edgar Ansel Mowrer, *Long Island Star-Journal*, January 23, 1961

238 *Chicago Tribune*, January 13, 1961

239 "Cuban Fiasco Upsets Latins—Survey Finds Officials Were Disappointed." *Chicago Tribune*, August 5, 1961

240 *New York Times*, June 10, 1961

241 *New York Times*, January 29, 1969

242 *Chicago American*, November 5, 1961

243 *New York Times*, February 20, 1962

244 *New York Times*, December 14, 1959

245 Quoted in Marquis Childs' column, *Chicago Sun-Times*, November 12, 1963

246 *Chicago Tribune*, July 6, 1966

247 *Chicago Tribune*, July 13, 1966

248 *Chicago Tribune*, July 25, 1966

249 "Thais Fear Fall of Laos To Reds," by Robert Trumbull, *New York Times*, June 10, 1961

250 *Long Island Star-Journal*, August 22, 1961

251 According to *The New York Times*, August 6, 1959 (dispatch from Paris by Robert C. Doty), Georges Bidault, former French Premier and Foreign Minister, "contrasted the present position with the firmness with which the Eisenhower Administration, at its debut, proclaimed the objective of the 'roll-back' of communism."

It is apparently this change in U.S. policy which led him to the conclusion that "the two-power meetings could be 'the beginning of the capitulation of the free world.'"

252 The interview took place at Cape Cod, Mass., on November 25, 1961. (The full text was published in *The Chicago Tribune* of November 29, 1961)

A natural complement of this interview is the article published in *Izvestia*, the Soviet official daily (editor Adzhubei), commenting on the interview, published in *The New York Times* of December 4, 1961

253 A letter released in October 1970 by The Youth International Party (Yippies) called for a "fall offensive" against "Amerika": . . . "We are not just 'attacking targets'—we are bringing a pitiful helpless giant to its knees." (*Chicago Tribune*, October 7, 1970, "Yippies Warn Fall Offensive Is Starting")

254 This inability of many of our liberal policy-makers is rooted in the obsession with the hope that "on certain fundamentals we can find a common language because we have a common interest." Quoting these words of Mr. Herter, *The Chicago Tribune* (editorial, "Secretary Herter Pleases Pravda," December 7, 1959) commented: "When a secretary of state thinks that a nation dedicated to liberty can agree with communism on fundamentals, it is time to start wondering if he is an evangel of victory thru surrender."

Index